PLACE, CULTURE AND IDENTITY

ESSAYS IN HISTORICAL GEOGRAPHY IN HONOUR OF ALAN R. H. BAKER

EDITED BY IAIN S. BLACK AND ROBIN A. BUTLIN

Géographie historique

Collection fondée et dirigée par Serge Courville

La collection « Géographie historique » regroupe des scientifiques reconnus et accueille tous les chercheurs préoccupés de donner une dimension spatiale à leurs analyses historiques, quelle que soit leur discipline. Elle rassemble des textes destinés à donner ses fondements à la géographie historique québécoise et à faire connaître l'expérience et l'espace québécois.

Titres parus

La cartographie au Québec, 1760-1840, par Claude BOUDREAU, 1994.

Introduction à la géographie historique, par Serge COURVILLE, 1995.

Espace et culture/Space and Culture, sous la direction de Serge COURVILLE et Normand SÉGUIN, 1995.

La sidérurgie dans le monde rural : les hauts fourneaux du Québec au XIXe siècle, par René HARDY, 1995.

Peuplement et dynamique migratoire au Saguenay, 1840-1960, par Marc ST-HILAIRE, 1996.

Le coût du sol au Québec, par Serge COURVILLE et Normand SÉGUIN, 1996.

Naviguer le Saint-Laurent à la fin du XIXe siècle. Une étude de la batellerie du port de Québec, par France NORMAND, 1997.

La bourgeoisie marchande en milieu rural (1720-1840), par Claude PRONOVOST, 1998.

Paysage, mythe et territorialité : Charlevoix au XIXe siècle. Pour une nouvelle approche du paysage, par Lynda VILLENEUVE, 1999.

Les idéologies de développement régional : le cas de la Mauricie 1850-1950, par René VERRETTE, 1999.

À la façon du temps présent : trois siècles d'architecture populaire au Québec, par Paul-Louis MARTIN, 1999.

Jacques-Rousseau 1905-1970, Bio-bibliographie, par Camille LAVERDIÈRE et Nicole CARETTE, 1999.

Le Québec, genèses et mutations de territoire, par Serge COURVILLE, 2000.

Place, Culture and Identity: Essays in Historical Geography in Honour of Alan R. H. Baker, edited by Iain S. BLACK and Robin A. BUTLIN, 2001.

Hors collection

Paroisses et municipalités de la région de Montréal au XIXe siècle (1825-1861), sous la direction de Serge COURVILLE, avec la collaboration de Jacques CROCHETIÈRE, Philippe DESAULNIERS et Johanne NOËL, 1988.

Entre ville et campagne : l'essor du village dans les seigneuries du Bas-Canada, par Serge COURVILLE, 1990.

PLACE, CULTURE AND IDENTITY

ESSAYS IN HISTORICAL GEOGRAPHY IN HONOUR OF ALAN R. H. BAKER

EDITED BY IAIN S. BLACK
AND ROBIN A. BUTLIN

Les Presses de l'Université Laval

Les Presses de l'Université Laval reçoivent chaque année du Conseil des Arts du Canada et du ministère de la Culture et des Communications du Québec une aide financière pour l'ensemble de leur programme de publication.

Canadian Cataloguing to Publication Data

Main entry under title

Place, culture and identity : essays in historical geography in honour of Alan R. H. Baker

(Géographie historique)

ISBN 2-7637-7807-0

1. Historical geography. I. Baker, Alan R. H. II. Black, Iain S. III. Butlin, Robin A. IV. Series.

G141. P52 2001   911   C20019440806-4

Supervision
Serge Courville

Cover page
Charaf El Ghernati

Cover illustration
Blois (1875) ; Paris, Dépôt de la Guerre. Reproduced courtesy of the Royal Geographical Society, London (Map Library, France VFS. S. 22.)

Infography
Chantal Gaudreault

Distribution de livres Univers
845, rue Marie-Victorin
Saint-Nicolas (Québec)
Canada G7A 3S8
Tél.: (418) 831-7474
ou 1 800 859-7474
Téléc.: (418) 831-4021
http:/www.ulaval.ca/pul

Eurospan University Press Group
3 Henrietta Street
Covent Garden
London   WC2E 8LU UK
Tél.: 44 (0) 20 7240-0856
Fax:44 (0) 20 7379-0609
info@eurospan.co.uk

UBCPress
University of British Columbia
2029 West Mall
Vancouver, british Colombia
Canada, V6T 1Z2
Phone: (604) 822-5744
Fax:(604) 822-6083

ALAN R. H. BAKER

NOTES ON CONTRIBUTORS

Iain Black is Lecturer in Geography at King's College London

Mark Billinge is Lecturer in Geography at the University of Cambridge

Robin Butlin is Professor of Historical Geography at the University of Leeds

Mark Cleary is Professor of Geography at the University of Plymouth

Serge Courville is Professor of Geography at Université Laval, Quebec

Richard Dennis is Reader in Geography at University College London

Michael Heffernan is Professor of Historical Geography at the University of Nottingham

Philip Howell is Lecturer in Geography at the University of Cambridge

Brian Osborne is Professor of Geography at Queen's University, Ontario

Chris Philo is Professor of Geography at the University of Glasgow

Jean-Robert Pitte is Professor of Geography at Université de Paris-Sorbonne

Joe Powell is Emeritus Professor of Historical Geography at Monash University and Visiting Fellow at the Australian National University, Canberra.

Tim Unwin is Professor of Geography at Royal Holloway, University of London

Preface

On the 18th and 19th of September 1998, a group of some fifty scholars and friends of Alan Baker gathered at Emmanuel College Cambridge to celebrate his sixtieth birthday (slightly in advance of the actual date). The conference, entitled 'Explorations in Historical Geography', was held not only to celebrate Alan's attainment of that particular and notable chronological milestone, but also to celebrate his long and distinguished role as researcher, writer, teacher and companion in the study of Historical Geography. That these scholars came from as far afield as Canada, the United States, India, Japan and China, as well as France and the U.K. provided further testament to the high esteem with which Alan is held by his peers. There were, in addition, many expressions of good wishes sent by colleagues unable to attend.

Those at the conference experienced a stimulating and wide-ranging set of academic papers, many addressing themes close to Alan's own interests. These included: Historical Geographies of France; Historical Geographies of Food, Agriculture and Rural Society; Methodologies of Historical Geography; Colonial and Postcolonial Geographies; and the Historical Geographies of Power, Culture and Identity. It was thought fitting to commemorate both this specific event and our broader appreciation of Alan's work and interests by producing a set of essays as a *festschrift*. We have, therefore, sought in this collection of essays to draw from the many excellent papers presented at the conference a selection which touches on Alan Baker's enduring interest in the Historical Geography of France and of France in the wider world. Coupled with these papers are two thought-provoking methodological pieces which address, in different ways, Alan's distinctive contribution in the general area of methodological debate in Historical Geography. One paper, that by Mark Cleary, could not be presented at the conference for various logistical reasons, but has been included given its obvious relation to the theme outlined here.

We would like to thank the following individuals for their help and advice in the transition of this book from a selection of conference papers to a dedicated *festschrift* volume. Sarah Black and Mike Heffernan gave much energy, time and commitment to help us set up the conference in Cambridge and to ensure that it ran smoothly. We would also like to thank all those attending for making it such an enjoyable occasion, and to all the contributors for the cheerful responses to all our queries and prompting over the last three years. We owe a great debt of gratitude to Serge Courville, of Université Laval, Quebec. In addition to presenting a paper at the conference and writing his own contribution for the volume, he has provided constant support, interest and enthusiasm for the publication of this *festschrift* within the Géographie Historique Series of the Laboratoire de géographie historique of the University Laval, a component of the Centre interuniversitaire d'études québécoises. We would like to thank Serge warmly for all his help and patience. And finally our deepest thanks to Alan Baker himself, who through his friendship, support, wisdom and wit over many years has proved such a stimulating and enjoyable companion on many journeys of exploration and discovery of Historical Geography.

Iain Black   *Robin Butlin*

Table of Contents

Chapter One

ALAN R. H. BAKER

Historical Geographer

IAIN S. BLACK AND ROBIN A. BUTLIN

One of the means by which scholastic communities have traditionally honoured their most distinguished members is by the presentation of a *festschrift*. We continue this tradition with the following set of essays for Alan Baker, an outstanding scholar in the field of historical geography. We do so in recognition of his major contributions to research and published scholarship, to teaching and postgraduate supervision and to the editing of an outstanding journal and specialist book series, together with his energetic promotion of national and international colloquia and scholarly exchanges. We celebrate in these essays too, not only an outstanding scholar but also an exceptionally kind and generous friend, whose scholarly and material hospitality and whose thoughtful consideration for others are boundless. The book is a small thematically focused offering of our debt to Alan (shared by many others who have expressed their strong support for the purpose of this work) in recognition of his impressive achievements in the past, and in further anticipation of major work to come.

In the second half of the twentieth century and the opening years of the twenty-first, Geography as an academic subject, like many other social science and humanities disciplines, has changed remarkably and on the whole beneficially in character. The traditional fascination with and the explanatory challenges afforded by the infinite variety of place and landscape, together with a continuing engagement with maps as descriptors of distributions and symbolic representations of complex processes, has continued throughout this period. Changes have occurred in the technical and conceptual means of selecting and representing data, and there has been response – inevitably varied – within Geography itself to the opportunities offered by quantitative data and statistical modes of analysis. Additionally there has been increasing variety of more subjective but equally significant conceptual and analytical tools, with accelerating interest in, for example, post-colonial, gender, cultural and political perspectives. The historiography of these changes in the discipline is well documented.

Historical geography has not only reflected these changes, but has often been at the leading edge of experiment and change, as reflected in the work and research trajectories of innovative scholars such as Alan Baker. Alan's undergraduate training and postgraduate research experience in the Geography Department at University College London provided a firm base for his future work. Historical geography was, and still is a great strength in that department, notably through the late Clifford Darby, Bill Mead, the late Terry Coppock, Hugh Prince, Tony French, David Harris, Jim Johnson, David Lowenthal, with later appointments of David Robinson, Frank Carter and Hugh Clout. The fundamentals of historical geography were well understood and taught, in terms of archival and field evidence, of fieldwork and comparative national and international case studies. All this and more in an institution with ready access to major national libraries and archives, where visitors to the department were numerous, and where lively and contentious debate was a characteristic.

The link with Clifford Darby was important, both at University College London, and Cambridge. Darby, a distinguished scholar, had an ability to locate and encourage outstanding academic talent, and built up a strong department at University College London, to which Alan Baker was appointed as lecturer at the conclusion of his doctoral research. Darby moved in 1966 to the Chair of Geography in Cambridge, where he appointed Alan Baker, Mark Billinge, Robin Donkin, Harold Fox, Robin Glasscock, Derek Gregory, John Langton, Mark Overton and Richard Smith – all historical geographers – as lecturers. Darby's meticulous use of archives, his comprehensive knowledge of a very wide range of relevant literature, and his carefully crafted style of writing were doubtless influential on the young Alan Baker and other postgraduate students and colleagues. Alan mentions these in his obituary for Darby, published in 1992: "Darby conveyed to his graduate students the necessity for circumspection in the use of historical sources, for pragmatism in research methodology, for careful attention to issues of literary style and written expression, and for an awareness of the relevance of work by economic historians and of the importance of retaining nonetheless one's integrity as an historical (economic) geographer".[1] The talent so nurtured inevitably found new pioneering paths to tread, leading to ways and views substantially different from those of the master historical geographer[2] and, perhaps coincidentally (perhaps not), to a rapidly developing role for Alan as the promoter and enabler of an unashamed *avant-garde* in historical geography, active in Cambridge and elsewhere. Inevitably this following of new trails led to difficulties of rapport, but the basic influence of Darby was positive.[3] He encouraged colleagues to publish results of their detailed research and also syntheses: exemplified in Alan Baker's chapter on 'Changes in the Later Middle Ages' in the Darby-edited book *A New Historical Geography of England* (1973). That book was perhaps the last of the major syntheses in a more traditional *genre* of historical geography with which Alan would be associated. Darby's "initial stimulus" as an "intellectual mentor" is acknowledged in the Preface to Alan's *Fraternity Among the French Peasantry* (1999). It is to the memory of Alan's parents, together with that of H. C. Darby, that the book is dedicated.

Field systems and theory: Kent, England and the making of medieval landscapes

Alan's Ph. D. research, under the supervision of Clifford Darby, was on aspects of the medieval agrarian historical geography of his home county – Kent. The thesis itself – 'The field systems of Kent' (1963) formed the basis of a significant group of twelve or more journal articles, of some work on other counties such as Sussex and Derbyshire, and of wider-based publications on England, Britain and Ireland. This extensive and influential research had strong archival and documentary bases, and where appropriate included field evidence and discussion of practical aspects of farming, including ploughing techniques. An early major paper – 'Open Fields and Partible Inheritance on a Kent Manor'[4] is a good example of his extensive and expert use of archival material. The paper is mainly concerned with the evaluation of two propositions advanced by the historian M. D. Nightingale: "that Kentish open fields were common fields, i.e. a product of co-operative ploughing and subject to common grazing, and that partible inheritance had ceased to be the popular custom in Kent by the end of the eleventh century".[5] The paper partly confirms the first of these, and refutes the second. In doing so, it draws on evidence, *inter alia*, from the Kent Archives Office, The Public Record Office, manuscripts from Gillingham Corporation and from Gillingham Public Library, material from Lambeth Palace Library and Canterbury Cathedral Library, together with a range of published sources. Most of the manuscript sources were in medieval Latin, and from them Alan derived an informative set of statistics, which in turn were used as a basis of ingeniously produced and mapped reconstructions of the layouts of holdings. The range of linguistic and interpretative skills required would, at the time, have been regarded as quite normal (though now quite rare among geographers), but the quality of synthesis analysis, and explanation was exceptional.

A capacity for synthesis and re-evaluation is also demonstrated in a paper published in 1965 on H. L. Gray's *English Field Systems* (1915, re-printed in 1959).[6] In only a few pages, the essential components of Gray's models of evolution of regionally distinctive types of field systems are outlined and assessed in the light of more recent research. A brief agenda is set out for further work ("The hare which Gray set off has not yet been caught"[7]), including firm advocacy of the use of the retrospective method. Thus: "Since 1915, surprisingly few studies of field systems have been both undertaken and presented retrospectively. But of this Gray would have been convinced: the great attack on field systems should be conducted by working backwards through their past. For this attack, Gray's *English Field Systems* is the surest of salients".[8] The goal here identified is exemplified in *Studies of Field Systems in the British Isles* (1973), jointly edited with Robin Butlin,[9] where the retrogressive approach was followed in most of the chapters. This collection covered most of England, Scotland, Wales and Ireland. A notable *lacuna* was the South-West of England. Provision had been made for coverage of this region by a distinguished young postgraduate (now a greatly respected senior scholar), but the publishers took a conservative view, and a potentially significant contribution was excluded at the book's planning stage. The book as a whole was well received both as a synthesis of past and prognosis for future work. It remains, particularly in its regional detail, a major text on the subject. Alan Baker's own chapter, 'Field Systems of Southeast England' is a masterly synthesis. It opens with a quotation from Gray's *English Field Systems,* moves to a detailed discussion of the changing field systems of Kent, which is then followed by a shorter comparative analysis of the field systems of Surrey and Sussex. The reconstructions, including the graphic representations, are logical, imaginative, and convincing.

To the considerable skills evidenced in the historical reconstructions described above should be added mention of Alan's gift of acute observation – perhaps with the eye of an artist – and a style of writing that combines economic and compelling prose with a predictable invitation to challenge and debate. The combination of these talents has without question contributed to the wide dissemination of an impressive range of new and provocative ideas, both through informal debate and through publication.

The inquisitive ideologue

Questions of methodology and ideology have been central in Alan Baker's work in historical geography, and are particularly conspicuous in his research and writing from the late 1960s and early 1970s onwards. Interest in the retrogressive method in history, rooted in the work of the French historian Marc Bloch, has already been mentioned. A brief speculation on "The Future of the Past", written with three others following a lively discussion one evening, after a research seminar at University College, in Bertorelli's restaurant in Soho (the outline, if memory serves correctly, having been drafted on a paper table napkin) helped to accelerate a trend.[10] Major reflections and examples of methodologies and ideologies in historical geography were combined in a volume of reprints of seminal articles in historical geography, published in 1970 and co-edited with J. D. Hamshere and J. Langton.[11] The general aim was to look at the problems posed by historical source materials used by historical geographers and to review the methodological problems and possibilities associated with them. The editors, in their introduction, accepted the importance of empirical analysis, but then rehearsed some interesting ideas about theory, the formulation of hypotheses, and the systems concept. In some ways this was symbolic of the beginning of a more conscious engagement of historical geographers in Britain and elsewhere with a variety of developing theories, particularly and appropriately of the dynamics of location, and also involvement in what became known as the Quantitative Revolution. A contemporary review and prediction of changes in the ideologies and methodologies of historical geography was that of Hugh Prince, in his seminal paper of 1971: "Real, imagined and abstract worlds of the past".[12]

The long and complex processes of engagement by historical and human geographers with ideologies and methodologies, which continue to the present and doubtless into the future, cannot and need not be rehearsed in great detail here. What is important to our purpose here is that Alan Baker has, for a period of more than thirty years, been at or ahead of these frontiers, both as innovator and disseminator of knowledge. Initial engagements with systems theory and some of the immediate possibilities for quantitative methods led on to broader advocacy of imaginative ideological exploration and evaluation of the ideas of historical geographers outside Britain. In the edited book *Progress in Historical Geography* (published in 1972), Alan Baker's first chapter – "Re-thinking Historical Geography" – is sub-divided into indicative sections on: 'The challenge of change'; 'Explorations in other disciplines'; 'Statistical approaches in historical geography'; 'Theoretical approaches in historical geography'; 'Behavioural approaches in historical geography'; and 'Prospect of the past'. The start of the first chapter is mildly apocalyptic in tone. "It is, paradoxically, the future that matters most in the study of historical geography. For a discipline to flourish it has to be flexible. But the future is not usually regarded as the province of the historical geographer. Any discussion of the changing nature of historical geography, of the necessity for adaptation, will be admittedly partial, personal and possibly idiosyncratic. None the less, historical geography is a profession. Those who profess a religious faith recognize that their profession dies unless it is renewed by frequent rediscovery of its reason for being. In the case of historical geography the need is for a re-thinking of its philosophy and methodology".[13] Curiously no summary or prescriptive conclusion was provided for the book as a whole, with the individual chapters on nine different countries and regions left, in a sense, to speak for themselves.

Ideological and methodological matters were not discussed in isolation from empirical research. Alan's research from the late 1960s – in effect after the move from University College, with Darby, to Cambridge – was shifting rapidly towards nineteenth-century rural France and the geography of its post-Revolutionary voluntary associations. The standardized national archive and statistical sources for France provided opportunity for both quantitative and qualitative research, and appealed to a scholar with a talent for intellectual precision and organizational efficiency. More will be said on this later. At about the same time, Alan was energetically engaged in a broader dissemination of the themes of historical geography, both through more general syntheses such as the highly successful book *Man Made the Land. Essays in Historical Geography*, co-edited with Brian Harley and published in 1973, and through the initiation of what began life as the *Studies in Historical Geography* series, published initially by David and Charles, from 1970-1974. Brian Harley was also co-editor of the series. Four books were published under this imprint. The series was for a short period published by Dawson in Kent, with eight books published between 1976-1980, and since 1982 by Cambridge University Press, with 32 books in the series by the Press to date. The books in the series show a commendably catholic view of historical geography, and include titles of primarily ideological and methodological interest together with others of thematic and regional interest. The standards set are very high, as is the quality of physical production: great credit is due to the editorial panel and to the members of Cambridge University Press responsible for commissioning and publishing this very fine scholarly series.

Alan's own publications in the field of methodology and ideology in historical geography further developed from the late 1970s through the 1980s and the 1990s. Of particular interest and influence were three books in the *Studies in Historical Geography* series, co-edited with Mark Billinge, Derek Gregory and Gideon Biger respectively. The first of these was *Period and Place: Research Methods in Historical Geography*, published in 1982.[14] The editorial preface indicates that the book was produced to give account of papers and discussions at a symposium in Cambridge, organized under the auspices of the International Geographical Union's Working Group on Historical Changes in Spatial Organization. Alan Baker had been a prime mover in the attempt, through this working group, to bring historical geography more actively within the activities of the IGU. The thirty-one short papers were divided between six sections: developments in historical geography; reconstructing past geographies; the identification and interpretation of geographical change; behavioural approaches to the study of geographical change; theoretical approaches in historical geography; and historical sources and techniques. This was a very balanced collection, covering both traditional and newer approaches, and it gave an idea, particularly in the behavioural and theoretical sections, of some future directions. Alan Baker, in his paper 'On ideology and historical geography' advocated a more intensive and critical engagement by historical geographers with ideology and with the new insights offered by innovative work in other disciplines. He stated that: "Since the mid-1960s, however, there has been a flurry of publications concerned with the methodology of historical geography and a reflexive critique is undoubtedly being undertaken, albeit by a minority of practitioners".[15] In the supporting endnote the articles cited are all by himself (a series of pieces from *Progress in Human Geography* for 1977, 1978 and 1979), an indication of his position as a pioneer in this field. He led on to a consideration of the value of Marxist perspectives in historical geography, pointing to the challenges posed by Marxist to non-Marxist historians through their work in Britain and other European countries. The implications and prospects for this in terms of humanistic perspectives, particular practice, generalizations, total historical geography and progress and praxis were outlined and evaluated with characteristic boldness and concise insight. The Cambridge Geography Department at that time was an energetic debating forum for such ideas, not least on account of Derek Gregory's explorations of ideology, agency, action and structure in human geography and Mark Billinge's explorations of phenomenological approaches to historical geography.[16]

This link was continued in Baker and Gregory's edited *Explorations in Historical Geography. Interpretative Essays* (1984). This was very much a Cambridge product, with innovative essays contributed by the editors and by their colleagues Mark Billinge, Mark Overton and Richard Smith. Alan Baker's own essay, reflecting in part his strong interest in the historical geography of France, is titled 'Reflections on the relations of historical geography and the *Annales* school of history', and is a critical and compelling historiographical analysis of the *Annales* school of French historians and of French historical geography.[17] A prescriptive section appears towards the end, strongly supportive of the structural and social historical geography evidenced in the essays in the book, and leading helpfully to a demonstration of its application by reference to his own work on fraternity in the French countryside during the nineteenth century. The book ends with an informative (but less than theatrical) 'exploratory discussion' between Alan Baker and Derek Gregory on 'Some *terrae incognitae* in historical geography'.

In many respects *Explorations* was an important and influential work, sounding a call to a greater involvement with new intellectual opportunities in historical geography in Britain and elsewhere. A demonstration of the possibilities presented came with the publication, again in the Cambridge series, of *Ideology and Landscape in Historical Perspective*, the outcome of a conference in Jerusalem in 1989. *Ideology* was edited with an Israeli colleague, Gideon Biger, and prefaced by a powerful essay on ideology and landscape by Alan himself. Sub-titled 'Essays on the meanings of some places in the past', it demonstrated the variety of representations of landscapes to be found through, for example, maps, writings, relict features, settlement and political processes and paintings.

Debate in historical geography

The 1970s and 1980s were particularly exciting times in which to practice historical geography. Although university finances in Britain were becoming more difficult and the general number of academic appointments declining, activity in historical geography developed in exciting ways, in terms of an increasing range of perspectives, opportunities for innovation by different interest groups, and for publication.[18] Additional opportunities were developing at an international level, including the establishment of the CUKANZUS conferences from 1975 and the IGU Working Group from 1976. Many international links were, of course, developed by individual initiative. Among the most thoughtful and influential of these were the consistent efforts made by Alan Baker to link historical geographers from overseas to the Cambridge department by inviting them as visitors. It is nigh impossible to list the many countries from which they came, but we are personally aware of visits to Cambridge by scholars from China, Japan, India, Singapore, Australia, South Africa, Canada, the United States, Israel, France, Sweden, and Germany. In addition, Alan made a number of visits to centres with research interest in historical geography, for example in Eastern Europe, in Japan and China. Both processes resulted in valuable interchanges of ideas and in publications. Alan himself published accounts of historical geography in some of the countries he visited, and also accounts of the state of historical geography in Britain.[19] Whether the basis of visits to Cambridge by overseas scholars was formal or informal, guests have inevitably been welcomed and catered for by kind, thoughtful and deeply considerate hospitality by Alan and Sandra Baker and by Emmanuel College, Cambridge. To these must be added the large number of British and Irish historical geographers who have attended the Friday night Occasional Discussions in Historical Geography.

Opening the speculative encounter between himself and Derek Gregory, in 'Some *terrae incognitae* in historical geography', Alan Baker remarked "that debate should be a central concern of historical geographers is … the premise on which this collection of essays is based".[20] It has already been noted how this consistent concern to foster a critical exchange of ideas regarding the sources, methods, philosophies and ideologies of historical geography has been a hallmark of Alan's teaching, research and writing over many years. An important space for such debate was created on the 18 October 1968, when the first Occasional Discussion in Historical Geography was held in Cambridge. In the following thirty years no less than two hundred and forty papers have been presented to this forum, including twelve by Alan himself.[21] From the beginning, the discussions were seen as both *informal* and *irregular* – hence the title 'Occasional' – and each followed a dinner held with the speaker and discussants. The series was initiated by Alan Baker, Harold Fox and Jack Langton with the early meetings held, according to Baker "in a variety of private basements, flats and houses in Cambridge, including a memorable Discussion led by Paul Koroscil on cultural and historical geography in North America, at 60 Storey's Way, the home of Clifford Darby".[22] Their location, from early 1971 until the summer of 1999, however, was in Alan Baker's room in Emmanuel College.

A key feature of the Discussions has always been a commitment to frank, open, and sometimes combative, debate. But the purpose has always been to interrogate the theoretical frameworks and empirical substance of the various papers presented with a view to their improvement as pieces of historical geography. Many of the papers first presented at the Occasional Discussions have gone on to publication as significant papers in the *Journal of Historical Geography* and elsewhere. The atmosphere of collegiality and conviviality of these occasions owed much to Alan's powers of organisation and attention to detail, always supported by the other historical geographers at Cambridge.[23] Leaders of Occasional Discussions have been overwhelmingly from Britain and, in particular, from Cambridge itself. Such facts may suggest to historical geographers outside the Cambridge circle a rather insular preoccupation with the fostering of 'a Cambridge School'. Yet consultation of the list of speakers who have presented over the last thirty years reveals scholars from New Zealand, Canada, Australia, Denmark, the United States, France, Germany, South Africa, Israel, Japan and India, as well as from the United Kingdom and Ireland.[24] Nor have all the speakers been 'historical geographers' in the narrow, disciplinary sense of that term: they have included economic and social historians, archaeologists, anthropologists, sociologists and geomorphologists.[25]

Alan became Editor of the *Journal of Historical Geography* in 1987, a position he held until 1996. During his tenure, Alan's editorial mission was shaped by two of his principal concerns as an historical geographer: first, to increase the visibility of the sub-discipline in both interdisciplinary and international terms; and, secondly, to encourage and foster critical debate more explicitly though its pages. Yet he was sensitive to the context within which he assumed editorial control, taking care to situate his own agenda for change with reference to the *Journal's* continuing scholarly traditions. The *Journal*, published by Academic Press, had been established by John Patten and Andrew

Clark in 1975, and the tradition of editing jointly from Britain and North America continued via the efforts of David Ward, Robert Mitchell and Hugh Prince. In his first editorial, Baker recalled Patten and Clark's original prospectus: "to reflect and to foster progress in historical geography, to provide an international focus and an interdisciplinary forum for those who have something to say about the geography of an area at some time past. Their approach to historical geography was eclectic and liberal: no particular dogma about the nature of historical geography was to be promoted: the study of no problem, period or place in the past was to be prohibited; and the *Journal* would welcome not only articles based upon scholarly research but also essays concerned with the philosophy and methodology of historical geography".[26]

Alan Baker indicated his desire to build upon these foundations, ensuring that the *Journal* would not become preoccupied with policing disciplinary boundaries or carving out a distinctive niche for historical geography in isolation from broader trends in the social and human sciences. Thus, he continued, "the *Journal*'s doors are open wide to articles concerned separately or jointly with analysis and synthesis, with description and explanation, with action and structure, with individual and collective understandings, experiences and interpretations of places in the past as well as with their mental and material cultural geographies".[27] This indicated an open, catholic stance to the field, where empirical and theoretical approaches to the study of the past would be welcomed equally with attempts to understand their philosophical and ideological constitution, as both representations of and with material foundations in, past historical geographies. The commitment to interdisciplinarity was underlined by a desire to foster links with not only traditional companions in history and archaeology, "but also many anthropologists, demographers, economists, ethnologists, sociologists and other specialists", while not ignoring the need for a renewal of connections with the wider discipline of Geography itself, both contemporary human geography and physical geography.[28] Baker ended his editorial with a plea for historical geographers to pay much closer attention to the construction of their accounts of places in the past. In this respect the *Journal* would, therefore, "welcome both essays addressing the central problem of geographical description, and critical discussions of sources, techniques and methodologies".[29] Writing better historical geography should be a common aim therefore, but one which assumed a greater importance in efforts to communicate with those outside the relatively narrow confines of the scholarly community.

Between 1987 and 1988 Alan Baker initiated a series of interventions in debates over the purpose and practice of historical geography within a broader canvas of historical problems within the historical and human sciences. These ranged from Paul Glennie's consideration of the transition from feudalism to capitalism; the debate between Derek Gregory and Jack Langton on the regional geography of England during the industrial revolution; Gerry Kearns's critique of world-systems theory and the debate between Richard Dennis and David Harvey on the relations between theory and evidence in the prosecution of historical geography.[30] Of these, the debate between Gregory and Langton in particular provoked interest and comment from a wide range of historians and historical geographers.[31] Yet 1988 can be seen as a high-water mark for the creation of an explicit space for debate within the pages of the *Journal*. The final issue of that year saw Gillian Rose and Miles Ogborn discussing feminism and historical geography but it was not until 1994 that a further specific polemical debate was engaged with, by Robert Mayhew, on the contextualising of intellectual history.[32]

The concern to push debate in historical geography, in this explicit sense, to the top of the *Journal*'s agenda can only be regarded as a partial success, therefore. Whilst reaction to work published in historical geography (and elsewhere) continued, of course, in the time-honoured fashion of critique, reassessment and challenge within subsequent academic papers, the intellectual challenge of interrogating accepted and contentious claims to historical geographical knowledge shifted to a series of extended book review articles.[33] In 1997 Alan Baker's tenure as Editor of the *Journal* passed to Michael Heffernan, after ten years at the helm. In his first editorial Heffernan, one of Baker's former research students, neatly summed up the influential role of his predecessor, drawing attention to the "skill and sensitivity" with which he had handled the editorial role, whilst remaining true to his "characteristically expansive vision of historical geography and of the *Journal*'s place as the natural home for the published record of the discipline".[34]

Studies of rural communities in nineteenth-century France

For a period of over thirty years Alan has developed a strong and productive interest in the historical geography of post-Revolutionary rural France. The particular focus has been the historical geography of voluntary associations in the *Département* of Loir-et-Cher, substantially as represented in the materials in the departmental archives at Blois. Some years ago the Bakers purchased a 'stone tent' (as they describe it) in the Beauceron village of Mulsans, near Blois in the middle Loire Valley, from which many archival and field excursions have ventured forth over the years, often in the company of colleagues and students from Cambridge. The combination of detailed explorations in the archives with Alan's keen eye for place and people in places has resulted in a large number of exemplary and highly stimulating articles on this region in the nineteenth and early twentieth centuries.

The contrast, afforded by this research engagement with French peasantry and rural life in the past, with the metropolitan sophistication of London and the intellectual context of Cambridge, is interesting. Has this research and location, at least in part, perhaps reflected a need and opportunity to become more closely involved with and to dig deeper into human nature and process than is possible from locations within polite urban academic societies? Familiarity, through residence in a village in Loir-et-Cher for twenty-five years, with active, changing rural life in France has undoubtedly given different perspectives and perhaps senses of priority.

The fruits of this research have recently been gathered together in a *magnum opus: Fraternity Among the French Peasantry. Sociability and Voluntary Associations in the Loire Valley, 1815-1914*.[35] Prefaced by a contextual review of past and current portrayals of peasants and peasantry in nineteenth-century France, the themes of the book then follow a logical and informative sequence, from the theory and practice of fraternal association and the character of Loir-et-Cher in the nineteenth century to a detailed analysis of individual associations: insurance societies, mutual aid societies, fire-fighting corps, anti-phylloxera syndicates, and agricultural associations. Many new maps were drawn, mainly based on archival data, and the book is also sensitively illustrated with a wealth of evocative contemporary photographs, gleaned from archives and private collections. The concluding chapter reviews the overall patterns of timing and spacing of voluntary associations in Loir-et Cher, and ends with a review in the context of France as a whole. This is a pointer to current and future work on voluntary associations in a wider range of representative French regions, the results of which will doubtless be published in many more articles and books. *Fraternity Among the French Peasantry* has, deservedly, been well reviewed. For his distinguished research on the historical geography of France, Alan was honoured in 1997 by the French Government as a *Chevalier dans l'Ordre des Palmes Académiques*. In 1999 he was awarded the degree of D. Lit. by the University of London for his work in this field.

Conclusion: a total historical geographer

Alan Baker has played a major role in the understanding and promotion of historical geography, in Britain, France, and many other parts of the world. This has happened because of the rare combination of his exceptional intellectual gifts with a creative vision, a deep concern for academic and other communities and their individual members, together with a flair for writing and the dissemination of knowledge. Alan's influence is worldwide. He has played an important strategic role at Emmanuel College, Cambridge, as a Fellow, as Senior Tutor, and for a short period as Vice-Master. He was a highly effective and innovative Head of the Geography Department in the University of Cambridge for five years, and has had a major role in the co-ordination of the evaluation of Geography through the Cambridge University Schools Examination Board, including work submitted for the *Baccalauréat*. Alan is an outstanding teacher, whose lecture and field courses in historical geography at Cambridge, including those on France, North America and the Methodology of Historical Geography, have been innovative and exemplary. His lectures have always been clearly structured and presented, well-informed and challenging. His students have particular recollections of his course on the historical geography of France, with its powerful evocations of the nature of peasant life through readings of Zola's novels, especially *La Terre*. Alan's gifts as a teacher in the field have been effectively demonstrated in his field courses to Blois, and his excursions to the Yorkshire Dales for first-year geography students at Emmanuel College.

Leading scholars have an influence that extends beyond their published writings and undergraduate teaching, of course. In this Alan is no exception. For more than thirty years he has been actively and successfully supervising postgraduate students at Cambridge. His combination of an imaginative contextualisation of theories and debates, careful attention to detail and, above all, a deep concern for the welfare of his research students has resulted in no less than sixteen Ph.D.'s and two M. Litt degrees (see Appendix 2). Characteristically, it has resulted in as many friends. The range of topics covered and the diversity of approaches adopted are testament to Alan's belief in providing a liberal and supportive research environment within which individual solutions to research problems could be worked out. Eschewing a more dogmatic model of the relationship between supervisor and supervised, Alan always treated his students as equal partners in the conduct of research and, while his hand is no doubt evident in every thesis produced, the final product was always very much theirs.

Given Alan's own research interests discussed above, it is not surprising to discover the range of research undertaken by successive research students (see Appendix 2). Six were primarily concerned with field systems, agriculture and the evolution of the rural economy in England and Ireland between the Middle Ages and the early twentieth century; six with various aspects of urban and rural France between the eighteenth and twentieth centuries; remaining topics focused on the dynamics of settlement evolution, and the historical geography of urban and regional change in England, Spain and Australia between the sixteenth and the twentieth centuries. The diversity through time and across space embodied in these research theses is a tribute to a scholar whose historical and geographical imagination, energy and enthusiasm is remarkable. The influence of Alan's teaching and guidance continues: no less than nine of his former research students hold University posts, five of them as Professors, whilst he is continuing to supervise doctoral students.

We look forward with confidence to his continuing and varied contributions to the field of historical geography.

Acknowledgement

We are grateful to Michael Heffernan for his comments on a first draft of this chapter.

NOTES

1   A. R. H. Baker, Henry Clifford Darby 1909-1992, *Transactions, Institute of British Geographers* N.S. **17** 4 (1992) 497.

2   *Ibid.*, 498.

3   See, for example, the comments in A. R. H. Baker, Editorial: Legacie, or an enlargement of the discourse of historical geography [after Samuel Hartlib, 1651], *Journal of Historical Geography* **15** (1989) 1-3.

4   A. R. H. Baker, Open fields and partible inheritance on a Kent Manor, *Economic History Review* Second Series, **XVII** 4 (1964) 1-23.

5   *Ibid.*, 1.

6   A. R. H. Baker, Howard Levi Gray and *English Field Systems:* An Evaluation, *Agricultural History* **39** 2 (1965) 86-91.

7   *Ibid.*, 6.

8   *Ibid.*

9   A. R. H. Baker and R. A. Butlin (Eds), *Studies of Field Systems in the British Isles* (Cambridge 1973).

10 A. R. H. Baker, R. A. Butlin, A. D. M. Phillips and H. C. Prince, The future of the past, *Area* **4** (1969) 46-51.

11 A. R. H. Baker, J. D. Hamshere and J. Langton (Eds), *Geographical Interpretations of Historical Sources. Readings in Historical Geography* (Newton Abbot 1970).

12 H. C. Prince, Real, imagined and abstract worlds of the past, *Progress in Geography* **3** (1971) 1-88.

13 A. R. H. Baker (Ed.), *Progress in Historical Geography* (Newton Abbot 1972) 11.

14 A. R. H. Baker and M. Billinge (Eds), *Period and Place: Research Methods in Historical Geography* (Cambridge 1982).

15 A. R. H. Baker, On ideology and historical geography, in *ibid.*, 235.

16 See D. J. Gregory, *Ideology, Science and Human Geography* (London 1978); D. J. Gregory, The discourse of the past: phenomenology, structuralism and historical geography, *Journal of Historical Geography* **4** (1978) 161-173; M. D. Billinge, In search of negativism: phenomenology and historical geography, *Journal of Historical Geography* **3** (1977) 55-67.

17 A. R. H. Baker, Reflections on the relations of historical geography and the *Annales* school of French history, in A. R. H. Baker and D. Gregory (Eds), *Explorations in Historical Geography. Interpretative Essays* (Cambridge 1984) 1-27.

18   See H. C. Prince, *Geographers Engaged in Historical Geography in British Higher Education 1931-1991*, Historical Geography Research Series, Number 36 (London 2000).

19   For example, A. R. H. Baker, Historical geography in Czechoslovakia, *Area* **18** (1986) 223-228; *idem*, Historical geography in Canada, *Journal of Historical Geography* **17** (1991) 92-94; *idem*, Historical geography: an essay on its basic characteristics, *The Deccan Geographer* **30** 2 (1993) 13-21; *idem*, Agendas for historical geography: reflections upon an International Conference for Historical Geography, Beijing, P. R. China, 16-20 July 1996, *Journal of Historical Geography* **22** (1996) 479-483.

20   A. R. H. Baker and D. Gregory, Some *terrae incognitae* in historical geography: an exploratory discussion, in Baker and Gregory, *op. cit.*, 180.

21   *30 Years of Cambridge Occasional Discussions in Historical Geography 1968-1998* (University of Cambridge: Department of Geography, 1998).

22   A. R. H. Baker, Twenty years of "Discussions" in historical geography, *Historical Geography* **18** (2) 3. See also A. R. H. Baker, Cambridge Occasional Discussions in Historical Geography 1968-1988, *Historical Geography* **19** (1) 7-12.

23   See Baker, Twenty years of "Discussions" *op. cit.*, 3, where he notes that between 1968 and 1988 "there have been 161 Discussions, accompanied by the consumption of more than one thousand bottles of claret and burgundy".

24   30 Years of Cambridge Occasional Discussions, *op. cit.*

25   Baker, Twenty years of "Discussions", *op. cit.*, 4.

26   A. R. H. Baker, Editorial: the practice of historical geography, *Journal of Historical Geography* **13** (1987) 1.

27   *Ibid.*

28   *Ibid.*

29   *Ibid.*, 2.

30   P. Glennie, Debate: the transition from feudalism to capitalism as a problem in historical geography, *Journal of Historical Geography* **13** (1987) 296-302; D. Gregory, Debate: the production of regions in England's Industrial Revolution, *Journal of Historical Geography* **14** (1988) 50-58, J. Langton, Debate: the production of regions in England's Industrial Revolution: a response, and D. Gregory, Reply, *Journal of Historical Geography* **14** (1988) 170-176; G. Kearns, Debate: history, geography and world-systems theory, *Journal of Historical Geography* **14** (1988) 281-292; R. Dennis, Review article: faith in the city?, *Journal of Historical Geography* **13** (1987) 310-316, D. Harvey, Comment: the production of value in historical geography, *Journal of Historical Geography* **14** (1988) 305-307 and R. Dennis, Comment in reply: by the waters of Babylon, *Journal of Historical Geography* **14** (1988) 307-308.

31   See, for example, I. Black, Geography, political economy and the circulation of finance capital in early industrial England, *Journal of Historical Geography* **15** (1989) 366-384; P. Hudson, The regional perspective, in P. Hudson (Ed.), *Regions and Industries: A Perspective on the Industrial Revolution in Britain* (Cambridge 1989) 5-38; R. A. Butlin, Regions in England and Wales *c.* 1600-1914, in R. A. Dodgshon and R. A. Butlin (Eds), *An Historical Geography of England and Wales* (Second Edn: London 1990) 223-254.

32   See G. Rose and M. Ogborn, Debate: feminism and historical geography, *Journal of Historical Geography* **14** (1988) 405-409 and R. Mayhew, Debate: contextualizing practice in intellectual history, *Journal of Historical Geography* **20** (1994) 323-328.

33   See, for example, C. Earle, Historical geography in extremis? Splitting personalities on the postmodern turn, *Journal of Historical Geography* **21** (1995) 455-459.

34   M. Heffernan, Editorial: the future of historical geography, *Journal of Historical Geography* **23** (1997) 1. See also: D. Meyer, Editorial, *Journal of Historical Geography* **22** (1996) 1, where he records that "it is a pleasure to work with Alan Baker who has done so much to make the *Journal of Historical Geography* a premier international journal".

35   A. R. H. Baker, *Fraternity Among the French Peasantry. Sociability and Voluntary Associations in the Loire Valley, 1815-1914* (Cambridge 1999).

Chapter Two

RECONCILING GEOGRAPHIES, REPRESENTING MODERNITIES

RICHARD DENNIS

"Only connect ..." E. M. Forster's famous aphorism on the title page of *Howards End* drew attention to the benefits of engaging positively with those different from ourselves.[1] We might equally, if less ambitiously, use his words as an injunction to the practitioners of different traditions in historical geography to empathise with and respond to one another's different ways of seeing and interpreting the past, to effect a reconciliation of different historical-geographical cultures, thereby also reaffirming the status of Geography as an integrative discipline. To this end, my essay comprises three main sections: on the practice of historical geography; on the concept of 'modernity' as a unifying theme for much historical geography; and an extended illustration of how different approaches to historical geography can be integrated through a discussion of contrasting modes of representation of the same 'space of modernity', in this case 'Oxford and Cambridge Mansions', a briefly fashionable block of 'French flats', erected on the margins of London's West End in the late nineteenth century.

Practising historical geography

My starting point is a series of reflections on the practice of historical geography over the decades since Alan Baker, John Hamshere and Jack Langton assembled their *Geographical Interpretations of Historical Sources*, at the height of the positivist revolution in geography, and since Alan Baker first wrote about *Progress in Historical Geography*, discussing the roles of quantification and model-building, theory and the study of perceptions in historical geography.[2] This was a very 'modern' conceptualization of historical geography, predicated on hypothesis-testing and the use of a scientific method in the social sciences. In my own field of urban historical geography it involved the 'testing' of urban ecological theory, including zonal and sectoral models of urban structure and social area theory which posited a disaggregation of distinct dimensions of economic, family and ethnic status in the spatial structuring of cities. The data were culled from census enumerators' books, tax assessment records and city directories for cities of different sizes and at different periods in the past. The aim was to position cities along a continuum from 'pre-modern' to 'modern'.[3] Historical demographers likewise compared their empirical findings to the dictates of gravity models and distance-decay curves; and students of settlement patterns, frontier colonization and innovation diffusion employed simulation models in which the deterministic rules of social physics were tempered by probability.[4] Yet, as Baker anticipated, "Mathematical techniques will probably never be so widely used in historical geography as elsewhere in geography: its practitioners tend to be non-mathematical by inclination as well as by training, and much historical data is not amenable to mathematical analysis".[5] Nevertheless, he expected the future of historical geography to be more quantitative, as well as more theory-driven, than its past.

In practice, quantitative analysis, applying statistical tests of significance to the results of correlations, regressions, analyses of variance and the like, found few adherents among historical geographers, but a continuing empirical tradition favoured the mapping and tabulation of descriptive statistics; and some limited uses of location theory were matched by attempts to apply systems theory to historical problems.[6]

Writing in the context of the late 1970s growth of humanistic geography, the Canadian historical geographer, Cole Harris, advocated the cultivation of a "historical mind" which was "open, eclectic … sensitive to motivation and value" but far from purely humanistic. Harris' historical mind also embraced "factual accuracy" including the use of statistical compilations and analysis, and was "enthusiastic for hard data" and "ready to make explicit use of appropriate theory".[7] In Harris' own case, the espousal of theory subsequently led him to focus on questions of power and modernity, building on the theoretical insights of Foucault, Habermas, Mann and Giddens; not 'testing' concepts such as structuration, but using them as "ideas that lurk … in the background of research" and continuing to advocate, and practise, "a historical geography that is both immersed in data and sensitive to general literatures".[8]

But Harris' all-embracing eclecticism, his distaste for prescriptive methodology and his call "to deemphasize technique and resurrect learning"[9] could also be interpreted as elitist, or at least patrician. He lay most emphasis on the researcher's acquisition of experience and familiarity with their chosen society and landscape, and his conclusion that "there is no methodological palliative to replace years of study and creative intelligence"[10] runs contrary to all the bureaucratically imposed wisdom about training in 'research methods' and the expectations of 'academic audits' and 'research assessment exercises' for instant and quantifiable results.

In theory, comprehensive forms of training in methods should at least have guaranteed new generations of graduate students capable of both quantitative and qualitative methods of analysis. In practice, historical geography has increasingly been dominated by cultural theory and qualitative, mainly textual and visual, sources. By the 1980s 'narrative' was back in fashion, now an artful 'strategy' rather than the unconscious storytelling which had been perceived by 1960s positivists as providing only "loose, weakly explanatory, non-rigorous modes of temporal explanation";[11] and 'imagined geographies' found new respectability under the umbrellas of 'iconography', 'social construction' and 'representation', and especially by substituting for 'imagined' the more affirming 'imaginative'.[12] All of this would be fine if the new cultural geography was perceived, both by colleagues and students, as just one way of doing historical geography. In practice, it seems to be assumed that all historical geography is now cultural geography.

This absorption of historical geography into cultural geography, as for example in the creation in many British geography departments of 'Cultural and Historical Research Groups' (albeit sometimes merely packaging to impress external assessors), implies that the only contemporary human geographers to whom historical geographers relate are 'cultural', and that the agenda for historical geography focuses only on issues such as identity, consumption, (post)colonialism, and heritage, that are the fashion in cultural geography. By definition, too, historical geography is defined as 'qualitative' because cultural geography is 'qualitative'. Other kinds of historical geography, and especially anything quantitative, are marginalised or, at best, partitioned into a separate territory of 'Historical-GIS' where, with a few honourable exceptions, the emphasis has been more on technical wizardry than the historical significance of the questions being asked or the patterns being generated. As somebody who began as a quantitative urban historical geographer, who took some time to discover art and literature and politics, but has latterly wanted to see those different sources and different methodologies as complementary, not alternative, whose enthusiasm for the eclecticism of Cole Harris' 'historical mind' remains undiminished,

I want to re-assert the importance of a diverse historical geography which gives equal value and attention to different approaches.

It is often claimed that one of the strengths of Geography as a teaching discipline are all those 'transferable skills' and 'key skills' which make graduate geographers attractive to a wide range of potential employers. Geographers, we say, are good with words *and* figures *and* graphically; good at problem-solving on their own and working as members of teams, in the laboratory or the field. Yet, in practice, most students, given the choice, opt either for a preponderance of 'technical' courses, in which they are rarely expected to write discursively or interpretatively, or for mostly 'cultural' courses, where they never need calculate a percentage let alone engage in any more serious numerical analysis. Not only external assessors but undergraduates perceive historical geography as a subset of cultural geography – so most of the students who take courses or opt to pursue research in historical geography are less than expert in numerical skills. This, in turn, has implications for the future of the sub-discipline if it is ever hoped to recruit researchers and teachers with anything more than expertise and interest in cultural questions and qualitative sources and methods.

My aim, therefore, is the re-integration of quantitative and qualitative perspectives. This is partly a matter of reflexivity – how do qualitative sources provoke quantifiable investigations of the generality of individual accounts and experiences, and how do quantitative analyses stimulate studies of attitudes and experiences, of what the numbers *mean*? But it impinges on at least two areas of recent methodological debate in human geography: an increased interest in 'multi-method analysis' and a concern for methods of 'validation', such as 'triangulation', to demonstrate the 'rigour' of qualitative analysis, or to confirm the generality or acceptability of interpretations, especially to 'user-groups' who may be sceptical of qualitative methods, such as in-depth interviews and ethnographies.[13]

In a series of papers in *Professional Geographer* devoted to 'Multi-method research' in population geography, John McKendrick noted that "method is only one of a number of 'multiple' strategies", to be considered alongside the employment of multiple theoretical frameworks and multiple writing styles, and Elspeth Graham differentiated between multiple research methods, multiple forms of data collection, and multiple methods of data analysis or interpretation.[14] McKendrick also contrasted research "more appropriately conceived as a series of discrete projects of different methods", where different methods are used to address related but different questions, with research where "more than one method is used to address a particular research question" which may be conceived as "a variation on the principle of triangulation".[15]

Rather as the most interesting aspect of regression analysis is often the identification of residuals – observations that do not conform to the overall trend and which therefore demand particular attention – so the value of triangulation is not only to confirm the same results by the use of different methods or sources, but, more provocatively, to "tease out meaningful inconsistencies", not discarding contradictory findings but seeking to reconcile them.[16] Likewise, Baxter and Eyles comment that "verification based solely on appeals to conventional wisdom [the fit with existing literature] ... may be counterproductive to the development of new wisdom"[17] which is surely the point of worthwhile research.

Baxter and Eyles are primarily concerned with contemporary research and the scepticism with which research methods such as unstructured interviews and discussion groups are often regarded by those trained in scientific method, but their arguments are also applicable to historical applications of ethnographic method, to oral histories, iconographies and the use of unique textual and visual sources of evidence. They place particular emphasis on "the notion of credibility", which they define as "the degree to which a description of human experience is such that those having the experience would recognize it immediately and those outside the experience can understand it".[18] Asserting that "triangulation is one of the most powerful techniques for strengthening credibility", they distinguish at least four different kinds of triangulation, involving multiple methods, sources, investigators and theories.[19] "Investigator triangulation" is where different researchers (such as different interviewers or, in historical research, different archival transcribers or different readers of the same text) investigate the same phenomenon and compare results. In what ways does the interpretation – whether of a will or a painting – depend upon the characteristics (including, to invoke Cole Harris again, the experience) of the interpreter? Here, however, we are veering away from 'credibility' towards 'dependability': "Credibility refers to the accurate representation of experiences while dependability focuses attention on the researcher-as-instrument, and the degree to which interpretation is made in a consistent manner."[20]

How do these debates affect historical geography? Prior to the cultural turn, historical geographers generally paid more attention to sources than to method, tracking down new sources which were assumed to speak for themselves. Then, challenged from within historical geography especially by Brian Harley's interest in the power relations within which cartographic sources were situated, but quickly extending his questions to quantifiable sources such as censuses and tax records previously assumed to offer an objective account of past reality, we became alert to issues of representation.[21] But while multiple readings of texts – and of landscapes as texts – became acceptable, the same generosity was not extended to quantitative sources. Numbers were the product of unequal power relations and therefore unacceptable; words and images were equally the product of individual experience, bias, ideology and inequality, and therefore – apparently – all the more interesting! Meanwhile, we have paid less attention to different varieties of method, implicitly assuming that method is commonsense, that experienced researchers can be trusted to use their sources sensibly. I am *not* arguing for a new fetishization of method – not after my celebration of Cole Harris' anti-method! – but at the very least, these debates about multiple methods, triangulation and credibility should make us more self-conscious about the practice of historical geography. How do we conceptualize the research *process*? Where do our research questions come from? And how do we envisage the researcher's role: as experimental scientist, as creative artist, as detective (and, if so, as painstaking, literal minded, private investigator, methodically piecing together different strands of evidence, or as lateral thinking, speculative, Sherlock Holmes)?

Modernity

The image of the detective is an appropriate one to carry with us into the second part of this paper, on 'modernity' in historical geography. The detective, like the *flâneur*, is an archetype of modernity, observing, classifying, ordering, but apart, either inconspicuously merging with the crowd, or positioned just out of sight, or in disguise, playing out one of numerous multiple identities. 'Modernity' has been a keyword in the historical geographer's lexicon over the last decade or more, whether on its own or in collaboration with globalization, imperialism, colonialism or postcolonialism.[22] While a few human geographers have dismissed modernity's blandishments, many more have been attracted by the term's multiple identities: from the path-breaking research agendas of David Harvey, Allan Pred, Mike Watts and Miles Ogborn to recent textbook reinforcement in Brian Graham's and Catherine Nash's *Modern Historical Geographies*.[23] Despite his own caution against "regarding associations as part of some controversial 'modernising' process, or even as a sign of 'modernity'", Alan Baker's work on the voluntary associations of Loir-et-Cher can also be considered a study of rural modernity, not only the modernization expressed through economic, political and technological change, but also the local and societal attitudes and responses to, and experiences of, modernization.[24]

Urban historical geographers have been using 'modern' in a theoretical way for a long time: think of David Ward's paper on "Victorian cities: how modern?" published in 1975, which explored the spatial implications of debates on class formation and class consciousness then current among social historians.[25] Much of the research undertaken in the 1970s was less sophisticated and more mechanistic than Ward's, involving a crude conceptualization of cities differentiated by class or ethnicity into zones and sectors: the more segregated the classes, or the more distinctive the social areas, the more modern the city.[26] But this was to focus on only one dimension of modernity – the development of order, classification, segregation and specialisation in the modern city – and, of course, to reinforce that narrow focus by adopting 'modern' methods of classifying cities, social areas and people, such as the calculation of indices of dissimilarity, or the use of factorial ecology. Moreover, the data on which these analyses were based were the product of modern ideologies and methods of measurement: censuses and tax assessments as instruments of the modern nation-state, and street directories as aids to modern business. The origins of the census – in Britain in 1801 – parallel the rise of panoptical thinking and the equation of knowledge with power.[27]

Yet modernity, as Marshall Berman insisted, involved empowerment as well as constraint, discipline and surveillance: the attempt by people to become subjects as well as objects of modernization, to make themselves 'at home' in a modern world, establishing an "intimate unity" between "the modern self and the modern environment".[28] If an earlier generation of urban historical geographers, trained in a Conzenian tradition of urban morphology,[29] were good on the modern built environment, and quantitative geographers were good on spatial structures, neither had much to say about the modern self. This, of course, is what cultural geographers have been so good at; but in concentrating on questions of consciousness and identity they have too often neglected the spatial and material structures within which identities were constructed and performed. Moreover, the evidence of modern identity – the realist novel, new forms of art, a popular press – were just as much the product of modernization as were censuses and social surveys.

My argument is, therefore, that 'modernity' provides an ideal vehicle for the integration of the cultural, the social, the political and the economic; and also of quantitative and qualitative approaches. Even if we restrict ourselves to different contemporary representations of modernity, we need to consider not only art and literature, but also new mentalities of ordering the city through mapping, measurement and social survey.

It may be argued that the looseness and ambiguity of 'modernity' is a fatal weakness. Every age and place can claim to be modern, and recent research has been concerned to push back the boundaries of modernity from Berman's focus on the nineteenth and early twentieth centuries, through the 'early modern' (a term which gains new layers of meaning when we start to think what it was about, say, seventeenth-century London that warranted the adjective 'modern'), at least to Renaissance Italy; and also to discover alternative, rural and colonial, modernities, and alternative experiences of modernity, through the eyes of women, children, the poor – all those groups hitherto marginalized by a concentration on male, middle-class experience.[30] However, the focus on 'modernity' advocated in this essay is less about a place or a period than about a method for integrating studies of modernization and modern experience, 'representations of space' (both the models of present-day historical geographers and the images and ideals of contemporaries) and 'spaces of representation' (how people on the ground occupied space in everyday practice).[31]

The illustration I present in the remainder of this chapter may seem to retreat from what I have just outlined. It is set firmly in the classic period of modernity – the late nineteenth century, among an upper middle-class population in one of the most technologically and economically 'modern' cities in the western world. Moreover, the principal protagonists were male, although, as I shall argue, the implications for women's experience of modern urban life were profound. But I am presenting this particular example primarily as an illustration of method, and as a blueprint for teaching undergraduates and masters' students in the practice of research in historical geography.

Among precedents for this study, Mona Domosh used a case study of the New York World Building, erected in Lower Manhattan in 1890, to illustrate a multi-layered approach to landscape interpretation;[32] but while she referred to the need to situate her primarily symbolic interpretation in the context of economic and technological change, her own evidence was drawn principally from newspaper and magazine reports and illustrations, and she relied on existing accounts of, for example, land values and skyscraper technology that were not specific to the building. Her approach was certainly multi-scale and contextualised in a variety of economic, political and cultural arenas, but it was not really multi-method. Closer in spirit to my own approach is Deryck Holdsworth's critique of landscape studies in which, while commending the subtlety of cultural interpretations by Domosh and others, he also asserts the importance in his own work of "corporate archives, fire insurance plans, asssessment records, property transfer records, mortgage records, and the manuscript census to try to make visible, to bring out of concealment, what is not visible in today's landscape".[33] Holdsworth effectively demonstrates the wisdom of Alan Baker's advice that "productive research demands a committed, long-term relationship with an interrelated family of sources".[34] However, my objective is not merely the understanding of *landscape*. I am more concerned with the connections between modern landscapes and modern society. Consequently, I move between literary, architectural, social-scientific, cartographic and visual discourses, to explore how they informed or contradicted one another, then, and how they provoke questions of one another in our analysis, now.

Oxford and Cambridge Mansions: 'French Flats' in Victorian London

Literary Discourse

George Gissing (1857-1903) was not a 'modern' novelist in the sense of literary modernism, but he was very interested in, if frequently appalled by, modern society, and his novels, often set in London, are full of references to modern phenomena, new technology, new business practices, new women, and new environments, not least the contemporary fascination for, and cynicism towards, living in so-called 'French Flats'. Whatever might be acceptable in Paris, or even in Glasgow and Edinburgh, living in flats ran counter to English ideals of domesticity, family and property.[35]

Gissing situated several of his more bohemian and nouveau riche characters in flats. In *In The Year of Jubilee* (1894), we encounter the independently minded Beatrice French, establishing the South London Fashionable Dress Supply Association to sell cheap imitations of the latest fashions to suburban women of pretensions but no taste. Beatrice's habits revealed her to be the archetypal 'new woman': she displayed an interest in the stock market, a penchant for cigarettes – a special brand for women from a shop in the Haymarket – and a desire to live in a flat: "something convenient and moderate… A bachelor's flat". In due course this materialized, on the second floor of a block of recently (late 1880s) completed flats in Brixton, then a middle-class suburb. She packed the small flat overfull with fashionable bric-a-brac and upholstery. There was a lack of pure air, making for a "decidedly oppressive" atmosphere, compounded by the spread of cooking smells, a "disadvantage attaching to flats".[36]

In *The Odd Women* (1893), Mrs Luke Widdowson, "a handsome widow of only eight-and-thirty", occupied a flat in Victoria Street, a street first laid out in the 1850s as part of a government-sponsored slum clearance scheme designed to eradicate the 'Devil's Acre', linguistically as well as visually a classic example of modernity's 'other'.[37] By the late 1880s, when Gissing set his story, Victoria Street was lined by blocks of imperially named flats: Prince's Mansions, Queen's Mansions, Edinburgh Mansions, Members' Mansions (to attract members of parliament). Mrs Widdowson used her flat to entertain "a heterogeneous cluster of pleasure-seekers and fortune-hunters, among them one or two vagrant members of the younger aristocracy". In pursuit of her objective to marry into a title, she "lived at the utmost pace compatible with technical virtue". Her flat was as crowded as Beatrice French's, only more expensively; and she could afford to purify the air: "Luxurious fashion, as might have been expected, superabounded; perfume smoothed the air."[38]

The plot of *The Odd Women* hinged on the ambiguity of public and private space in another block of flats, in Bayswater, where two of the principal male characters – Bevis and Barfoot – each had flats. Monica, the young wife of Mrs Widdowson's dour brother-in-law, becomes infatuated with Bevis, but when she goes to visit him, she panics at the presence of strangers coming and going on the stairs, and knocks instead on the door of Barfoot, whom she knows to be out, having just seen him leave the building. One of the strangers, a private detective hired by her jealous husband, naturally assumes that the innocent Barfoot must be the object of her affection and does not bother to follow her back inside the building when she returns later with a note for Bevis.[39]

All these flats were in localities where flats were commonplace by the late 1880s, but in none of these cases did Gissing identify a specific building. However, in *The Whirlpool* (1897), the childless Hugh and Sibyl Carnaby, the latter "devoted to the life of cities, wherein she shone", return from travelling the world – the civilization of Honolulu and the savagery of Queensland – to take up residence in a flat in 'Oxford and Cambridge Mansions' – a real block of flats, erected in stages between 1880 and 1882, just outside Edgware Road Station.[40] The building was divided into twelve blocks, each containing six suites (one per floor) and arranged around a common staircase. In contrast to "the foreign system" of "only one entrance, invariably a stately *porte-cochère*", the building followed the American system which "does away with the very satisfactory palatial element of the foreign flat, but … seems to answer our singular English ideas of privacy".[41] *The Builder* observed that "The site being rather confined and of a peculiar shape, some blocks are smaller than others; the smallest, however, contain six rooms, and the largest nine rooms in each suite" (Figures 1, 2).[42]

A recurrent theme in *The Whirlpool* was the 'servant problem' – the increasing difficulty of obtaining trustworthy servants and the attractiveness of flats which required few if any servants to run them. In fact, the novel opened with the report of a robbery at the Carnabys' then residence in Hamilton Terrace, St John's Wood, evidently an 'inside job' since it coincided with the disappearance of their housekeeper.[43] Later in the novel, the widowed Mrs Frothingham, whose husband had committed suicide following the collapse of his Britannia Loan, Assurance, Investment & Banking Company, enthused about her move into a flat in Swiss Cottage:

FIGURE 1
Oxford and Cambridge Mansions, 1883.

Source: City of Westminster Archives Centre.

*But I'm sure it is possible to be too civilised – to want too many comforts, and
become a slave to them. Since I have been living here, Mr Rolfe, you can't think
how I have got to enjoy the simplicity of this kind of life. Everything is so easy;
things go so smoothly. Just one servant, who can't make mistakes, because there's
next to nothing to do. No wonder people are taking to flats.*[44]

In conclusion, she assured her visitor that "most happiness is found in simple
homes". By contrast, in the Carnabys' flat in Oxford and Cambridge Mansions: "Here
was no demonstration of the simple life; things beautiful and luxurious filled all
available space, and indeed over-filled it ..."[45]

Architectural Perspectives

Gissing wrote in 1896, but set the Carnabys' move into the mansions in 1889, when
they would still have been new and fashionable places in which to live.[46] Indeed, they
attracted considerable attention in the architectural press when they – and the
neighbouring, Hyde Park Mansions, actually nowhere near Hyde Park – first opened,
because F. E. Eales, the son in the architectural firm of C. Eales & Son, which designed
the blocks, was one of the leading advocates of flats in London. Addressing the
Architectural Association early in 1884 on "The Arrangement of Buildings in Flats",

FIGURE 2
Oxford and Cambridge Mansions, Ground Plan.

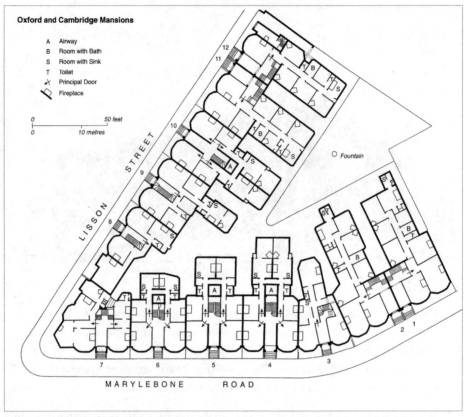

Source: *The Builder*, **XLIV** (February 3, 1883); Goad Fire Insurance Plans, 1902, 1930 (City of Westminster Archives Centre)

he discussed such critical modernist issues as the need for segregation within flats. To ensure a proper separation of eating, sleeping and working areas, "[t]he correct and best arrangement, where possible, is to have the bedrooms separated from the kitchen and servants' part by the reception-rooms".[47] Eales' ideal suite comprised "three good rooms in front, consisting of dining-room, drawing-room, and best bedroom", a total of four bedrooms, kitchen and offices, bathroom and two water-closets, one of which could be in the bathroom (a practice decried by the editor of *The Builder*, George Godwin, as "most disagreeable, unsuitable, and uncivilised"), the other "in the neighbourhood of the servants' part". "The two principal rooms should be so arranged that they can be thrown into one, as occasion may require", using folding or sliding doors or revolving wooden shutters.[48]

In practice, only two rooms in each suite in Oxford and Cambridge Mansions faced onto the street. Many of the rooms overlooked 'areas' (ventilation shafts) or deep, narrow yards between the buildings (Figure 2), little different from the conditions pertaining in working-class model dwellings, such as the Farringdon Road Buildings so roundly condemned by Gissing in *The Nether World* (1889).[49]

Eales assumed that the occupants of his flats would be middle-class families, but one discussant of his paper thought that "[t]hose who would be most likely to take up their residence in these buildings would be people without families, and those who had artistic and professional occupations ... what seemed to be required would be small suites of rooms suitable for diminutive families and for bachelors". In response, Eales conceded that "Flats were not suited for children. It was most disagreeable to be always meeting them on the stairs." Nor, opined another questioner, were they appropriate for "invalids and old people" who "would not be able to walk downstairs, and would be too nervous to use the lifts".[50] In fact, no passenger lifts were included in Oxford and Cambridge Mansions, although they were installed in the adjacent Hyde Park Mansions, completed a year later. Eales was concerned that the cost of providing an elevator (and an attendant) would be about £800 per annum, yet to attract tenants away from suburban living annual rents could be set no higher than £150-200. It was clearly not viable to provide a separate elevator for each block of six suites.[51]

While it was important to differentiate between family space and servants' space, it was also undesirable to have a completely separate staircase for servants and tradesmen, lest servants from different flats engaged in gossip and in other ways misbehaved on the back stairs, a Parisian abomination most graphically illustrated in Zola's *Pot-Bouille* (1882).[52] Segregation had to be reconciled with surveillance. Eales preferred to install dumb-waiters so that coal and groceries could be hoisted up to flats on upper levels, but he did not offer any solution for the problem of masters (and, presumably, mistresses, although all the discussions in the architectural press were conducted on the [erroneous] supposition that tenants were all male) and servants meeting on the main staircase.[53] French practice was also condemned by some of his audience. Mr J. A. Gotch noted that in France:

> the same attention was not paid to sanitary matters as in this country. The whole
> French feeling, in regard to domestic matters, was essentially different to what it
> was here. The concierge did not mind living in a room having no communication
> with the open air, and with entirely borrowed light; whereas, in this country, we
> should not like to house any human being in that manner.[54]

Eales also disliked the idea of resident concierges or janitors, "either of whom requires two rooms at least allotted to him, and either of whom is an expense", preferring a simple tablet in each entrance hall, with names, suite numbers and in-out signs – an Oxbridge staircase, in fact.[55] True to this proposal, there were no *resident* hall porters or attendants listed among the residents of Oxford and Cambridge Mansions in the 1891 census.

One person who *was* listed in 1891 was William H. White, architect and secretary of the Royal Institute of British Architects. Then a 53-year old bachelor, White's personal history confirms his candidacy as the ideal apartment-house tenant, almost as if he had walked out of a Gissing novel! His father had been a doctor in the Bengal Medical Service. After becoming an associate of the RIBA in 1864, White practised in Paris for several years until, fleeing the Franco-Prussian War, he moved to India, working for the Public Works Department of the Indian government in Calcutta. In 1873, he returned to London as an examiner in architecture at the Royal Indian Engineering College, quickly immersing himself in the activities of the RIBA and in architectural journalism. In 1878 he was appointed secretary of the institute and editor of its publications, retaining these positions until his death in 1896.[56] But it was not just as an artistically minded bachelor, with both colonial and continental experience, that White is of interest. Drawing on his experience of Parisian life, White was also one of the most vociferous advocates of flat-living in London in the 1870s and 1880s, writing regularly in *The Builder* as well as in the RIBA's own journals.

In November 1877, White addressed the RIBA on "Middle-Class Houses in Paris and Central London", claiming an authority on the subject unequalled by any other English member of the Institute, based on "a residence of ten consecutive years in middle-class Paris houses". He invoked a tradition of flat-living that dated back to the *insulae* of Cicero's Rome, extending to France "even before Palladio's time" and to seventeenth-century Scotland. Interestingly, he avoided using the word 'flat' as much as possible, preferring to label the apartments as 'houses'. We could interpret White's strategy as one of minimizing the modern, stressing the continuity of modern flats with a romanticised past and eschewing a modern vocabulary likely to alienate his audience. Thus, in describing a typical modern Second Empire Parisian apartment building, he referred to each storey above the ground floor as a 'house' of about eight rooms, extending round three sides of a courtyard from a hall which opened off the principal staircase to back stairs at the end of a servants' corridor. The courtyard was reached through an archway from the street, sufficient to accommodate carriages, which could stop to discharge their passengers under cover of the arch directly at the foot of the main stairs. A two-room porter's lodge also opening onto the archway was positioned to overlook stairs, entrance and courtyard. Most servants for all the 'houses' would sleep on the top floor, under the slope of the mansard roof, and accessed by the back stairs.[57] The only difference between the building described by White and that in which Zola set *Pot-Bouille* is that White envisaged only one family per storey, whereas Zola located at least two households on each floor. In contrast to the chaotic collision of residents' social and sexual lives in Zola's fictional building, White claimed that the arrangement in his typical Paris apartment house allowed each family to maintain its privacy. His fellow architects might claim that London was a city of single-family houses, but in practice, throughout central and inner London, most houses were subdivided: most Londoners were lodgers, sharing staircases, kitchens and toilets in a far from private fashion.

White blamed British fear of change for the failure to provide modern apartments in London. Referring to the Duke of Bedford's estate, and especially to houses in Bedford Street, Covent Garden, where White himself lived prior to the building of Oxford and Cambridge Mansions,[58] he noted the insistence on maintaining narrow (18-feet) lots, even when leases expired and redevelopment was undertaken. Yet, above the ground-floor shops, pairs of houses had sometimes had holes cut in the fireproof party walls to allow leaseholders to cross between adjacent buildings. How much more sensible it would be to redevelop such terraces with 'houses' arranged horizontally. He even suggested building just the fireproof shell of a new building, the staircase, elevator and plumbing for toilets, and then letting prospective tenants specify "the distribution of rooms in the different residences", an 1870s forerunner of today's loft-living! Still anxious to avoid the dreaded word 'flat', he concluded by emphasising that his proposals would offer "not barracks, taverns, or co-operative hotels, but – purely and simply – homes".[59]

In many respects, Oxford and Cambridge Mansions failed to live up to White's blueprint – there were no elevators, no archway for alighting in the dry, no grand entrance staircase. Yet he remained a tenant of flat 8B from the building's opening in 1881 until his death fifteen years later.

Social Statistics

While we can use the census to identify a few sample individuals, whose personal life histories may be more or less amenable to historical detective-work, we can also use it in a more systematic way, to qualify, refute or confirm the accounts provided by Gissing and other commentators, and to raise new questions with which to interrogate textual representations. Altogether, the 1891 census for Oxford and Cambridge Mansions enumerated 62 households, a total of 204 persons. Most flats

TABLE 1

Age structure of residents, Oxford and Cambridge Mansions, 1881-1891

Age	1881				1891			
	Males	Females	Serv'ts	Total (%)	Total (%)	Males	Females	Serv'ts
0-9	6	5	-	15	5	5	6	-
10-19	1	2	5	11	15	8	4	18
20-29	4	9	6	26	28	11	20	26
30-39	7	8	2	23	19	11	16	11
40-49	4	3	-	10	16	8	17	7
50-59	3	2	1	8	10	6	9	5
60-69	1	2	-	4	6	2	8	2
70+	2	-	-	3	2	3	1	-
Total	28	31	14	73	204	54	81	69

Source: 1881 census (RG11/152/28-29); 1891 census (RG12/99/94-98)

contained three or four inhabitants; the largest households included most of the handful of children living in the mansions, and, in one case, five 'visitors'. In total, only twelve households included anybody under 16 years old, two of whom were servant girls. Three more were 'visitors', and one a 'boarder'. There was only one baby and he had been born to a family who seem to have been 'passing through': they were listed in neither ratebook nor directory compiled a few months before and after the census. But most households, like the Carnabys in *The Whirlpool*, were childless. Yet ten years earlier, there had been just as many children aged 0-9 in the 22 households then enumerated in the partially completed building as there were in 1891 in the full complement of 62 households (Table 1). Evidently, the unsuitability of flats for small children had to be proved by experience.[60]

The Carnabys had returned from touring the world. The census tells us only where residents had been born. But among the inmates at Oxford and Cambridge Mansions in 1891 were two single women born in Jamaica, a banker's clerk whose wife was from the West Indies, a colonial broker's agent from Tasmania, an elderly widower from Calcutta, another spinster from India, a stock exchange dealer from the Punjab, women from Buffalo and Niagara, and several household heads of continental European birth – from Denmark, Holland, Rotterdam, Oporto and Paris. There were also children born in Cairo and Cape Colony, evidence of further colonial connections on the part of British parents; and wives and their sisters and visitors from Dresden, Augsburg, Hamburg, Luxembourg, Belgium and Boulogne. Most servants were from

TABLE 2

Birthplace of residents, Oxford and Cambridge Mansions, 1881-1891

Birthplace	1881				1891			
	Heads	Other Family	Servants	Total (%)	Total (%)	Heads	Other Family	Servants
Foreign	5	2	-	10	14	12	15	2
London	1	3	3	10	9	4	6	8
Rest of England	8	17	1	36	29	16	26	17
Rest of British Isles	8	15	10	45	48	24	32	42
Total	22	37	14	73	204	56	79	69

Source: 1881 census (RG11/152/28-29); 1891 census (RG12/99/94-98)

rural counties of England, but two households employed Swiss servants. Excluding servants, exactly 20 per cent of those resident in Oxford and Cambridge Mansions on Census Day, 1891, had been born outside the British Isles. The pattern had already been set by the advanced guard of occupants who had moved in by April 1881: five of the first 22 household heads had been born outside the British Isles (Table 2). Here was a cosmopolitan population, reflecting London's role as an imperial city, and the role of flats – in particular – in providing either a temporary foothold or, especially for widows, a permanent home in the metropolis.

However, in other respects the character of residents changed dramatically during the building's first decade. In 1881, only two out of 22 household heads were women; 17 were married men. There was no reason to doubt White's and Eales' assumption that flats were for men and their families. But ten years later, among 56 heads of household present on census day were 13 spinsters, 9 widows, and 4 married women with no husband present.[61] Nine households were headed by bachelors and three by widowers. Married couples, like the Carnabys, constituted fewer than a third of all households (Table 3). This was much closer to the image of flat-dwellers presented in *The Odd Women* and *In The Year of Jubilee*. Yet there was little evidence of young, independently minded, "new women" like Beatrice French. Only three female heads were aged under 30, and only two were recorded with any kind of occupation: a 26-year old "vocalist" and a 52-year old "journalist". The vast majority were "living on their own means".

Not that all of the men were more productively employed! Certainly there were few people in trade, and proportionally more in 1881 than 1891. The earliest residents included retired military officers, artists in music and stained glass, a classical tutor (not too different from how Gissing earned most of his money in

TABLE 3

Marital status of heads of household, Oxford and Cambridge Mansions, 1881-1891

Marital Status	**1881**			**1891**		
	Male	Female	Total (%)	Total (%)	Male	Female
Single	2	1	**14**	**39**	9	13
Married	17	-	**77**	**39**	18	4
Widowed	1	1	**9**	**21**	3	9
Total	20	2	22	56	30	26

Source: 1881 census (RG11/152/28-29); 1891 census (RG12/99/94-98)

the early 1880s), and two lawyers, but also iron and wine merchants and a grocer. By 1891, the professional and leisured classes had increased relative to the handful of merchants, a commercial traveller, a tailor and an upholsterer, who were the only people 'in trade'. Of course, it might be anticipated that the better-off would wait until all the building work had been completed before taking up leases, and that there may have been some short-term financial incentives to attract the first, more modestly endowed tenants.[62]

What is clear is that few of the first tenants stayed for very long. Of the 22 households listed in April 1881, only five were present just over five years later, including both female tenants. By 1891, there were only two survivors. Focusing in more detail on the heads of household recorded in the 1891 census, residential persistence rates were higher – 28 per cent were still in residence five years later, and the same proportion of tenants had been resident for at least five years (i.e. since 1886) – but still modest by the standards of other studies of middle-class persistence (Table 4).[63] But the study of mobility is complicated because it is likely that many tenants would also have had a house in the country (hence the head-less, servant-only households recorded in the 1891 census), or may even have moved away for a year or more, temporarily removing their names from the street directory and subletting their flats. We can infer such a process from attempting to link entries in censuses and directories, but we can gain direct evidence from letters and diaries, such as those written by Gissing during his tenancy of a flat at nearby Cornwall Residences. No fewer than ten households listed at Oxford and Cambridge Mansions in directories for both 1891 and 1892 were absent on Census Day, while others reappeared after absences from the directories for several years.[64] Among Gissing's correspondents, Edith Sichel, who had inherited a substantial legacy on the death of her father in 1884, had a house in Chiddingfold, Surrey, and a flat in Barkston Mansions, Earl's Court. Gissing himself occupied his flat on successive three-year leases, which obliged him to pay rent – in his case a modest £10 per quarter – for the full three-year period even if he decided to vacate the flat well before the expiry of the lease. His letters are full of increasingly desperate attempts to find a tenant to help recoup some of the costs during his lengthy absences on Mediterranean tours.[65] For the well-off, and even for the less well-off, like Gissing, modernity meant an ability to come and go, and also a desire to move house in line with changing circumstances and opportunities, a fluidity which challenges the historical geographer so accustomed to mapping the fixity of spatial patterns.

Another indication of the modest, and possibly transient, status of the earliest tenants was the comparative absence of resident domestic servants in 1881: an average of only 0.64 resident domestic servants per household. Ten years later, there was an average of 1.11 servants per household, including two male servants, six housekeepers and 17 cooks. Eleven households made do without any servants, 35 had one resident domestic, but 14 had two, and two households employed 3 servants: not quite the simplicity urged by Mrs Frothingham but still modest compared to some other blocks, such as Albert Hall Mansions, next to the Royal Albert Hall, which recorded an average of 2.5 servants per household. However, it was probable that households which did not employ a live-in servant still benefited from the services of daily help or a

TABLE 4

**Residential persistence of heads of household,
Oxford and Cambridge Mansions, 1881-1897**

Sample	1881 census	1882 directory	1884 directory	1887 directory	1891 census	1892 directory	1893 directory	1897 directory
				% heads resident in:				
1881 census (n=22)	100	86	32	23	9	5	5	9[1]
1891 census (n=57)	4[2]	9[2]	19	28	100	81	61	28

Source: 1881 census (RG11/152/28-29); 1891 census (RG12/99/94-98); Kelly's Post Office Directories for London, 1882-1897.

1   One tenant, absent in 1892 and 1893, had returned to the building by 1897.

2   Building only partially complete in 1881-82.

Directories were compiled in the months immediately preceding the year to which they refer, e.g. 1882 directory would have been compiled in late 1881.

Censuses were normally conducted in April.

FIGURE 3

The area around Oxford and Cambridge Mansions, Marylebone, from Charles Booth's
***Descriptive Map of London Poverty* (1889)**

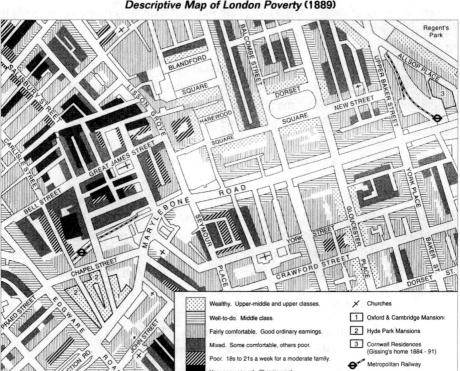

charwoman. Even the impecunious Gissing could not survive without Mrs King, whom he paid four to five shillings per week.[66]

Visualization

1889 – the year when the Carnabys moved to Oxford and Cambridge Mansions – was a momentous year in London history; it marked the first elections to the newly established London County Council but also the first edition of Charles Booth's 'Descriptive Map of London Poverty'.[67] Much has been written about Booth's survey. Here I can merely note its value in any teaching about 'modernity' and any discussion about the ideological nature of quantitative surveys: the value-laden way in which the data were collected (working with information provided by school-board officers, whose job was to ensure that children attended school regularly, a discipline most urgently required in poorer areas of the metropolis, what could Booth really have

FIGURE 4

Oxford and Cambridge Mansions c. 1910. As depicted in *Residential Flats and Chambers to Let*, advertising brochure, no date.

Source: City of Westminster Archives Centre.

learnt about middle-class and childless families living in buildings such as Oxford and Cambridge Mansions?); the scale of presentation (whole blocks or streets assigned to one category, thereby implying a false degree of social homogeneity within, and of segregation between streets); the naturalizing colour scheme (gold for wealth, black for crime-related poverty); the panoptical rationale for mapping.[68] To the south and west of Edgware Road lay streets, squares and crescents of uniformly high status, but within their immediate neighbourhood, Oxford and Cambridge Mansions and Hyde Park Mansions stood out as an island of wealth, abutting 'fairly comfortable' streets, yet only a few hundred yards from some of the 'black spots' which connect Booth's mapping to other Victorian conceptualizations of 'slums' and the redemptive possibilities of surgery to remove them from the body of the city (Figure 3).[69]

Booth's was not the only visual representation of Oxford and Cambridge Mansions. Not only was the building featured in *The Builder* soon after its completion (Figure 1), but it also appeared in an advertising brochure produced by the managing agents, Consolidated London Properties Ltd, in about 1910-12 (Figure 4).[70] These two illustrations display contrasting versions of modernity. The 1883 depiction played down any disruptive modernity, portraying a 4-square block, apparently regular and symmetrical, ultra-respectable, the street outside replete with evidence of domesticity including children and a dog. The mansions were modern compared to the Georgian and vernacular buildings on the margins of the illustration, but unlikely to shock. Face on, they could be mistaken for a row of tall town-houses, a collision of French mansard and Dutch gables atop an Elizabethan façade! The later advertisement was desperate to assure prospective tenants of the building's continuing modernity, presenting it in the classic ocean-liner perspective beloved of skyscraper illustrators. But the accompanying text exposed the building's inferiority compared to its neighbour. Oxford and Cambridge Mansions had "tradesmen's and coal lifts"; its location was "adjoining Hyde Park Mansions". Hyde Park Mansions had passenger lifts, two w.c.s in each apartment, a listed telephone number and a "central position, very convenient for City and West End", "Near Marble Arch". Visual assertions of modernity can sometimes prove evidence of its absence.

Conclusion

I have tried to interweave a variety of contemporary sources – maps, social survey, architectural drawings and essays, photographs, census returns, street directories, ratebooks, fiction, letters, diaries – all focused on what today appears as a very ordinary Victorian building, passed unnoticed by thousands of Londoners every day as they travel in and out of central London on the Circle Line and along Westway and the new and old Marylebone Roads. Questions raised by Gissing's novel and by architectural treatises – about the lifestyles and characteristics of flat-dwellers and their servants – find confirmation and qualification in the analysis of censuses and directories; some apparent contradictions – the silence of architects compared to the fascination shown by novelists concerning the situation of women in flats – are explained, at least in part, by studying the changing composition of the blocks' population over time; while we can make more sense of the patterns revealed by mapping and statistical tabulation when we encounter personal accounts of the diurnal and life-cycle time geographies of individual residents. In themselves, flats were one component of modernity: embodying the architectural and technological up-to-date, rooted in new ideologies of spatial planning, and both accommodating and stimulating new lifestyles and new social structures. In many places flats engendered resistance and conflict; everywhere they provoked artistic, scientific and behavioural responses as they intruded on the consciousness of social commentators, passers-by and visitors as well as inmates. In partnership with other, equally modern, elements in the urban landscape – model dwellings and suburbs, gin palaces and museums, railway stations and station hotels, tram lines and telegraph wires, sewers and subways, lofts and sweatshops, warehouses and department stores, cemeteries and botanical gardens, infirmaries and universities, banks and office blocks, fire stations and police stations, city halls and music halls – they contributed to cities that were both more segregated into specialist zones and more integrated and interconnected than ever before. Indeed, starting from a single building, the trail of sources and questions can quickly lead us all over the city, offering new insights into perceptions, attitudes, *mentalités* and *genres de vie*.

Even in this extended illustration many more trails could have been followed. Statistical tabulations only acquire meaning through comparisons with similar enumerations of other spaces: what sex-ratios, or family structures, or birthplaces, or mobility rates characterised people who rented rooms, or occupied suburban villas, or town-houses? The continental and imperial connections merit further attention. The everyday life of residents and their neighbours' reactions could be explored through reports in local newspapers of social activities, 'at homes', burglaries, announcements of families coming and going for the season, and letters to the editor, thereby shifting emphasis from 'representations of space' on which I have concentrated to 'spaces of representation' (though, still, of course, mediated by what the press deigned to report).

Oxford and Cambridge Mansions are not unique. Similar combinations of literary, cartographic, visual and quantitative sources exist for numerous buildings in modern cities. As a teaching device, the focus on one building or one small area brings together a range of sources and methods; as a research method, the focus on selected 'spaces of modernity' is equally productive, taking the case study not so much as an illustration of a neatly pre-packaged theory, but opening up a huge range of questions for further research that require, and demonstrate the efficacy of, a catholic approach to historical geography.

Acknowledgements

Thanks are due to the staff of both Westminster Archives Centre and Kensington & Chelsea Local Studies Library for their assistance, especially Jill Barber, Education Officer at Westminster and Carolyn Starren, Local Studies Librarian at Kensington, who have enthusiastically cared for successive cohorts of UCL students practising what I have preached above. More formally, I am grateful to Westminster Archives Centre for permission to reproduce illustrations of Oxford and Cambridge Mansions (Figures 1 and 4), and to Elanor McBay of the Cartographic Unit, Department of Geography, UCL, who prepared the ground plan and map (Figures 2 and 3).

NOTES

1   E. M. Forster, *Howards End* (London 1910).

2   A. R. H. Baker, J. Hamshere and J. Langton (Eds), *Geographical Interpretations of Historical Sources* (Newton Abbot 1970); A. R. H. Baker, Rethinking historical geography, in A. R. H. Baker (Ed.), *Progress in Historical Geography* (Newton Abbot 1972) 11-28.

3   See, for example, the papers in *The Victorian City*, theme issue of *Transactions of the Institute of British Geographers* **NS 4** (1979) 125-319.

4   W. Norton, *Historical Analysis in Geography* (London 1984).

5   Baker, Rethinking, 17-18.

6   R. A. Butlin, *Historical Geography: Through the Gates of Space and Time* (London 1993), chapters 3 and 4.

7   R. C. Harris, The historical mind and the practice of geography, in D. Ley and M. Samuels (Eds), *Humanistic Geography* (Chicago 1978) 123-37.

8   Cole Harris, Power, modernity, and historical geography, *Annals of the Association of American Geographers* **81** (1991) 671-83.

9   Harris, The historical mind, 133.

10   *Ibid.*, 136.

11   D. Harvey, *Explanation in Geography* (London 1969) 422, quoted in Baker, Rethinking, 13.

12   Milestones on this route include H. C. Prince, Real, imagined, and abstract worlds of the past, *Progress in Geography* **3** (1971) 4-86; D. Cosgrove and S. Daniels (Eds), *The Iconography of Landscape* (Cambridge 1988); D. Gregory, *Geographical Imaginations* (Oxford 1994).

13   J. Baxter and J. Eyles, Evaluating qualitative research in social geography: establishing 'rigour' in interview analysis, *Transactions of the Institute of British Geographers* **NS 22** (1997) 505-25; J. H. McKendrick, Multi-method research: an introduction to its application in population geography, *Professional Geographer* **51** (1999) 40-50.

14   *Ibid.*, 46; E. Graham, Breaking out: the opportunities and challenges of multi-method research in population geography, *Professional Geographer* **51** (1999) 76-89.

15   McKendrick, *op. cit.*, 42.

16   *Ibid.*, 43.

17   Baxter and Eyles, *op. cit.*, 509.

18   *Ibid.*, 512.

19   *Ibid.*, 514.

20   *Ibid.*, 517.

21   B. Harley, Historical geography and its evidence: reflections on modelling sources, in A. R. H. Baker and M. Billinge (Eds), *Period and Place: Research Methods in Historical Geography* (Cambridge 1982) 261-73; *idem*, Maps, knowledge, and power, in Cosgrove and Daniels, *op. cit.*, 277-312.

22   See the increasingly elaborate entries for 'modernism' and 'modernity' in successive editions of *The Dictionary of Human Geography*: R. J. Johnston, D. Gregory and D. M. Smith (Eds), *The Dictionary of Human Geography: Third Edition* (Oxford 1994) 386-92; R. J. Johnston, D. Gregory, G. Pratt and M. Watts (Eds), *The Dictionary of Human Geography: Fourth Edition* (Oxford 2000) 510-16.

23 N. Thrift, *Spatial Formations* (London 1996); D. Harvey, *Consciousness and the Urban Experience* (Oxford 1985); *idem, The Condition of Postmodernity* (Oxford 1989); A. Pred, *Recognizing European Modernities* (London 1995); A. Pred and M. Watts, *Reworking Modernity* (New Brunswick, NJ 1992); M. Ogborn, *Spaces of Modernity: London's Geographies 1680-1780* (New York 1998); B. Graham and C. Nash (Eds), *Modern Historical Geographies* (Harlow 2000).

24 A. R. H. Baker, *Fraternity among the French Peasantry: Sociability and Voluntary Associations in the Loire Valley, 1815-1914* (Cambridge 1999). The quotation is from page 316.

25 D. Ward, Victorian cities: how modern? *Journal of Historical Geography* **1** (1975) 135-51.

26 For a critical review, see R. Dennis, *English Industrial Cities of the Nineteenth Century: A Social Geography* (Cambridge 1984).

27 E. Higgs, *A Clearer Sense of the Census: The Victorian Censuses and Historical Research* (London 1996).

28 M. Berman, *All That Is Solid Melts Into Air: The Experience of Modernity* (London 1982) 132; *idem,* Why modernism still matters, in S. Lash and J. Friedman (Eds), *Modernity and Identity* (Oxford 1992) 33-58.

29 J. W. R. Whitehand (Ed.), *The Urban Landscape: Historical Development and Management: Papers by M.R.G. Conzen* (London 1981).

30 C. Nash, Historical geographies of modernity, in Graham and Nash, *op. cit.*, 13-40.

31 H. Lefebvre, *The Production of Space* (Oxford 1991).

32 M. Domosh, A method for interpreting landscape: a case study of the New York World Building, *Area* **21** (1989) 347-55.

33 D. W. Holdsworth, Landscape and archives as texts, in P. Groth and T. W. Bressi (Eds), *Understanding Ordinary Landscapes* (New Haven, CT 1997) 44-55.

34 A. R. H. Baker, "The dead don't answer questionnaires": researching and writing historical geography, *Journal of Geography in Higher Education* **21** (1997) 231-43.

35 A. Sutcliffe, Introduction, and J. Tarn, French flats for the English in nineteenth-century London, in A. Sutcliffe (Ed.), *Multi-Storey Living* (London 1974) 1-18 and 19-40; S. Marcus, *Apartment Stories: City and Home in Nineteenth-Century Paris and London* (Berkeley 1999).

36 G. Gissing, *In The Year of Jubilee* (London 1894) 78-9, 200-1, 8, 276, 212, 274-5 (page references are to the 1994 Everyman edition).

37 On the necessity of defining 'anti-modern' or 'pre-modern' scapegoats in projects of modernization, see L. Nead, From alleys to courts: obscenity and the mapping of mid-Victorian London, and M. Ogborn, This most lawless space: the geography of the Fleet and the making of Lord Hardwicke's Marriage Act of 1753, both in *New Formations* **37** (1999) 33-46 and 11-32.

38 G. Gissing, *The Odd Women* (London 1893) 117-8 (page references are to the 1980 Virago edition).

39 *Ibid.*, 246-8.

40 G. Gissing, *The Whirlpool* (London 1897) 170-3 (page references to the 1984 Hogarth Press edition). Oxford & Cambridge Mansions was not listed in Kelly's Post Office Directory for 1881 (published in December 1880), but in the (April) 1881 census, five of the twelve blocks which comprised the mansions were occupied. In the directory for 1882, eight blocks were occupied, and by 1883 (December 1882) the whole building was in use.

41 Flats at home and abroad, *The Builder* **XLIV** (February 3, 1883) 135-6.

42 Oxford and Cambridge Mansions, *The Builder* **XLIV** (February 3, 1883) 140.

43 Gissing, *The Whirlpool*, 5-6.

44 *Ibid.*, 107.

45 *Ibid.*, 107, 172.

46 Gissing was living in Epsom, south of London, while working on *The Whirlpool*, but from December 1884 until January 1891 (i.e. during the period when the novel was set), he lived at 7K Cornwall Residences, Baker Street, a 3-room flat only 5 minutes walk from Oxford & Cambridge Mansions. That he had long been interested in the mansions is evident from a letter to his sister, dated October 20, 1889, in which he referred to "some people who lived in one of the aristocratic flats I showed you near Edgware Road". It transpired that he had been invited to participate in a Shakespearian Society reading at the home of the Fennessys, 6 Hyde Park Mansions, across the street from Oxford & Cambridge Mansions. Despite his own modest circumstances, he cultivated friendships with well-off middle-class families, partly through acting as private tutor to their children. For details of Gissing's life, see M. Collie, *George Gissing: A Biography* (Folkestone 1977); J. Halperin, *Gissing, A Life in Books* (Oxford 1982); and P. F. Mathieson, A. C. Young and P. Coustillas (Eds), *The Collected Letters of George Gissing Volumes One – Nine* (Athens, Ohio 1990-1996). The letter of October 1889 is in *Volume Four*, 129. There is a lightly fictionalised description of his own flat in Cornwall Residences in his novel, *New Grub Street* (London 1891) chapter 4.

47 Houses in flats, *The Builder* **XLVI** (March 8, 1884) 352.

48 *Ibid.*, 352-3. Godwin's comment is in a footnote to the article reporting Eales' paper.

49 *The Builder* **XLIV** (February 3, 1883) 149; G. Gissing, *The Nether World* (London 1889) 274 (page reference to the 1973 Everyman edition).

50 The arrangement of buildings in flats, *The Builder* **XLVI** (March 15, 1884) 386.

51 Houses in flats, *The Builder* **XLVI** (March 8, 1884) 351; No. 6 Hyde Park Mansions, Edgware Road, *The Builder* **XLIX** (October 17, 1885) 532.

52 E. Zola, *Pot-Bouille* (Paris 1882); variously translated as *Piping Hot!* (1886), *Restless House* (1953) and, most recently, by Brian Nelson, as *Pot Luck* (Oxford 1999). For a commentary on the novel, see Marcus, *op. cit.*, 166-98.

53 Houses in flats, *The Builder* **XLVI** (March 8, 1884) 352.

54 The arrangement of buildings in flats, *The Builder* **XLVI** (March 15, 1884) 386.

55 Houses in flats, *The Builder* **XLVI** (March 8, 1884) 353.

56 *Directory of British Architects 1834-1900* (compiled by A. Felstead, J. Franklin and L. Pinfield on behalf of British Architectural Library, R.I.B.A.) (London 1993), 987; *The Times* (October 22, 1896) 3.

57 W. H. White, Middle-class houses in Paris and central London, *The Builder* **XXXV** (November 24, 1877) 1166-70.

58 In Kelly's Post Office Court Directory for 1881, White was listed at 23 Bedford St, Covent Garden, one of the houses featured in his 1877 paper.

59 White, *op. cit.*, 1170.

60 Census enumerators' returns for Oxford & Cambridge Mansions are to be found at RG11/152/28-29 (1881) and RG12/99/94-98 (1891).

61 Six households comprised only servants, with no 'head' present on Census Day.

62   Although no evidence of rents and management practices at Oxford & Cambridge Mansions has come to light, we may infer minimum rents by comparing rateable values recorded in local rate books. Gissing's 3-room flat at Cornwall Residences had a rateable value of £22. He paid £40 per annum in rent. Rateable values for flats in Oxford & Cambridge Mansions were mostly concentrated between £40 and £80, implying rents of £75-150 p.a.

63   Dennis, *English Industrial Cities*, chapter 8; R. M. Pritchard, *Housing and the Spatial Structure of the City* (Cambridge 1976); C. G. Pooley, Residential mobility in the Victorian city, *Transactions of the Institute of British Geographers* **NS 4** (1979) 258-77.

64   For example, Mrs de Wilton was listed in block 6 in 1884, 1887 and 1897, but not in 1891-2-3.

65   Mathieson, Young and Coustillas, *op. cit.*, Volume Three, 207-44, 297, 308; Volume Four, 17, 28, 109. On Sichel, see Volume 4, 113, 131-2, 138 and P. Coustillas (Ed.), *London and the Life of Literature in Late Victorian England: The Diary of George Gissing, Novelist* (Hassocks 1978) 167, 170.

66   Mathieson, Young and Coustillas, *op. cit.*, Volume 2, 358 and Volume 3, 237.

67   D. Reeder (Ed.), *Charles Booth's Descriptive Map of London Poverty 1889* (London 1987).

68   K. Bales, Charles Booth's survey of *Life and Labour of the People in London 1889-1903*, in M. Bulmer, K. Bales and K. Sklar (Eds), *The Social Survey in Historical Perspective, 1880-1940* (Cambridge 1992) 66-110; C. Topalov, The city as *terra incognita*: Charles Booth's poverty survey and the people of London, 1886-1891, *Planning Perspectives* **8** (1993) 395-425.

69   F. Driver, Moral geographies: social science and the urban environment in mid-nineteenth century England, *Transactions of the Institute of British Geographers* **NS 13**, 275-87; S. B. Warner, The management of multiple urban images, in D. Fraser and A. Sutcliffe (Eds), *The Pursuit of Urban History* (London 1983) 383-94.

70   *Residential Flats and Chambers to Let*, undated pamphlet (c. 1912), Westminster City Archives.

Chapter Three

THE 'TOTAL ENVIRONMENT'

and Other Byways of Historical Geography

CHRIS PHILO

Introduction

This chapter will present a small piece of geographical 'detective work', pursuing
what I am happy to term certain 'byways' in the historiography of historical geography,
and as such the paper reveals my own antiquarian fascination with the musings of
past and often relatively forgotten geographers. The byways in question are ones that
concern the notion of the 'total environment', as linked to conceptions of the 'physical
environment' and, much more saliently, the 'human environment'. My ambitions are
not solely antiquarian, however, since my excursions here into dusty old geographical
texts are also meant to open a window on theoretical matters which are very much on
the present agenda of historical geographers (and, indeed, of human geographers
more generally). The final part of my paper will therefore address such theoretical
matters in the light of the byways explored initially, and also, appropriately enough,
in the light of Alan Baker's own most thoughtful of essays from the 1984 *Explorations
in Historical Geography* volume.[1]

Kirk anticipated: a paper from 1940 (and some related writings)

The hinge of my account is a paper which, to the best of my knowledge, has been
entirely overlooked in writings on the historiography of historical geography: a paper
published in the journal *Geography* in 1940 by two authors, Stanley Jones and Frank

Walker,[2] two individuals who, it would have to be admitted, would not normally be remembered for their theoretical contributions to the discipline. Yet, in my view, their 1940 paper, entitled 'The concepts of human and total environments', perhaps does deserve at least a footnote when discussing a rather better-known passage of disciplinary history: namely, William Kirk's celebrated formulations revolving around what he referred to as the 'behavioural environment'. As developed in his two similar papers of 1952 and 1963,[3] Kirk effectively challenged mid-century geographers to take seriously, as Frederick Boal and David Livingstone put it, "worlds of meaning in a world of facts".[4] In short, and as is familiar, Kirk distinguished between, on the one hand, a 'phenomenal environment' supporting the entire panorama of natural and humanly-created things ("a world of facts") and, on the other hand, a 'behavioural environment' wherein the facts of this external reality were organised into conceptual 'patterns and structures' peculiar to particular peoples in particular times and places ("worlds of meaning"). In the process he aimed to show "the integration of mind and nature",[5] thereby demonstrating the unity of human and physical geography, as well as seeking to rescue the idea of 'environmental determinism' from the seductions of possibilism. Central to this vision was a borrowing from Gestalt psychology concerned with the 'organised wholes' emergent in the minds of human individuals and groups, a holistic position,[6] and it is likely that the borrowing was heavier than Kirk explicitly acknowledged (witness the similarity between his famous diagrams and one drawn by Kurt Koffka in 1935[7]). Much has of course been subsequently claimed about the role of Kirk in prompting 'behavioural' and 'perceptual' turns in academic geography,[8] quite rightly, while some effort has been expended (most obviously in John Campbell's exhaustive 1989 survey[9]) in tracing the intellectual influences on, and antecedents of, Kirk's two papers.

As far as I can tell, though, nobody has commented on the remarkable extent to which this humble 1940 paper by Jones and Walker anticipated Kirk's later formulations. Jones and Walker opened their paper with a nod to an observation from A. J. Herbertson to the effect that: "[e]nvironment … is not merely the physical circumstances among which we live, important though those are. It … is found to be more complex and more subtle the more we examine it. There is a mental and spiritual environment as well as a material one".[10] Herbertson himself was never able to develop the implications of this statement, so they argued, given that his approach was so concerned to set humanity within the overwhelmingly physical frame of his 'natural regions' (a point also made forcefully many years later by H. J. Fleure,[11] and it is probably relevant that Jones had studied with Fleure at Aberystwyth). Instead, Jones and Walker wrote as follows:

... many workers have continued this emphasis [on the physical side of things] and delayed a full realisation that the 'mental and spiritual environment' constitutes in itself a body of facts comparable with the facts of the physical environment and that their analysis must become a vital feature of all geographical interpretation. The failure to recognise the essential nature of this 'human environment' has led to an oversimplification of geographical arguments and to an entire misconception of the real nature and philosophy of our subject.[12]

They hence introduced the concept of the 'human environment', the historiographic roots of which I will probe shortly, and they defined this as "the sum total of contemporary thought, whether economic, social, religious or political".[13] Elaborating, they also insisted that it should be taken to include "the whole stream of human ideas, whether in the form of accumulating customs and traditions or in the form of occasional flashes of individual genius".[14] This realm of thought, custom and genius was reckoned to be most obviously expressed within "definite human organisations" such as church, monarchy and state, which are "themselves capable of limiting or guiding the actions of individuals or groups of individuals in their interactions with the physical environment".[15] It should be evident that this construction is extremely close to that of Kirk's 'behavioural environment', even if being less developed in terms of theorising how thought becomes organised into seemingly coherent shapes (for Kirk, *Gestalten*). (It is of course close to many other concepts well-known to geographers, notably that of *mentalité*, and I am tempted to say that it carries within it something akin to Michel Foucault's understanding of 'discourse':[16] but I cannot elaborate such parallels here.)

In addition, Jones and Walker argued that:

Geography to us is ... a study of what, for want of a better word, we shall call the 'total environment'. This total environment is composed of two interacting bodies of fact, the physical environment as it is usually understood, and the human environment as we have defined it above ... The essential central theme of geographical philosophy ... must be derived from serious and considered studies of the interactions of the human and physical environments within the total environment. This is something more than a general theory of Holism, because such studies of total environment are our only means of determining the issues raised by problems previously expressed in terms of 'man [sic] and his environment', and without a realisation of this fuller concept of the total environment little advance can be made in the subject.[17]

Jones and Walker duly coined the term 'total environment' as the synthesis of an external 'physical environment' and an internal 'human environment', the latter being an 'environment' *within* humans, albeit bound up with organised forms of social existence, that allows them to experience, reflect upon and act toward the more physical aspects of their surroundings. The holistic ambitions of this vision need underlining, notably given a further statement about "the study of the total environment ... involving the difficult task of interpreting the sum total of complicated and interrelated processes".[18] Once again, the closeness of this construction to Kirk's ideas – at one point in his 1963 paper Kirk posited an all-encompassing 'geographical environment' which looks much like what Jones and Walker mean by the 'total environment' – is really quite marked. To summarise, then, the triad of 'geographical', 'phenomenal' and 'behavioural environments' posited by Kirk certainly does seem to be anticipated by the triad of 'total', 'physical' and 'human environments' posited by Jones and Walker.

In the rest of their 1940 paper, Jones and Walker illustrated the utility of their concepts through an outline historical geography of England, in the course of which they endeavoured to show how a changing 'human environment', the changing thought-worlds (as we might say) sustained by members of key social institutions, fed into changing geographies on the ground of agriculture, industry, settlement and trade. They thereby touched upon the 'Romanisation' of England, the "preconceived ideas of land utilisation and the seeds of a feudal plan of society"[19] associated with the Anglo-Saxons, "the idea of feudal superiority"[20] and the granting of 'privileges' to particular lordships and towns under the Normans, and on and on into the more modern fostering of "economic individualism".[21] Throughout they emphasised the changing 'human environment', in the sense of changing perspectives on individual, community and society, specifically on questions of individual liberty in relation to the role of institutions (including everything from the state to trades unionism), and all as playing back upon how humans react to and act upon the 'physical environment'. It was all done very sketchily, inevitably for a paper only lasting seven pages, and it is really quite a strange effort, almost like a short lesson in English social and political history rather than a piece of geographical writing; but it *is* intriguing, and does offer an unusually early 'idealist' version of historical geography attuned to how the underlying ideas base of a given society might impact upon its material geographical productions.[22]

This 1940 paper appears to be the only one which Jones and Walker wrote together, while they overlapped in the Department of Geography at Bristol, although it is possible to unearth many of their individual writings from both before and after 1940.[23] (See Figure 1 for a collage of materials culled from various of their works.) Having consulted these writings, I am confident in saying that the 1940 paper was an almost unique attempt at meta-theoretical reflection for both of them. There are some hints of Jones thinking more conceptually about time and space, notably an enticing reference to a paper called 'Time and the social geographer' which he gave at something called the Willans Lecture in 1966,[24] and in an earlier paper of 1949 Jones even suggested – paralleling what his one-time teacher Fleure claimed about regions as 'corridors of time'[25] – that there was a need to develop "a greater understanding of regions as the segregations in space of the processes of time".[26] It should nonetheless be added that the heart of this 1949 paper remained a solidly (and conventionally) empirical study of the Gold Country of the Sierra Nevada, California, emphasising how certain settlements in this region had changed over time (specifically 'gold towns' turning to fruit packing and lumber packing to sustain themselves economically). Jones concluded here that empirical evidence of this kind demonstrated the "complex relationships between human societies and their physical environments",[27] and he thereby reprised, albeit in only a very limited fashion, themes from the 1940 paper about how the physical and the human aspects of regions and settlements articulated one with the other. There are a few quirky moments in the respective publication records of both Jones and Walker, most obviously in Jones's piece reporting on archaeological evidence for the domestication of the horse,[28] but there is still little indication throughout their corpuses of any explicit or obvious return to the key concepts of 'human environment' and 'total environment'.

This being said, traces of a concern for the 'human environment', understood in the sense of the 1940 paper, can be gleaned in a handful of places. Perhaps the best-known text by either of its two co-authors, Walker's substantial 1939 monograph on the *Historical Geography of Southwest Lancashire*,[29] displays more of a sustained interest than might be expected in questions of religion and hence in the contested religious dogmas which played out in sixteenth- and seventeenth-century Lancashire (notably in the context of the Civil War as it affected the county).[30] Indeed, the close of Chapter III and much of Chapter IV revolved around the distinction between a basically Protestant Southeast Lancashire and a rather more Catholic Southwest Lancashire,[31] including a remark that "[s]uch remarkable contrasts between adjacent regions, and the intense hatreds to which they gave rise, were an obvious source of danger".[32] Exploring the geography of hatred here, emerging "from the totally different religious history and outlook of Southwest and Southeast Lancashire",[33] certainly took Walker a long way into the "worlds of meaning" and a long way from more orthodox 'geographical' accounts of regional settlement patterns, agricultural systems and industrial endeavour.[34] Moreover, he talked about how "a strictly material explanation of Southwest Lancashire becomes impossible since the outlook of a very

FIGURE 1

Collage of materials from work by Stanley Jones and Frank Walker

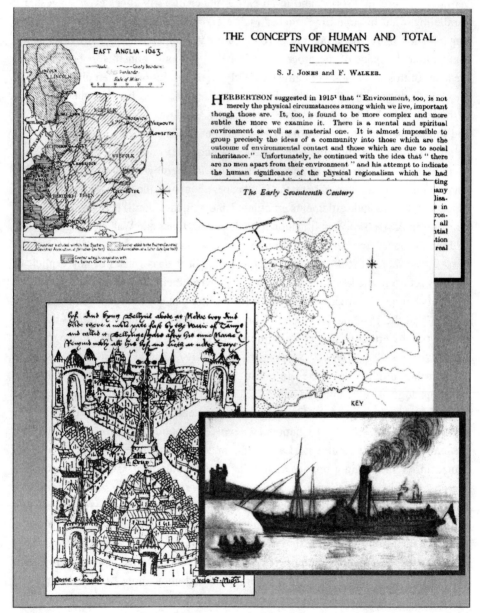

large proportion of the population was determined by purely personal factors",[35] thus proposing that a geographical study should take cognisance of individual beliefs, loyalties, hopes and fears (the realm of meaning again).[36] He even consulted the autobiography of one Adam Martindale, which "preserved a record of the attitude and outlook of an ordinary man who lived in the completely rural district around Rainford",[37] and his attention at this point to the 'outlook'[38] of a very ordinary historical person long predates more theorised attempts by historical geographers to extract everyday 'structures of meaning' from the historical record.[39] [40] Turning to Jones and the 'human environment' concept, it is evident that his 1946 paper on the growth of Bristol spoke of the ideas, 'interests' and 'ideologies' which impacted on the 'bare skeletons' of city morphology (the buildings and layout), and whose "place in environmental studies [therefore] cannot lightly be denied".[41] In a later and somewhat parallel essay on the historical geography of Dundee, he used and quoted from historical sources such as the Charter of 1327 issued by King Robert to the burgesses of the city, thereby giving some sense of prevailing views held by a particular social institution (the Scottish monarchy).[42] [43] Yet these fragments from both Jones and Walker – fascinating as they are – hardly amount to the sustained reconstruction of 'human environments' as seemingly demanded by the 1940 paper, and the thoughts, customs and genius of people, whether as individuals or in groupings, still remain as frustratingly shadowy presences at the margins of the writings concerned.

Traces of a concern for the 'total environment', understood as in the 1940 paper, can also be found in some of their writings. The ostensible ambition of Walker's 1939 monograph was to compose a synthetic[44] account of the various factors which together arguably render Southwest Lancashire a distinctive regional entity, thus

Sources (clockwise):

S. J. Jones and F. Walker, The concepts of human and total environments, *Geography* **25** (1940), p.18.

F. Walker, *Historical Geography of Southwest Lancashire before the Industrial Revolution* (Manchester 1939), Map on p. 71 (entitled 'Southwest Lancashire convicted recusants (based on the recursancy rolls for 1628 and 1641)', giving an impression of Catholic sympathies within the region).

S. J. Jones, Historical geography of Dundee, in S. J. Jones (Ed.), *Dundee and District* (Dundee Local Executive Committee of the British Association, Dundee 1968), Plate 13 between p. 272 and p. 273 (entitled 'Passenger steamer sent by North British Railway Company to serve Tayport and Broughty Ferry after the collapse of the first Tay Bridge in 1879').

S. J. Jones, The growth of Bristol: the regional aspects of city development, *Transactions and Papers of the Institute of British Geographers* **11** (1946), Figure 7 on p. 66 (a town 'plan' of Bristol prepared by Ricart, Town Clerk, in 1479).

F. Walker, Geographical factors in the Civil War in East Anglia, *Geography* **24** (1939), Map on p. 77 (entitled 'East Anglia 1643', and showing relationships of counties to the 'Eastern Counties Association', formed in 1642 and entailing a 'defensive alliance' in support of Parliament against royalist uprisings).

promulgating "the existence of a permanent natural or geographical region in the southwestern part of the county [Lancashire]".[45] He duly wrote an 'evolutionary' narrative of regional formation, the emphasis on time anticipating Jones's later observations[46] (see above), in which the physical characteristics of the region (notably its peat mosses and related 'remoteness') were seen as playing through into distinctive regional contours of settlement, agriculture, industry and even religion and politics. As he put it:

> *The later development of well-marked regional characteristics in religion, politics and social organisation forms an organic growth from the original simple historical reactions to the primitive physical conditions of this part of Lancashire, and we may regard the final 'individuality' of the region as the product, not only of its permanent physical character and orientation, but also of the* whole *[my emphasis] course of its earlier history.*[47]

The stress here on 'everything coming together', on the meshing of physical and human phenomena to produce a region's 'individuality', does sound something like the 'total environment' thinking of the 1940 paper (albeit the regional element was less prominent in the latter). This being said, my own reading is that such thinking remained in unacknowledged tension with Walker's parallel wish to immerse himself more fully in the minutiae of quite specific matters such as "[t]he influence of the Derby family, especially on the religious history of Southwest Lancashire", or "[d]etails of the warfare in Lancashire and the reasons for the sudden collapse of the Royalist party".[48] His regional synthesis thereby remained rather more fragmented, less homogeneous in its execution, than some of his more programmatic comments in the 1939 text, particularly in conclusion, might have implied was the case.[49] Turning to Jones and the 'total environment' concept, it is apparent that in several papers tackling particular places such as Bristol, Dundee or the Gold Country of California's Sierra Nevada,[50] he occasionally hinted at bringing together the many different elements which shape local and regional character, yet he was just as likely to pick upon a particular theme, a small aspect of a whole place such as the Somerset paper industry or the Bristol cotton industry,[51] as he was to try filling in a total picture. In various of their studies, then, both Jones and Walker arguably did edge towards offering an overall reconstruction of 'total environments',[52] but in practice a more pragmatic, limited and humble approach always tended to prevail. As Jones admitted when contemplating everything that he really ought to include in his portrayal of Dundee's historical geography from the eleventh century to the present day, "discussion must be confined to a few topics selected on the basis of their interest to the geographer".[53]

The impossibility of a 'total' perspective was surely here being recognised, if reluctantly, a point to which I will return in conclusion.

Jones and Walker preceded: a text from 1927

In a footnote to their paper, Jones and Walker indicated that the term 'human environment' had been used before in economic history, and that "care should be taken to distinguish between the previous use of the term and the new significance which we place upon it in geographical interpretation".[54] More specifically, they noted its use in a 1927 textbook entitled *Human Environment and Progress* by one W. R. Kermack.[55] On consulting this textbook, I was surprised to find that it carried the subtitle *The Outline of World Historical Geography*, and to realise that it was another of those works from the earlier part of the century explicitly concerned with trying to insert a geographical sensibility into the practice of historical inquiry (and it expressly referenced the likes of Huntington, Semple, George and Fleure).[56] Beginning with a claim about 'citizens of the world' needing to develop "some knowledge of world history", he argued that:

> *The unity of world history ... is becoming recognised, as that of world geography long has been. At the same time, the influence of geography upon history has been more closely studied. It would seem, then, that one of the best ways to approach world history is through world geography; and this book attempts to trace their connection throughout its course.*[57]

The result was clearly a work of 'geographical history', a term that Kermack himself used elsewhere (see below), although here he happily deployed the term 'historical geography' for precisely this project of tracing the influence of geography (chiefly physical geography) on history (human history):

> *The aim of Historical Geography is to explain all aspects of the life of man [sic] in the past, political, economic, social, intellectual, so far as they were affected by, or as they affected, his geographical environment at different periods. Its account of this relationship should trace all its changes down to the threshold of our own times, when it merges with Human Geography. Thus it will mainly draw its material on the one hand from history, on the other from physical geography.*[58]

This being said, Kermack was clear that "[r]ecognition of the ways in which geographical environment has influenced historical events does not at all mean that what is called a 'materialist' view of history is taken".[59] Indeed, while for him the term 'human environment' seems to have meant little more than the physical environment in which human beings are inevitably situated, and which shapes their lives, he veered toward a perspective akin to that of Jones and Walker when acknowledging the role of human knowledge in allowing people an independent creative role in making their own worlds. In a statement which bore the stamp of a Vidal or a Febvre, he duly talked about an increasing knowledge of physical-environmental 'conditions' which "enables [people] to utilise them, and, exploiting them instead of being controlled, to rise above them to fuller progress".[60]

He did not really explain as such the objectives of his 'world historical geography', its insistence on an orientation toward the whole *world*, although the sense conveyed was that a thoroughly comparative approach, one prepared to examine a diversity of physical environments and their differing influences on human history, was essential in allowing plausible conclusions to be reached. In his Part I, on 'The principles of historical geography', he quickly entered into what was then familiar reasoning about "geographical factors ... select[ing] the type of men and women best fitted to survive under certain conditions, and thus make likely the inheritance of their special qualities, mental or physical, by later generations".[61] This led him into a discussion of "the moulding of racial types by environment", complete with comparative claims about the differing physiologies and even 'mental development' evolved by different peoples in different parts of the world.[62] Further observations then followed on the influences of climate, natural resources (such as food supply), physical 'frontiers' and the like, before he switched into some reflections on the historical geographies of such anthropological types as 'hunter-palaeolithic man' (who had to achieve "some accumulation of [surplus] wealth, over and above the bare essentials of existence"[63]), 'nomad herdsman' and 'cultivator', as well as offering intriguing notes on the trading city-states of Ancient Greece, before leaping into more detail on 'the industrial nation-state' (feeding into subsequent chapters on, for instance, the geographical conditions of the British Empire: see below). The scope of his meanderings indicated that Kermack did intend to produce a 'world historical geography', although his interest in processes occurring at a world scale was demonstrated empirically rather than being secured more theoretically (as in the case of Jones and Walker on the 'total environment').

I know virtually nothing of Kermack himself – I suspect that he was an Edinburgh school teacher, but I may be wrong – although it is possible to find a number of other published books by him. Of particular interest is his 1913 book entitled *The Historical Geography of Scotland*,[64] wherein he declared that his hope was "to explain the connection of the geography of Scotland with the history of Scottish nationality. It is believed to be [the] first attempt, however inadequate, to do so, on a scale larger than that of the lecture or magazine article".[65] In the preface to a second edition of 1926, he added that "[w]hen it was published in 1913, this book was the only one in existence on the subject of the Historical Geography of Scotland. It still remains so...".[66] This book is almost entirely forgotten now, although versions of its first two chapters which appeared in the *Scottish Geographical Magazine* in 1912[67] are recalled as "the first time" that "[t]he term 'historical geography' was applied to the Scottish context".[68] Kermack's angle, unsurprisingly, was to provide a clear account of how the location of Scotland, the configuration of its land and the character of its physical environment have all shaped 'The making of Scotland' (the title of his Chapter I), and this meant that he wrote at length on particular 'racial qualities' of the Scots, as protected in part by the peculiarity of physical-geographical circumstances, which have entered into their 'national individuality' and distinctive 'national history'.[69] Two later books, *Nineteenth Centuries of Scotland* and *The Scottish Highlands: A Short History (c.300-1746)*,[70] continued his interest in showing how "the course of events [in Scottish history] was influenced by the distribution of highland and lowland, valley and mountain ... the stage upon which the drama of history was played".[71] These were obviously not works of 'world historical geography', adopting a much more local (and partisan) focus, but there is one other book by Kermack in which the grander design is to an extent present: namely, his earlier text entitled *The Expansion of Britain from the Age of the Discoveries: A Geographical History*.[72] As he explained at the outset, "[t]his book is an attempt, on a small scale, to look, from a geographical point of view, at the history of the settlement and growth of the great Dominions of the British Commonwealth, and the foundation and expansion of the Indian Empire".[73] His account of this imperial 'geographical history' was very factual, albeit interspersed by notes of celebration about the greatness of the British imperial project, and the book might repay further attention from the standpoint of those who are currently teasing out the complicity of academic geography in the excesses of European imperialism and colonialism.[74] For my purposes in the present paper, however, it only remains to remark that the ambitious vistas of 'world historical geography' signalled in 1927 rarely surfaced anywhere else in Kermack's corpus; and that, even in the 1922 study of Britain's geographical expansion, he confessed to doing no more than writing 'on a small scale'.

The incomplete universe, or the impossibility of 'totalising historical geography'

I want now to conclude this chapter by connecting its antiquarian concerns to key broader themes of geographical theorising, and in the process to revisit Alan Baker's 1984 piece 'Reflections on the relations of historical geography and the *Annales* school of history'.[75]

Baker's chief purpose here is to consider the root concepts and motivations of the *Annalistes*, and to examine the extent to which the geographical (or, as they might say, the 'geohistorical') concerns of scholars such as Bloch, Braudel and Febvre (with their evident Vidalian overtones) have then played back upon the works of those who more specifically define themselves as historical geographers (principally in France, but also in the Anglophone world). Baker usefully reviews aspects of the *Annales* school, notably the interest in *mentalités*, the 'collective consciousness' associated with given peoples (not just elites) in given places, and he describes the attempt "to unravel layers of meaning, and hence of understanding ... employing interpretative theories from cognate disciplines to do so".[76] Quarrying such seams of meaning and understanding could be taken as a more sophisticated version of what Jones and Walker meant by reconstructing past 'human environments', as too could Baker's subsequent thoughts in the 1984 paper about the possibility of borrowing from J. P. Sartre's 'progressive-regressive method' (as linked into the latter's accommodations between Marxism and existentialism). According to Baker, Sartre envisaged a recursive movement between the material qualities of given situations ('objectivity') and the realm of human interpretations ('subjectivity'), itself embedded within a related movement 'back and forth' between social structure and human individual (the dynamic of the former being all about appropriating a surplus and promoting the common good; that of the latter being all about overcoming scarcity and preserving individual freedoms).[77] At the same time, so Baker argues,[78] Sartre highlighted the contribution of "groups, organisations and institutions" (ranging from the family to the state) within these twin movements, chiefly because of "their vital role in social change and social control, [and] in the allocation of scarce resources (including time and space)".[79] Baker sees here the framework for 'a truly social historical geography',[80] which he briefly deploys to outline what a 'social historical geography' of nineteenth-century rural France might look like,[81] clarifying in the process his ongoing interest in the groupings, communities and *syndicats* ('fraternities') of rural France which effected a distinctive local articulation of social transformations and individual struggles.[82] In the essentials of this vision, with the concern for "definite human organisations"[83] and when spotlighting a recursive movement between "human actions and material things, subjects and objects",[84] [85] Baker effectively echoes (while certainly refining) the claims of Jones and Walker's 1940 paper.

A further connection, meanwhile, obviously resides in the issue of totality which figures throughout Baker's 1984 paper. He never uses the term 'total environment', but he clearly asks questions about research which aims to disinter "the *sum total* [my emphasis] of complicated and interrelated processes" (a phrase from Jones and

Walker[86]). This is unavoidable given that one invention of the *Annalistes* has been "the study of total history, a synthesis based upon interdisciplinary analyses and upon the interpretation of historical patterns, processes and structures, both ideational and artefactual".[87] 'Total history', *histoire totale*, is hence a name frequently attributed to the efforts of the *Annalistes*. Baker duly describes this 'totalising' style of work, its grand synthetic and comparative ambitions, its "imaginative sweeps" combined with "a close attention to detail",[88] and he also states that "[t]he all-inclusive nature of total history quite simply meant that no problem, source or technique could legitimately be omitted from the ultimate synthesis".[89] This being said, he acknowledges that in practice not every study could embrace every possible "problem, source or technique", and he adds that the hypothetically 'limitless' "range of concerns" open to the *Annalistes* has tended to be narrowed down to a certain collection of (still broad-brush) themes such as the elucidation of past *mentalités*.[90] The logic of Baker's piece, nonetheless, is to propose that the 'totalising' style of the *Annalistes* could usefully be translated into the inquiries of at least some historical geographers (and another feature of the paper is a tempered criticism of French historical geographers for failing to do precisely this). At one point Baker explicitly declares "the need to totalise historical geography", notably when urging that historical geographers should embrace not just humanity's "conflict with nature" but also its "personal struggle with 'conscience' and … social struggle with 'class'".[91] Similarly, in the course of exploring Sartre's ideas, he indicates that, as well as class, the struggles of many different kinds of social groups "demand the attention of those whose concern is with total historical geography".[92] He thus comes close to positioning 'total historical geography' quite expressly as academic geography's equivalent of the *Annalistes'* 'total history'.

While I have much sympathy for this line of reasoning in Baker's paper, particularly as he brings it to bear in his proposals for grounded research on the geographies of fraternity in the French countryside, his claims do carry with them a problem or two which I will now consider in closing. Firstly, near the end of his paper Baker appears to derive a concept of 'social totality' from Sartre, as when positing that "Sartre's progressive-regressive method involves going back and forth from the social totality to the individual",[93] and it is this concept of 'social totality' which runs through his subsequent fraternity in the forest materials, as when talking about how the *syndicats* "mediated between the individual farmer and [their] social totality".[94] Indeed, it is this concept of totality as 'social totality' which he probably has in mind when explicitly naming 'total historical geography' (an historical geography attentive to 'social totality'), in which case what is being advocated is more specific, with a narrower remit, than a 'total historical geography' fully-formed in the image of the more inclusive take on totality associated with the *Annalistes*. Baker is arguably using the terms 'total historical geography' and 'social historical geography' interchangeably at this juncture, while introducing the device of Sartre on 'social totality' effectively recasts what 'total' means here away from what it meant earlier in his piece when discussing the *Annales* school. The result is not, therefore, a fully-fledged 'totalising' of historical geography.

This is not a criticism from me, since I am happy about the proposal to 'socialise' historical geography but less sure about the goal of seeking to 'totalise' it: and this is where I move to a second concern arising from Baker's paper. Baker reflects briefly on the relationship of Michel Foucault to the *Annales* school, and writes as follows:

> ... *Foucault is integrating and extending the ideas of Annalistes and Marxists about the character of historical transformations, building upon 'total history' what he terms a 'general history' in which the key notions required by historical research are no longer those of consciousness and continuity, nor those of sign and structure, but those of the event and the series as being materially based, discontinuous and unpredictable.*[95]

This is a canny observation, since in certain respects Foucault's vision of 'general history' certainly does draw key ideas from the *Annalistes*, notably their imagining of history occurring in different 'series', across different 'levels' and being punctuated by different 'temporalities'. Moreover, the case is explicitly made by C. C. Lemert and G. Gillan that Foucault is directly inspired by the sensitivity of the *Annalistes* to matters of geography, distribution and space.[96] (They do go on to argue, though, that he neglects the sensitivity which the *Annalistes* also display for the more messy realities of places, regions and countries.[97]) Yet it is vital to appreciate that, while Foucault may be building what he terms 'general history' with some tools derived from the 'total history' of the *Annalistes*, he is actually setting his face determinedly *against* what he personally means by 'total history' or 'totalising' history. This is obvious from the appended introduction to *The Archaeology of Knowledge*, where he argues that:

> *The project of total history is one that seeks to reconstitute the overall form of a civilisation, the principle – material or spiritual – of a society, the significance common to all the phenomena of a period, the law that accounts for their cohesion – what is called metaphorically the 'face' of a period.*[98]

It is also one which "suppose[s] that between all the events of a well-defined spatio-temporal area, between all the phenomena of which traces have been found, it must be possible to establish a system of homogeneous relations", and that "one and the same form of historicity operates upon economic structures, social institutions and customs, the intertia of mental attitudes, technological practice [and] political behaviours".[99] Foucault trenchantly criticises this version of 'total history', regarding it as insensitive to the particularities of history, steamrollering over details and difference, and smoothing out the jagged edges (notably the shards of contestation, struggle and resistance) which are perhaps the most interesting things to be found in the swirl of what has gone before. It is hence precisely in *reaction* to such a 'totalising' history that he formulates his 'general history', one designed from the first moment of conception to preserve the awkwardness of the past, and it is telling that he contrasts the two endeavours as follows:

> *A total description draws all phenomena around a single centre – a principle, a meaning, a spirit, a world view, an overall shape; a general history, on the contrary, would deploy the space of a dispersion.*[100]

The reference to deploying 'the space of a dispersion' is compelling, and elsewhere I explore at greater length its implications – ranging far beyond being merely a use of spatial metaphor – within, and to some extent beyond, Foucault's own corpus of theoretical writings and substantive studies.[101]

The implication for my purposes here, however, is simply that Foucault's critique of 'total history', or perhaps better of 'totalising' history, leaves questionmarks beside any statement about needing "to totalise historical geography"[102] (particularly since it was partly an alertness to the complications of geography that initially spurred Foucault to challenge the 'totalising' of history). Thus, any programmatic statements by geographers about needing to think in terms of totalities, whether it occurs in Kirk's turn to Gestalt holism, in Jones and Walker's 'total environment', Kermack's 'world historical geography' or Baker's 'total historical geography', should perhaps be confronted by a measure of Foucauldian scepticism about their claims (which is not necessarily to say that they should then be discarded as a matter of course). Such an scepticism obviously squares with the more general questioning currently being directed at all manner of 'grand theories', 'big pictures' and 'metanarratives' within the social sciences and humanities, and some commentators would doubtless position it under the sign of a 'postmodernism' hostile to Enlightenment constructs of Order, Truth and Reason.[103] Many contentious matters are now being aired on these terrains of debate, of course, and there are many, notably but not exclusively Marxist geographers such as David Harvey,[104] who are very hesitant, often with an eye to the political-ethical implications, about jettisoning the notion of totality from their work. Even so, maybe a distinction can be made between retaining some notion of totality, an imagined sense of the overall interconnections comprising a totality wherein ecological, economic, political, social and cultural forces do come together, and expecting to discern the complete array of empirical 'bits and pieces' which theoretically agglomerate to constitute that totality. The latter are always too abundant, too dispersed, too confused with the specificities of one another in given spaces, places and networks, ever to be neatly caught in the 'totalising' gaze. As Patrick Grim admits in a book which is no postmodern diatribe,[105] but rather a patient philosophical inquiry into "the logical impossibility of *totalities* of knowledge and truth",[106] to all practical intents and purposes the 'universe' for us cannot be anything but 'incomplete':

> *Consider finally the opening lines of the* Tractatus *[by Ludwig Wittgenstein].*
> *'The world is a totality of facts'. The suggestion that runs the length and breadth*
> *of the results I want to explore is that there ultimately* can *be no totality of facts.*
> *There can thus be no closed world of the form the* Tractatus *demands. If we think*
> *of the universe in terms of its truths, the universe itself, like any knowledge or*
> *description of it, is essentially open and incomplete.*[107]

Even so, this does not stop Grim[108] wondering about a wholly 'alternative' logic which *will* enable us to glimpse that 'totality of facts', to operate in effect with a notion of totality, despite such a logic being nowhere obviously present in existing thought systems. What this suggests is that maybe, after all, it is not so wrong to dream about being able to know a 'total environment', a 'social totality' or a 'total (or 'world') historical geography', but that for the moment we have little choice but to produce studies which are – as Mark Billinge puts it at the end of an essay achieving far more than most in this respect – "necessarily brief, partial and sketchy".[109]

Acknowledgements

Thanks to all those who commented supportively on the version of this chapter that I delivered at the 'Explorations in Historical Geography' Conference in Honour of Alan Baker, held at Emmanuel College, University of Cambridge, September 1998. Thanks as well to the editors of this book, Iain Black and Robin Butlin, for their patience and assistance. More specifically, I must thank Peter Haggett and Jack Langton for their invaluable personal communications, and Allan Findlay for digging out autobiographical notes on Stanley Jones. In addition, thanks are due to Les Hill for his creativity and skill in preparing the figure. I would also like to take this opportunity to underline my more personal thanks to Alan Baker for his generosity to me over the years with his time, advice, debate and conviviality.

NOTES

1   A. R. H. Baker, Reflections on the relations of historical geography and the *Annales* school of history, in A. R. H. Baker and D. Gregory (Eds), *Explorations in Historical Geography* (Cambridge 1984) 1-27.

2   S. J. Jones and F. Walker, The concepts of human and total environments, *Geography* **25** (1940) 18-24.

3   W. Kirk, Historical geography and the concept of the behavioural environment, *Indian Geographical Journal* **Silver Jubilee Edition** (1952) 152-160; W. Kirk, Problems of geography, *Geography* **48** (1963) 357-371.

4   F. W. Boal and D. N. Livingstone, The behavioural environment: worlds of meaning in a world of facts, in F. W. Boal and D. N. Livingstone (Eds), *The Behavioural Environment: Essays in Reflection, Application and Re-evaluation* (London 1989) 3-17.

5   *Ibid.*, 16.

6   The influence of Gestalt psychology is clearly present throughout Kirk, 1952, *op. cit.* and Kirk, 1963, *op. cit.*, and he reflected further on its contribution in W. Kirk, The road from Mandalay: towards a geographical philosophy, *Transactions of the Institute of British Geographers* **3** (1978) esp. 390. See also J. Campbell, The concept of 'the behavioural environment', and its origins, reconsidered, in Boal and Livingstone (Eds), *op. cit.*, esp. 46-58; C. Philo, Thoughts, words and 'creative locational acts', in *ibid.*, esp. 214-216.

7   Kirk's well-known diagrams are extremely similar to one depicting the relations between the 'geographical' and 'behavioural environments' found in K. Koffka, *Principles of Gestalt Psychology* (London 1935), Figure 2, 40: see Philo, *op. cit.*, 214.

8   This link has been debated on several occasions, but see Campbell, *op. cit*, esp. 59-61.

9   *Ibid.*,

10   A. J. Herbertson, Regional environment, heredity and consciousness, *The Geographical Teacher* **43** (1915) 149.

11   H. J. Fleure, Recollections of A. J. Herbertson, *Geography* **50** (1965) 348-349.

12   Jones and Walker, *op. cit.*, 18.

13   *Ibid.*

14   *Ibid.*, 18-19.

15   *Ibid.*, 18.

16   See Philo, *op. cit.*, esp. 216-224, for a discussion of parallels in the thought of both Kirk and Foucault, and where I ponder the value of a 'discourse-orientated behavioural geography'.

17   Jones and Walker, *op. cit.*, 18-19.

18   *Ibid.*, 24. The concept of 'holism' was also central to Kirk's thinking, in part thanks to his borrowings from Gestalt psychology: see Philo, *op. cit.*, 215-216.

19   Jones and Walker, *op. cit.*, 19.

20   *Ibid.*, 20.

21   *Ibid.*, 23.

22   On the project of an 'idealist historical geography', see L. Guelke, *Historical Understanding in Geography: An Idealist Approach* (Cambridge 1982). Revealingly, Guelke is clearly able to position his own ideas as a development from Kirk's concept of the 'behavioural environment': see L. Guelke, Forms of life, history and mind: an idealist proposal for integrating perception and behavour in human geography, in Boal and Livingstone, *op. cit.*, 289-310.

23   It will be helpful here to sketch out the basic academic biographies of both scholars:

   Stanley Jones: Having studied under and with H. J. Fleure in the Department of Geography at Abersytwyth, Jones held a lectureship in the Department of Geography at Bristol between 1928 and 1946. In 1935-1936 he was a Fellow at the University of California, Berkeley, studying under Carl Sauer and A. L. Kroeber, and in 1939 he returned briefly to Berkeley as a Visiting Lecturer. In 1946 he moved to be Head of Department in the Department of Geography at University College (Queen's College from 1954), Dundee, then attached to the University of St. Andrews, and he was in charge of this department during the period (c.1967) when the University of Dundee became independent, being appointed to the founding Chair of Geography in the 'new' department in 1968. He retired in 1975 and died in 1990. (This information derives from H. Jones, Obituary, *Contact* **13** (1990) 13, and from bibliographical notes kindly provided by Allan Findlay.)

   Frank Walker: Having studied under and with P. M. Roxby in the Department of Geography at Liverpool, Walker took a lectureship in the Department of Geography at Bristol in the 1930s and stayed there for the remainder of his academic career, being a Senior Lecture at the time of publication of his 1972 book (see below) and dying there 'in harness' subsequently (Haggett, pers. comm., 20/05/2000). (This information derives from a personal discussion with Peter Haggett, who remembers Walker as a 'warm, welcoming and generous man'.)

24   S. J. Jones, 'Time and the social geographer' (1966), referenced in H. Jones, *op. cit.* Sadly, I can find no trace of this paper as yet.

25   H. J. Fleure and H. Peake, *The Corridors of Time* (London 1927-1930, a series of books).

26   S. J. Jones, The Gold Country of the Sierra Nevada in California, *Transactions and Papers of the Institute of British Geographers* **15** (1949) 138. Such an account of the entanglings of time and space (history and geography) anticipates the likes of Doreen Massey talking about 'space/time': see D. Massey, Politics and space/time, *New Left Review* **196** (1992) 65-84.

27   S. J. Jones, 1949, *op. cit.*, 138.

28   S. J. Jones, The domestication of the horse, summary of paper in *Report of the British Association for the Advancement of Science, Bristol Meeting, September 1930* (London 1931) 371. I can find no trace of the full paper. Given some of my own recent work – see C. Philo and C. Wilbert (Eds), *Animal Spaces, Beastly Places: New Geographies of Human-Animal Relations* (London 2000) – I was delighted to find that Jones was an early exponent of a more cultural 'animal geography' (almost certainly reflecting the influence on him of Sauer from his time at Berkeley).

29   F. Walker, *Historical Geography of Southwest Lancashire before the Industrial Revolution* (Manchester 1939). This is a fairly well-remembered text – it is cited, for instance, in H. C. Darby, On the writing of historical geography, 1918-1945, in R.W. Steel (Ed.), *British Geography, 1918-1945* (Cambridge 1987) 126 – and Jack Langton (pers.comm., 19/10/1999) describes it as "a super book, bringing together physical and human geography, with lots of original maps of Catholics, land use, population & c. from primary sources". It was doubtless an influence on Langton's own substantial study of Southwest Lancashire – J. Langton, *Geographical Change and Industrial Revolution: Coalmining in Southwest Lancashire, 1590-1799* (Cambridge 1979) – although it is not explicitly referenced.

30   Walker made extensive use of primary sources, which he scanned in part for what they could reveal about the thought-worlds of contemporaries. For instance, he makes use of "the multitudinous news-letters, petitions and reports which were issued by the Parliamentary side on the eve of the [Civil] War" (Walker, *op. cit.*, 84), as well as consulting such personal records as autobiographies from the past.

31   Walker suggested that the 'conservatism' in religion of Southwest Lancashire "related to [the region's] geographical remoteness and isolation from the main centres of reforming influence", whereas in Southeast Lancashire "the existence of textile trade connections with London and the continent naturally led to contact with advanced forms of Protestantism" (Walker, *op. cit.*, 65). He also speculated on how the missionary zeal of Roman Catholic priests, their 'secret mission' of keeping alive the 'old religion', was aided in the cut-off rural districts of Southwest Lancashire: they "could lie hidden and carry out their task in the isolated country houses of the Roman Catholic gentry in a way that would have been clearly impossible in districts where the population was centred on a small number of towns or large villages in which a fairly rigid control would be possible" (*ibid.*, 67).

32   *Ibid.*

33   *Ibid.*, 84.

34   His broader narrative does, all the same, propose that the outcome of the Civil War shaped the subsequent social and economic fortunes of the neighbouring regions (with specific mention of the differing industrial developments arising subsequently): see *ibid.*, esp. 127-133.

35   *Ibid.*, 92.

36   He was particularly interested in the differing stances of 'noblemen' towards the Crown, and in the webs of obligation which then influenced the propensities of the lesser gentry (and indeed of more humble people) in deciding which religion to practise and which side to take in the Civil War: see *ibid.*, esp. 92-96. Walker's fascination with the 'human environment' of the Civil War surfaced in another paper – F. Walker, Geographical factors in the Civil War in East Anglia, *Geography* **24** (1939) 171-181 – where he considered the regional 'spirit' as connected to the 'motives' of political rebellion and religious reform (encompassing shifts of 'outlook' occurring through time) shaping the course of the Civil War in Eastern England.

37   *Ibid.*, 95.

38   The frequent use of the term 'outlook' in Walker's text is revealing, since it seeks to identify something like a wider 'world view' or even more personal stances on a given issue: it thereby suggests a definite conceptual link through to notions of the 'human environment'.

39   Various texts reflect on the 'humanising' or 'peopling' of historical geography, the attempt to recover the thoughts, ambitions, prejudices, hopes and fears of the human occupants of past periods and places, noting tensions between approaches seeking to rescue individual people from 'the condescension of posterity' and those seeking to reconstruct more collective ideologies or discourses: see D. Gregory, *Regional Transformation and Industrial Revolution: A Geography of the Yorkshire Woollen Industry* (London 1982), Chaps. 1 and 6; D. Gregory, Historical geography, in R. J. Johnston, D. Gregory and D. M. Smith (Eds), *The Dictionary of Human Geography* (Oxford 1986, Second Edition) 194-199.

40   Mention should be made of Walker's 1972 text – F. Walker, *The Bristol Region* (London 1972) – which contained small elements of 'human environment' thinking. He noted here that "there have been periods when some degree of regional identity might be discerned" (*ibid.*, 1), and he also displayed a concern for "a growing number of organisations" such as the South West Economic Council whose own words and reports seemingly supported a coherent regional vision. This latter claim echoed a previous paper – F. Walker, Economic growth on Severnside, *Transactions and Papers of the Institute of British Geographers* **37** (1965) 1-13 – which drew heavily on views expressed in 'in-house' reports produced by British planners, utilities and corporations.

41 S. J. Jones, The growth of Bristol: the regional aspects of city development, *Transactions and Papers of the Institute of British Geographers* **11** (1946) 83.

42 S. J. Jones, Historical geography of Dundee, in S. J. Jones (Ed.), *Dundee and District* (Dundee Local Executive Committee of the British Association, Dundee, 1968) esp. 264.

43 In one co-authored study – W. W. Jervis and S. J. Jones, The village of Congresbury, Somerset, *Geography* **19** (1934) 105-114 – Jones drew on specific primary sources such as village surveys and Overseers' accounts to reconstruct an unusual system of land tenure and land management associated with the 'common meads' (known as 'the Dolmoors'). In so doing, he reconstructed some local 'land customs' which one might describe as ingredients of the local 'human environment'.

44 Interestingly, Jack Langton (pers.comm., 19/10/99) suggests that the efforts of Jones and Walker might be described as sitting within "the tradition of synthetic historical geography". There is much more that could be argued about the character of such a tradition, specifically as it emerged *contra* (and often opposed by) a more analytical version of historical geography concerned with themes to be traced systematically in their spatial patterns set within limited periods of time.

45 Walker, 1939, *op. cit.*, 136.

46 He expressly talked about "the evolutionary aspect of regional geography" (*ibid.*), and thereby underscored the importance of time, change and evolution to his vision of historical geography. This being said, the root logic of his project was to detect stabilities in the regional distinctions (most obviously those between Southwest and Southeast Lancashire) apparently persisting through time, even if the precise bases for these distinctions might vary from one period to the next, and he concluded that "there is throughout its history a sufficiently strong sense of continuity to justify the description of this corner of the county [Southwest Lancashire] as a natural region" (*ibid.*, 138). The centrality of time to the thinking of both Jones and Walker possibly owed something to the influence of Carl Sauer, with whom Jones had studied and maybe corresponded, perhaps on the coat-tails of Sauer's links with Francis Grave Morris, the British geographer to whom he stated that historical geography was 'the apple of my eye': thanks to Peter Haggett (pers.comm., 20/03/2000) for this information. The broader context for these considerations is rehearsed in M. Williams, 'The apple of my eye': Carl Sauer and historical geography, *Journal of Historical Geography* **9** (1983) 1-28.

47 Walker, 1939, *ibid.*, 137.

48 These are both headings from the contents pages of *ibid.*, vii-viii, and they are much more specific, enmired in historical details and nuances, than might be expected from a study in regional synthesis with some ambition of reconstructing past 'total environments'.

49 Similarly, and despite furnishing a highly comprehensive if somewhat stultifying account in his text on the Bristol region – Walker, 1972, *op. cit.* – he confessed that "homogeneity can hardly be regarded as a regional characteristic" (*ibid.*, 1), and found himself concentrating elsewhere (eg. Walker, 1965, *op. cit.*) much more on specific aspects of the city-region to do with industrialisation and planning.

50 As well as three papers already referenced – Jones, 1946, *op. cit.*; Jones, 1949, *op. cit.*; Jones, 1968, *op. cit.* – see S. J. Jones, The historical geography of Bristol, *Geography* **16** (1931) 175-186.

51 S. J. Jones, The cotton industry in Bristol, *Transactions and Papers of the Institute of British Geographers* **13** (1947) 61-79; S. J. Jones and W. W. Jervis, The paper-making industry in Somerset, *Geography* **15** (1930) 625-629.

52 Intriguingly, both authors – S. J. Jones, Dundee from the air, *Scottish Geographical Magazine* **78** (1962) 15-16; F. Walker, The geographical interpretation of air photography, in G. Taylor (Ed.), *Geography in the Twentieth Century: A Study of Growth, Fields, Techniques, Aims and Trends* (London 1953, Second Edition: Walker's chapter was only added to this edition) – showed an interest in the possibilities that aerial photography hold for geographical research. Maybe something could be made of their concern for observing the world from above in relation to their prior thoughts about the 'total environment', given

that the critique of 'ocularcentricism' – an orientation which has been prevalent throughout geography's history: see D. Gregory, *Geographical Imaginations* (Oxford 1994), esp. Chaps.1 and 2 – identifies a 'totalising' gaze which seeks to lay bare all of the phenomena of the world as if in an exhibition. Martin Jay is someone who has both critiqued this ocularcentricism in Western thought *and* explored the history of conceptions of 'totality' within Western Marxism: see M. Jay, *Marxism and Totality: The Adventure of a Concept from Lukács to Habermas* (Berkeley 1984); M. Jay, Scopic regimes of modernity, in H. Foster (Ed.), *Vision and Visuality* (Washington 1988) 3-23.

53 Jones, 1968, *op. cit.*, 260.

54 Jones and Walker, *op. cit.*, Footnote 2, 18.

55 W. R. Kermack, *Human Environment and Progress: The Outline of World Historical Geography* (Edinburgh and London 1927).

56 I discuss something of these earlier inquries into 'the history behind geography' in C. Philo, History, geography and the 'still greater mystery' of historical geography, in D. Gregory, R. Martin and G. Smith (Eds), *Human Geography: Society, Space and Social Science* (London 1994), 252-281.

57 Kermack, *ibid.*, v.

58 *Ibid.*, 1.

59 *Ibid.*, vi.

60 *Ibid.*

61 *Ibid.*, 2. Yes, women *did* get a mention here.

62 *Ibid.*, 7 and 1-12.

63 *Ibid.*, 18-19.

64 W. R. Kermack, *Historical Geography of Scotland* (Edinburgh and London 1913).

65 *Ibid.*, no pagination.

66 W. R. Kermack, *Historical Geography of Scotland* (Edinburgh and London 1929, Second Edition), no pagination.

67 W. R. Kermack, A geographical factor in Scottish independence, *Scottish Geographical Magazine* **28** (1912) 31-35; W. R. Kermack, The making of Scotland: an essay in historical geography, *Scottish Geographical Magazine* **28** (1912) 295-305.

68 I. Adams, A. J. Crosbie and G. Gordon, *The Making of Scottish Geography: 100 Years of the RSGS* (Edinburgh 1984) 25.

69 Kermack, 1913, *op. cit.*, 3.

70 W. R. Kermack, *Nineteenth Centuries of Scotland* (Edinburgh and London 1944); W. R. Kermack, *The Scottish Highlands: A Short History (c.300-1746)* (Edinburgh and London 1957).

71 Kermack, 1944, *op. cit.*, 3.

72 W. R. Kermack, *The Expansion of Britain from the Age of the Discoveries: A Geographical History* (London 1922).

73 *Ibid.*, 2.

74 See, for instance, M. Bell, R. A. Butlin and M. Heffernan (Eds), *Geography and Imperialism, 1820-1940* (Manchester 1995); F. Driver, Geography's empire: histories of geographical knowledge, *Environment and Planning D: Society and Space* **10** (1992) 23-40; A. Godlewska and N. Smith (Eds), *Geography and Empire* (Oxford 1994).

75   Baker, *op. cit.*

76   *Ibid.*, 7.

77   *Ibid.*, 21-23.

78   Intriguingly, this is a link here back to that curious political history element of Jones and Walker, *op. cit.*: their concern for changing 'political' views of what comprise social responsibilities and individual liberties.

79   Baker, *op. cit.*, 22.

80   *Ibid.*, 22 and 26.

81   *Ibid.*, 23-27.

82   Baker has produced a number of individual studies dealing with particular groupings in the nineteenth-century French countryside: see, for example, A. R. H. Baker, Ideological change and settlement continuity in the French countryside: the development of agricultural syndicalism in Loir-et-Cher during the late-nineteenth century, *Journal of Historical Geography* **6** (1980) 163-177; A. R. H. Baker, Devastation of a landscape, doctrination of a society: the politics of the phylloxera crisis in Loir-et-Cher (France), *Wutzburger Geographische Arbeiten* **60** (1983) 205-217; A. R. H. Baker, Sound and fury: the significance of musical societies in Loir-et-Cher during the nineteenth century, *Journal of Historical Geography* **12** (1986) 249-267. These studies are now gathered together and contextualised in A. R. H. Baker, *Fraternity Among the French Peasantry: Sociability and Voluntary Associations in the Loire Valley, 1815-1914* (Cambridge 1999).

83   This phrase derives from Jones and Walker, *op. cit.*, 18. In his paper on the growth of Bristol, Jones paid particular attention to such organisations, which he termed 'social influences', and he wrote as follows: "[t]he interrelationships between social influences and morphology is important because it brings into true perspective the function of the social organisations and institutions of which buildings are just the bare skeletons" (Jones, 1946, *op. cit.*, 83). He also talked about 'monastery, castle and town' being such organisations, "as being, 'in the social sense', separate units" (*ibid.*).

84   Baker, 1984, *op. cit.*, 22.

85   This recursivity also surfaced in Jones's paper on the growth of Bristol, accenting the way in which 'old ideologies' formulated in one period, perhaps in response to one particular set of physical surroundings, may continue to have an influence on the development of new surroundings at a later date. As he explained, "the maintenance of an eighteenth-century outlook in the critical opening years of the nineteenth century, an outlook which had no place for a changed economic pattern and the rise of new rivals, did much to jeopardise Bristol's position in the present-day world" (Jones, 1946, *op. cit.*, 83).

86   Jones and Walker, *op. cit.*, 24.

87   Baker, 1984, *op. cit.*, 4.

88   *Ibid.*

89   *Ibid.*, 7.

90   *Ibid.*

91   *Ibid.*, 21.

92   *Ibid.*, 22.

93   *Ibid.*

94   *Ibid.*, 24.

95   *Ibid.*, 10.

96   C. C. Lemert and G. Gillan, *Michael Foucault: Social Theory as Transgression* (New York 1982).

97   *Ibid.*, esp. 97-98: see also C. Philo, Foucault's geography, *Environment and Planning D: Society and Space* **10** (1992) esp. 154-155.

98   M. Foucault, *The Archaeology of Knowledge* (London 1972) 9.

99   *Ibid.*, 9-10.

100   *Ibid.*, 10.

101   Philo, 1992, *op. cit.* (reprinted in M. Crang and N. Thrift (Eds), *Thinking Space* (London 2000) 205-238).

102   Baker, 1984, *op. cit.*, 22.

103   Within the geographical literature there are now numerous elaborations of this 'postmodern challenge', such as: G. Benko and U. Strohmayer (Eds), *Space and Social Theory: Interpreting Modernity and Postmodernity* (Oxford 1997); P. Cloke, C. Philo and D. Sadler, *Approaching Human Geography: An Introduction to Contemporary Theoretical Debates* (London 1991), Chap. 6; M. Dear, The postmodern challenge: reconstructing human geography, *Transactions of the Institute of British Geographers* **13** (1988) 262-274; D. Gregory, Areal differentiation and postmodern human geography, in D. Gregory and R. Walford (Eds), *Horizons in Human Geography* (London 1989) 67-96; J. P. Jones III, W. Natter and T. R. Schatzki (Eds), *Postmodern Contentions: Epochs, Politics, Space* (New York 1993).

104   D. Harvey, *The Condition of Postmodernity: An Enquiry into the Origins of Cultural Change* (Oxford 1989); D. Harvey, *Justice, Nature and the Geography of Difference* (Oxford 1996).

105   P. Grim, *The Incomplete Universe: Totality, Knowledge and Truth* (Cambridge, Mass. 1991). The closest parallel to this book in the geographical literature, broadly conceived, is probably the *Birds* half – complete with its excursion through 'many-valued logics' – of G. Olsson, *Birds in Egg/Eggs in Bird* (London 1980).

106   Grim, *op. cit.*, 1.

107   *Ibid.*, 3.

108   *Ibid.*, esp. 126-129.

109   M. Billinge, Hegemony, class and power in late-Georgian and early-Victorian England: towards a cultural geography, in Baker and Gregory, *op. cit.*, 67.

Chapter Four

FROM MONTPELLIER TO NEW ENGLAND

John Locke on Wine[1]

TIM UNWIN

On the 28th May 1677, an Englishman travelling along the Loire valley in France, recorded in his diary:

> *From Amboise to Blois 10 leagues. We rode it at a litle more then foot pace in 4 1/2 hours, soe that I beleive it scarce 15 English miles. The way al along upon the bank of the Loir, the vally much the same as that between Tours & Amboise. Several chasteaux on both sides the valley on the riseing ground. Bloys stands high upon the north side the river & seems to be a very healthy place. The Three Merchants a good house, but 30s. per repas.[2]*

Sixteen months later he was in Bordeaux, from where he had ridden out into the countryside of the Graves. Here, he encountered a landscape full of vines, and chanced to stop and talk with a peasant woman. His diary for the 15th September 1678, recalls their conversation with great detail and clarity:

> *Talkeing in this country with a poore paisant's wife, she told us she had 3 children; that her husband got usually 7 s. per diem, findeing himself, which was to maintein their family, 5 in number. She indeed got 3 or 3 1/2 s. per diem when she could get worke, which was but seldome. Other times she span hemp, which was for their*

clothes & yeilded noe mony. Out of this 7 s. per diem they 5 were to be mainteind,
& house rent paid & their taile, & Sundays & holy days provided for.

For their house which, God wot, was a pore one roome & one story open to the
tiles, without window, & a litle vineard which was as bad as noe thing (for though
they made out of it 4 or 5 tiers of wine – 3 tiers make 2 hogsheads – yet the labor &
cost about the vineard, makeing the wine & cask to put it in, being cast up, the
profit of it was very litle) they paid 12 ecus per annum rent & for taile £4, for
which, not long since, the collector had taken their frying pan & dishes, mony not
being ready.

Their ordinary food rie bread & water ...[3]

The traveller was none other than John Locke, one of the key figures of seventeenth-century European philosophy, and widely acknowledged as one of the fathers of the Enlightenment.[4] He was to visit Blois again at the beginning of August 1678, commenting at some length on the various houses nearby that belonged to the king and the nobility. For the purposes of this volume celebrating Alan Baker's contribution to historical geography, Blois is a special place. It was the home town of Roger Dion, one of the great figures of French historical geography,[5] and author of the classic *Histoire de la Vigne et du Vin en France des Origines au XIXe Siècle*.[6] This provides one important connection with the viticultural theme of this paper. However, Blois is also the town near where Alan Baker chose to buy a house, and from whence he has explored the surrounding region and archives, producing a wealth of important papers on the historical geography of the Loir-et-Cher, and indeed on its viticultural and wine making traditions.[7] Many of those contributing to this book first became enthused with the historical geography of France through the lectures he shared with us at the University of Cambridge, imbued with his knowledge and love of the area. This chapter thus seeks to build on this tradition, and to explore what a seventeenth-century Englishman can tell us about wine making and grape growing in France just over three hundred years ago. It begins with a short account of the context of Locke's travels in France, and then proceeds to examine his understanding of viticulture and wine making, the economics of the wine trade, and the wider significance of his writings on wine.

John Locke's travels in France, 1675-1679

The place of France in Locke's life
John Locke was one of England's greatest philosophers. Born in 1632, he lived through the tumultuous years of the Civil War and Restoration, was a significant figure in the 'Glorious Revolution' of 1688, and lived on into the eighteenth century, dying at a ripe

old age in 1704. Best known for his *Two Treatises of Government* (1689) and his *Essay Concerning Human Understanding* (1690), he wrote a number of other important tracts and essays, including *A Letter Concerning Toleration* (1689), and *Some Thoughts Concerning Education* (1693). Locke is widely acknowledged as the principal founder of philosophical liberalism, and, together with Bacon, of English empiricism. His ideas were of fundamental importance to the emergence of the Enlightenment, and he played a central role in shaping the ways in which modern Europeans have thought. For geographers, he is of particular significance, because of the importance that he placed on the environment in the shaping of knowledge. Moreover, he was of the firm belief that geography had a crucial role to play in education. He thus commented in his *Thoughts Concerning Education* that

> Geography, *I think, should be begun with: For the learning of the Figure of the* Globe, *the Situation and Boundaries of the Four Parts of the World, and that of particular Kingdoms and Countries, being only the Exercise of the Eyes and Memory, a child with pleasure will learn and retain them: And this is so certain, that I now live in the House with a Child, whom his Mother has so well instructed this way in* Geography, *that he knew the Limits of the Four Parts of the World, could readily point, being asked, to any country upon the Globe, or any County in the Map of* England, *knew all the great Rivers, Promontories, Straits, and Bays in the World, and could find the Longitude and Latitude of any Place, before he was six Years Old.*[8]

Most studies of Locke's life and works pay remarkably little attention to the time he spent in France.[9] In general, this period is treated as but an interlude in the development of his more significant political and philosophical thought. However, while there he compiled a fascinating diary,[10] and in 1679, partly based on this, he also wrote an even lesser known work, his *Observations upon the growth and culture of vines and olives: the production of silk: the preservation of fruits*, which was first published in 1766 almost a century after his travels.[11] In these texts, Locke reveals himself to have been a detailed observer of contemporary French viticultural and wine making techniques, of political and economic changes affecting the wine trade in the latter part of the seventeenth century, and of French society in general.

On his return from France, Locke re-entered Shaftesbury's service. However, a short while later in 1683 he once again left England in fear of his life, this time settling in Amsterdam.[12] He was to remain in Holland throughout James II's reign, moving to Rotterdam in 1687, and returning only in 1689, the day before William and Mary were offered the throne. Locke's *Two Treatises of Government*, although not published until 1689, seem to have been first drafted as early as 1681. In these, Locke argued vehemently that if a ruling body offends against natural law it should be overthrown. It was just these sentiments that came to play such a significant role a century later in the American Declaration of Independence and in the French Revolution. Having completed his other major works shortly after his return to England, he spent the last decade of his life defending his often controversial views, eventually retiring to Oates in Essex, where he lived at the home of Sir Francis and Lady Masham until his death.

The reasons for Locke's travels in France

The precise reasons for Locke's travels in France still remain unclear. The most widely accepted explanation is that he went there because of his poor health. Indeed, on arrival he travelled rapidly to Montpellier, a health resort specialising in the treatment of phthisis (consumption), the disease from which he thought he suffered. It was also home to a sizeable British community.[13] However, in the 1660s it had become increasingly common for members of the Royal Society to travel abroad, and it is quite possible that Locke chose to use this opportunity to travel to France to develop his own political and philosophical ideas through discussion and debate with scholars from a rather different background to those with whom he was familiar at home.[14]

It is also possible that there were other reasons for his travels. In 1666 Locke had made the acquaintance of Anthony Ashley Cooper, Baron Ashley (later Lord Shaftesbury), who subsequently became his friend and patron, and Shaftesbury's grandson writing in 1704 commented that his grandfather had sent him abroad at a time of political intrigue, and that Locke's "health served as a very just excuse".[15] It is probable, therefore, that, with Shaftesbury falling out of favour at Court, and Locke coming under suspicion of involvement in the Whigs' efforts to remove the Earl of Danby from power as the King's Chief Minister, he chose to leave the country rather than risk the chance of being arrested.[16] He returned only in 1679, by which time Shaftesbury had returned to power and was leading the parliamentary campaign to exclude James Duke of York from succeeding to Charles II's throne.[17]

For whatever reason, Locke left Dover on 14th November 1675, at the age of 43 and in the company of George Walls, who was later to become a canon of Worcester and St. Paul's. He had previously briefly visited Paris in the autumn of 1672, and was therefore not unfamiliar with French society. Following a ten-day stay in the capital, he headed south by diligence, boat and horseback to Montpellier, where he was to remain for the next fifteen months (Figure 1). While living at Montpellier, he undertook several excursions to the surrounding towns such as Sète and Aigues-Mortes which, for example,

FIGURE 1

John Locke's journeys in France

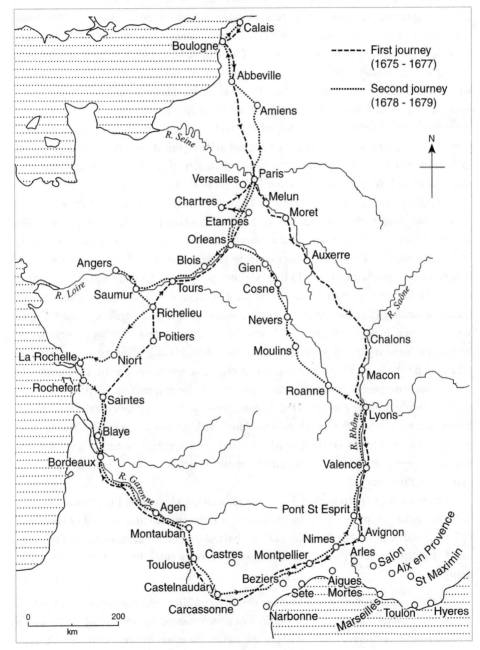

he visited in March 1676. In April of that year, he also visited Arles, Marseilles, Aix-en-Provence and Avignon, together with a number of other towns encountered on route. In March 1677, he returned to Paris to take charge of Caleb Banks, son of Sir John Banks, and he was subsequently to remain in the capital for more than a year. His route north from Montpellier took him by Toulouse, Bordeaux and Poitiers, and his diary provides vivid descriptions of his journey. While in Paris he met a number of scientists, and also occasionally acted in his capacity as a physician. In July 1678, he embarked with Caleb Banks on a second journey, this time down the Loire, across country to the new naval port at Rochefort, and thence south to Bordeaux and Montpellier. From there they went to Lyons, and had hoped to travel on to Italy, but the weather apparently prevented the journey. They therefore returned to Paris, this time preferring to cut across to Orleans via Roanne and Moulins, rather than retracing Locke's earlier southerly journey through Auxerre, Chalons and Macon (Figure 1).

Lough emphasises the importance of Locke's diary, noting that "There is indeed little to compare with it in the way of English travellers' accounts of seventeenth-century France".[18] However, it is a somewhat arbitrary account, and for a full study of Locke's time in France it is necessary to supplement it with the correspondence that he maintained with friends in England and elsewhere.[19] As an English account of French agriculture, though, there is nothing to compare with it until Arthur Young's travels a century later. As far as viticulture and the wine trade are concerned, Locke visited France during a highly significant period, coming just after the emergence of important new styles of wine, such as the New French Clarets and sparkling Champagne, both of which represented a changed emphasis on the investment of capital in wine production rather than merely in the acquisition of profit through trade.[20] While Locke did not visit Champagne, and passed only briefly through Burgundy, his stays in Bordeaux provided him with interesting insights into the New French Clarets, and his sojourn in Montpellier, an important centre of seventeenth-century science, enabled him to gain a wealth of detail about viticulture and wine making in Provence.

Based on his experiences in France, and drawing closely on his journals written to date, Locke completed his *Observations upon the growth and culture of vines and olives* ..., and dedicated them to the Earl of Shaftesbury on 1st February 1679. Typically, there is no mention of this in his diary, with the only entry for that date, a Sunday, being:

> *Mr Toinard shewd me a new systeme of our Tourbillion wherein the center of the sun described a circle of the turbillion in which it made its periodical circuit in six months & Mercury moved about the sun as the moon doth about the earth.*[21]

Locke's knowledge of grapes, viticulture and wine making

Locke's most detailed knowledge of French methods of grape growing and wine making comes from the practices he encountered while living in Montpellier. In some ways this is unfortunate, since most of the exciting developments in the wine trade taking place at that time were occurring in the north and west of the country. These were fuelled by the changing demands of Parisian society, as well as by the expanding markets of northern Europe. Locke's views can thus best be seen as a description of more traditional methods of wine making, as yet relatively uninfluenced by these internal and external forces. He does, though, provide useful insights into the grape varieties he encountered, the methods by which they were grown, and the wines into which they were made.

Grape varieties

While in Montpellier, Locke on several occasions visited the Jardin des Plantes, which had been founded by Henri IV in 1593 and was the oldest in France. From these visits as well as his travels elsewhere he was able to produce a list of some 41 sorts of grapes that were known to him from the surroundings of the town.[22] He proceeds to describe several of these in some detail, noting for example that the Tarret was "a black, very large, but not very sweet grape, and therefore used only for wine; wherein it gives a very large quantity, but not much strength".[23] His favourite red grape was apparently the Espiran, which he described as a "round, black, very sweet and very wholesome grape ... I think them one of the best fruits in the world. These alone of all the red grapes, make good wine by themselves; but they plant them not in so great quantities as the other sorts, because in hot and dry seasons they will dry up before they are ripe".[24]

Locke's descriptions of the grapes indicates that he had a clear knowledge of the linkages between grape varieties and wine making practices. As with the Tarret noted above, large grapes, with a high volume to skin ratio, tend to produce quite light wines, with low tannin content, and low ageing potential. His understanding of wines made from a single grape variety is also well indicated by his comments on the wine now known as Muscat de Frontignan: "Musquat blanc, or white muscat; this is usually planted and pressed alone, and makes the wine we usually call Frontiniac, from Frontignan, a town on the Mediterranean, near two or three leagues from Montpelier, where the most and best sort of this wine is made. It is a pleasant grape, and early ripe, before the ordinary sorts; but they are not near so good to eat as the espiran, being apt to fume to the head and make it ache".[25]

Most of the grape varieties described by Locke can readily be traced to modern varieties, although it is not always clear precisely which ones he intends. The Tarret is thus the Terret Noir, the Clarette is the Clairette, the Piquepoul the Piquepoul Noir, the Servan the Servin Blanc, and the Unio blanquo the Ugni Blanc or Trebbiano.[26] However, Locke's descriptions are focused very much on the diversity of grape varieties that he encountered in Languedoc-Roussillon, and he fails to note the tendency for other French vineyard areas in the latter part of the seventeenth century to be concentrating on specific grape varieties, as with the Cabernet Sauvignon and Merlot in the Bordeaux region, or the Pinot Noir in Burgundy.[27] These important varieties somewhat surprisingly fail even to get a mention in his account.

Throughout his time in France, Locke maintained close links with his friends in England, and on the 7th February 1676, only just a little over a month after his first arrival in Montpellier, his diary records that he sent a box of eight varieties of vine to Shaftesbury:

> *I sent this day away into England a box of vines of the following sorts:*
> 1. *Muscat.*
> 2. *Spiran, both black & green.*
> 3. *Picardan.*
> 4. *Corinth*
> 5. *Marokin.*
> 6. *St. John's.*
> 7. *Crispata.*
> 8. *Claret.*[28]

It is not clear precisely why Locke chose these particular varieties, since the consignment included some vines good for wine, others good for eating, and some good for both. It was also not restricted to varieties then unavailable in England, because Locke specifically mentions that the Corinth was already found there, and he guessed that the Crispata, so-named because of its jagged leaves, was none other than the parsley grape known at home. It is possible, therefore, that the choice represented vines that his new acquaintances in Montpellier considered would do well in England. This single indication of him sending vines home does, though, suggest that Locke had a practical intent during his stay in France, and that he was concerned to make the best use of his time there to the benefit of his friends in England.

Methods of viticulture and the influence of the physical environment on wine qualities

Locke provides a detailed account of where and how the grapes were planted, cultivated, and pruned, noting that varying practices were adopted in different parts of France. Thus in the region between Bordeaux and Cadillac, he commented on 26th September 1678 that "the vineards are set thus: 2 rows of vines & then between them 3 or 4 times that breadth of ploud land for corne. This way, I suppose, the grapes have more both direct & reflex sun & ripen better".[29] In contrast, around Montpellier, he notes that "They set them exactly in quincunx, & the rows are in some places 4, in some 5 pans distant, I suppose according to the difference of the ground or grape" (7th February 1676).[30]

These quotations indicate Locke's sound understanding of the need for different vines to be grown under different conditions, and of the importance of the physical environment in influencing the quality of wines.[31] In his *Observations ...*, he comments that "They plant their vineyards both in plains and on hills, with indifferency; but say that on hills, especially opening to the east or south, the wine is best: in plains they produce most".[32] However, it is in his diary that he discusses this subject in most detail:

> *The goodnesse of their wine to drink seems to depend on two causes, besides the pressing & ordering the fermentation. One is the soyle they plant in, on which very much depends the goodnesse of the wine; and this is a constant rule, setting a side all other qualities of the soyle, that the vineard must have an opening towards east or South, or else noe good is to be expected. The other is a mingling of good sorts of wine in their vineyards, for they seldome make red wine of red grapes alone; it wil be too thick & deepe coloured except the Spiran which, they say, will make good wine by its self, but to make their red wine pleasant & delicate, they use to mingle a good quantity of white grapes with the red* [28th February 1676].[33]

The former practice of planting vines on southerly facing hillslopes in order to maximise the amount of sunlight and warmth is common today, but that of intermixing vines has become unfashionable. Indeed, the use of white grapes in red wine making suggests either that tastes in the late-seventeenth century were for particularly light and soft wines, or that the pressing methods then used made wines from red grapes excessively tannic, and thus unpalatable when drunk young.

On his travels, Locke specifically recognised the great local diversity in vineyard soils, both in the Montpellier region, and also in Bordeaux. In his diary, he thus commented on 29th February 1676 that "to make their wine, they generally plant of all these sorts togeather (except the Muscat) in their vineyards, & upon the skilfull mixture of these, next to the property of the soile, the goodnesse of their wine does much depend, but the soile is so considerable that two fields which only a ditch parts, doe one yield good wine & the other constantly bad".[34] In referring to the vineyards used to make Arnaud de Pontac's wine at Haut-Brion, which had then become highly fashionable as one of the New French Clarets in the London market, he comments in his *Observations* ... that "the vien de Pontac, so much esteemed in England, grows on a rising open to the west, in a white sand mixed with a little gravel, which one would think would bear nothing at all; but there is such a particularity in the soil that at Mr. Pontac's near Bourdeaux, the merchants assured me that the wine growing in the very next vineyards, where there was only a ditch between, and the soil, to appearance, perfectly the same, was by no means so good".[35]

Viticulture is notoriously labour intensive, and Locke describes many of the seasonal activities encountered in the vineyard. In several places, for example, he comments on vines being planted and pruned in winter. On 7th February 1676, he thus notes that "In setting the vines, they dig the ground sometimes all over, sometimes only in trenches where they set them. They set the cutings about 18 or 20 inches into the ground & leave only 2 knots [buds] above ground. The next yeare at pruning they cut them soe that, if conveniently there can, there may be 4 shoots the next year neare the ground, at least 3 spreading severall ways, that in the succeeding years may be, as it were, the old stock out of which the shoots are to sprout".[36] Vines were propagated by layering, and if a gap occurred they dug a trench from a neighbouring stock, and lay a piece of vine along it, which would then form a new plant.[37] This method, he was told, ensured that the vines would fruit the next vintage, whereas with cuttings it was necessary to wait three or four years.[38] Interestingly, he comments that decisions over the time for planting and pruning were in part governed by the phases of the moon. Thus in his diary for 29th February 1676, he noted that "They usually plant about this time of the yeare in the quarter before the full",[39] and that "in pruning their vines they observe to do it in one year in the new and another in the old of the moon, or else they say they will grow too much to wood".[40]

For fertilizer, pigeons' dung and hens' dung were the preferred sources of nutrients, and Locke was told that they were "an improvement that will increase the quantity without injuring the goodness of their wine".[41] He goes on to note, though, that horse dung, or that from any other beast was detrimental to the quality of wine. He continued: "This they have so strong an opinion of at Gaillac, a place about thirty leagues from Montpelier, that, if a peasant there should use any but bird's dung about his viens, his neighbours would burn his house; because they would not have the wine of that place lose its reputation".[42] This is a fine indication of local attempts at ensuring quality control long before the introduction in the twentieth century of formal *Appellations d'Origine Contrôlée* regulations. If all else failed, Locke commented that "I have been told that a sheep's horn buried at the root of a vien will make it bear well even in barren ground. I have no great faith in it, but mention it, because it may so easily be tried".[43] This last statement reflects both his scepticism and also his recognition of the importance of the experimental method.

From grapes to wine

Locke's account of wine making was less comprehensive than his descriptions of grape growing, but it nevertheless provides useful insights into traditional methods of French vinification in the seventeenth century. In order better to achieve ripe fruit, he comments that "When the grapes are ready to turn, they go into the vineyards, and there taking four, five or six of the neighbour shoots, twist them together at the top; and thus the shoots all through the vineyard, being as it were tied toether, stand upright, whereby the grapes have more sun, and perhaps too the sap is hindered from running into the wood and leaves".[44] This is nothing other than an early form of canopy management, designed to maximise the amount of light and warmth reaching the grapes as they ripen.[45] He was also well aware that older vines produced better quality wines, although in lesser quantity than young vines. He thus comments that "A vineyard, from its planting, will last fifty, eigty, or an hundred years. The older the vineyard, the fewer the grapes, but the better the wine. New planted vineyars produce more, but the wine is not so good: it is generally green, *i.e.* more inclining to verjuice".[46]

Locke describes the actual method of wine making very similarly in both his diary and his *Observations* ... In the former, on 3rd December 1676, when it was snowing hard in Montpellier, he took the opportunity to summarise what he had learnt so far about wine making.[47] When the grapes are ripe, he emphasised that it was important to vinify them immediately so that they do not spoil. Everything, grapes, husks and stalks were placed on a grate above the cuve, where they were then trodden. Once in the cuve, they were left for between one and three days depending on the character of the wine to be made: "the longer it works, and the more stalks are in it (for sometimes they put them in not at all) the rougher and deeper coloured will the wine be, but keep longer".[48] The must was then put into barrels to continue 'working', "filling up the working vessel every day with some of the same must kept on purpose, for it wastes much in working".[49] The remains left in the cuve (the marc) were then pressed to make a rough and coarse sort of wine for the servants.

Locke notes that many different kinds of vat were used for wine making. In some places they were made of wood, but around Montpellier they were usually simply holes in the ground lined with plaster of Paris. He was decidedly unimpressed by the lack of cleanliness in wine making:

> *In the kuve (which is made use of but once a year) as well as all other parts of their making wine, they are, according to their manner, sufficiently nasty: the grapes often are also very rotten, and always full of spiders. Besides that, I have been told by those of the country, that they often put salt, dung, and other filthiness, in their wine, to help, as they think, its purging. But, without these additions, the very sight of their treading and making their wine (walking without any scruple out of the grapes into the dirt, and out of the dirt into grapes they are treading) were enough to set one's stomach ever after against this sort of liquor.*[50]

Locke notes various practices that were used to 'improve' the quality of wines.[51] In particular he comments that "When they have in mind to have some of their wine fine sooner than ordinary, they put in a cask a pretty good quantity of shavings of fir, and, in some places, of hazel, and with it they sometimes put some whole white grapes".[52] He also notes local superstitions concerning the ease with which wine can be turned to vinegar. Thus on both 11th July and 14th August 1676 there is an entry which states that "A little bread or oil mixed with must turns wine to vinegar; but iron laid on barrels keeps wine or bear from souring by thunder, as also it does milk, if put on the thing that covers it".[53] He repeats the same in his *Observations ...*,[54] and appears to accept these comments at face value.

Wine qualities

It is rather surprising, given his detailed comments on viticulture and wine making, that Locke makes so few statements about the qualities of different French wines. In scattered places he does comment on the character of particular wines, but even when he was in Paris, and thus likely to come across the most prestigious wines then available in the capital, he makes no mention of the wines he was drinking. Indeed, on his various visits to inns and hostelries, he is much more concerned with the comfort of the lodgings, and the price that he was charged, than with the quality of the wines.[55] This is in stark contrast to some of his English contemporaries, such as Pepys, who provided extended commentary on the wines in their cellars.[56] Nevertheless, he does make some interesting observations about wine quality, and he was particularly impressed by the wines of St. Chignan de la Corne (St. Chinian) that he encountered on his journey from Montpellier to Beziers and Castres in February and March 1677. These he described on 1st March as "the best wine I have met with on this side Paris".[57] While in Bordeaux, he commented on 5th April

1677 that the best wine was "that of Medoc or Pontac",[58] thus seeming to confuse the generic wines of the Médoc with those of the single property of Arnaud de Pontac. On his way up the Loire on 27th May of that year, while at Amboise he noted "A la Corne excellent coole wine, but make your bargain before hand or expect an extraordinary reconing".[59] Two days later, he also commented that at Clery there was "a sort of wine cald Genotin which is not bad".[60] In Saumur, he recorded on 18 August 1678 that the white wine was not only good, but also plentiful, at Pouly (Pouilly-sur-Loire) on 21st November 1678 he commented that "the wine is excellent good, & the soyle where the vineards are, full of litle stones soe as one would think it a very barren soyle', and he twice noted the fame and quality of the wines of Hermitage on the Rhône.[61]

The economics of the wine trade

Throughout Locke's diary there is evidence of the economic malaise affecting rural France in the 1670s. He particularly comments on the widespread discontent with the increased levels of taxes being imposed by Louix XIV's government, although sometimes these complaints seem to be exaggerated. While Locke noted with approval the beneficial improvements introduced by Colbert, he was also a keen observer of the continuing decline in agricultural prices that affected France during the latter part of the seventeenth century.

He notes with clarity the effects of the combination of falling prices and higher taxation on the wine trade. At Angers on 26th August 1678 he recorded that "The wine that was formerly sold here for 4s. per pinte is now sold for 1s.",[62] and at Orleans on 24th November 1678, he noted that "A tun of wine holding two poinsons which contein 400 pints, is sold here now, vessell & all, for £7, the vessell itself being worth neare the mony, & this not bad or decayd wine, but that which is very good".[63] The effects of taxation on the peasantry of Bordeaux have already been noted, but when at Saumur on 18th August 1678 he also observed its effects on townspeople, commenting that they sell the white wine "for 18 deniers la pinte at their boushons, i.e. where people in privat houses sell their own wine by retail, & of these 18 deniers per pinte the King hath 10 deniers for excise & the proprietor 8 d. for his wine".[64]

The practice whereby people sold wine by retail at their own houses was recorded by Locke in detail in his *Observations* ...:

> It is usual to set fig-trees, pear-trees, &c. up and down in their vineyards, and sometimes I have seen olive-trees. Here at Montpelier, as in other parts of France, it is no discredit for any man to hang out a bush at his door, and sell his wine by retail, either to those that fetch it out of doors, or will come and drink it at his

house; for which they usually, for that time, set apart a room or quarter of the house, and have a servant on purpose to attend it. This I have known both gentlemen and churchmen do, But whoever, in Languedoc, sells his own wine at his house, must not afford his customers so much as a bit of bread, or any thing else, to eat with it; for then it will come under the notion of a cabaret, or common drinking-house, and their tax or excise overtake them. I mention Languedoc, because in other parts of France they who sell their own wine by retail are not excused from paying the king a part of what they sell it for.[65]

These examples indicate the overall heavy burden of taxation, the regional variation in its imposition, and the general decline in agricultural profitability from which those involved in growing grapes and making wine suffered. However, to these misfortunes must be added the effects of war, to which Locke also refers. While in Tours on 6th August 1678, he thus comments that wine "was worth here formerly 80 or 90 £ & now since the warre it is worth but 30 £; and their wine here now they sell by retails for 18d. per pinte".[66] Likewise, on 20th September in the same year while in Bordeaux, he observed that "The present prohibition in England much troubles them, which, joynd to the Dutch warre, makes the wine here now worth but about 25 ecus per tunneau, which formerly there sold for between 40 & 50, which was the price of the best sort of Graves wine, except Pontac which was sold for 80 or 100, & some others of a peculiar note".[67]

Locke is scathing about the recent fashion for the wines from this region, and the effects that the English had had on elevating the prices. He thus commented on his visit to Bordeaux and the Haut-Brion property of Arnaud de Pontac in May 1677 that the prices for Pontac's wines were then selling "at 100 escus per tun", although "It was sold some years since for 60, but the English love to raise the market on themselves".[68] He noted further that the best wines from the Médoc were then selling for 80 or 100 crowns a tun, but that "For this the English may thank their own folly for, whereas some years since the same wine was sold for 50 or 60 crowns per tun, the fashionable sending over orders to have the best wine sent them at any rate, they have, by striveing who should get it, brought it up to that price. But very good wine may be had here for 35, 40 & 50 crowns per tun".[69] This is a fine example of the importance that fashion played in shaping the wine trade in the latter part of the seventeenth century, and of how producers who made appropriate investments in their production of wine were able to go against the trend of falling agricultural prices.

John Locke as a commentator on French viticulture and wine making in the late seventeenth century

In his comprehensive history of French vineyards, Lachiver draws a key distinction between what he calls *Les vignerons de tradition* (wine makers of tradition) and *Le temps des créations* (the time of creations) in the seventeenth and early eighteenth centuries.[70] Locke's account of French viticulture and wine making very much refers to the first of these, and it is somewhat surprising that he does not comment at any real length on the considerable changes in wine making practice that were occurring at that time in France. In part, this is probably because he gained most of his information in Montpellier, and that he only passed very rapidly through Burgundy and did not visit Champagne at all. While he comments briefly on the emergence of the new wines of Bordeaux, his emphasis is significantly on the vineyards rather than in the winery. Indeed, throughout his journeys he seems to have focused mainly on what he could see and gather from people working in the fields, rather than from what he could learn from speaking to the owners of the vineyards themselves. In the case of Arnaud de Pontac's vineyard, he was handicapped further by his inability to understand the Gascon language.

Nevertheless, as a commentator on the traditional viticultural and wine making practices of the areas he visited, he does indeed appear to have been an accurate reporter. He closely reflected French opinion about the importance of soils and the physical environment in influencing wine quality, he showed a keen awareness of the wider agrarian decline that farmers were encountering at that time, he recorded accurately the methods of vine cultivation and propagation, and he shows some knowledge of the relatively recent development of brandy production in the country. He likewise provided highly pertinent comments on the role of fashion in shaping the English market for the quality wines of the Médoc.[71]

English interests in French viticulture

Locke's account of viticulture and wine making must also be seen in another light, and that is in the context of English aspirations to develop vineyards of their own, particularly in North America. As early as 1609, English settlers had made wine from local indigenous grapes in Jamestown, and further encouragement came from Lord Delaware who sent French vines and *vignerons* to Virginia in 1619.[72] Elsewhere, "Governor John Winthrop of Massachusetts was granted Governor's Island in Boston harbour in 1632 for the planting of vines, Lord Baltimore attempted to cultivate them in Maryland in 1662, and William Penn brought Spanish and French vines to the new colony of Pennsylvania in 1683".[73] But none of these enterprises proved to be successful.

Against this background, the editor of Locke's *Observations* ... in the eighteenth century, hints at one of their key purposes. Not only was Locke providing information for Shaftesbury's possible use in developing vineyards in England, but he was also discovering material which could be of use in developing British production of commodities in North America which had previously necessitated trade with southern European states. As the editor, G.S., notes,

> *Our commerce with Spain and Portugal, and other countries, will subsist under every change of government or inhabitants, whilst we are in want of the productions of their soil and industry.*[74]

He goes on to comment that:

> *However populous and great, industrious and rich, the settlements in the vast continent of America become, this the mother-country may for ever be connected with it more intimately than the southern nations, by encouraging the growth and production of vines and olives, silk and fruits, which cannot advantageously be raised in England.*[75]

In conclusion, he states:

> *The editor cannot take his leave of the reader without observing, that very important services have been done to America, by a plan of government drawn up for the province of Carolina by Mr. Locke, under the direction of that eminent and able statesman the first earl of Shaftesbury; and by the present earl of Shaftsbury, as an active and zealous trustee for the colony of Georgia; from which, in time we may expect a considerable quantity of raw silk will be imported into England.*[76]

Locke was indeed actively involved in discussions and debates over property rights in America, and served as secretary to the Lords Proprietors of Carolina between 1668 and 1675, during which time he was closely involved in drawing up the 1669 *Fundamental Constitutions of Carolina*.[77] While there is no direct evidence to suppose that the main purpose of his time spent in France was specifically to acquire information that would be of benefit to the economy of Britain and its colonies in North America, there is little doubt that the experiences gained on his travels, and recorded in part in his journal and letters, would have been of considerable interest to those seeking to reduce Britain's dependence on the produce of European states, such as France, with which the country was periodically at war.

Conclusion

The central purpose of this paper has been to provide an exposition of John Locke's account of French viticulture and wine making in the late 1670s. In so doing, though, it has highlighted that there were many other aspects to his life than merely his philosophical and political writings on human understanding and good government.[78] Locke's journal provides important insights into his wider character, and particularly his sense of humour and fun as in describing the odours under the long gallery windows at the Château of Fontainbleau (25th September 1677), or in the following comment on his boat journey on the Saône from Châlons to Macon on the 19th December 1675: "In the boat we played for doubles, at which, I having won 3d., the French were willing to avoid paying. M. l'Abbé and a woman lay in the same chamber, as the first night, and so 2 or 3 nights after".[79] These, and similar comments elsewhere, reveal him to be a much more human and colourful character than he sometimes appears.

Nevertheless, Locke's comments about viticulture and wine-making, and particularly the aspects of the wine trade that he fails to discuss, suggest that his visit to France was not entirely innocent. While it seems likely that Locke did indeed leave England in part because he wanted to avoid possible arrest, and in part for his health,[80] he used the opportunity well to gain valuable information about French technological developments and agricultural activities which could have been of benefit to his interests in North America. He left for France only shortly after ceasing his work for the Lords Proprietors of Carolina in 1675, and his account of vines, olives, silk production and fruit preservation in his *Observations* ... gives every appearance of having been specifically designed as a report on the ways in which the French undertook these activities. In short, it could readily have been used as a manual by those wishing to undertake similar activities elsewhere. Moreover, if one of the intentions of his diary was to serve as a notebook for the collation of such practical information, it is scarcely surprising that he did not bother to comment at any length on such ephemeral things as the wine fashions then prevalent in Paris. This suggests that his interest might well have been to find out how best to grow vines, or for that matter to produce silk, so that he could pass this information on to those interested in developing production of these commodities in the British colonies in North America. Locke himself became a Commissioner for Trade in the 1690s, and in this capacity was actively involved in preparing a report on the problems of Virginia together with recommendations for reform in 1697. His experiences in France placed him in good stead to undertake such economic and commercial activities.

Another aspect of Locke's journeys in France which has not yet been explained fully is precisely why he travelled on the routes that he did. It is entirely reasonable to suppose that his choice of Montpellier was indeed for his health, since it was a popular resort with the English, particularly those who suffered from consumption. It was also famous for its Medical Faculty, which was of interest to Locke given his own medical background. However, the presence of the Jardin des Plantes, and the cultivation nearby of a wide range of Mediterranean crops, meant that it was also an ideal place for him to study plants which he thought would be suited to cultivation in North America. If his main interest had been in vines or plants suitable for growing in England, he would have been better served by studying northern French agriculture. On his way south in 1675, he chose the most direct route, but it is unclear why he decided to return north again via Toulouse, Bordeaux and the Loire when he set off for Paris in March 1677 to take charge of Caleb Banks. There is certainly nothing in his journals which hints at a reason, and his correspondence is likewise of little avail. This northwards journey was troublesome, and he had to rest for six weeks at Agen having been hit over the head by a pole in the boat in which he was travelling, and succumbing subsequently to violent headaches, and what he later described as a tertian ague. Despite his illness, he made a specific effort to visit Arnaud de Pontac's property of Haut-Brion in the Médoc, and wrote at some length about the wines of the region. Pontac's wines were then the most famous available in the London market, and it is just possible that his decision to visit Bordeaux was in part influenced by a desire to see if he could learn anything about how they were made. Subsequently, on his journey back down to Montpellier the following year, it is salient to note that he seems specifically to have gone out of his way to visit the new naval port of Rochefort, commenting at some length on the town's defences and the construction of ships, just as he had done previously at Marseilles and Toulon.

This is not to claim that the main reason for Locke's journeys was agricultural espionage, but it is to suggest that he used his time in France to the very best advantage, and that his interests in viticulture and wine making were more than purely scientific. Locke's diaries and his *Observations upon the growth and culture of vines and olives: the production of silk: the preservation of fruits* indicate that he was very much more than just a philosopher and a theoretician of revolution. They show him to have been an able and accurate observer of technological and scientific progress, as well as someone with a keen commercial interest in the wine trade. Living in France for three and a half years, he gained valuable insights which were later to prove of practical benefit to his interests in North America and in his role as a Commissioner for Trade.

NOTES

1   This chapter builds on a paper first presented at the conference to celebrate Alan Baker's birthday held in Cambridge in September 1998. An earlier, but closely similar, version was published in *The Locke Newsletter*, 29, 1988, and a version has appeared as: The viticultural geography of France according to John Locke, *Annales de Géographie* **614-615** (2000) 395-414. I am very grateful to all those who have commented on the manuscript, as well as to Justin Champion, Mark Goldie and Roland Hall all of whom have provided valuable advice concerning Locke's interest in wine.

2   J. Lough (Ed.) *Locke's Travels in France 1675-1679* (Cambridge 1953) 148.

3   *Ibid.,* 236-237.

4   R. Ashcraft, *Revolutionary Politics and Locke's 'Two Treatises of Government'* (Princeton 1986); R. Ashcraft, *Locke's Two Treatises of Government* (London 1987); M. Goldie, John Locke's circle and James II, *The Historical Journal* **35** (3) (1992) 557-586; J. Marshall, *John Locke: Resistance, Revolution and Responsibility* (Cambridge 1994).

5   A. R. H. Baker, Historical novels and historical geography *Area* **29** (3) (1997) 269-273.

6   R. Dion, *Histoire de la Vigne et du Vin en France des Origines au XIXe siècle* (Paris 1959) (republished Flammarion, 1977).

7   See for example, A. R. H. Baker, Ideological change and settlement continuity in the French countryside: the development of agricultural syndicalism in Loir-et-Cher during the late-nineteenth century, *Journal of Historical Geography* **6** (1980) 163-177; A. R. H. Baker, Devastation of a landscape, doctrination of a society: the politics of the phylloxera crisis in Loir-et-Cher (France) 1866-1914, *Würzburger Geographisches Arbeiten* **60** (1983) 205-217.

8   J. Locke, *Some Thoughts Concerning Education*, J. W. Yolton and J. S. Yolton (Eds), (Oxford 1989), 235.

9   See for example, W. M. Spellman, *John Locke* (Basingstoke 1997); although note the more extensive coverage in M. Cranston, *John Locke: a Biography* (London 1957).

10 Lough, *op. cit.*

11 J. Locke, Observations upon the growth and culture of vines and olives: the production of silk: the preservation of fruits, in *The Works of John Locke*. A new edition, corrected. In ten volumes, Vol. X (London 1823) 323-356.

12 See Goldie, *op. cit.*

13 Cranston, *op. cit.*

14 R. Illiffe, Foreign bodies: travel, empire and the early Royal Society of London. Part I. Englishmen on tour, *Canadian Journal of History* **33** (1998) 357-385; see also R. Illiffe, Foreign bodies: travel, empire and the early Royal Society of London. Part II. The land of experimental knowledge, *Canadian Journal of History* **34** (1999) 23-50.

15 University Library, Amsterdam, Remonstrants' MSS. J. 20; Cranston *op. cit.,* 159.

16 For Locke's involvement in political action see Ashcraft *op. cit.,* and D. Wooton (Ed.) *Political Writings of John Locke* (New York 1993), but also Goldie's *op. cit.*, cautionary critique.

17 Spellman, *op. cit.*

18 Lough, *op. cit.,* xxiv.

19 It should be noted, though, that Locke's diary is extremely valuable for a wide range of purposes other than a study of viticulture and the wine trade, including research on modes of transport, the quality of the

inns, buildings and monuments, social conditions, technological change, science, the practice of medicine, his own health, the effects of taxation, and the situation of the Huguenots. Lough, *op. cit.*, provides a full commentary.

20 For introductory accounts of French wine making at this time see T. Unwin, *Wine and the Vine: an Historical Geography of Viticulture and the Wine Trade* (London 1996); M. Lachiver, *Vins, Vignes et Vignerons: Histoire du Vignoble Français* (Paris 1988); T. Brennan, *Burgundy to Champagne: the Wine Trade in Early Modern France* (Baltimore 1997).

21 Lough, *op. cit.*, 256.

22 Locke, *Works, op. cit.*, 332.

23 *Ibid.*

24 *Ibid.*, 332-333.

25 *Ibid.*, 333.

26 For grape varieties see P. Galet, *Cépages et Vignobles de France* (Montpellier 1958-1962); P. Viala, *Traité Général d'Ampelographie* (Paris 1909); and J. Robinson, *Vines, Grapes and Wines: the Wine Drinker's Guide to Grape Varieties* (London 1986).

27 Unwin, *op. cit.*

28 Lough, *op. cit.*, 28.

29 *Ibid.*, 239.

30 *Ibid.*, 29.

31 For a wider discussion of terroir see T. Unwin, El terrer I la Geografia del vi, *Treballs de la Societat Catalana de Geografia* **45** (1997) 257-274; also J. E. Wilson, *Terroir: the Role of Geology, Climate and Culture in the Making of French Wines* (London 1998) and S. Haynes, Geology and wine 1. Concept of terroir and the role of Geology, *Geoscience Canada* **26** (1999) 190-194.

32 Locke, *Works, op. cit.*, 329.

33 Lough, *op. cit.*, 51.

34 *Ibid.*, 52.

35 Locke, *Works, op. cit.*, 329; a similar account is given in his diary for 14th May 1677 Lough *op. cit.* 143.

36 Lough, *op. cit.*, 29; see also Locke, *Works, op. cit.*, 330.

37 Locke, *Works, op. cit.*, 330.

38 Lough, *op. cit.*, 21.

39 *Ibid..*, 52.

40 Locke, *Works, op. cit.*, 330-331; see also journal entry for 20th March 1677, Lough *op. cit.*,136.

41 Locke, *Works, op. cit.*, 331.

42 *Ibid.*

43 *Ibid.*; a similar statement is also found in his diary for 19th May 1677, Lough *op. cit.*, 144.

44 Locke, *Works, op. cit.*, 332.

45 For modern methods of canopy management see R. Smart and M. Robinson, *Sunlight into Wine: a Handbook for Winegrape Canopy Management* Adelaide (1991).

46   Locke, *Works, op. cit.,* 330.

47   Lough, *op. cit.,*117; see also Locke, *Works, op. cit.,* 334-335.

48   Locke, *Works, op. cit.,* 334; see also Lough *op. cit.,* 117.

49   Locke, *Works, op. cit.,* 334.

50   *Ibid.,* 335; see also Lough, *op. cit.,* 117 for a very similar description.

51   In 1669 Walter Charleton had delivered a fascinating paper to the Royal Society, which outlined the numerous fraudulent practices that were used to improve the qualities of wines, W. Charleton, *The Mysterie of Vintners. Or brief discourse concerning the various sicknesses of wines, and their respective remedies, at this day commonly used* (London 1669).

52   Lough, *op. cit.,* 117; see also Locke, *Works, op. cit.,* 335.

53   Lough, *op. cit.,* 104.

54   Locke, *Works, op. cit.,* 335-336.

55   Typical of his comments about lodging were his views on the accommodation in which he stayed at Lacie le Bois [Lucy-le-Bois] some 15 leagues from Auxerre on 16th December 1675: "We lay at Lacie le Bois, 15 Leagues, where we had miserable lodging, but that must be borne with in France", Lough, *op. cit.* 2. In contrast, he records on 12th April 1676 that the Hostel de Malt in Marseilles was "the fairest inn I ever saw", Lough *op. cit.,* 76.

56   Unwin, *Wine and the Vine, op. cit.*

57   Lough, *op. cit,.* 126.

58   *Ibid.,* 142.

59   *Ibid.,* 148.

60   *Ibid.*

61   *Ibid.,* 221, 248, 245.

62   *Ibid.,* 225.

63   *Ibid..,* 250-251.

64   *Ibid.,* 221.

65   Locke, *Works, op. cit.*, 336-337.

66   Lough, *op. cit.,* 214.

67   *Ibid.,* 238.

68   *Ibid.,* 143; for a detailed account of the history of Haut-Brion see A. Briggs, *Haut-Brion* (London 1994); see also R. Pijassou, Le marché de Londres et la naissance des grands crus médocains (fin XVIIᵉ siècle-début XVIIIᵉ siècle) *Revue Historique de Bordeaux* (1974) 139-150; R. Pijassou, *Un Grand Vignoble de Qualité: le Médoc* (Paris 1980).

69   Lough, *op. cit.*, 142.

70   Lachiver, *op. cit.*

71   It can also be noted that Locke's account actually precedes most of the classic French descriptions of wine making regions, such as Arnoux's dissertation on Burgundy published in 1728 or Godinot's account of Champagne dating from 1722. For a wider discussion of such sources see Brennan *op. cit.,* and Lachiver *op. cit.*

72   Unwin, *Wine and the Vine, op. cit.*; T. Pinney, *A history of Wine in America: from the Beginnings to Prohibition* (Berkeley 1989); H. G. Lee and A. E. Lee, *Virginia Wine Country* (White Hall, Virginia 1987).

73   Unwin,*Wine and the Vine, op. cit.,* 249.

74   Locke, *Works, op. cit.,* 325.

75   *Ibid.,* 326

76   *Ibid.,* 325-326.

77   J. Tully, Rediscovering America: the *Two treatises* and aboriginal rights, in G. A. J. Rogers (Ed.), *Locke's Philosophy: Content and Context* (Oxford 1994); see also Cranston, *op. cit.,* Spellman, *op. cit.,* and H. Lebovics, The uses of America in Locke's second treatise, *Journal of the History of Ideas* **47** (1986) 567-581.

78   See for example J. Locke, *Essays on the Law of Nature* (Oxford 1954); T. Unwin, The end of the Enlightenment? Moral philosophy and geographical practice, in J. Proctor and D. M. Smith (Eds), *Geography and Ethics* (London 1999) 263-274.

79   Lough, *op. cit.,* 3, 172.

80   D. Wootton (Ed.) *Political Writings of John Locke* (New York 1993). It is also possible that he acted as an agent of the Whigs who were opposed to Charles II. While in Paris he served as physician to Lady Northumberland, the wife of the English Ambassador, Ralph Montagu, and was thus in a position to have good knowledge of the latter's thoughts and actions. See also Cranston *op. cit.*

Chapter Five

A Sacred and Contested Place

English and French Representations of Palestine in the Seventeenth Century

ROBIN A. BUTLIN

"Pray for the peace of Jerusalem: they shall prosper that love thee".
Psalm 122:6.

Introduction

Palestine or the Holy Land has been a centre of religious, political, ethnic and cultural engagement for over two thousand years. As a focus of three of the world's major religions, Christianity, Judaism and Islam, it carries in its historical geographies a multiplicity of both constant and changing meanings, including historic and alarming contemporary experiences of religious and territorial dispute. It has been controlled by major Middle Eastern and European imperial powers, from before the time of the Roman Empire, through the period of the Ottoman Empire, to the period of European imperialism from the late nineteenth century and the resurgence of powerful territorial disputes from the twentieth century onwards. These potent new nationalist trends have often had tragic outcomes, though there have also been experiences of hope and peace.

Over long periods of time, conflicting political, religious and territorial ideologies in Palestine were (and continue to be) of major concern to European scholars, merchants, religious leaders, monarchs and state administrators. Their interests have variously focused on the physical remains of past civilizations, on the detailed cultural characteristics of the indigenous peoples, such as language, society, manners and customs, housing, economy, and on the nature of religious belief systems, and on prospects for European-Levant trade.

For the historical geographer and the historian, the accounts by these scholars, pilgrims, soldiers, traders, diplomats, and curious travellers who visited or lived in Palestine, including their illustrative maps and engravings, provide sources for attempted constructions of the essences of its 'legendary topography'[1] and its changing scenes of life, in addition to the complex ideologies represented and experienced in this region.

The focus in this essay is on images of Palestine, as represented in the accounts by various English and French scholars who were writing about and in some cases travelling to the Levant in the seventeenth century. The images and perspectives afforded by individual accounts and exegeses are reviewed against backgrounds of seventeenth-century change in political relations, in theologies, in commercial goals, and in intellectual and cultural discourses. The accounts of the travellers from England and France generally cover larger areas of the Levant than Palestine itself, but the focus here will be on their images of that particular region.

Historical geographies and ideologies of Palestine, present and past

In spite of the considerable distance in time between a seventeenth-century past and an early twenty-first-century present, it is impossible not to link one with the other, particularly in relation to ideological questions, which are profoundly significant for historical geography and the specific place/regional problems under consideration. Much of the valuable work and publication of historical geographies of recent and more distant pasts of Palestine has come from Israeli geographers. In their researches and publications particular reference is made to questions of cartographic history, scientific investigation (especially from the nineteenth century), and ideologies and practices of land allocation and of settlement and economic development.[2] This type of work has largely – almost inevitably – been set within powerful and difficult agendas of national identity, rehearsed and implemented at both regional and global scales. Meinig has recently commented on the problems and possibilities of writing national historical geographies. In a *festschrift* for a leading Israeli historical geographer,

Yehoshuah Ben-Arieh, he writes: "The nation-state is a powerful shaping influence on human affairs and it may deserve our allegiance on many grounds, yet we should not simply accept it as a rigid, stable, final stage in the political division of earth-space. The historical geographer must be alert to various kinds of group identities that may not be congruent with the national territory."[3] This sort of problem certainly faces those who write on aspects of past and present geographies of Palestine, not least on account of the failure hitherto to accommodate to an adequate degree the experiences and contributions of the Palestinians.

Narratives of national identity as experienced and described internally and externally have been a significant part of the work of Edward Said on his Palestine homeland. Narratives of evolving national identities are by character strongly contested, with the memories that feed them often being highly inventive. In the late twentieth and early twenty-first centuries, as Said has recently indicated, it is necessary to emphasize "the extent to which the art of memory for the modern world is both for historians as well as ordinary citizens and institutions very much something to be used, misused, and exploited, rather than something that sits inertly there for each person to possess and contain".[4] Said in the same essay uses Jerusalem and Palestine, as represented by European Renaissance paintings and interpretations of physical sites and landscapes, as "an indication of how geography can be manipulated, invented, characterized quite apart from a site's merely physical reality".[5] Said picks up strongly on the ideas of Whitelam[6] who seeks to demonstrate, in effect, an attempted editing-out from some major recent works on the history of Palestine of the diversity of peoples who inhabited this complex region from the earliest times, including the Palestinians. Meron Benveneti's *Sacred Landscape. The Buried History of the Holy Land since 1948* is also an important statement about the need to have a much greater balance between the preservation and identification of sites of importance to Israeli and Palestinian cultures.[7]

The purpose of the above comments is two-fold. Firstly to show the difficulties of dissociating images and memories of the past, recent and distant, from the images and ideologies of the present. Secondly, to draw attention to the wide range of ideologies and approaches to the experience of a territory, either directly or remotely, that derives from cultural, political and belief systems, some of which no longer survive. The distinction between the early modern past and the present in this second respect is not necessarily as great as the distance in time would have us expect. Ideologies associated with Zionist and Palestinian aspirations in the twentieth and twenty-first centuries have deep, powerful, and conflicting consequences. That is not to say, however, that the views and beliefs of those studying, travelling and writing in the seventeenth century were not of comparable significance in their own local, national and international worlds. There are, of course, many discontinuities between the seventeenth and the twenty-first centuries, but there are also elements of continuity, many of them ideological.

One such area is that of the religious symbolism of the land seen as holy by at least three different religious traditions and the memories, imaginations, experiences and literatures associated with them.[8] One of the stronger traditions linking, in effect, religious belief and the geography of a specific place, conspicuously the Holy Land, is that of what has become known as 'sacred geography'. Within the western Christian tradition this goes back to early historical time and includes the work of Bishop Eusebius of Caesaria from the early fourth century. The tradition of the recreation of the biblical – mainly topographical – background to the events of the Old and New Testaments continued through the Middle Ages and into the early modern period. By the seventeenth century it had been further fed by the effect of the Reformation, mainly but not exclusively within the Protestant tradition, on the authority of the Bible and the maps included in early reformed editions.[9] The Jesuit Order in France also reflected this enthusiasm for the reconstruction of sacred geography in its training and education curricula.[10]

The tradition continued in the eighteenth and nineteenth centuries, with an increasingly scientific basis of investigation, in archaeology and botany, for example, additionally prompted by European geostrategic interest. A significant event was the founding of the Palestine Exploration Fund in 1865. This, Moscrop contends, was part of a British imperial mission, conscious or otherwise, effected in the Holy Land, as elsewhere, by mapping and scientific investigation, particularly of sites of the Old Testament. "The loss of the Jerusalem bishopric to a Prussian nominee in 1846 had been a blow to British pride. The appearance of the PEF in 1865 allowed Britain again to capture the high ground of imperial religious control," to which can be added the obtaining of information for military and strategic interests, especially through topographic mapping.[11]

The rediscovery of the Holy Land in the nineteenth century, as Ben-Arieh has termed it,[12] owed much to the competing interests of European powers and the United States in the geostrategic position of the region, and was reflected in the establishment of institutes of archaeological research. Silberman has observed that "It is interesting to note that the geographical distribution of the various societies' activities closely reflected their nations' spheres of interest in the Holy Land. The British work concentrated on sites in the south and in Sinai, in strategic proximity to the Suez Canal; the Americans initially concentrated in Transjordan which remained, by agreement with the British, an American preserve. The French Dominicans concentrated on Jerusalem, with its many church establishments and religious associations. And German activity centred on Galilee and the Jezreel Valley, conveniently close to the Haifa-Dera's spur of the Hijaz railway, built under the supervision of German engineers".[13]

Elements of sacred geography and the historical geographies of past landscapes and societies have continued to occupy scholars into the twentieth and twenty-first centuries, with similar ties to a range of personal and national ideologies.

The seventeenth century provides, therefore, an interesting period, part-way through the long Western involvement in the Levant, from which to view and evaluate impressions of life and landscape in Palestine and its neighbouring regions. The period here considered was one in which the Ottoman Empire underwent a change that more greatly emphasized local administrative structures and responsibilities than central ones, and some Ottoman commentators were critical of this diversion from the 'classical' Ottoman tradition. They were followed in this view by Western scholars, who argued that control became less certain, leading to an amalgam of turbulence, corruption, lack of interest in remoter territories, and, according to some commentators, general decay and decline.[14] In practice, the processes and chronologies of change, including the beginnings of decline in the empire's strength, were much more complex. Although with de-centralization of authority there could be corruption through the buying of offices, the administrative system on the whole worked well, within the oversight of central government.[15]

Nonetheless one of the distinct impressions given by many European visitors to Palestine, and notably in descriptions of landscapes, is that of the decaying and ruined relict features of periods of former (pre-Ottoman) greatness. It is also manifest in, and bound up with, some of the frequent and less sensitive analyses of the nature of Islam and Islamic culture. These accounts were usually penned by Europeans (many of whom did not speak Arabic or Turkish) with Turks and Arabs, and frequently Jews, being assigned to what was regarded as an irredeemable cultural Otherness. This view had evolved from the incorporation of the Christians' sacred places into the Ottoman Empire, and was based on a range of medieval European interpretations of Islam, which incorporated the growing fear of Christian conversions to Islam, partly in order to secure office within the Empire.[16] This process of alienation of sacred territory to another culture was seen as the prime reason for the neglect of important historical sites and for what was deemed to be its general economic and moral decay. There were some exceptions among European writers to this particular evaluative tendency. The agendas of the large numbers of European commentators were complex, and represent both individual and national characteristics, together with common and differing scholastic, religious belief and knowledge systems.

The focus hereafter will be on the lives, memories, experiences, religious and cultural belief systems of a diverse group of French and English scholars and writers experiencing the power of the Holy Land either through direct experience of travel or indirect scholarly appraisal, mainly via biblical exegesis, in the course of the seventeenth century.

Orientations and perspectives

The sources used in this essay for identifying images of the Holy Land are accounts and exegeses produced by men, and they derive from west European Christian traditions. Accounts by women would undoubtedly give greater variety of perspective: the problem is that for this period such accounts are extremely rare. An area for future work is the representation by women of what Billie Melman has called, in a book of that title, *Women's Orients*.[17] Melman, however, recognizes the difficulty imposed by the fact that such accounts are very rare before the eighteenth century. She states that : "What little evidence that we do have about women's travel to the eastern Mediterranean before 1717 suggests that it was exclusively religious. The modern 'secular' discourse erupted after more than fifteen centuries of silence. Richard Bevis [*Bibliotheca Cisorientalia*[18]] lists only one travelogue by a woman between 1500 and 1763 and three between 1763 and 1801, compared with some 240 books between 1801 and 1911".[19]

To this must be added the important observation that although this essay is written from a Western European, essentially Christian, perspective, a wide range of Judaic and Islamic perspectives must also be recognized. There is still much work to be done in this respect, preferably on a comparative basis, and there have been some helpful beginnings.[20]

Dramatis personae

The agencies of connection, in this particular study, to the vanished worlds of Europe and Palestine in the seventeenth century are a group of theologians, travellers and traders from England and France. Their experiences reflect Catholic and Protestant traditions, differing national interests, and the perspectives of theologians, merchants and humanists. There are many more whose writings could be considered, but the group chosen offers at least a starting base for analysis of seventeenth- and early eighteenth-century experiences and images of Palestine.

In order of years of birth they are George Sandys (1578-1644), Samuel Bochart (1599-1667), Thomas Fuller (1608-1661), Pierre-Daniel Huet (1630-1721), Jean de

Thévenot (1633-1667), Laurent d'Arvieux (1635-1702), and Henry Maundrell (1665-1701).

George Sandys (1578-1644)[21]

George Sandys was born at Bishopthorpe Palace in York on 2nd March 1578, the ninth child and seventh son of Edwin Sandys, Archbishop of York since 1577. His father the archbishop was educated at Cambridge, becoming vice-chancellor in 1553, and Master of St Catherine's Hall in 1547. He was strongly involved in the Protestant cause, was imprisoned in the Tower at the time of Queen Mary, and left with his wife and young son for exile in Europe until the Queen's death, when he became Bishop of Worcester, of London, and then Archbishop of York. The archbishop was a man of stubborn temperament and deep conviction.

One of George Sandys' godparents was George, third Earl of Cumberland, who fought against the Armada. His older brother, Sir Edwyn Sandys, a friend of Richard Hooker, was a Member of Parliament and an active member of the East India Company and later of the Virginia Company, with which George Sandys was later associated.

George Sandys, it is thought, was educated at St Peter's School close to York Minster up to the age of eleven, though nothing is known of the nature of that schooling. He went at 11, in 1589, a year after the death of his father, to the University of Oxford. Initially registered at St Mary's Hall, he and his brother rapidly transferred to Corpus Christi College. Two of their older brothers had been there before them. The president of the College, William Cole, had been in exile with their father. Their curriculum would have involved lectures and disputations in Greek, Latin, possibly theology, logic, natural philosophy, mathematics, and morals.

It is not clear how long Sandys stayed at Oxford, but it cannot have been later than October of 1596, when he was admitted to membership of the Middle Temple in London. It is likely that he studied law for at least two years. By 1609 he had moved to Canterbury, and his circuit of residences after this were Kent, Oxfordshire and London.

In May 1610 he set off on a journey to the Eastern Mediterranean, much of the evidence for which derives from the book which he wrote about this experience. *A Relation of a Journey begun An. Dom. 1610. In Four Bookes. Containing a Description of the Turkish Empire, of Egypt, of the Holy Land, of the Remote Parts of Italy and Ilands adioyning* was published in 1615 and is based on his travels in these regions, his route taking him to the Middle East via France and Italy. The *Relation* was widely read, and had nine editions including translations from 1615-1673. Sandys subsequently was an officer of the Virginia Company, before he retired to live in England in his later years.

Samuel Bochart (1599-1667)[22]

Bochart, son of a Protestant pastor René and his wife Esther, was born at Rouen in May 1599, studied theology at Rouen and then took courses at the Protestant Academy at Saumur. He became a pastor in Caen in 1625, and made a major impact as a strong debater, controversialist and oriental linguist, and as a writer on various aspects of 'Sacred Geography'. The first of the two parts of his *Geographia Sacra* was published in 1646, and the whole work had a major scholarly impact. Figure 1 is a map from the first part of this work, and relates to his theory of the origin and spread of the human race after the Noahtian flood. He was invited to visit Queen Christina of Sweden in 1652, and took with him the young P.-D. Huet, who had been impressed by his work. In 1663 he published *Hierozoicum, sive Historia Animalium Sanctae Scripturae*, an analysis of biblical references to animals. He was a member of the Academy at Caen, and in 1660 was deputy for Normandy at the Synod of Loudon. He died of apoplexy during a debate at Caen on May 16 1667. His early links with Huet, across a major religious divide, were profitable and constructive, but after the visit to Sweden a number of issues divided them. These included his criticism of Huet's edition of and commentary on a manuscript of a commentary on St Matthew by the Greek theologian Origen (185-c.254 A.D.), and their respective views on the biblical evidence for the location of the Garden of Eden.

Thomas Fuller (1608-1661)[23]

Thomas Fuller was born in the village of Alwincle in Northamptonshire in midland England in 1608, and at the age of twelve became a scholar at Queen's College, Cambridge, becoming a B. A. in 1625, and an M. A. in 1628. He was appointed in 1630 by the Master and Fellows of Corpus Christi College, at the age of twenty-two, to the curacy of St. Benet's Church in Cambridge, and in 1631 became a Prebendary of Salisbury Cathedral in Wiltshire. In 1635 he became a Bachelor of Divinity in Cambridge, having continued to reside there, and in 1634 was presented to the living of Broadwinsor in Dorset, where he married his first wife.

His son was born in 1641, but his wife died in the same year, and Fuller went to live in London, where he remained until 1660, preaching at the Inns of Court and at the Chapel Royal, Savoy from 1641-1643. From the beginning of his clerical career he had published sermons, and verses, followed by *The History of the Holy Warre* [The Crusades] in 1634, and *The Holy (and Profane) State* in 1639. He followed the Royalist cause and various aristocratic patrons as chaplain in the English Civil War (1642-9) and was ultimately appointed 'chaplain in extraordinary' to the King (Charles II), after the Restoration in 1660. His major published works during the Civil War

FIGURE 1
Samuel Bochart, *DescriptioTerrarum in Quas Dispersunt Structures Turris Babel*.
This map, from Bochart's *Geographia Sacra pars prior* (Caen 1646),
illustrates the lands to which the descendants of Noah dispersed.
Map reproduced by permission of the Department of Manuscripts and
Special Collections, University of Nottingham.

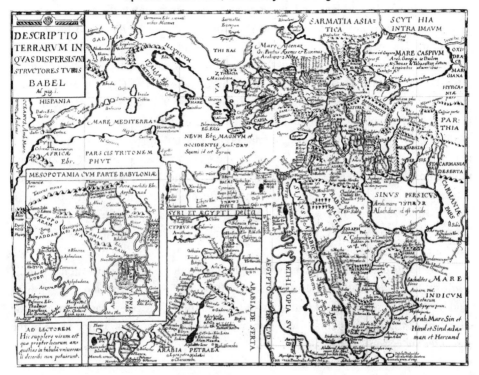

were *Good Thoughts in Bad Times* (1645), and *A Pisgah-Sight of Palestine* (1650). These were followed after the war by two of his most famous works: *A Church History of Britain; with a History of the University of Cambridge* (1655), and *The History of the Worthies of England*, published after his death, in 1662.

Pierre-Daniel Huet (1630-1721)[24]

Huet was born at Caen on February 8th 1630. He was orphaned early in his life, his father dying when he was two and his mother when he was six. He was placed in the guardianship of a mathematician uncle, and after his death with his aunts in Rouen. From the age of thirteen his studies at the Jesuit college at Mont-Royal included philosophy, Latin and mathematics (he also had a strong interest in astronomy), and at seventeen he commenced the study of law. His reading, however, of the *Geographia Sacra* of Samuel Bochart, published in 1646 and 1651,[25] prompted him to extend his studies to include Greek and Hebrew in order to gain better understanding of biblical antiquity. He subsequently added the study of Syrian and Arabic. He accompanied Bochart on a visit to Queen Christina of Sweden in 1652, and travelled back through Holland, in whose scholarly publications and active economy he took great interest. Because of the Anglo-Dutch wars, he was obliged to stay at the Dutch frontier for two years. He spent much time after 1654 on his edition of Origen, and visited Paris each year for study in libraries and, for other scholarly and social contacts, including visits to the salons. He founded an Academy of Sciences at Caen in 1662, which corresponded with the Royal Society in London, and was supported financially by Colbert. In 1670 he became assistant tutor to the Dauphin, son of Louis XIV. In 1674 he was elected a member of the Académie Française, and in 1676 was ordained priest.

He was appointed Abbot of Aunay, on the Orne in Normandy, in 1678 and took up his post in 1680. Thereafter he was nominated to the See of Soissons, and in 1685 appointed Bishop of Avranches (though not formally accredited from Rome until 1692). In 1699, after intense work in his diocese, he was nominated by the king as Abbot of Fontenay near Caen, but took up residence in the Jesuit house in Paris, where he died at the age of 90.

The focus here, within his astonishingly wide range of erudition which included philosophical disputation and reflection, will be on his work in sacred geography and on his links with other orientalists and other biblical exegetes, partly through the 'Republic of Letters'. Mention will also be made of his treatise on Dutch trade in the seventeenth century.

Jean de Thévenot (1633-1667)[26]

Thévenot was born in Paris. He was the nephew of the famous French traveller Melchisadech Thévenot (1620-1692). His father left him a large fortune and Thévenot travelled in Europe from 1652. In 1664 he left Marseilles for a journey to the Levant. His *Relation d'un Voyage fait au Levant* was published in Paris in 1664.

Laurent d'Arvieux (1635-1702)[27]

D'Arvieux came from a Tuscan family, whose surname was Arveo (modified to Arviou) and which had moved to Provence in the sixteenth century, and settled near Marseilles. Marseilles was the French focus for the Levant trade, in which members of Laurent's family were involved. In 1650 he began work in the office of his prosperous cousins Bertandié, and in October 1653 sailed with one of them to Smyrna via Genoa, Leghorn, and Malta, reaching Smyrna fifty-nine days later.[28] He spent twelve years in the Levant, travelling and mastering a range of languages including Turkish, Arabic, Persian, Hebrew and Syrian. He went to the Holy Land in Lent of 1660, via Jaffa, spending, as was the custom, Holy Week in Jerusalem and its environs. Subsequent to his return to Marseilles in 1665, he had various other diplomatic and consular engagements on behalf of Louis XIV and Colbert, in Tunis, Constantinople, Algiers, and from 1679 at Aleppo. He returned to France in 1686. He was made Chevalier of the Order of St. Lazare in 1673. He provided, in 1670, the details of Turkish dress and custom for Molière's *Le Bourgeois Gentilhomme*. He had major interests in commerce and trade with the Levant, and his facility with language gave him access to and considerable knowledge of Ottoman society and administration, particularly in his mission to the Turabey at Mount Carmel in 1664. His notes of his journeys were published in Paris in 1717 by La Roque, and a major edition in seven volumes edited by P. Labat was published in 1735: *Mémoires du Chevalier d'Arvieux, Envoyé Extraordinaire du Roy à la Porte, Consul d'Alep, d'Alger, de Tripoli, & autres Échelles du Levant.*

Henry Maundrell (1665-1701)[29]

Henry Maundrell, Oxford-educated and an ordained priest, was appointed as chaplain to the Levant Company at Aleppo where he remained until his death in 1701. Like many Levant Company chaplains he had a keen interest in the history and antiquities of the region. His account of a pilgrimage to the Holy Land, published posthumously in 1703 with the title *A Journey from Aleppo to Jerusalem at Easter AD 1697*, is regarded as a fine piece of writing and useful source of information.

The merchants' worlds of Western Europe and the Levant

One of the prime motives for an expanding European interest in the Levant in the late sixteenth and the seventeenth centuries was the anticipated profit to be made from investment, by the state (mercantilism) and private money, in commerce and trade. This was allied to geostrategic positioning for the protection of trading bases and routes. There was an expansion of trade with the Ottoman Empire by the English, Dutch and French, starting in the sixteenth century, when capitulations or trading privileges were granted: first to the French in 1536 and 1569, and later to the English and Dutch. The capitulations system developed from the grant of permission by the Ottoman rulers to non-Ottoman subjects for regulated trade within the empire, with a view to Ottoman benefit from imports and presumably also from exports. According to Moscrop, "In order to foster trade and contact with the non-Moslem world, seventeenth-century sultans had granted certain privileges to representatives of non-

Moslem states at the Porte at Constantinople. The privilege related to the rights of foreign nationals to be set apart from the laws and practices of Turkey and to be subject to the jurisdiction of their own embassies".[30] They were not permanently fixed privileges, and had to be re-negotiated at various times by European states such as England, France and the Netherlands. The capitulations granted to France in 1536 were based on earlier models of agreements with Venice and Genoa, and in turn were used as a model for trading agreements with other European countries.[31]

The primary goods exported from the Levant were raw materials such as cotton, silk and mohair, and silk and cotton yarn.[32] Competition between the three powers (and initially with the Italians), for the trade of the Mediterranean, reflected a struggle for commercial supremacy at the heart of what Wallerstein has called the core of the modern world-system. Wallerstein claims that from 1651 to 1672 the English and the French were both concerned in eliminating Dutch commercial advantage, after which they focused their attention on each other. The chronologies of development of the role of the Levant in Wallerstein's theory of the rise of the world-system are debatable, but one proposal is that the Ottoman Empire as a whole, including the Levant, became part of the world-economic system in the seventeenth century.[33] The evidence cited to prove this thesis included, as Wagstaff has stated, "the granting of the first Capitulations (with France in 1569, England 1580, Netherlands 1612), and the establishment of the first French, Dutch and English consulates in the Ottoman Empire (French 1523, England 1581, Netherlands 1613). It is principally the chronology of these events, and their coincidence with the first phase of expansion for the European world-economy (put by Wallerstein at 1450-1650), which suggested that the incorporation of the Ottoman Empire into the European world-economy could have taken place in the seventeenth century".[34] According to Wagstaff, however, Wallerstein was wrong in this assertion, both in terms of chronology (such incorporation did not take place until the nineteenth century) and also the orientation of Ottoman trade, which was more strongly linked to the Indian Ocean than to Western Europe.[35]

Both England and France (and the Netherlands) established Levant Companies for the purpose of realizing the trade potential of the Near East, this in turn the by-product of a strategy to link to Indian Ocean trade through the Eastern Mediterranean, particularly for spices and Iranian silk.[36] The Dutch were actively involved from the late sixteenth century in attempts to compete for Far Eastern trade with the Portuguese and Spanish. In some respects the 'Dutch Model' of development of overseas trade, as it is sometimes termed, seems to have been a driving competitive force for both Britain and France.[37]

The English Levant Company began in effect with the accreditation of the first English Ambassador, as a merchant, to the Ottoman Porte in 1581, with special protection given to English merchants. This was followed by the Turkey Company being licensed in the reign of Elizabeth, and the Levant Company, as it became, received its charter in 1590, part of a sequence of trading companies that included the East India and Muscovy companies.[38] The English presence in the Levant was enhanced through the establishment of consulates and groups of merchants, at various places, including Smyrna and Aleppo.[39] These colonies of merchants, many of them quite small, at the port and major trading cities, and usually operating under the judicial authority of and representation by consuls and vice-consuls, were the bases of European trade with the Levant. The English termed these merchant colonies *factories*, and the French *échelles*.

The appointment of scholarly chaplains, usually from Oxford, to the English factories in these places facilitated both the gathering and relaying of manuscripts and materials in Arabic and the production of accounts of travel in the Levant, such as that of Henry Maundrell, in his *A Journey from Aleppo to Jerusalem at Easter A. D. 1697*.[40]

English commercial activities through the creation of regional trading companies were paralleled by France, and the involvement of the major European nations in greater trading links with the Levant, including Palestine, together with the existing religious significance of the region, spurred further visits and descriptions from the mid-sixteenth century onwards. Broc has suggested, for example, that the signature of the Capitulations between Suliman the Magnificent and François I produced new facilities for French travellers and gave protection to those who were botanists, archaeologists, soldiers, merchants or pilgrims. While the travellers still remained strongly pious, they extended their interests to antiquities and the languages, religion and customs of the inhabitants of the Ottoman Empire in and beyond the Levant.[41]

Under Louis XIV and the policies developed by his controller-general of the realm, Jean-Baptiste Colbert (1619-1683), concerted effort was made to increase national self-sufficiency and profit, through a mercantilist philosophy which included the granting of trading monopolies to companies trading with the colonies and other potentially lucrative locations.[42] The French Levant Company was established for the first time in 1670, following the West Indies Company (1662), the East Indies Company (1664), and the Northern Company (1669). The notion of such a company had quite a long gestation, partly, it is thought, through Colbert's interpretation of the relative roles of the state and of private capital in the financing and control of the successful English Levant Company.[43] The fall in French trade with the Levant resulted in later attempts at reformation by Colbert, and the establishment of agencies through the new company in Smyrna, Cairo and Aleppo by 1671. The attempts to stimulate trade by the export of Languedoc cloth failed, and the French Levant Company company was liquidated in 1678, to be revived again shortly afterwards.

French trade in the Mediterranean in the seventeenth century was changing in character, having lost some of the major trade in Oriental goods, including spices, which were declining in quantity on the Gulf and Red Sea routes from Asia and which were being bought and sold increasingly by the English and the Dutch. Marseilles, however, strengthened its trading links with the Levant, and became France's most important Mediterranean port. East has stated that : "In the latter decades of the seventeenth century Marseilles absorbed almost the whole of French trade in the Levant... A new quay was built; its harbour was dredged; its near-by islands were used for quarantine stations and for the discharge of cargoes; and its population increased to between 75,000 and 1,000,000 by 1700. It developed a number of industries on the basis of imported raw materials: soap was made with soda from Syria and olive oil from the Levant, since the supplies of Provence itself were insufficient".[44] The sailing time, on the lighter French vessels operating from the southern ports, varied from fifteen to thirty days out and longer on the way back, on account of the weight of the cargo.[45] Cohen has stated that by the end of the seventeenth century France was the only European country left trading significantly with Palestine, the English being more interested in the territory to the north and the Dutch trade of small amount: "Thus, the bulk of the Palestinian trade was in French hands. The chief commodity was cotton. Palestinian cotton, which was very highly regarded in Europe, was exported to France in a number of forms (carded, spun, etc.). Although cotton was grown also in the Ramle-Lydda area, the best quality fibre was considered to come from the Galilee ('Cotons d'Acre'). The increasing French demand for Palestinian cotton at the end of the 17th and the beginning of the 18th Century, and the considerable profits which were to be made from exporting this to France, encouraged the Sidon and Acre merchants to get hold of as much of this as possible".[46] Other sources of cotton at this time included the Aegean Islands and the hinterland of Smyrna in Anatolia.[47]

The nature of European trade with the Levant is described in two works by authors considered in this chapter: in Huet's study of Dutch commerce, and in the account by Laurent d'Arvieux of his travels and residence in the Levant. It is against the background of French opportunities in the Levant trade that the perspectives of Laurent d'Arvieux, who was created French Consul at Aleppo in 1679, and where he remained until 1686, should be seen. D'Arvieux, wherever he went, made opportunity to review and comment on a variety of economic and cultural issues, including the nature and extent of goods traded from the regions of the Levant, and the potential for further trade with France. P.-D. Huet, though he never travelled to the Levant, had a detailed statistical knowledge of French trade, which he compared with that of England and the Netherlands in particular. Both embraced similar mercantilist philosophies of national advancement for France through trade and industry, though their scholarly interests and sources were otherwise very different.

Huet's *Le Grand Trésor Historique et Politique du Florissant Commerce des Hollandois dans tous les États et Empires du Monde* was first published in Rouen in 1712, and in English translation in London in 1718. It is principally concerned with the reasons for the superiority of the Dutch as a trading nation, and the political consequences of this for France. Much of the detail given relates to the seventeenth century. The key in the Huet thesis is the relationship between commerce and national status and power. His motives for writing are that he has been asked by his friends at the Académie Française to write "something upon Trade, which might give them a general Idea of it as regards politics", and because, he claims, commerce seemed to be so little understood in France.[48] He outlines the importance of commerce and agriculture as the foundations of the state economy, and the links between naval and state power. He praises French achievements in the seventeenth century, and attributes the decline of Spanish power to reduction in its trading activity. He also states that: "We *Frenchmen* have been reproached (and perhaps not without some reason) that the genius of our Nation was not proper for a foreign Commerce, being greatly weary of all Undertakings that require solid and continuous application", but he indicates that there are nonetheless people of commercial ability in France.[49] Chapter XII of his thesis deals with the relative strengths and particular details of Dutch, English and French Mediterranean trade, and the need for heavily armed escort naval vessels for the merchant ships to offset the dangers posed by the "Corsairs of Barbary".[50]

The accounts by D'Arvieux of trade in the Levant are largely first-hand, given the nature of his interests, employments and travels, in contrast to those of Huet. D'Arvieux's first encounter with the Levant was with Smyrna in Anatolia, where there was a well-established French trading settlement, and which he reached after a journey from Marseilles in December 1653. In Smyrna he learned of the extensive overland trading contacts with Persia, India and Asia, and also applied himself to understanding the Turkish language (also Arabic, Persian, Hebrew and Syrian) and customs.[51] In Palestine he was not actively involved in trade. He visited Acre in 1658, and in 1660 went to the Holy Land as a pilgrim. He does comment, on both visits, on the state of and opportunities (or lack of them) for trade with France. In 1658 he speaks of the poor state of the buildings of Acre, but also of the growing of wheat, rice and vegetables in the vicinity and the production of ashes (*cendres*), exported for the manufacture of glass and soap in France. In 1660 he landed at Jaffa, the main point of landing for pilgrims en route to Jerusalem. There he comments on its poor state, but mentions the presence of merchants. Later he comments on the lack of opportunity for business in Jerusalem.[52] On a visit to Mount Carmel, he describes the productive potential of the rich soil, the cultivation of melons and the raising of deer, cattle, and sheep.[53] Like Sandys, he bemoans the demise of the land and settlements from a former state, but D'Arvieux is always looking at the potential of the land. Part of the problem of the trading potential for Palestine was that its maritime Plain was not greatly endowed with natural harbours. George Adam Smith, writing in the late nineteenth century in his *Historical Geography of the Holy Land*, describes it in the following way:

> "*The whole Maritime Plain possesses a quiet but rich beauty. If the contours are gentle the colours are strong and varied. Along almost the whole seaboard runs a strip of links and downs, sometimes of pure drifting sand, sometimes of grass and sand together ... Such a plain, rising through the heat by dim slopes to the long persistent range of blue hills beyond, presents today a prospect of nothing but fruitfulness and peace. Yet it has been one of the most famous war-paths of the world. It is not only level, it is open. If its coastline is so destitute of harbours, both its ends from wide and easy entrances. The southern rolls off upon the great passage from Syria to Egypt ...*"[54]

The only ports in the seventeenth century were Jaffa, Acre, and Carmel. Jaffa was the port for the inland town of Ramleh (modern Ramla), which in turn acted as an *échelle* and a staging point for pilgrims to Jerusalem. Jaffa was in a very poor state in the seventeenth century, with virtually no habitable buildings and a very small port guarded by Turks sent by the *pasha* of Gaza. Though improvement was noted at the end of the century, it was still frequently attacked from the land and from the sea.[55]

The trading potential of Acre, once a major medieval port, had been badly affected both by political circumstance and neglect, and parts were covered in wind-driven sand. According to Lewis, "Acre had been a great port in the Middle Ages, and the scene of the last stand of the Kings of Jerusalem, but by 1658 it was nothing but a heap of ruins half buried in drifting sand, its harbour so incumbered with fallen masonry and so dangerous that most ships anchored under the lee of Mount Carmel, in spite of the fact that they were exposed to the raids of pirates".[56] Nonetheless, the French, the Dutch and the English used it as a place of purchase and shipment of goods. In 1700 the French were the only European residents, and had acted as factors for the English and Dutch merchants based at Aleppo until the controversial appointment of a Dutchman as joint Dutch and English vice-consul in 1700.[57] Acre was a port of export of cottons from Galilee and of the ash, made through burning aromatic herbs, which was sent in large quantities to Marseille and Venice for the production of soap and glass. Rice and wheat were also produced in the region around Acre, and periodically exported.[58]

Hazardous journeys

One of the problems encountered by all travellers to and in the Levant, both at sea and on land, was the constant danger of attack and robbery. For merchant vessels, their crews and passengers, the danger was ever present, along the shipping routes from the western to the eastern Mediterranean. The character and geography of local and 'international' privateering and piracy in this region was complex. It included: the activities of ships owned or licensed as privateers by the Knights of Malta; English and French, Dutch and Italian privateers; and Barbary corsairs, licensed by the governors of the North African Ottoman principalities. Their terms and frequency of activity depended in part on whether they were Christian or Muslim, and the state of political relations between Western European states.[59]

D'Arvieux, like many others, experienced this type of hazard at first hand, the efforts of Colbert to introduce a convoy system to protect French merchant ships, like that of the British and Dutch, having conspicuously failed, not least because of the individualism of the French merchant captains and their dislike of naval officers.[60] The ship on which d'Arvieux was sailing from Sidon (Seide) to Acre in March 1660, en route to Jerusalem for the Easter services, was attacked by what is described as a pirate ship (presumably a privateer) and looted. D'Arvieux, bearded and dressed as a Turk, persuaded the captain to release their ship, and they continued to Acre.[61] Thévenot had a similar experience in May 1658, as "a passenger on board a ship close inshore off Mount Carmel, a favourite pirate hunting ground. When it became obvious that the pirate they had sighted was about to board them, the crew dived overboard and swam ashore, leaving the passengers to their fate", but Thévenot convinced the captain to release them the following day, on the grounds that they had little worth taking.[62]

George Sandys, earlier in the seventeenth century, suffered, as did most travellers to the Holy Land, from a natural hazard: a storm at sea. On leaving Acre for Sidon by the English ship *Trinity* after his visit to the Holy Land at Easter 1610 they experienced a severe storm, and had to ride out the very heavy seas in great discomfort until they could be brought ashore in a skiff.[63] D'Arvieux also gives an account of the natural hazards of sea travel. In February 1658, en route from the Nile to Acre, the *caique* on which he sailed had to await in the Nile delta until the Nile itself could cut through the accumulated sand that had been blown by the wind into the channel, which it had blocked. Once at sea, the combination of a gale and poor seamanship on the part of the Greek captain put them at risk, until, comforted by tots of brandy, invocations of the aid of the saints of several different nations, and aided by the expertise of a French merchant captain travelling as a passenger, they landed at Tyre and went overland to Acre.[64]

Once they had reached the coast of Palestine, travellers had continually, as had their guides, to be on the lookout for armed attacks, and frequently made detours to avoid trouble. They were expected to pacify local Ottoman administrators with gifts. They also had to travel through some harsh and difficult environments. Thus, for example, Sandys describes the route from Ramleh to Jerusalem, in the higher hill region: "The passage exceeding difficult; streighten'd with wood, and as it were paved with broken rocks: which by reason of the raine then falling, became no less dangerous to our Camels", the area also being unsafe, in his opinion, because of the inhabitants being "theeves, as are all the Arabians".[65] D'Arvieux, taking the coastal road from Acre at the start of his journey to Jerusalem, observes: "Ce passage est presque toujours dangereux. Les Arabes se cachent derrière ces morceaux de sable, [et] dès qu'ils découvrent quelqu'un, ils montent sur leur cavalles, [et] vous joignent dans un instant". They were deterred, he states, only by the sight of firearms.[66]

Piety and pilgrimage

An important element of the experience of French and English travellers to Palestine in the seventeenth century was that of personal belief and piety, expressed in their representations of their experiences and reflections when on pilgrimage to the holy sites, including Jerusalem. Sandys, Thévenot, D'Arvieux and Maundrell each offer different views and emphases in their accounts.

The general pattern of visits, which had long been the case with Christian pilgrims, was to visit Jerusalem and surrounding sites at Easter, and many of the descriptions focus on the various religious ceremonies, and the places in which they were conducted (especially the Church of the Holy Sepulchre). After Easter the tradition was for an escorted journey to the Jordan, sometimes to the Dead Sea, and to other holy places such as Bethlehem and Nazareth.

The restriction on travel by the Ottoman authorities was a significant common experience. As Haynes puts it: "The traveler could not wander freely over the landscape: he was almost always confined to the network (ship, embassy, and caravan) which assured him a tolerable degree of safety. Understandably, his narrative was also confined to a well-beaten path".[67] This largely on account of the personal dangers encountered in travel, but there were other restrictions. The Ottoman authorities, for example, tightly controlled arrangements for visits to Jerusalem in particular. Responsibility for western Christian pilgrims to the holy city had been placed in the hands of the Franciscan Pater-Guardian of Jerusalem, and pilgrims were required to stay in the monastery and submit to their control when travelling in and near to the city.[68] A certificate of visits to the holy places was a compulsory purchase for pilgrims, and this, together with the unfamiliar rituals of Catholic and Orthodox religious observances, posed particular problems for Protestant visitors like Sandys. Money was raised by the friars through various charges, including that for the installation of pilgrims as Knights of the Holy Sepulchre. Sandys laments the control of access by the Turks to the Church of the Holy Sepulchre: "O who can without sorrow, without indignation behold the enemies of Christ to be the Lords of this Sepulcher! and who at festivall times sit mounted under a Canopie, to gather money of such as do enter: the profits arising therefrom being farmed at eight thousand Sultanies".[69] Sandys' concerns at such matters, however, do not outweigh the intensity of his religious experience of Jerusalem in particular. Although he generally writes in a controlled and somewhat dispassionate way, the effect of Jerusalem and his experience with his companions during the Easter celebrations, witnessed over several days' confinement in the Church of the Holy Sepulchre is clear, including his writing of a "hymne to my Redeemer".[70]

D'Arvieux visited the Holy Land in 1660, together with a group of French and Dutch merchants and religious who wanted to spend Easter in Jerusalem. He expressed disappointment at the lack of opportunity for business in Jerusalem in order to cover his expenses of travel, and in general seems to have been sceptical about the country and its state.[71] He received the Order of Knight of the Holy Sepulchre, and subsequently visited the River Jordan and Jericho, the Mount of the Forty Days, the Dead Sea, Bethlehem, Hebron, and Nazareth.

Thévenot's visit, at Easter 1665, paralleled those of the others mentioned here. He spends much time in his account describing the Church of the Holy Sepulchre and the Easter services, together with visits to holy places outside the city. These included a visit by a large group of European pilgrims to the River Jordan, accompanied by a major Ottoman escort of 300 cavalry and 200 foot-soldiers.[72]

Henry Maundrell went as a pilgrim to the Holy Land at Easter 1697, and gives a long account of the experience. Of the group of accounts considered here his is the only one by an ordained minister. "There being several Gentlemen of our Nation (fourteen in number) determined for a visit to the *Holy-Land* at the approaching Easter, I resolved, tho' but newly come to Aleppo, to make one in the same design: considering that it was my purpose to undertake the Pilgrimage some time or other, before my return to *England*...".[73] They entered the Church of the Holy Sepulchre on Good Friday, March 26th : "The Pilgrims being all admitted this day, the church doors were lock'd in the evening, and open'd no more till Easter Day; by which we were kept in a close, but very happy confinement, for three days. We spent our time in viewing the Ceremonies practis'd by the Latins at this Festival, and in visiting the several holy places; all which we had an opportunity to survey, with as much freedom and deliberation as we pleased".[74] He gives a general description of the church, saying that full details are to be had in the earlier descriptions and measurements provided by "our Learned sagacious Country-man Mr Sandys".[75] He discusses the divisions of responsibility between the various sects for the management of the Church of the Holy Sepulchre, and its topography "or places consecrated to a more than ordinary veneration, by being reputed to have some particular actions done in them, relating to the Death and Resurrection of Christ".[76] He describes the Easter service in the manner of an observer rather than participant, and follows it with an account of the city walls.

On Monday, March 29th, Easter Monday, "the Mosolem or Governour of the City set out, according to custom, with several Bands of Souldiers to convey the Pilgrims to *Jordan*. Without this guard, there is no going thither, by reason of the Multitude and Insolence of the Arabs in these parts. The fee to the Mosolem for his Company and Souldiers upon this occasion, is twelve Dollars for each Frank Pilgrim, but if they be Ecclesiastics, six; which you must pay, whether you are dispos'd to go to the Journey or stay in the City".[77] They went to the Mount of Olives, and Bethany, to Jericho and to the River Jordan and the Dead Sea. Their devotions at the Jordan were disturbed by shots fired by a group of Arabs, "but at too great a distance to do any execution".[78] At the Dead Sea he states that he could find no evidence of "those Cities anciently situate in this place; and made so dreadful an example of the divine vengeance ...",[79] though he was assured by the Pater-Guardian and the Procurator of Jerusalem that they had previously seen such ruins. He subsequently visited Bethlehem.

Maundrell's account contains many interesting and accurate details of the places visited and the ceremonies experienced, of topography and of agriculture. His writing exhibits a tolerance of religious practices of other Christian sects, with the exception of the Greek ceremony of the Holy Fire, yet curiously does not give much evidence of strong personal feelings about Jerusalem and the holy sites and his own religious convictions.

Theologies, humanities and republics of letters

The question of the location of important sacred places, conspicuously in Jerusalem, and their character at various times in the biblical past, is a strong element in the writings about Palestine by both visitors and non-visitors alike. The significance and symbolism of biblical events was increasingly judged by scholars' ability to relate them to real places on the ground, and in some cases to attempt a local verification through a primitive form of archaeological investigation. This is not simply an issue, however, of the veracity of travellers' accounts. As with the accounts of non-travellers, such as those of Thomas Fuller, both types of representation of the past and present landscapes and symbolism of the Holy Land must be seen within a great complexity of personal beliefs and broader cultural contexts. They also have links with the literary sources, in addition to various versions of the Bible, from which they drew information and illustrations, including maps.

Some illustration of the cultural and ideological issues involved can be given by brief consideration of the context in which the name Holy Land was used. The name itself derives from its Christian spiritual origins, enforced by European activity at the time of the Crusades. In the sixteenth and seventeenth centuries, though the numbers of Christians varied widely from place to place, from none to up to about thirty per cent of the population,[80] the assumption generally made by travellers was that Christian influence in the Ottoman Empire was limited, and many accounts reflect the sense of despair at the decay of the sacred sites and the decline of Christian influence. Hence the use of the name Holy Land was problematic. Sandys, for example, reflects this contrast in his *Relation of a Journey*, in what Haynes sees as a dilemma of "two mythic visions. In one of them Palestine labours under a dark curse, is 'anathemated', is to be contemplated with horror; in the other it really is a Holy Land. These two visions interfere with each other, each keeping the other from gaining ascendancy. Out of their interference comes Sandys' objective and historical treatment of Palestine, which permits him to avoid making a choice. He will still use the name 'The Holy Land', but under protest, holding it at a philological distance. The meaning of the Holy Land is that it once had a sacred meaning which has been withdrawn".[81] The sensitivity of the use of the term is also reflected by Fuller in the title and contents of his *Pisgah-Sight of Palestine* (1650), where Palestine is the name preferred. Fuller's sensitivity, as Sandys', is partly a Protestant one: a concern amid the religious fluxes of mid-seventeenth-century England at not being closely associated with Catholic causes and controversial issues of Protestant faith. He thus describes his *Pisgah-Sight* as "a parcell of Geography touching a particular description of *Judaea*; without some competent skill wherein, as the blind *Syrians* intending to go to *Dothan*, went to *Samaria*; so ignorant persons discoursing of the Scripture, must needs make many absurd, and dangerous mistakes. Nor can knowledge herein, be more speedily and truly obtained, then by particular description of the tribes, where the eye will learn more from a Mappe, then the eare can learn in a day from discourse".[82] In the introductory section of Chapter Two (*The different names and bounds of Judaea*), he lists the various names by which Palestine had been called: The Land of Canaan, The Land of Promise, The Land of Judah and Israel, Judaea, and the Holy Land. Of the last of these, Fuller tellingly comments: "But fear makes me refrain from using this word, lest whilest I call the Land holy, this age count me superstitious."[83] It is the usefulness of the proffered geography of Palestine, not to salvation but to "the true understanding of the History of the Bible",[84] that is important to Fuller in his production of the book. He and others were caught up in the conflict between the scripture-based Puritans and the High Church party under Laud, especially in the period from c.1630 to the start of the Civil War in 1642. Fuller himself, a Royalist and Calvinist, was a man of great moderation, and was scrupulously anxious to avoid the extremes of Puritan, Anglo-Catholic and Roman Catholic belief. His attempts to write a factually-based historical geography or topography are reflected clearly in his *Pisgah-Sight*, and in the nature of his reaction to the attack on his *Church History* (1655) by Peter Heylyn. According to Drabble, "Heylyn was a narrow ideologue who appraised all men, past or present, by Laudian standards. How different was the approach of Thomas Fuller, who, judging all men by their 'piety, painfulness, learning and patience', avoided the more perjorative term 'Puritan' and divided Nonconformists into the 'mild and mannered', the 'fierce and fiery'". [85]

Such concerns at the implications of the use of the name Holy Land seem to have been less of a problem to the French scholars and travellers included in this account. Huet, D'Arvieux, Thévenot, and Bochart, who use both 'La Terre Sainte' and 'Palestine' seemingly, and understandably, without the same reservations as the English.

The reactions of Protestant travellers to the codes and religious observances of Muslim, Jewish, Catholic and Orthodox believers were in part also conditioned by the relations between churches. A general observation is that, in relation to what might be described as ecclesiastical geopolitics, European Protestant travellers and commentators on the Holy Land tend to a sympathy with the orthodox Eastern churches as opposed to their Roman counterparts. This was on account of what were regarded as the heresies of Rome and its active proselytizing in the Levant in the sixteenth and seventeenth centuries, and illustrated by the sending of priests by the eastern churches to train at Oxford during this period.[86] The capitulations granted to the Levant Company from the late sixteenth century had facilitated contact "with the Muslims, and particularly with the Arabic-speaking Christians of the Eastern Church".[87] The relations more broadly between Christian, Jew and Muslim cannot be discussed at length here, but it is worth drawing attention to some of the other issues involved. The Christian study of Islam was frequently uninformed, inaccurate and misleading, evidencing its polemic purpose of protecting the Christian faith. In the period after the Reformation there are further complexities in relation to the comparison by Catholic authors of Protestantism with Islam, the fierceness of Protestant hostility to Islam, and periodic Protestant aspirations for anti-Catholic power alliances with the Ottomans.[88] More positive scholarly outcomes included a conspicuous Protestant contribution to Arabic studies, in Holland and England in particular, partly for better understanding of the context of Old Testament Hebrew text, partly for better understanding of eastern churches, and partly as a practical aid to commerce in the region.[89] These were sometimes linked, as illustrated by Archbishop Laud's endowment of the first chair of Arabic at the University of Oxford in 1636 (the endowment being made permanent in 1640).[90]

Both English and French accounts of Palestine reflect complex perspectives of late Renaissance humanism and Reformation theology and their engagement with geography, history, cosmography, chorology and topography. Major theological and cosmographic issues were discussed in their own right by theologians and travellers, but they were often linked with practical aspects of landscape description and the consideration of commercial prospects.[91] Maps were significant contributions to the broad array of representations and debates, especially as illustrations of aspects of sacred geographies, including the territories of the tribes of Israel and the locations of important biblical sites.[92]

Sandys' *Relation of a Journey* symbolizes some of the significant aspects of what might be termed Protestant humanism. The book is dedicated to Prince Charles, in accordance with the conventions of the time, and the dedication itself suggests much about the purpose of the book. In essence, it is a digest of English Christian Renaissance humanism, in which, as Haynes puts it "History is displayed to us as a moral spectacle, illustrating a simple paradigm: a happy state is violated by sin, and retribution follows".[93] The lands visited are alleged to have declined from their once glorious and civilized states, much of this attributed to the Islamic influence.

The title page of the book [Figure 2] is decorated by an engraving by Francis Delaram, showing as allegory figures representing the places that he had visited,

FIGURE 2

Title page of G. Sandys *A Relation of a Journey begun An: Dom: 1610* (London, 1615). Reproduced by permission of the Brotherton Library (Special Collections), University of Leeds.

located around an architectural structure of a classical style. On the left is a Turk, with an orb of the world and a yoke in his hands. Opposite, *Isis sive Aegyptus*, with objects relating to the mysteries of ancient Egypt, and standing, ostensibly, in opposition to the Turk. The lozenge below is of a Cumaean Sybil outside her cave, with a Virgilian inscription. Above the centre is Christ above the Mount of Olives, "flanked by the guardian angels of Christian humanism, Veritas and Constantia ...".[94] Haynes states that: "The engraving is a fine expression of the contents of the book, and of the allegorical and symbolic imagination behind it. The figures represent great powers in the history of the West, figures of mystery and danger as well as of human values and divine promise ... Four books, four countries, four personifications, each out of a different tradition: this is the scheme of the *Relation*".[95]

The text has a prefatory map, which is like many of its time, but its exact source is not clear: it may have been a compilation by the publisher or Sandys himself from other maps available at the time. The rest of his illustrations are based on those of Giovanni Zuallardo, a pilgrim of Belgian origin [his Belgian name was Jean Zuallart] who visited the Holy Land in 1586, and produced a book, published in Rome in 1587. This was called *Il devotissimo viaggio di Gerusalemme*, and had many splendid illustrations.[96]

The nomenclature of the map is interesting, for it gives no indication of Ottoman or Arab control, using quite old place-names. This, Haynes has argued, may be more an indication of Sandys' awareness of the readers' geographical senses "formed by an education in the classics and the Bible, which left an abiding interest in the ancient places. The modern places one ... 'Babylon' is on the map, but Baghdad is not. Not a map for mariners or merchants, then, but for an educated reader seeking general knowledge. The map represents neither the ancient nor the modern worlds, but the interests of its readers, and the world Sandys describes".[97]

A significant aspect of the humanistic context of seventeenth-century accounts of the Holy Land, both for England and France, was the extensive network of personal and bibliographical links, between scholars of different nationalities and regional affinities and of differing theological traditions. The links within the learned worlds of Western Europe were acknowledged through the use of the phrase 'Republic of Letters'. This was particularly true from the mid-seventeenth century (though the concept dated from the fifteenth century), and reflected the rapid increase in institutions of learning, including academies, learned societies, and learned journals, together with the active promotional interests of governments and monarchs in the advancement of learning.[98]

The Académie Française was founded by Cardinal Richelieu in 1653, following the tradition of the early Italian academies such as Rome (1601), and the philosophy of the Englishman Sir Francis Bacon (1561-1626), for co-operative and experimental learning programmes.[99] The programme developed by Colbert, *Surintendant des Batîments du Roi*, for a system of paid cultural patronage, starting in 1663, extended beyond France, and added to the collaborative nature of scholarship in the seventeenth century and to the reputation of Louis XIV as a patron of scholarship and the arts: "insofar as Louis XIV became acknowledged as the monarch to whom scholars from all over Europe looked for cultural patronage, his reputation would be advanced".[100]

P.-D. Huet is a good example of a scholar operating in a dense network of contacts, within and outside France. He eagerly sought the opinions and bibliographical advice from European scholars, was a member of the Académie Française (elected in 1674), and received patronage from Louis XIV and Colbert. In August 1686 he entreated the Huguenot Étienne Morin, who had fled to the Netherlands after the Revocation of the Edict of Nantes, to inform him of new books being published there. Many European scholars followed developments in publishing in the Netherlands closely, because of the efficacy of the book trade and the freedom of the Press, and in consequence frequently sent their manuscripts there for publication.[101] He actively engaged in correspondence and debate with fellow scholars, which led in some cases, almost inevitably, to dispute and controversy. One of the saddest examples is his falling out with his friend the Huguenot pastor Samuel Bochart, initially over Bochart's dispute about Huet's omission of a section while copying the manuscript of Origen in the library of Queen Christina of Sweden. This led, according to Huet, to Bochart's warning to Protestant scholars in Europe that Huet had faked part of the passage copied.[102]

In the late seventeenth century he became disillusioned with the development of literary journals, on the grounds that he considered journals to be for "those who do not want to give themselves to the trouble of reading the entire books".[103] His Protestant colleague Samuel Bochart also operated within a national and international web of scholarly exchanges. Laplanche clearly demonstrates how Bochart, although operating from a 'provincial' base, with his extensive knowledge of the libraries of Paris, his invitation to Sweden to advise Queen Christina, his links with Northern European Protestant scholars, and his studies at Leiden, Oxford, and Saumur, "can be numbered among the Protestant scholars of European standing, who gave particular shape to Protestantism north of the Loire in the seventeenth century".[104]

The involvement of other English and French writers on theological and topographical aspects of the Holy Land depended more on reference to the writings of others, less frequently as a result of direct contact or correspondence. Thomas

Fuller, whose idea for a book on the topographic background to the Bible had started with his scene-setting in his earlier history of the Crusades (*The Historie of the Holy Warre*, 1634), in addition to the ancient geographers and historians such as Strabo, Josephus and Eusebius, cites the work, inter alia, of Samuel Bochart (*Geographia Sacra*), Sir Walter Raleigh's *The Historie of the World*, the Mercator atlas, Camden's *Britannia*, Adrichom's *Theatrum Terrae Sanctae*, and Biddulph's *Travels*.

By definition, perhaps, the actual travellers to the Holy Land, such as Sandys and D'Arvieux, had less need for other sources of information, in view of their own direct experience, than those who wrote without having visited the place.

Antiquities and topographies

These early accounts of Palestine are useful as reflections of the state of factual knowledge of the country and its antiquities and of the cultural contexts in which they were represented. Silberman, writing of the connotations of seventeenth-century archaeological interest, for example, ascribes one of the earliest excavations in the Holy Land to "the French adventurer Laurent D'Arvieux, who reported the discovery of a colossal statue – which he mistakenly identified as the image of the Philistine god Dagon – at Gaza in 1659".[105] To this type of what Bliss, in his account of early archaeology in the Holy Land, terms "short descriptions of the country, ordinarily visited", to which he adds the D'Arvieux accounts of Chateau Pelerin, Caesarea, Ascalon, and the remains in the Dead Sea of what were deemed to be the vestiges of five destroyed cities.[106] Individual travellers showed varied interest in the antiquities of particular parts of the Levant. Maundrell, according to Bliss's analysis, in his *Journey from Aleppo to Jerusalem in 1697* provides detailed and accurate accounts of the Syrian coast North of Beirut, but he showed relatively less interest in the Holy Land and added little to what was already known about Jerusalem.[107] Maundrell himself acknowledges his debt to Sandys' descriptions of Jerusalem (though there is of course a time gap of eighty years between their accounts). Sandys himself, in his *Relation of a Journey* provides both first-hand and partially derived accounts of the antiquities of the Holy Land. Figures 3 and 4 show a stylized landscape between Jerusalem and Bethlehem and a plan of Jerusalem, both derived from Zuallart. The genealogy of geographic, historic and cartographic information in late medieval and early modern accounts of the Holy Land is a subject of considerable potential.[108]

The quality of topographic and general geographical description by these English and French travellers is high. They are without exception acute observers, and their accounts offer important bases for understanding their perceptions of the places they

FIGURE 3

**The way between Jerusalem and Bethlehem, from G. Sandys *A Relation of a Journey begun An: Dom: 1610* (London, 1615).
Reproduced by permission of the Brotherton Library (Special Collections), University of Leeds.**

A. *Ieruſalem.*
a. *The ruines of Dauids tower.*
B. *Berſhebas fountaine.*
C. *The Turpentine tree.*
D. *The tower of Simion.*
E. *The Ciſterne of the Sages.*

Q 4

F. *The*

visited, and the broader theological and intellectual contexts in which they and their readers lived. Sandys, describing part of the journey from the coast to Jerusalem, states that "From hence to Jerusalem the way is indifferent even. On each side are round hills, with ruines on their tops; and valleys such as are figured in the most beautifull land-skips. The soil, though stony, not altogether barren, producing both corn and olives about inhabited places".[109] D'Arvieux has a sharp eye both for ruins and for areas that were productive or had productive potential, the latter including the environs of Bethlehem, and Mount Carmel. Equally, he has a sensitivity to the darker side of the landscape experience, evidenced in his pilgrim ascent of the 'Mountain of the Forty Days' (*Quarantain*) – the Mount of Temptation, near Jericho,

FIGURE 4

Jerusalem, from G. Sandys *A Relation of a Journey begun An: Dom: 1610* (London, 1615).
Reproduced by permission of the Brotherton Library, University of Leeds.

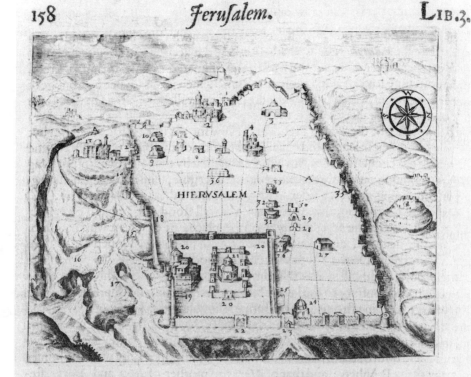

158   *Jerusalem.*   LIB.3.

1. *The gate of Ioppa.*
2. *The Castle of the Pisans,*
3. *The Monastery of the Franciscans.*
4. *The Temple of the Sepulcher.*
5. *A Mosque, once a collegiat Church where stood the house of Zebedeus.*
6. *The iron gate.*
7. *The Church of S. Marke where his house stood.*
8. *A Chappell where once stood the house of S. Thomas.*
9. *The Church of S. Iames.*
10. *The Church of the Angels where once stood the pallace of Annas the High Priest.*
11. *The Port of Dauid.*
12. *The Church of S. Sauiour, where stood the pallace of Caiphas.*
13. *A Mosque, once a goodly Temple there standing, where stood the Cœnaculum.*
14. *Where the Iewes would haue taken away the body of the Blessed Virgin.*
15. *Where Peter wept.*
16. *The fountaine Siloe.*
17. *The fountaine of the Blessed Virgin.*

18. *Port sterquiline.*
19. *The Church of the Purification of the Blessed Virgin, now conuerted into a Mosque.*
20. *The court of Solomons Temple.*
21. *A Mosque, where stood the Temple of Solomon.*
22. *The Golden gate.*
23. *The gate of S. Steuen.*
24. *The Church of Anna, now a Mosque.*
25. *The Poole Bethesda.*
26. *Where the pallace of Pilate stood.*
27. *Where stood, as the say, the pallace of Herod.*
28. *Pilats arch.*
29. *The Church of the Blessed Virgins swouning.*
30. *Where they met Simon of Cyrene.*
31. *Where the rich Glutton dwelt.*
32. *Where the Pharise dwelt.*
33. *Where Veronica dwelt.*
34. *The gate of Iustice.*
35. *Port Ephraim.*
36. *The Bazar.*
37. *The circuite of part of the old City.*

a place hallowed by the cells of ascetics and saints, and by tradition and imagination: "It is the most frightful mountain I have ever seen, particularly from the side by which we climbed it. Scarped, and almost steep as a wall ... dry, burnt, and so sterile that no blade of grass can grow on it from base to summit. It took us an hour by a narrow little path of rolling pebbles to arrive at a stairway cut in the rock ... after which we had to climb a seven-foot rock face by putting our feet in holes and hanging on to projections," and thence, via a narrow path with "live rock on one side, a horrible precipice on the other", to the summit, a difficult experience from which he recovered only after drinking two cups of wine after his descent.[110]

Maundrell is a gifted describer of landscape. He gives an interesting account of the evidence of agricultural terracing, in support of his thesis that in the past Palestine had been more productive and supported a larger population : "Of this form of culture you see evident footsteps, wherever you go in the Mountains of Palestine. Thus the very Rocks were made fruitful. And perhaps there is no spot of ground in this whole Land, that was not formerly improv'd, to the production of something or other, ministring to the sustenance of human life".[111] Maundrell's descriptions, in contrast to those of the others reviewed here, are full of scriptural references and links. He visits the Dead Sea: "Coming within about half an hour of the Sea, we found the ground uneven, and varied into hillocks, much resembling those places in England where there have been anciently Lime-kilns. Whether these might be the Pits at which the Kings of *Sodom and Gomorrah* were overthrown by the four kings, *Gen.* 14.10. I will not determine".[112]

Questions of Paradise

Both those who travelled to the Holy Land in the seventeenth century, and notably those theologians who conducted their biblical researches from their home countries, engaged with a range of contested topics and issues which were eagerly discussed, debated and cross-referenced on a transnational scale. In spite of the waves of religious turbulence and their tragic consequences experienced in many regions of Western Europe, including France and England, over this period, scholarly exchanges through a 'Republic of Letters', as shown above, were sustained well into the eighteenth century. These exchanges often crossed and seemingly ignored denominational divides, focusing as they did on issues of the geographies and topographies of the Holy Land and its neighbouring regions, as reflected in the sacred literatures, including versions of the Christian Bible.

Three of the key general areas of debate were the geographical location of the Garden of Eden, or Earthly Paradise; the location of Mount Ararat and the circumstances and consequences of Noah's Flood; and the Tower of Babel. Here we will discuss some of the issues raised by French and English Scholars on the subject of the location of the Garden of Eden, or Earthly Paradise/*Paradis Terrestre*. The basis of the interest and exegesis of this subject in the seventeenth century, as in the Middle Ages before, was the text of the Old Testament Book of *Genesis*, especially Chapter 2 vv.8-15, in which Adam and Eve are placed by God in the Garden of Eden. The medieval belief that this was a real place on earth was demonstrated in part by its location on medieval world maps. As Scafi has indicated, "A picture of the earth with the Garden of Eden is making visible the divine order of creation. It is at once a confession of the transcendent craft of God operating on terrestrial space, and of the limits of human reasoning. The sort of map-making which engages with theology in this way discloses a vision of the world which goes far beyond the frame of the human domain. Mapping Paradise is an act of faith in the sacred text".[113] The questions posed by the biblical text, for which cartographers and theologians long sought answers, related to the location of the Garden of Eden, and the identity and courses of the four rivers flowing from Eden. While the names and courses of two of the rivers- Tigris and Euphrates, were known, those of the other two rivers, the Pishon and the Gihon, were not.[114] Scafi suggests that the Garden of Eden disappeared from world maps about 1500 A.D.[115], but that thereafter, as a result of the Reformation and increasing interest in the authenticity and geographies of the biblical text, there was renewed interest at more local scales. Maps of the possible locations of the Garden of Eden appear in many of the seventeenth-century accounts of the historical geography of the Holy Land and of world history. A map of the location of the Garden of Eden, derived from a Calvin commentary on the *Book of Genesis*, published in French in 1553, was reproduced in the 1560 London edition of the Geneva Bible.[116] Thus " The presence of maps from Calvin's commentary on Genesis was one sign of the commitment of the editors of the Geneva Bible to a historical reading of the Bible. Maps, which claimed to show the exact situation of places named in scripture, seemed to prove that the Bible told a continuous story about the real world. They justified a literal reading of the text, by showing how it corresponded to presumed geographical facts".[117] The Garden and its symbolic representation of the fall of humans from divine grace through a lost paradise was a matter of deep theological significance and debate, which enhanced interest in the subject. With the voyages of exploration and discovery of the fifteenth century, hopes developed that the actual location of the original Garden of Eden might be discovered, though ideas of its location embraced many different parts of the world. The question of its location remained of interest in the seventeenth century, and large numbers of texts engaged in discussion of its theological, etymological, and geographical implications. The idea continued in to the Enlightenment, with the increasing use of empiricist geography to reconcile the tensions between scripture and scientific reason.[118] Prest has argued that the attempt to recreate a lost Paradise Garden was one of the seminal influences on the origins of the botanic garden in the seventeenth century.[119]

Paradis Terrestre in the writings of Bochart and Huet

Two of the French scholars whose work is being reviewed here – Huet and Bochart – were interested in the question of the location of the Garden of Eden, or *Paradis Terrestre* as they called it. The relevant works are: Bochart's *Geographia Sacra seu Phalag et Chanaan*, the first part of which, Phalag, was published in Caen in 1646, with later editions in 1674, 1681, 1692, 1707 and 1712, and Huet's *Traité de la Situation du Paradis Terrestre* which was first published in 1691. Figure 5 shows the title page of Huet's work, with Moses pointing out the location of *Paradis Terrestre* on a map. Bochart and Huet were working in different theological traditions, but had many issues of common interest in the sacred geographies of the biblical past.

Bochart's *Geographia Sacra* had a wider objective than Huet's *Traité*. The first part, *Phalag*, deals with the dispersion of people across the world (in effect the genealogies described in *Genesis:10* after the great Flood, much of it concerned with the building of Noah's Ark and the Tower of Babel. "The work continued with an account of the history of the Flood, explaining that paradise, and the first human settlement, had been in Babylonia; that the Ark had come to rest on the highest peaks of Assyria, the Gordiaei, which were to the east of the Taurus Mountains, and that the original language, Hebrew, had decayed in various ways since the time of the dispersion of peoples".[120] It was illustrated with maps, including one showing *Edenis sui Paradisi Terrestris Situs* – the location of Paradise at the confluence of the Tigris and Euphrates.[121] The second and longer part, *Chanaan* (1651), is concerned with the diffusion of Phoenician language and settlement colonies, developing his thesis that the spread of peoples across the world all linked back to Noah's sons and their families, traceable by various versions of Hebrew. One of his concerns, albeit leading to some fanciful etymological conclusions, was in the history of language and its use to trace the history of the colonization of the world. Bochart's *Geographia Sacra* was widely admired. It made a major impact on contemporary scholarship, not least on the thinking of P.-D. Huet, who having read the work determined to study Hebrew and Arabic in order to facilitate his study of sacred geography.

Huet, as reflected in the *Traité*, is described by Massimi as a man whose life was divided between travels in search of manuscripts and scholarly information and

FIGURE 5
Title Page from P.-D. Huet, *Traité de la Situation du Paradis Terrestre*.
This work was first published in Paris in 1691. This version is from
the seventh edition of 1701, published in Amsterdam.
Reproduced by permission of the British Library (shelfmark g.19518: p.d.Huet).

FIGURE 6

**Map showing the location of Paradis Terrestre,
from P.-D. Huet, *Traité de la Situation du Paradis Terrestre*.
This work was first published in Paris in 1691. Seventh edition of 1701,
published in Amsterdam.
Reproduced by permission of the British Library (shelfmark g.19518: p.d.Huet).**

correspondence with other contemporary scholars, a man *'préencyclopédique'* in his curiosity and epistemologically a contemporary of the scholars of the Renaissance. He was primarily devoted to the use of his science to prove the superiority of Christianity[122] and worked in the tradition, characteristic of the period from the Renaissance to the early eighteenth century, of the use of the Bible as a source of historical, geographical and scientific information, involving the engagement of theological with scientific discourse, but relying essentially on the biblical text. Huet firmly located the Garden of Eden in the lower reaches of the rivers Tigris and Euphrates : "Je dis donc que le Paradis terrestre estoit situé sur le canal que forment le Tigre et l'Euphrate joints ensemble, entre le lieu de leur jonction, et celuy de la séparation qu'ils font de leurs eaux, avant que de tomber dans le Golfe Persique",[123] and produced an accompanying map (Figure 6). He asserts that one of the key questions is the identity and course of the river Pishon, and gives a detailed appraisal and historiography of earlier works on the matter. He discusses the views of classical scholars such as Strabo and Ptolemy, but moves to more recent exegeses in the works of 'Schikard' [sic] of Tübingen, Kircher the Jesuit, Calvin, and Seeliger, all of whom, not surprisingly, he holds to be mistaken in their identification of its location. He himself locates the river close to *Charila* in Arabia, as a branch of the Euphrates which falls into the Persian Gulf on the side of *Catif* and the Isle of *Baharan* (presumably Bahrein).[124]

His confidence in the matter emerges clearly, here cited from an early eighteenth-century English translation: "it will be sufficient to propose my own [location] and to shew not only that it perfectly agrees with Moses' description and the ancient geography, but also that it is the only one which answers it, and that whosoever will look for another will fall into insuperable difficulties".[125] He calls Bochart's work on the matter seriously into question, stating that Bochart had three times changed his mind on the subject – "Pour le sentiment de Mr. Bochart sur le lieu du Paradis Terrestre, je me souviens bien de luy avoit ouï dire, qu'il avait changé trois fois d'opinion" – and that in fairness he had waited twenty-four years after Bochart's death before making his critique.[126] He asserts that when Bochart originally put forward what he claimed to be a definitive opinion on the location of Paradise, he had barely started his work on the subject, and had cited his treatise on animals, which Huet claims that Bochart only wrote a long time later. This critique marks the sad consequence of the disruption in friendship between the two men, which in earlier years had been so productive, as their correspondence shows. Huet's work, like that of Bochart, was extensively cited by other European scholars, and disputed by others.

Conclusion

This examination of a series of English and French writings on Palestine or the Holy Land from the seventeenth century illustrates both the difficulties of and the possibilities for the understanding of historical geographies of the region in that fascinating period. The complex belief and cultural systems incorporated consciously and sub-consciously in individual accounts link to major theological, political and commercial issues embracing relations between Western Europe and the Eastern Mediterranean. In this case the main forms of evidence for the understanding of these systems are the early and later versions of printed texts of contemporary accounts, including maps and other symbolic illustrations, which have been evaluated in the contexts of near-contemporary and later critical scholarship. While affording important and interesting evidence of past landscapes and cultures, their study inevitably and properly necessitates a drawing into a wide and complex range of ideologies. While most of the ideologies considered here are those from the past, the influence of present concerns on our understanding of this small but powerfully evocative territory is inescapable. Such perspectives are entirely accordant with Alan Baker's consistent advocacy of the incorporation of ideological issues in the production of historical geographies, and it is to Alan that this essay is respectfully and gratefully dedicated.

Acknowledgements

I am deeply grateful to Professor J. M.Wagstaff for his expert comments on an earlier draft of the text, and for his most helpful suggestions, particularly in relation to various complex matters of the history and geography of the Ottoman Empire. I also thank the staff of the Special Collections section of the Brotherton Library, University of Leeds, and of the Rare Books and the Humanities Reading Rooms at the British Library, London, for their help and assistance.

NOTES

1   M. Halbwachs, *La Topographie Légendaire des Évangiles en Terre Sainte; Étude de Mémoire Collective* (Paris 1941).

2   R. Kark (Ed.), *The Land that became Israel. Studies in Historical Geography* (Jerusalem 1989); Y. Ben-Arieh, *The Rediscovery of the Holy Land in the Nineteenth Century* (Jerusalem/Detroit 1979); R. Rubin, Ideology and landscape in early printed maps of Jerusalem, in A. R. H. Baker and G. Biger (Eds), *Ideology and Landscape in Historical Perspective* (Cambridge 1992) 15-30.

3   D. W. Meinig, National historical geographies: necessities, opportunities, cautions, in Y. Ben Artzi, I. Bartel and E. Reiner (Eds), *Studies in Geography and History in Honour of Yehoshuah Ben-Arieh* (Jerusalem 1999) 87.

4   E. Said, Invention, memory, place, *Critical Inquiry* (Winter 2000) 179. I am grateful to Dr David Pierce for drawing my attention to this reference.

5   *Ibid.*, 180.

6   K. W. Whitelam, *The Invention of Ancient Israel: the Silencing of Palestinian History* (New York 1995).

7   M. Benvenisti, *Sacred Landscape. The Buried History of the Holy Land since 1948* (Los Angeles 2000).

8   Halbwachs, *op. cit.*

9   R. A. Butlin, Ideological contexts and the reconstruction of Biblical landscapes in the seventeenth and early eighteenth centuries: Dr Edward Wells and the historical geography of the Holy Land, in Baker and Biger, *op. cit.*, 31-62.

10   F. de Dainville, *La Géographie des Humanistes* (Paris 1940).

11   J. J. Moscrop, *Measuring Jerusalem. The Palestine Exploration Fund and British Interests in the Holy Land* (London 2000) 2-3.

12   Y. Ben-Arieh, *The Rediscovery of the Holy Land in the Nineteenth Century* (Jerusalem/Detroit 1979).

13   N. A. Silberman, Power, politics and the past: the social construction of antiquity in the Holy Land, in T. E. Levy (Ed.), *The Archaeology of Society in the Holy Land*, second edition (London and Washington 1998) 15.

14   J. Goodwin, *Lords of the Horizons. A History of the Ottoman Empire* (London 1998) xiv. A more guarded view of the question of the complexities of Ottoman decline from the sixteenth and seventeenth centuries is to be found in S. J. Shaw, *History of the Ottoman Empire and Modern Turkey*, vol. I (Cambridge 1976).

15   See, for example: S. Faroqhi, *Approaching Ottoman History* (Cambridge 1999); A. Singer, *Palestinian Peasants and Ottoman Officials. Rural Administration Around Sixteenth-Century Jerusalem* (Cambridge 1994).

16   J. Tolan, Introduction, in J. Tolan (Ed.), *Medieval Christian Perceptions of Islam* (New York and London 1996), xii.; N. Daniel, *Islam and the West. The Making of an Image* (Oxford 2000).

17   B. Melman, *Women's Orients. English Women and the Middle East, 1718-1918* (Michigan 1992).

18   R. W. Bevis, *Bibliotheca Cisorientalia: an Annotated Checklist of Early English Travel Books in the Near and Middle East* (Boston, Mass. 1973).

19   Melman, *op. cit.*, 10.

20   See, for example, J. Scott and P. Simpson-Hously (Eds), *Sacred Places and Profane Spaces. Essays in the Geographics of Judaism, Christianity, and Islam* (New York 1991); Daniel, *op. cit.* Bernard Lewis, *Islam and the West* (New York 1993).

21   Sources of biographical information include: R. B. Davies, *George Sandys Poet-Adventurer* (London 1955); B. Penrose, *Urbane Travelers* (Philadelphia 1942) 158-172; J. Hayes, *Humanist as Traveler : George Sandys's Relation of a Journey begun An. Dom.1610* (London and Toronto 1986); *Dictionary of National Biography*, vol. 50 (London 1897) 283-286.

22   Major biographical sources include : *Dictionnaire de Biographie Française*, Tome Sixième (Paris 1951-1954) 743; F. Laplanche, *L'Écriture, le Sacré et l'Histoire, Érudits et Politiques Protestants devant la Bible en France au XVIIIᵉ siècle* (Amsterdam 1986); A. Goldar, *Impolite Learning. Conduct and Community in the Republic of Letters 1680-1750* (New Haven and London 1995).

23   Sources of information on Fuller's life include: W. Addison, *Worthy Dr Fuller* (London 1951); D. B. Lyman, *The Great Tom Fuller* (Berkeley 1935); J. E. Bailey, *The Life of Thomas Fuller, D. D.,*

with Notices of His Books, his Kinsmen and his Friends (London 1874); J. E. Bailey, Palestine geography in the seventeenth century, *Palestine Exploration Fund Quarterly Statement* (1875) 51-7.

24   Major sources of biographical data include: *Nouvelle Biographie Générale* (Paris 1858) 380-390; F. Gégou, *Lettre-traité de Pierre-Daniel Huet sur l'Origine des Romans. Édition du Tricentenaire, 1669-1969,* (Paris 1971) 11-42; P.- J. Salazar, Introduction et notes, P.-D. Huet, *Mémoires (1718)* (Paris 1993); Goldar, *op. cit.*

25   S. Bochart, *Geographia Sacra seu Phalag et Chanaan* (2 parts, Caen 1646, 1651).

26   See *Biographie Universelle. Ancienne et Moderne*, tome 45 (Paris, 1826), 383-5. The major publication by Thévenot is: *Relation d'un Voyage fait au Levant: dans laquelle il est curieusement traité des États, Sujets au Grand Seigneur, des Mœurs, Religions, Forces, Gouvernemens, Politiques, Langues et Coutumes des Habitans de ce Grand Empire* (Paris 1665).

27   W. H. Lewis, *Levantine Adventurer. The Travels and Missions of the Chevalier d'Arvieux, 1653- 1697* (London 1962); *Dictionnaire de Biographie Française, Tome Treizième* (Paris 1939) 1229-1230.

28   Lewis, *op. cit.,* 11-16; *Mémoires du Chevalier d'Arvieux, Envoyé Extraordinaire du Roy à la Porte, Consul d'Alep, d'Alger, de Tripoli, & autres Échelles du Levant.* , Ed. J. B. Labat (Paris 1735) 7 vols.

29   Sources for Maundrell's life and work include: 'W. P. C.', Henry Maundrell, *Dictionary of National Biography* (London 1894) 92-3; Butlin, *op. cit.,* M. A. Hachico, English Travel Books about the Near East in the eighteenth century, *The World of Islam*, new series, **9** (1964) 42-44.

30   Moscrop, *op. cit.,* 8.

31   S. J. Shaw, *History of the Ottoman Empire and Modern Turkey, Volume I: Empire of the Gazis: The Rise and Decline of the Ottoman Empire,1208-1808* (Cambridge 1976) 97.

32   J. M. Wagstaff, *The Evolution of Middle Eastern Landscapes. An Outline to A. D. 1840* (Beckenham 1985) 203.

33   J. M. Wagstaff, The role of the eastern Mediterranean (Levant) for the early modern European world-economy 1500-1800, in H.-J. Nitz (Ed.), *The Early Modern World-System in Geographical Perspective* (Stuttgart 1993) 329-30.

34   *Ibid.,* 330.

35   *Ibid.,* 337-339; and personal communication.

36   I am grateful to Professor J. M. Wagstaff for this point and information, also for the reference : B. Masters, *The Origins of Western Economic Dominance in the Middle East: Mercantilism and the Islamic Economy in Aleppo, 1600-1750* (New York 1988).

37   P. Haudrière and G. Le Bouëdec, *Les Compagnies des Indes* (Rennes 1999) 6-7. The Dutch East Indies Company (V.O.C.) was created in 1602, after initial attempts to send ships to trade directly in the East Indies, and became a major force in Dutch colonial activity and trade.

38   G. A. Russell, Introduction: The seventeenth century: The Age of 'Arabick', in G. A. Russell (Ed.), *The 'Arabick' Interest of the Natural Philosophers in Seventeenth-Century England* (Leiden 1994) 8.

39   Masters, *op. cit.*

40   Russell, *op. cit.,* see also P. M. Holt, The background to Arabic studies in seventeenth-century England, in *ibid.* 20-29.

41   N. Broc, *La Géographie de la Renaissance 1420-1620* (Paris 1986) 140. See also G. Atkinson, *Les Nouveaux Horizons de la Renaissance Française* (Paris 1936).

42   J. Merriman, *A History of Modern Europe from the Renaissance to the Present* (New York 1996) 289-90.

43 Lewis, *op. cit.,* 175-6.

44 W. G. East, *An Historical Geography of Europe* (London 1935) 365-6. East's information is from: P. Masson, *Histoire du Commerce Français dans le Levant au XVIIe siècle* (Paris 1896). See also: G. Rambert (Ed.), *Histoire du Commerce de Marseille, tome v, De 1660 à 1789: Le Levant* (Paris 1957).

45 East, *op. cit.*, 366.

46 A. Cohen, *Palestine in the 18th Century. Patterns of Government and Administration* (Jerusalem 1973) 11.

47 Information from Professor J. M. Wagstaff.

48 Anon, *A view of the Dutch trade in all the states, empires and kingdoms in the world: shewing its first rise and amazing progress after what manner the Dutch manage and carry on their commerce; their vast Dominions and Government in the INDIES, and by what means they have made themselves Masters of all the Trade of Europe. Translated from the French of Monsieur Huet.* (Second Edition, London 1722) i.

49 *Ibid.,* viii.

50 *Ibid.,* 105.

51 Lewis, *op. cit.,* 11-23.

52 D'Arvieux, *Mémoires du Chevalier D'Arvieux, Envoyé Extraordinaire du Roy* etc., Ed. J. B. Labat (Paris 1735) II, 96-98; 217-8.

53 *Ibid.,* 286-7.

54 George Adam Smith, *The Historical Geography of the Holy Land,* (London, 1894; the quotation is from the 16th edition 1910) 149.

55 Masson, *op. cit.,* 391.

56 Lewis, *op. cit.,* 55.

57 Masson, *op. cit.,* 389-90.

58 *Ibid.* 390.

59 Personal communication from Professor J. M. Wagstaff.

60 Lewis, *op. cit.*, 70.

61 D'Arvieux, *op. cit.*, 90-92; Lewis, *op. cit.,* 69.

62 Lewis, *op. cit.,* 71.; de Thévenot, *op. cit.,* 417-22.

63 Davis, *op. cit.,* 75-6.

64 D'Arvieux, *op. cit.,* 243-7; Lewis, *op. cit.,* 54.

65 Sandys, *op. cit.,*153.

66 D'Arvieux, *op. cit.,* 8-9.

67 Haynes, *op. cit.,* 50.

68 *Ibid.,* 105.

69 Sandys, *op. cit.,* 161.

70 *Ibid.,* 167.

71 Lewis, *op. cit.,* 73; D'Arvieux, *op. cit.,* 95; 217-8.

72   De Thévenot, *op. cit.,* 387-8

73   H. Maundrell, *A Journey from Aleppo to Jerusalem at Easter, A.D. 1697* (Oxford 1703; citations are from the 5ᵗʰ edition, Oxford 1732).

74   *Ibid.,* 68.

75   *Ibid.*

76   *Ibid.,* 69.

77   *Ibid.,* 78.

78   *Ibid.,* 82.

79   *Ibid.,* 84.

80   W.-D. Hütteroth and K. Abdulfattah, *Historical Geography of Palestine, Transjordan and Southern Syria in the late 16th Century* (Erlangen 1977).

81   Haynes, *op. cit.,* 108.

82   T. Fuller, *A Pisgah-Sight of Palestine and the Confines thereof with the Historie of the Old and New Testament acted thereon* (London 1650) 3.

83   *Ibid.,* 4. See also Haynes, *op. cit.,* 109-10.

84   Fuller, *op. cit.*, 3.

85   J. Drabble, Thomas Fuller, Peter Heylyn and the English Reformation, *Renaissance and Reformation* new series, 1979, **3**, 175.

86   I am grateful to Professor J. M. Wagstaff for making this point to me in comment on an earlier draft of this chapter.

87   Russell, *op. cit.,* 8.

88   Lewis, *op. cit.,* 85-6.

89   Russell, *op. cit.,* 8.

90   *Ibid.,* 9.

91   J. N. L. Baker, *The History of Geography: Papers by J. N. L. Baker* (Oxford 1963); F. de Dainville, *La Géographie des Humanistes* (Paris 1940); R. Mayhew, The character of English geography c. 1660-1800: a textual approach, *Transactions, Institute of British Geographers* **24** 4 (1998) 385-412; L. Cormack, *Charting an Empire. Geography at the English Universities, 1580-1620* (Chicago 1997).

92   E. Laor, *Maps of the Holy Land. A Cartobibliography of Printed Maps, 1475-1900* (New York 1986).

93   J. Haynes, *Humanist as Traveler* (London and Toronto, 1986) 18.

94   *Ibid.,* 15-16.

95   *Ibid.,* 16.

96   Laor, *op. cit.,* 188;

97   *Ibid.*

98   Goldar, *op. cit.*

99   D. J. Sturdy, *Louis XIV* (London 1998) 101-2.

100   *Ibid.,* 102.

101 *Ibid.*, 17, 33, 205.

102 P.-J. Salazar, Introduction et notes, to edition of P.-D. Huet, *Mémoires* (1718) (Toulouse 1993) 62.

103 Goldar, *op. cit.*, 55.

104 Translation from the French text of F. Laplanche, *L'Écriture, le Sacré et l'Histoire. Érudits et Politiques Protestants devant la Bible en France au XVIIIe siècle* (Amsterdam 1986) 250.

105 Silberman, *op. cit.*, 14.

106 F. J. Bliss, *The Development of Palestine Exploration* (New York 1906) 141-2.

107 *Ibid.*, 144.

108 For an idea of late medieval descriptions see: S. Yerasimos, *Les Voyages dans l'Empire Ottoman (XIVe – XVIe siècle). Bibliographie, Itinéraires et Inventaires des Lieux Habités* (Ankara 1991).

109 Sandys, *op. cit.*, 153.

110 Lewis, *op. cit.*, 75, translating from D'Arvieux, *Mémoires*, II, 201-202.

111 Maundrell, *op. cit.*, 65.

112 *Ibid.*, 83.

113 A. Scafi, Mapping Eden: cartographies of the earthly paradise, in D. Cosgrove (Ed.), *Mappings* (London 1999) 51.

114 *Ibid.*, 51-2.

115 *Ibid.*, 65.

116 J. Bennett and S. Mandelbrote, *The Garden, the Ark, the Tower and the Temple. Biblical Metaphors of Knowledge in Early Modern Europe* (Oxford 1998) 24. See also C. Delano- Smith and E. Morley Ingram, *Maps in Bibles 1500-1600* (Geneva 1991).

117 *Ibid.*, 24 -5.

118 C. W. J. Withers, Geography, Enlightenment and the paradise question, in D. N. Livingstone and C. W. J. Withers (Eds), *Geography and the Enlightenment* (Chicago 1999) 67-92; Butlin, *op. cit.*, 31-62.

119 J. Prest, *The Garden of Eden. The Botanic Garden and the Re-Creation of Paradise* (New Haven 1981).

120 Bennett and Mandelbrote, *op. cit.*, 192.

121 Laor, *op. cit.*, 89.

122 J.-R. Massimi, Montrer et démontrer: autour du *Traité de la Situation du Paradis Terrestre* de P. D. Huet (1691), in A. Desreumaux and F. Schmidt (Eds), *Moïse Géographe* (Paris 1988) 203-226.

123 P.-D. Huet, *Traité de la Situation du Paradis Terrestre* (Amsterdam 1701) 16-17.

124 *Ibid.*, Preface, 8-10.

125 P.-D. Huet, *A Treatise of the Situation of Paradise*. Translated from the French original [by T. Gale] (London 1694) 12.

126 Huet, *Traité de la Situation du Paradis Terrestre* (Amsterdam 1701) 11.

Chapter Six

LES ESPACES DE LA BONNE CHÈRE À PARIS À LA FIN DU XVIIIᵉ SIÈCLE

JEAN-ROBERT PITTE

Dans le Paris de la fin du règne de Louis XVI, les meilleurs cuisiniers, les meilleurs aliments et les meilleurs vins sont monopolisés par la Cour royale de Versailles et par la haute aristocratie. Celle-ci reçoit chez elle, en ses hôtels particuliers de Versailles et de sa région, des faubourgs Saint-Germain et Saint-Honoré, à l'Ouest de Paris, et encore un peu du Marais qui commence déjà à se démoder. Les cuisiniers et maîtres d'hôtel s'arrachent à prix d'or et prêtent leurs talents aux plus offrants. Ils n'hésitent pas à s'exiler, comme le font depuis la Renaissance tous les grands artistes d'Europe. Les fournisseurs, quant à eux, restent concentrés sur la rive droite, dans le quartier des Halles et ses environs. C'est là que tiennent boutique les bons mandataires et traiteurs de la capitale dont les correspondants de province dénichent les meilleures volailles et salaisons, les meilleurs pâtés (de foie gras, par exemple), fromages, vins et spiritueux, les ingrédients les plus rares, fruits exotiques, truffes, épices.[1] On trouve de tout à Paris, y compris du poisson très frais qui arrive de la Manche, de Dieppe en particulier, par les routes de la marée. La prospérité des professions de bouche dans la capitale ne tient pas seulement au poids d'une haute société éduquée dans l'art du raffinement des sens et du paraître. Dans l'ensemble les Parisiens mangent très bien, en quantité et en qualité. L'importance qu'ils accordent à la bonne chère est un trait caractéristique d'une culture catholique et d'une société où, depuis la fin du Moyen Âge, la centralisation croissante de l'État permet au peuple de côtoyer les puissants, de les voir vivre, c'est-à-dire parler, s'habiller, manger, et donc d'être influencé par leurs habitudes.[2]

C'est ce contexte qui explique l'apparition, dans la deuxième moitié du XVIIIe siècle, d'une institution majeure de la culture et de l'économie françaises, aujourd'hui répandue dans le monde entier sous des formes variées: le restaurant.

Les ancêtres du restaurant, ici et ailleurs

La définition la plus simple du restaurant est la suivante : c'est un lieu payant où l'on mange en dehors de chez soi. Or, de tels lieux existent depuis la plus haute Antiquité, probablement même depuis le Néolithique. À partir du moment où il y a eu agriculture et excédents agricoles, il y eût marché, déplacements de producteurs et de clients vers le marché et donc nécessité pour eux de se nourrir en dehors de chez eux, voire de bien se nourrir pour célébrer le succès d'une transaction et entretenir l'amitié. Il y avait donc probablement des lieux payants pour se nourrir en dehors de chez soi en Mésopotamie et en Egypte, longtemps avant notre ère. De tels établissements, d'un style très rustique, existent dans tous les pays pauvres de la planète : en Afrique, en Amérique Latine, en Asie du Sud et du Sud-Est, tant à la campagne qu'en ville. Ils sont ouverts à tous, même aux plus modestes des habitants et contribuent à la sociabilité des villages et des quartiers urbains. C'est, par exemple, le cas des *maquis*, ces petites gargotes des rues d'Abidjan.[3] En Chine, les cinquante années de maoïsme et la Révolution culturelle ne sont pas parvenues à tuer la cuisine de rue.[4] Bien au contraire, dans tous les bourgs et les quartiers des grandes villes, on rencontre quantité de petites roulottes et de boutiques minuscules dans lesquelles on prépare en général un seul plat. Ainsi pour obtenir un repas complet, il faut aller chercher un bol de soupe dans une boutique, des raviolis à côté, de la friture dans une autre encore. Toute l'Asie sinisée est marquée par ce phénomène : Vietnam, Corée et même Japon. À Taiwan ou à Singapour, les marchés de nuit sont de hauts lieux de l'animation et de la sociabilité urbaines. Des dizaines de micro-restaurants encerclent un ensemble de tables ; les clients achètent des plats à plusieurs d'entre eux pour constituer leur repas. C'est également le principe d'organisation des espaces de restauration des grands magasins coréens, à la différence des grands magasins japonais où les restaurants du dernier étage sont séparés les uns des autres et où le client ne peut composer son menu qu'à partir des plats servis dans chaque établissement. Dans les quartiers d'affaires des grandes métropoles japonaises, les salariés et même les cadres supérieurs apprécient de se rendre dans des roulottes où l'on prépare du *ramen* (soupe de nouilles), de l'*oden* (aliments variés bouillis au soja) ou des *gyoza* (raviolis sautés). Sur le front de mer et dans le port de Pusan, en Corée, des centaines de tentes et de baraques sont occupées par des restaurants tenus par des femmes qui servent du poisson cru. En Europe, les formes de restauration dans la rue ont un peu disparu, sauf pendant les fêtes : celle de la bière en Allemagne, le *Palio* de Sienne ou la *Feria* de Nîmes, par exemple.

Les établissements installés à demeure, dans des maisons construites en dur, existent dans les villes antiques du Bassin méditerranéen et dans toute l'Europe médiévale et moderne. Il s'agit de tavernes où l'on boit en abondance des boissons alcoolisées et où l'on consomme des nourritures simples. Les mentions de leur existence et les descriptions de leur atmosphère abondent dans les textes. L'iconographie dont on dispose à leur égard est immense et réjouissante. Le vin ou la bière y coulent à flots et l'on mange, sur de petites tables serrées ou sur de longues tables d'hôtes, dans une atmosphère propice à une sociabilité bruyante, joyeuse, parfois querelleuse, majoritairement masculine, mais agrémentée de la présence de quelques serveuses n'hésitant pas à dépenser, à l'occasion, des trésors d'affection pour leurs clients. L'équivalent existe en Afrique, dans les villages et les bourgs traversés par les routes et les pistes importantes. Les camionneurs qui s'y arrêtent ont été ces dernières années les principaux vecteurs de la propagation du SIDA.

Dans l'Europe d'aujourd'hui, subsistent des établissements populaires dans lesquels se maintient bien vivante cette tradition, modernisée et plus hygiénique que naguère. L'Italie fait peut-être exception, tant ce pays a été influencé par le 'restaurant' à la française, jusqu'en ses lieux populaires où, par exemple, on utilise toujours nappes et serviettes en tissu. Plus proches des modèles anciens sont les tavernes grecques, lieux chaleureux où l'on boit du vin résiné, accompagné de petits plats riches en huile (dans la tradition des *mezze* orientaux) que l'on sauce avec du pain, servi en abondance.[5] Ce sont des institutions fondamentales de la société grecque, des catalyseurs de l'art de la dialectique et de la passion politique que ce peuple cultive. En Espagne, la *bodega* est un peu similaire, avec ses *tapas* que l'on sert sur des tonneaux placés debout et que l'on mange avec ses doigts ou des petits bâtons en bois, en buvant du vin. En Angleterre, le genre est un peu différent. Le *pub* est toujours clos : pas de terrasse ou de débordement sur la voie publique dans une société marquée par le puritanisme. On y boit avant tout de la bière que l'on accompagne aux heures des repas de plats typiques, comme les *pies*, lesquels témoignent, par leur mode de présentation et de cuisson et par leur saveur sucrée-épicée, de la survivance de traditions culinaires médiévales en Europe du Nord et de l'influence indienne liée à l'histoire de l'Empire (curry, par exemple). En

Allemagne, la bière coule à flots dans les brasseries. Elle est accompagnée de pain bis, de charcuteries salées et fumées, de choucroute, de radis. On y parle fort, on y chante volontiers sur les airs que jouent les orchestres populaires dans lesquels les cuivres ont la part belle. Cette pratique triomphe en Bavière, durant les fêtes patronales de l'été et les fêtes de la bière en octobre, dans la vallée du Rhin, en hiver, pendant le carnaval. En Autriche, en particulier à l'automne, on va goûter le *heuriger* (vin nouveau) dans les tavernes (à Grinzing, par exemple, dans la banlieue de Vienne) en consommant des plats populaires. C'est une pratique qui existait dans les guinguettes parisiennes des bords de Seine ou de Marne (à Joinville-le-Pont, par exemple) ou dans les auberges de pêcheurs et de canotiers lyonnais, sur les rives de la Saône et de ses affluents. On y mangeait de la friture de gardon et d'ablettes, arrosée de petit vin blanc acidulé. Ces temples de la sociabilité bon enfant ont disparu et n'ont pas été remplacés. Certains sont devenus des restaurants de luxe. Dans le Nouveau Monde, le *saloon*, version libre du *pub*, a joué ce rôle au moment de la conquête de l'Ouest, mais le *fast food* qui l'a remplacé aujourd'hui n'en est qu'un très pâle avatar.

En France, l'histoire de l'alimentation en dehors de chez soi est beaucoup plus complexe. La grande cuisine, appelée à partir du début du XIXe siècle cuisine gastronomique, est liée à l'histoire culturelle et politique du pays. Avant la Révolution française, les gens de condition ne fréquentaient pas les salles communes des tavernes et des auberges, sauf à l'occasion de frasques de jeunesse. Lorsqu'ils voyageaient et qu'ils logeaient en ville, ils se faisaient livrer dans leur chambre des plats préparés dans les cuisines de l'hôtellerie ou de l'auberge, ou bien ils commandaient un repas de qualité à un traiteur ou à un pâtissier (préparant des plats en pâte, telles des tourtes, équivalent des *pies*). Au XVIIe siècle, se sont ouverts à Paris quelques cafés, une institution élégante, inspirée de l'Italie. Le premier, le *Procope*, fut ouvert à Paris en 1674. On y buvait des boissons exotiques et excitantes pour l'esprit : du café, du thé, du chocolat. On y servait aussi des glaces et des sorbets, mais on n'y mangeait pas à cette époque. Cela viendra seulement à le fin du XVIIIe siècle.

La cuisine raffinée, en revanche, on l'a dit, s'élabore au domicile des puissants. Les grands cuisiniers créatifs leur sont attachés et nomadisent à travers l'Europe, de cour princière en grande maison, à partir du XVIe siècle. Dès la fin du XVIIe siècle, la profession est dominée en Europe par les Français qui ont hérité de la grande cuisine de cour dont les recettes ont été élaborées à Versailles dans la première moitié du règne de Louis XIV.[6] Signalons que pendant longtemps, dans les châteaux, les palais, les hôtels particuliers, il n'existe pas de pièce spécifiquement réservée aux repas. La salle à manger apparaît timidement sous la Régence et sous Louis XV, avec la mode des petits soupers. C'est le XIXe siècle qui lui donnera toute sa place dans l'espace domestique en la distinguant du salon et de la chambre à coucher. Cette imprécision dans l'organisation de l'espace intérieur des grandes maisons survit dans un Palais comme l'Élysée à Paris. Les repas ne sont pas systématiquement servis dans la même pièce et chaque Président de la République tient à se démarquer de son prédécesseur en faisant tourner les fonctions des 'salons'. La 'salle des fêtes' sert aux dîners d'État, mais à bien d'autres cérémonies aussi.

La naissance du restaurant

Dans la forme que nous lui connaissons aujourd'hui, le restaurant apparaît à Paris sous le règne de Louis XVI. Il est issu de la *tavern* londonienne et du *club*, lieux d'un grand raffinement où se nourrit l'aristocratie anglaise lorsqu'elle séjourne à Londres. En effet, les membres de la Chambre des *lords* résidaient principalement à la campagne, sur leurs terres. Ils ne venaient à Londres que pour siéger. Ils logeaient alors dans des demeures relativement modestes, situation radicalement à l'opposé de la France où toute une partie de l'aristocratie, attirée par le roi et la Cour, après la Fronde, a délaissé la province et est venue construire de prestigieux châteaux et hôtels particuliers en Île-de-France. Dépourvus de train de maison à Londres, les *lords* anglais fréquentent donc des établissements payants où ils invitent leurs amis et retrouvent un petit air du luxe qui règne dans leurs demeures campagnardes : mobilier, vaisselle, argenterie, cristaux, linge de service, élégance du personnel y sont de grande classe. À défaut de trancher le débat quant à la qualité des mets,[7] il est certain que l'on boit du très bon vin dans ces établissements : du *french claret*, du porto, du sherry, du madère, par exemple. C'est ainsi que dès 1670 Jean de Pontac, fils du Président à mortier du Parlement de Bordeaux, tient une *tavern* à Londres, dans laquelle il sert le château Haut-Brion paternel.

Le modèle de la *tavern* passe la Manche à la faveur de l'anglomanie de la deuxième moitié du XVIIIe siècle. C'est l'origine du restaurant. Le premier établissement qui porte ce nom est ouvert vers 1765, près du Louvre à Paris, par un certain Boulanger qui a inscrit sur son enseigne : '*Venite ad me omnes qui stomacho laboratis et ego vos restaurabo*', soit : 'Venez à moi, vous tous qui avez faim et je vous restaurerai'. Il sert des 'bouillons restaurants', c'est-à-dire des consommés de viande fortifiants – dont le nom sert très vite à désigner ce type d'établissement – de la volaille, des pieds de mouton, des œufs, tous plats qu'il n'a pas le droit de vendre, dans la mesure où ils relèvent du monopole de la corporation des traiteurs. Boulanger est attaqué en justice, mais gagne son procès. C'en est fait des traiteurs. Les restaurants vont se multiplier au centre de Paris, dans le quartier du commerce, près des Halles et du Palais-Royal.

La Révolution accélère le phénomène. Les députés de la Constituante, en effet, disposent d'émoluments, mais pas de maison à Paris, pour la plupart d'entre eux. Par ailleurs, avec l'émigration des aristocrates, nombre de chefs de cuisine se retrouvent au chômage et ouvrent des maisons dans lesquelles ils servent les plats de cuisine savante qu'ils confectionnaient naguère pour leur maître. Certains établissements comme *Beauvilliers, Véry, Méot, Le Café de Chartres, Les Trois Frères Provençaux,* sont très connus en France et à l'étranger. Leur réputation est telle que les officiers des armées d'occupation qui déferlent sur Paris en 1815 se précipitent au Palais-Royal dont on sait, par ailleurs, que l'on y rencontre aussi les femmes les plus belles et les plus accueillantes de Paris. C'est chez *Les Trois Frères Provençaux* que l'on sert pour la première fois des plats méditerranéens, exotiques en diable à Paris : de la salade à l'huile d'olive, de la brandade de morue, de la bouillabaisse, des côtelettes à la provençale.

Les frères *Véry* sont des paysans lorrains qui ont visiblement réussi dans leur activité agricole. Ils achètent trois arcades du Palais-Royal en 1790, au centre de l'actuelle Galerie de Beaujolais, à côté du *Café de Chartres*, devenu depuis *Le Grand Véfour*, pour la somme de 196,275 livres.[8] Plus tard, ils migreront vers la terrasse des Tuileries. C'est là que mourra le vieux peintre Fragonard en 1806. Enfin, ils reviendront au Palais-Royal où l'établissement subsistera, traversant des fortunes variées, jusqu'au Second Empire.

La carte de Véry en 1790 : une interprétation historique et géographique

La Bibiothèque Historique de la Ville de Paris a acquis, voici quelques années, un magnifique exemplaire – le seul connu – de la carte de *Véry Frères, Restaurateurs, Maison Égalité, n° 83.* Ce document exceptionnel[9] date de 1790 (voir Figure 1). Compte tenu de certains plats qui y sont présentés (potage printanier, poulets nouveaux aux petits pois, haricots verts nouveaux, omelette aux fraises, abricots, framboises, compote de cerises), on peut admettre qu'il s'agit d'une carte de la fin du printemps, au mois de juin probablement. Elle est imprimée, ce qui laisse à penser que les propriétaires en faisaient imprimer plusieurs par an, peut-être une fois par saison, comme dans beaucoup de restaurants gastronomiques d'aujourd'hui. En revanche, un blanc est prévu dans la rubrique 'Entrées de poissons' – sous laquelle on trouve d'abord des poissons, puis ensuite des viandes en sauce et des légumes – pour que les plats du jour soient inscrits à la main. Trois plats sont indiqués sur l'exemplaire conservé : 'Limande frite ou sur le plat, Carlais[10] frit ou sur le plat, pigeon à la crapaudine'. Les prix mentionnés indiquent clairement qu'il s'agit d'un établissement

FIGURE I
La Carte du Restaurant Véry (1790).

VERY, Frères, RESTAURATEURS, Maison Egalité, N°. 83.

PRIX FIXE DES METS POUR UNE PERSONNE.

POTAGES.

Potage au vermichel.	4 10
Potage printanier.	4 10
Potage au riz à la purée.	4 10
Potage à la julienne ou aux choux	4 10
Trois pâtes au jus	7
Bouilli à la sauce ou sans sauce.	8
Rognon de mouton à la brochette au vin de Champagne.	9
Bouilli garni de légumes.	9
Artichaux à la poivrade.	7
Anchoix en salade.	5

PRIX DES VINS.

Vins Rouges et Blancs.

Vin de Bourgogne rouge et ordinaire.	9
Vin de Chably.	10
Vin de Beaune.	10
Vin de Volnay ou de Vosnes.	20
Vin de Paumard ou de Nuits.	20
Vin du clos Vougeot.	30
Vin du clos St George.	20
Vin de Champagne Roset.	20

	l. s
Vin de Mulseaux.	12
Vin de Champagne mousseux.	30
Vin de Bordeaux.	30
Vin de Grave et de Sauterne.	25
Vin de Barsac	25
Vin très-fin de Morachée.	25

LIQUEURS.

Marasquin le verre.	6
Vin de Malvoisie et Madere.	3
Vin de Malaga	3
Eau-de-vie vieille.	3 10
Anisette de Bordeaux de la veuve Brizard	3
Kersewaser.	3
Rhum.	2 10
Vin d'Alicante	3
Vin de Constance, demi-bouteille.	40
le verre.	4
Vin de Scervalle, *le verre.*	4
Vin de Calabre, le verre.	4

ENTRÉES DE POISSONS.

Matelotte d'anguilles et de carpes, garnie.	12
Tronçon d'anguille à la tartare.	12
Raie, sauce aux câpres ou au beurre noir.	12
Morue à la maître-d'hôtel.	12
Carpe frite 24 liv. la moitié	18
Maquereau frais à la maître d'hôtel.	18

ROTS ET SALADES.

Dindoneau rôti 8 liv le quart.	12 10
Pigeon de volière	18
Poularde fine 20 liv. (le quart).	22 10
Poulet normal 30 liv. (la moitié).	15
Salade de volaille aux anchois et cornichons.	18
Filet de bœuf piqué, rôti, sauce aux cornichons	12
Veau rôti chaud ou en gelée.	10
Salade nouvelle à l'huile de Provence.	8
Caille grasse rôtie.	10
Salade de laitue aux anchois ou aux œufs durs.	12

Canard aux choux ou aux navets 40 liv. le quart.	10
Deux côtelettes de mouton	7
Chapon au gros sel 90 liv. le quart.	22 10
Fricandeau à l'oseille ou à la chicorée.	10
Suprême de poulets nouveaux aux concombres ou aux petits pois.	15
Côtelette de veau piquée à l'oseille ou à la chicorée	10
Biftek aux choux ou aux pois.	10
Entre-côte de bœuf, sauce aux cornichons.	10
Blanquette de veau aux champignons.	10
Gigot braisé aux pois ou aux choux ou aux navets.	15
Tête de veau au naturel, 10 liv. ou en tortue.	15
Tourte à la financière.	15
Ris de veau glacé à l'oseille à la ravigotte ou à la chicorée.	12
Poitrine de mouton à la Sainte-Menehoult aux choux ou aux navets	15
Marinade de poulets nouveaux	15
Ragoût mêlé à la financière.	10
Poulet en fricassée garni de champignons, 30 liv. (la moitié).	15
Friteau de poulet, (la moitié)	15
Langue de veau en papillote ou sauce piquante.	10
Côtelette de veau en papillote ou aux fines herbes	10
Oreille de veau frite ou aux pois.	10
Cervelle de veau frite ou au beurre noir.	10
Palais de bœuf à la poulette ou à l'Italienne.	10
Poitrine de mouton aux choux aux pois, ou aux navets.	10
Tendron de veau à la jardinière ou à la poulette, ou aux pois.	15
Filet de bœuf piqué, sauce aux cornichons	12
Pied de veau au naturel, frit ou à la poulette	15
Poulet nouveau à l'estragon ou aux pois (la moitié).	15
Choux nouveaux au petit salé	18
Pigeon en compote aux petits pois	10
Caille en caisse.	10
Carbonade de mouton aux navets ou aux choux.	10
Foie de veau sauté à la ravigotte.	10
Côtelette de veau aux fines herbes.	10

ENTREMETS.

Regnet de pêches ou d'abricots	12
Artichaux à la sauce blanche ou au jus.	8
Fèves de marais.	10
Petits pois au beurre	10
Macédoine à la poulette ou sauté au beurre.	9
Epinards au jus ou à la crème.	8
Omelette aux fines herbes	8
Œufs au beurre noir.	8
Œufs brouillés au verjus,	8
Haricots verts nouveaux sautés au beurre ou à la poulette.	9
	12
Omelette soufflée.	15
Œufs à l'oseille	8
	8
Choux-fleurs nouveaux, sauce au beurre ou au jus	9
Concombre à la poulette ou au jus.	8
Chicorée au jus.	8
Navets au jus.	8
Artichaux à la barigoulle ou frits	10
Omelette aux fraises. ou seulement au sucre.	10

DESSERTS.

Abricot la pièce	2 10
Compote d'abricots	9
Compote de Cerises.	9
Fraises et sucre	10
Biscuit de Rouget.	3
Fromage de Neufchâtel.	2
Fromage de Gruyère.	2
Cerises de toutes espèces.	6
Fromage de Chestere	3
Fromage de Glosesterre	3
Franboises.	10

Café.	
Glace.	
Sorbec	5 10
Le bol de punch à l'eau-de-vie	25
Le bol au rhum.	30

Source: Bibliothèque Historique de la Ville de Paris.

de luxe. Les entrées les moins chères sont facturées 10 livres (à l'exception des 'côtelettes de mouton' qui valent 7 livres), le quart de 'Poularde fine' vaut 22 livres 10 sols. Rappelons qu'un loyer annuel moyen à Rouen à cette époque, ville réputée chère, est de 400 livres par an et qu'un ouvrier parisien gagne à cette époque entre une livre et une livre 20 sols par jour.[11] On a beau être situé dans la Maison Égalité...

Les rubriques des mets de la carte sont conformes aux habitudes gastronomiques du temps et comportent plusieurs chapitres : 'Potages, Entrées de poissons, rôts et salades, entremets, desserts'. Il est probable qu'une mention 'entrées de viande' ou 'autres entrées' a été oubliée par le rédacteur ou par l'imprimeur, puisqu'on passe sans transition du carrelet, dernier poisson de la liste, au pigeon, première viande. Selon les pratiques de l'époque, on trouve dans la rubrique 'Potages' des préparations liquides ou semi-liquides ('Potage au vermichel', 'potage au riz et à la purée', le pot-au-feu, intitulé 'Bouilli garni de légumes', probablement accompagné de son bouillon, mais aussi des plats qui auraient pu trouver place dans les chapitres 'Entrées' ou 'Entremets' : 'Rognon de mouton à la brochette ou au vin de champagne', 'Artichaux à la poivrade'. Le salé est mêlé au sucré dans les entremets ('begnets de pêches ou d'abricots', 'épinards au jus ou à la crème', 'artichauts à la sauce blanche ou au jus'). Les fromages sont mêlés aux préparations à base de fruits, aux pâtisseries sucrées et aux boissons exotiques dans les desserts (' fraises et sucre', 'Biscuit de Rouget', 'Fromage de Chestere', 'Sorbec', 'Café', 'Le bol de punch à l'eau de vie').

L'ensemble des plats semble haut en saveur et même assez relevé : les cornichons, les anchois, la sauce ravigotte ou la sauce piquante, la garniture à l'oseille et même le verjus qui accompagne une préparation d'œufs excitent le palais et représentent des vestiges des dilections gustatives du Moyen Âge français, analogues à celles qui sont restées vivantes dans l'Europe du Nord d'aujourd'hui. C'est la preuve que la révolution culinaire commencée au XVIIe siècle à Versailles n'est pas achevée à la fin du XVIIIe siècle. Elle survit même encore dans les plats des bistrots parisiens ou des bouchons lyonnais. Certaines maisons françaises, de tradition bourgeoise sans ostentation, ont encore aujourd'hui des cartes assez comparables à celle de *Véry*, le nombre des plats étant seulement réduit.

On remarque donc un mélange de recettes typiques de la cuisine populaire parisienne et de plats directement hérités de la cuisine de cour, peut-être déjà passée dans la deuxième moitié du XVIIIe siècle dans la cuisine des traiteurs, des pâtissiers et des premiers restaurateurs. Dans la première rubrique, citons le bouilli, les abats, tels l''Oreille de veau fritte ou aux pois', la 'Cervelle de veau fritte ou au beurre noir', le 'Foie de veau sauté à la ravigotte', la 'Raie, sauce aux câpres ou au beurre noir', les 'Choux nouveaux au petit salé'. Dans la deuxième catégorie, entrent les

'Trois pâtés au jus', le 'Chapon au gros sel' à 22 livres et 10 sols le quart, la 'Caille en caisse',[12] la 'Tourte à la financière', le 'Pigeon en compote ou aux petits pois', les 'Épinards au jus ou à la crème', l''omelette soufflée', le 'Sorbec'.[13] Il faut ajouter une troisième rubrique, celle des plats exotiques, ordinaires en leur contrée d'origine, précieux à Paris, parce que nouveaux et rares : les 'Anchoix en salade', la 'Salade nouvelle à l'huile de Provence', les fromages anglais 'de Chestere' ou 'de Glosesterre', suisses 'de Gruyère'.

La provenance des matières premières est révélatrice du caractère national et international de l'approvisionnement gastronomique de Paris, à la fin du XVIIIe siècle, phénomène qui ne fera que se renforcer au cours des deux siècles suivants. C'est tout particulièrement vrai en ce qui concerne les vins offerts au choix des clients. La liste est brève et éclectique. En ce qui concerne les vins français, elle révèle la domination écrasante du Bourgogne qui arrive par voie d'eau à cette époque à Paris. Sur 17 vins non liquoreux proposés, 11 sont des bourgognes,[14] 4 sont des bordeaux et 2 des champagnes. C'est beaucoup plus tard dans le XIXe siècle que ce monopole, dicté par le réseau navigable et le réseau commercial des marchands de vin, sera sérieusement entamé. En revanche, les 'Liqueurs', rubrique qui recouvre des vins naturellement moelleux, des vins mutés (ou renforcés en alcool) et des boissons distillées viennent de fort loin et sont vendues – chèrement – au verre : le 'Madère', le 'Malaga', l''Alicante', le 'Vin de Scetuvalle',[15] le 'Vin de Calabre', le 'Kersewaser',[16] le 'Rhum'. Le 'Vin de Constance', est vendu 40 livres la demi-bouteille, prix astronomique justifié par sa provenance sud-africaine.[17]

Conclusion

La carte du restaurant *Véry* représente bien la cuisine 'bourgeoise' parisienne, telle qu'elle survivra sans changement majeur de la Révolution à la fin du XXe siècle. Elle marie la tradition populaire gourmande d'une grande métropole où l'on a toujours aimé faire bonne chère et celle de la Cour royale. Par sa diversité et son mélange de simplicité et de haute technique, elle témoigne d'un aspect toujours vivant de la culture française, la gastronomie, laquelle doit beaucoup à Paris, incomparable vitrine internationale. Il serait passionnant de connaître la clientèle de *Véry*, à son origine, en 1790, sous la Terreur, sous l'Empire et dans le courant du XIXe siècle. Il est probable que l'on y trouverait l'essentiel de l'élite française et européenne. C'est toujours elle qui fréquente les restaurants triplement étoilés du *Guide Michelin*. Cependant, telle que composée en 1790, la carte de *Véry* mériterait aujourd'hui une étoile, au mieux, quelle que soit la perfection des préparations et 11 ou 12 sur 20 au *Guide Gault-Millau*. Autres temps, autres goûts, malgré tout, surtout en ce qui concerne les grands cuisiniers, toujours fébrilement en quête de nouveauté et voués à la disparition le jour où ils n'étonnent plus.

NOTES

1   J.-R. Pitte, L'approvisionnement gastronomique de Paris au début du XIXe siècle., *L'Art Culinaire au XIXe siècle. Antonin Carême.* Délégation à l'Action Artistique de la Ville de Paris (Paris 1984) 47-53.

2   J.-R. Pitte, *Gastronomie Française. Histoire et Géographie d'une Passion* (Paris 1991).

3   F. Leimdorfer dans A. Huetz de Lemps et J.-R. Pitte, (Éd.): *Les Restaurants dans le Monde et à Travers les Âges* (Grenoble 1990).

4   Lu Wenfu, *Vie et Passion d'un Gastronome Chinois* (Arles 1988).

5   M. Sivignon, dans Huetz de Lemps et Pitte, *op. cit.*

6   J.-L. Flandrin, P. et M. Hyman (Éd.): *Le Cuisinier François* (Paris 1983) ; B. Ketcham Wheaton, *L'Office et la Bouche. Histoire des Mœurs de la Table en France. 1300-1789* (Paris 1984).

7   S. Mennell, *Français et Anglais à Table du Moyen Âge à nos Jours* (Paris 1987).

8   R. Héron de Villefosse, *Histoire et Géographie Gourmandes de Paris* (Paris 1956).

9   Je remercie Luc Passion, Conservateur en Chef à la BHVP, d'avoir attiré mon attention sur ce document. Je remercie également la BHVP d'avoir mis une photographie de la carte à ma disposition en vue du présent article.

10   *Sic.* Il s'agit du carrelet. La carte est truffée de fautes d'orthographe, ce qui témoigne de l'extraction sociale des propriétaires et de leurs employés ou des négligences de l'imprimeur en cette période troublée.

11   Je dois ces informations à Jean-Pierre Bardet.

12   Chantée par Karen Blixen sous l'appellation « cailles en sarcophage » dans *Le festin de Babette.* Paris, Gallimard, 1961.

13   Sorbet.

14   « Mulseaux » est, en effet, probablement une déformation de Meursault et « Morachée » de Montrachet.

15   Peut-être un Porto.

16   Mauvaise graphie de *kirschwasser.*

17   Paul Claval a attiré mon attention sur cette interprétation. En effet, il est possible de trouver du vin aux environs de la ville de Constance, en Allemagne, mais celui-ci n'a jamais acquis une réputation internationale, à la différence de celui qui est toujours produit en Afrique du Sud.

Chapter Seven

THE NATURAL HISTORY OF THE OPERA HOUSE

Theatre, Audience and Socialization in
Nineteenth-Century Italy (with Parisian Asides)[1]

MARK BILLINGE

Overture (or settling the audience)

In 1891, Verdi wrote to his longtime friend and publisher Giulio Riccordi reflecting on
the latest alterations to the auditorium of the Teatro alla Scala in Milan: particular
amongst them the conversion of the fifth row of private boxes to make room for a larger
'public' gallery. He thoroughly approved:

> an excellent decision. The theatre is freed from a section of the audience that, by
> long tradition, was distracted, bored and turbulent; and in its place, it puts a
> great gallery of bourgeois spectators who will pay little individually and, when
> the opportunity arises, will enjoy themselves greatly. The public of the gallery is
> the best audience at La Scala.[2]

Verdi's enthusiasm – as ever a mix of artistic aspiration and shrewd business acumen
– was not universally shared; for the change – which had crept slowly and unevenly
through the theatres of Italy from the 1810s onwards – made explicit a *de facto*
reworking of certain fundamental assumptions about the lyric theatre, its clientele

and its place in public life; indeed about the nature of the opera (more strictly the *lirica*) itself. In the Scala rearrangements Verdi recognized something for which he had striven for much of his creative life: an emancipation of stage over auditorium, of audience over opera-goer, of performance over pretext. It was certainly a significant sea change, yet no artistic happenstance: the ecology of Italian society was evolving and, once again, the theatre – large or small, grand or provincial – was documenting its natural history. As John Rosselli would have it, in the ottocento "opera was an industry" and yet the theatre was more than its factory: it was "a microcosm of Italian life".[3]

The essay which follows seeks to explore only one aspect of the many-faceted relationship which bound stage to theatre, theatre to community and opera to civil rhetoric in an era when the public at large (particularly in Italy) attached to the local stage an importance which the late twentieth century would reserve only for the televisual media. It is part of a more general project which attempts to unravel the impact of the opera – as a cultural institution enjoying mass popular support – on local, regional and national identities. Its fundamental contention – that the lyric stage both mirrored and gave impetus to social development throughout the *ottocento* – has been set out in more generic form elsewhere but, in order to make intelligible what follows, it is necessary to offer the briefest sketch here.[4]

Intermezzo (or a moment to explain)

It is now widely recognized that one of the less ambiguous tasks for human geography is to examine the relationship between culture (in the sense of a shared body of recognitions and practices) and the people whose lives work through and, in turn, reproduce, its everyday constructions.[5] Culture – Raymond Williams famously reminded us – is not hieratic but 'ordinary': it is part of an ongoing *process* which sharpens and shapes our susceptibilities whilst responding plastically to shifting economic, social and political circumstance.[6]

This reflexive arrangement is, of course, no more or less true of conventionalized cultural genres, nor of the nineteenth century. It is not absurd, therefore to claim that the *lirica* in *ottocento* Italy should be seen as, at heart, a coherently social *and* political construction: social in that the opera was a form of collective activity which impacted upon the community at a variety of scales and helped, through participation, to give it shape and coherence; political in that it was responsible for the polemicising of opinion and, in addition, instrumental in the development and institutionalization of power relations at a variety of scales. Such effects could be felt *internally* through the recognition (or rather re-cognition) of status and social placement within a particular community (made explicit in the theatre itself), as well as *externally* through the rationalization of notions of 'otherness' to which challenges could be mounted or accommodations made. This was particularly true where the stamp of external authority was at its most insistent, for as well as promoting solidarity amongst the native citizenry (albeit with marked differentiation within) the opera could be deeply subversive. Indeed, it was at its most popular and most vital precisely where external domination and nationalist sentiment were the *leitmotivs* of civil life.[7]

If we can accept then (at least as a proposition) that the opera – and particularly the nightly experience of it in the theatre – was about the way in which citizens related to the communities in which they lived, and, later, discovered and negotiated the political world which more generally shaped their lives, then we must also accept that neither opera nor the theatres in which it was performed were the purely consumptive prescriptions, or elitist habits they have frequently been held to be.

Chorus (or a few opening salvos)

The more particular concerns of what follows is how, once established, such general recognitions can be deployed to make sense of the ways in which, in almost any Italian (in stark contrast to, say, any French) community the opera house became integral to and symbolic of the rhythms and concerns of ordinary life. To put it crudely, how and why did this exceptional affinity between a public and its chosen means of expression substantiate itself in practice: here, in the physical form of the theatre and the interior social world which it housed? There can be little doubt – given the almost ubiquitous presence of theatres in even the smallest and most provincial of towns – that something more than fashion, civic pride or the prospect of an evening 'out' propelled the process of their building.[8] Equally, something more than a stirring of entrepreneurship lured composers, patrons, and impresarios into an industry the precarious finances of which often proved little incentive in themselves.[9]

It is possible to consider the close (even symbiotic) relationship between a local population and its theatre in at least three ways[10]:

Firstly, at a level which might be described as 'atavistic', which is to say the most obvious and time-honoured relationship of the theatre to the community at large. Such a construction would note the strategic place of the opera house in the townscape as a noble or municipal expression of the town's stature as well as a political statement of its pretensions to local or wider control.[11] The opera house of a commune was frequently placed tactically – somewhere between (sometimes in) the *municipio* and the *chiesa*. In larger cities, it might express a direct connection to its most important patron, being attached physically to a Royal or Ducal Palace or placed in such a way as to leave no doubt as to whose private fiefdom it was. Lady Morgan, travelling in the 1820s more or less captured the flavour: "After the *Duomo* there is no shrine in Milan more attended, no edifice more prized as the Theatre of the Scala" she noted.[12] Stendhal, speaking of the gala re-opening of the San Carlo in Naples (which, incidentally, he did not attend) put it more politically, though no less aptly:

> *Standing once more in the theatre, I found again that sense of awe and ecstasy. If you search to the farthest frontiers of Europe, you will find nothing to rival it – what am I saying? Nothing to give so much as the vaguest notion of its significance. This mighty edifice, rebuilt in the space of three hundred days, is nothing less than a* coup d'état: *it binds the people in fealty and homage to their sovereign far more effectively than any Constitution. From prince to waiter, all Naples is drunk with joy.*[13]

Composers were neither indifferent to, nor – if they were astute – unexploitative of, the trickle-down effects association with a good house might bring. The composer Bellini – a Sicilian widely experienced in the politics of the mainland – noted that the theatre was not only the centre of social life but, before the 1848 revolution, was "the one field open to the manifestation of a public life – a substitute for a parliament or a free press".[14]

As Bellini recognized, matters of competition and civic pride certainly entered into the equation as far as the building of a theatre was concerned, but a fuller understanding of its continuing attraction in a civic context needs to take into account, for example, the stark lack of alternative venues for public association and the disputation of matters of day-to-day import. Theatres were often seen – not least by the judiciary and the policing authorities – as potential powder kegs; and in the Risorgimento years, particular operas would prove time and again their ability to provide the dreaded spark of ignition. Characteristically then, the theatre was subject to considerable scrutiny: both indirectly from public officials (for example, the censor and the local magistrate, as far as its general regulation was concerned), and directly from a militia interested equally with the maintenance of public order and the intelligence gathering opportunities which presence in the theatre afforded.[15]

At a second – 'architectural' – level, we are more concerned with the physical arrangements of the theatre and its implied ability to accommodate itself to, as well as to shape the social needs of, its public. Here the congruence between the internal spaces – in particular the relationship between stage and auditorium and the two in combination to the theatre as a whole – is the crux of the matter: for, by the late eighteenth century the opera house had evolved into an explicit and more or less universal design. Of course, the broad stability of this model was directly related to its functionality, so that – in the hands of masters such as Piermarini at La Scala[16] – the natural balance between aesthetic preference and practicality was paramount. Later, in the mid-nineteenth century – and the matter concerns us directly – the design of the house was altered. Such alteration necessarily speaks of a changing purpose, for little in the interior life of the theatre happened without underlying cause or significance. (It is with this aspect of the relationship that we are most concerned here).

And, finally, the affairs of the theatre involved matters of much wider import, indeed of national significance. The opera house was – as previously stated – a microcosm of the wider community: a distillation of its essence. Yet we must go further than even this reflective construction implies. I have argued elsewhere that the theatre is at heart (and at best) an interiorizing experience through which the audience is driven to self-examination by empathetic association with the fundamental tenets of the enacted drama.[17] In such circumstance, the theatre – as a physicality – dissolves leaving only the stage and its audience. Exploitation of this capacity was late in coming to the opera – arguably not much before the 1840s – though when it did come, it was to transform forever the cozy relationship between the theatre as a social space and the opera as a pretextual basis for other activity. The opera's transcendent capacity (in both an emotional and a geographical sense) is, therefore, key to its late nineteenth-century significance: for it was then that its language and content – as understood and internalized by individuals – catalyzed into a fully mature relationship between *the stage and the community at large*. This is at once the most intimate and personal of the relationships considered here, yet the one with the widest implication.

Recitative (or advancing the plot)

Recitativo secco

With the foregoing as context, we can now turn to more detailed matters: particularly the theatre's design. As suggested previously, the evolution of the form of the opera house – a series of stacked 'horse-shoes' – was no accident and it soon settled into a generally accepted though locally flexible design. Generic to all was the existence of three separate though inter-related spaces properly designated as: firstly the 'non-theatrical' space of the *anterior*, conventionally the social space of the house[18]; secondly the 'passive' space of the *auditorium* in which the public displayed itself and its social pretensions and in which [later] the audience – *as opposed to the opera-going public –*

FIGURE 1
**Cross Section and Ground Plan of the Teatro San Giovanni Grisostemo, Venice
(drawn by F Pedro)**

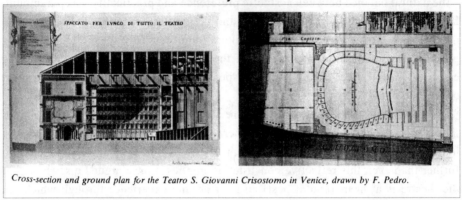

Cross-section and ground plan for the Teatro S. Giovanni Crisostomo in Venice, drawn by F. Pedro.

found its natural point of interest;[19] and finally the *stage* on which an initially pre-textual but later increasingly pertinent drama was enacted (see Figure 1).

Central to the present thesis is the contention that the relationship between these spaces varied both geographically (the difference between some Italian theatres was significant though nowhere near as great as the contrast between the Italian and the Parisian house) and over time. Thus in Italy – as the late *settocento* gave way to the *ottocento* – the emphasis began to shift from a strong focus on the anterior and auditorium to an increasing symbiosis between auditorium and stage. In this process, the areas of the anterior (never very grand) became more notably marginalized and retained only a residual socializing significance. The process as a whole was reflective of a deeper physical and emotional interiorizing though it was not, of course, without exteriorizing implication. In France (or more accurately Paris, for the theatre outside Paris – particularly in the South – was strongly connected to Italian models) the emphasis throughout the nineteenth century (and oblivious to its many regimes) remained much more firmly rooted in the relationship between anterior and auditorium with the former largely dominant throughout. Again, in contrast to the Italian theatre, the importance of the auditorium hardly changed at all as the century progressed, whilst the stage remained, at worst, insignificant and, at best, an incidental protagonist to the social drama enacted in the foyers and saloons. Here the process was physically more static and intellectually more superficial, carrying few of the transcendent implications of the Italian experience. Though the opéra (or rather conspicuous attendance at it) reinforced a certain cultural solidarity and demarcated the haves from the have-nots, it could claim little of the cultural and political fundamentality which marked its significance elsewhere. In short: in Italy, the opera house's legacy was that of social and political explosion (spreading significant ideas to the wider realm), whereas the Parisian experience was one of social implosion (drawing a favoured elite into closer contact only with itself). Eventually – to strain a metaphor – Italian Opera would cross the oceans, whereas French opera (particularly in its Meyerbeerian guise) would play on even as the Titanic sank.[20]

Recitativo accompagnato

It is clear then that (excluding the stage and backstage areas) two connected spaces defined the interior world of the opera house: the anterior and the auditorium.[21] We must now consider them in turn.

The **anterior** space was, in fact, not a single space at all, but rather a series of spaces made up of an entrance (foyer); a jungle of maze-like corridors which led to and from the boxes of the auditorium; (often but not always) a matching set of side rooms (or withdrafts) which serviced the boxes; and variously a saloon or large room in which the public could gather, converse and (more likely before the 1820s) gamble. The proportion of the theatre dedicated to these uses as well as the location, emphasis and rhythm of their connection varied considerably from theatre to theatre depending upon the whim of the theatre's main sponsor(s) as well as the dictates of local fashion (dukes for example tended to place more emphasis on their private boxes, communes on the more public spaces between them).

Figure 1 illustrates the ground plan and cross section of one of Venice's leading theatres of the early eighteenth century, whilst Figure 2 shows the footprints of five of Italy's leading mid-nineteenth-century theatres and immediately makes the different proportions of the theatres and the distribution of their interior spaces apparent. The Argentina – typical of Roman theatres under direct or indirect Papal control – had rather modest facilities all round; whilst the Canobiana and La Scala in Milan (commensurate with the Milanese's less attenuated social expectations) enjoyed more space throughout and particularly in the various private dressing rooms and withdrafts. The San Carlo, as befits a regal theatre, offered grand pretension on entrance, but less opportunity for communal intercourse within (social matters were subject to rather strictly regulated etiquette and important transactions took place in the regal box itself). In general the corridor spaces – which we must imagine bustling with the traffic of visitors, servants, soldiers and all manner of intrigue – were 'useful' in more senses than one: apart from their straightforward purpose in facilitating entrance and egress to the more functionally specific areas of the theatre, they were primarily the places to which box-holders resorted to relieve themselves when nature

FIGURE 2
Ground Plans of Five of Italy's Leading Theatres of the Ottocento

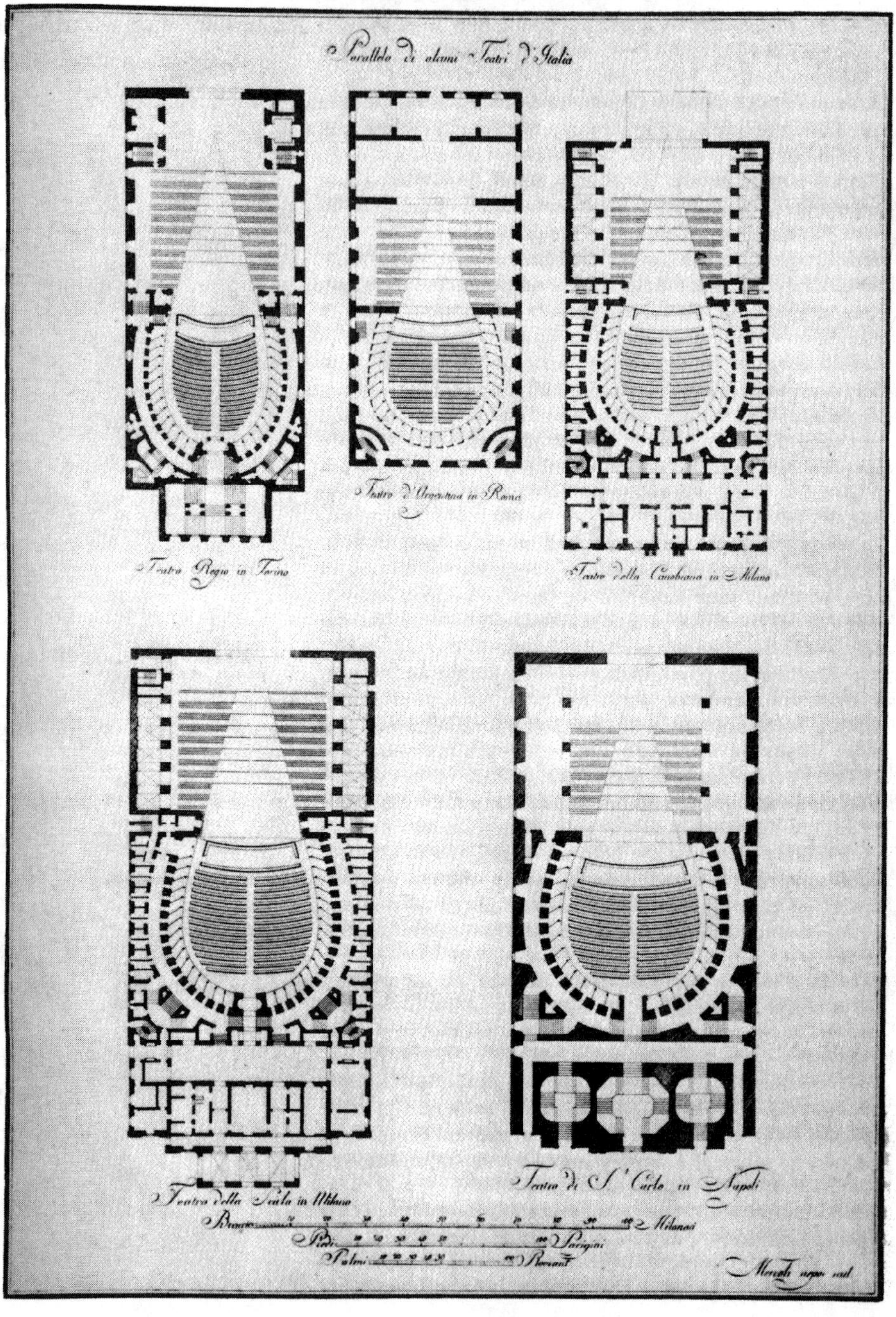

called. Buckets for this purpose were liberally distributed throughout their length. As contemporary accounts make clear, the theatre's corridors were often more fetid than the rankest street outside.[22]

The contrast with Garnier's Parisian theatre (and to some degree the Théâtre Italien) could hardly be more stark, for here the entrance, with its mirrored adjuncts and cavernous saloons, were not so much a prelude to an evening in the theatre but rather a proposition in themselves. It was possible, indeed quite common, to spend a whole evening in the theatre yet never enter – or even feel the need to enter – the auditorium (see Figure 3). For a time this was true of Italy too, though the difference lay in the nature of the alternative entertainments on offer. In Italy the draw was generally the *faro*, *rouge-et-noir* and *roulette* tables (monopoly concessions over which went to an impresario hand-in-hand with his opera permit), whereas in Paris it was largely a matter of conspicuous display in grand surroundings – a *tableau vivant* of the in-crowd passing time between the jockey club and supper.[23]

The **auditorium** too varied in size and splendour depending again on the capitalization of its building as well as the size of the town which it was expected to serve – not always the same thing. Relative to the building as a whole, it was the most consumptive of capital and the arena that (in Italy at least) was subject to the greatest critical scrutiny and the most significant adornment. Though, prior to the 1840s, the

FIGURE 3

Cross Section through the Palais Garnier

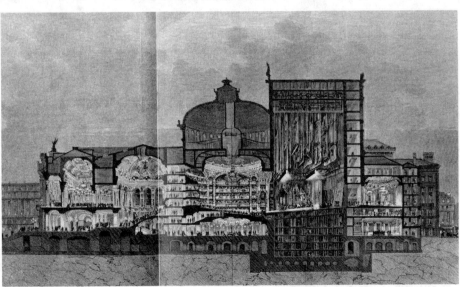

FIGURE 4
Interior of La Scala.

atmosphere within the auditorium – in particular the pattern of audience behaviour – related it more directly to the circus and even the bear pit than the contemporary salon, its pretensions to greatness were everywhere apparent in the relative luxury of its fittings and the comparative attention to detail in the design.

Almost worldwide after about 1820 (but, in the case of Italy, by the 1740s) the theatre's form followed a planimetric design (generally described as a horseshoe), which superimposed up to five tiers on top of each other. Each tier contained a series of private boxes ('*palchi*'), which at ground level ringed the pit or stalls: an unseated (or removable seat) area which could be put to other purposes when the opera season was concluded. The second row generally contained the grandest boxes and was crowned at its apex by the most noble box of all. Larger than any other, it was more conspicuous and more self-consciously grand. Further, in the better houses, it announced itself by a height extension which placed its ceiling at the same elevation as that of the boxes of the third tier (see Figure 4).

It is generally acknowledged that the earliest 'public' opera houses – notably those of Venice in the 1630s – established this basic design[24], whilst its elaboration is commonly attributed to Piermarini whose Milanese theatres (La Scala of 1770 and the smaller Canobbiana of 1776) are supreme examples of the genre,[25] even though they are by no means more elaborate than, say, the Teatro Communales of Bologna or Ferrara or (what is now) the Teatro Ponchielli in Cremona.[26] Clearly, once the opera had left the grand salon of the local Palazzo or Municipio, it demanded a more formal arena for its prosecution and the auditorium was, in a sense, an arrangement waiting to happen.

Aria (or reflections on the state of things *ossia* what on earth is going on here?)

Now that the general design of the house has been outlined, it remains to explain how it functioned and quite why it took on the particular characteristics it did. A variety of theses has been offered, especially with regard to the auditorium which, as we have seen, proved a broadly stable design over a very long period.[27] In the first instance three technical explanations are offered, each without comment.

The first concerns acoustics and argues that (stripped of its interior) the shape of the auditorium is a straightforward shoebox: a design characteristic of most if not all the world's finest concert halls and generally favoured by acousticians for its clarity and truthfulness.[28] However, acoustical theory also suggests that left to its own devices, such a symmetrical design hardens the overall sound picture by producing unwanted uniform reflections, so that it becomes necessary to disturb the sound waves by breaking up the space in some fashion. The traditional opera house does this, of course, in many ways. The rows of boxes with their internal dividing walls, the rounding of the space at its margins, the (often hemispherical) extension of its ceiling and the generally plush and absorbent furnishings all serve to de-symmetrize the angles and mellow the acoustic without disturbing its clarity. Thus, the theory goes, opera houses have evolved according to the 'soundest' and most democratic acoustic principles: perfect audibility for all. It is certainly true that many of the older Italian houses offer an unrivalled aural experience which – rather in the manner of a Greek amphitheatre – easily carries the voices, even above a Wagnerian orchestra, to the farthest recesses of the auditorium.

A second approach concentrates not on acoustics but on observation, arguing that the design of the house – particularly its serried ranks of comparatively shallow compartments surrounding the open area of the stage – permitted an intimate and almost uninterrupted view of the stage action, much as a 'theatre in the round' might offer today. In this sense, the auditorium might be considered a classic design with a number of lineal ancestors of which the usual suspects are the Teatro Olimpico of Vicenza (a hieratic semi-circular model) and the

FIGURE 5

The Teatro Olympico (Vicenza)

anatomy Theatre of Padova (a more pragmatic near-circular forebear). Again, both derived something from the amphitheatre, which is hardly surprising given the Renaissance's generally revivalist concerns (see Figures 5 and 6).

The third approach is a more or less straightforward conflation of the other two and draws upon the nineteenth-century concept of the panopticon, neatly inverting its logic to argue that the theatre is its reverse. The panopticon was a design proposed in the nineteenth century for the institutional observation of the sick, the mad and the criminal.[29] Its central proposition was that, properly arranged, a large number of people could be observed (and hence regulated) by a relatively small number of warders whose presence would be undetected by those being watched. Since inmates were unaware of whether they were being observed at any one time, the thesis argued that they would have continually to behave as that they were (see Figure 7).

FIGURE 6
The Anatomy Theatre (Padova).

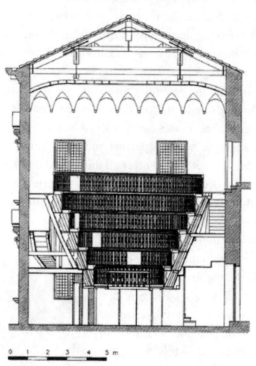

0 1 2 3 4 5 m

A reversal of this principle thus argues that the theatre offered, not the constant intrusive surveillance of the many by the few, but rather the open surveillance of the few (stage actors) by the many. Put another way: whereas in the panopticon a small number of privileged individuals were allowed unprecedented access to the normally private doings of the observed, the theatre offered to its whole audience a personalized sense of observing the most intimate moments in the life of the characters portrayed on stage. In this way, the physical arrangements of the auditorium conspired to a privatization of experience within the collectivized crowd, making the enacted drama 'uniquely' personal to any individual member of the audience who cared to tap in to what was on offer. It matters little that the panopticon was invented long after the theatre, for we might just as well say that the panopticon was a reverse theatre, the cathartic mechanics of which had been understood and practically instigated centuries earlier.

Such arguments take us some way into understanding the physical principles upon which the theatre might be held to have operated, though each is problematic,

FIGURE 7
The Panopticon.

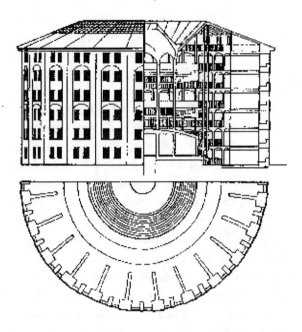

beyond the obvious (perhaps rather modern) knowledgeability they severally imply.[30] In the case of both the sight-line and panoptical arguments, for example, it is enough to note that the planimetric pattern of the opera-house was not a perfect circle or even semicircle but rather a variously distorted horseshoe; a fact which immediately throws such arguments out of kilter. The natural point of focus of a horseshoe is not the space between its opening or its epicentre, but rather the mid-point of the outer ring itself. As a result, sight-lines onto the open end are frequently not perfect but partial (or to use the proper theatrical term subject to a 'restricted view'). Add to this the problems of the all too frequent supporting pillars of the tiers and of elevation and, as any modern theatre-goer knows, from the boxes or gallery seats nearest the stage on the fourth or fifth tier, it is impossible to see anything save the orchestra and – occasionally – the top of a prima donna's soliloquizing head. Still, such seats often command a rather good view of much of the audience: a fact we will do well to remember when deciphering the auditorium further.

Beyond the particularities of such criticism, it is possible to make a more fundamental objection which brings us closer – at last – to the spirit of the age and society from which the opera sprang. This is to say that each of the arguments thus far advanced fails in its different way to make intelligible the vital connection between the theatre as a responsive institution and the general needs and concerns of the public it nurtured and embraced. Of course, it was a space with acoustical and other physical properties, but it was overwhelmingly a space manipulated by and for a public whose needs were much more broadly social than they were technical, and more instinctively participatory than they were consciously attentive.

Above all, each argument is flawed by a single presumption: that the audience was present in the auditorium primarily to observe or to listen to the performance on stage. Yet everything we know of the Italian theatre prior to about 1840 (and the French for some time thereafter) suggests that this was simply not so. We do better, in fact, when we recognize that the public was there for quite other reasons: to be seen and to be listened to; to be part of the communal drama which mere presence in the theatre inevitably generated. At best a local 'player', at worst a plain member of the crowd, everyone was an 'actor' and no-one a mere observer of the dim and distant events on stage. This is also to say that the collective audience (the public itself) was the true object and focus of the evening: something which the design of the horseshoe made both possible and manifest. For some – most notably the occupants of the noble box – their 'pole' position in the middle of the *piano nobile* granted a double advantage: they had the best possible view of the stage and the crowds ranged around them and yet they remained at all times conspicuously visible from almost any part of the auditorium (see Figure 8).

Contemporary evidence to support this view is widespread and strong. The composer Louis Spohr visited La Scala (according to Stendhal 'the city's Salon') in 1816 and observed that:

> *During the powerful overture, several very expressive accompanied recitatives and all the ensemble pieces there was such a noise that one heard hardly anything of the music. In most boxes cards were being played and in every part of the theatre there was loud talking. For a visitor who would like to listen attentively, nothing could be imagined more intolerable than this infamous din; however, from people who see the same opera perhaps thirty to forty times and who visit the city only for society no attentiveness can be expected.*[31]

The system of private boxes – in which the occupants behaved more or less as they wanted, and much as they would have done at home – gave force to the belief that an evening in the theatre was a matter of wining and dining, of conversation, reciprocal visitation and general social interaction[32] (see Figure 9).

FIGURE 8

Ground Plan of La Scala

(the Royal box is shown at the Southern end of the auditorium).

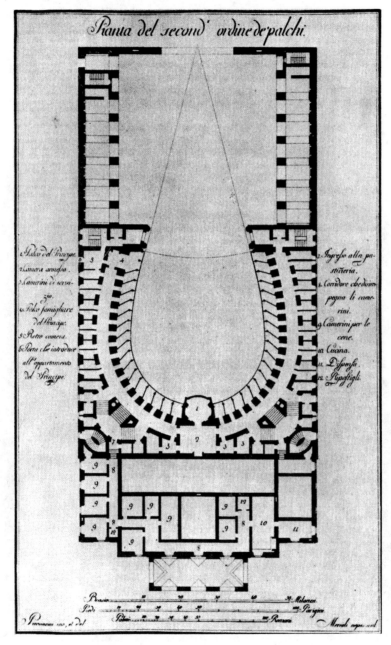

FIGURE 9
Interior of a Box at La Scala.

Add to this the uncouth loitering of soldiers, men on the make and women of easy virtue and it becomes evident that the normal traffic of social intercourse was little influenced, and even more seldom disturbed, by matters on stage, unless of course a particularly attractive ballerina, a favoured singer or a notably fetching aria caught the attention and stilled the incessant babble to a momentary hush. As late as 1849, *Il Mondo Illustrato* could caricature this pattern of behaviour knowing it to be based on an uncontestable truth[33] (see Figure 10).

Later, as I have argued elsewhere,[34] this changed, but during the formative years of the opera's ascent to general popularity, an audience was pretty much at liberty to do what it wanted. The provision of curtains, which could be drawn on the auditorium for greater privacy, further encouraged the notion that a box was a personal universe full of opportunity, intrigue and clandestine possibility.[35] Some took this further: Byron, for one, found the theatre an unrivalled place of assignation. When, in 1819, the Countess Teresa Guiccioli (whose adulterous affair with the poet had generally been conducted in his box at the Teatro La Fenice in Venice) was told by her furious husband that they were leaving the city, she needed to speak with Byron quickly. As William Weaver notes: "she knew exactly where to go: the opera house". A scene ensued (he happened to be in an all male box at the time) and it was doubtless more interesting to the public at large than the opera – as always, the wholly incidental backdrop to the real drama. Not inappropriately, that night it was Rossini's *Otello*.[36]

Cabaletta (or getting things moving again)

It is hopefully accepted by this stage that any satisfactory explanation of the theatre's attraction, significance and form needs to take careful account of the manner in which it addressed the needs of its clientele within the context of the general public's emerging social and political self-definition. That is to say, how it was both representative and reproductive of the community in which it was centred as an 'ordinary' culture. We must remember too that in the late eighteenth and early nineteenth centuries (in Italy and much of France outside Paris) the countryside remained a set of differentiated regions whose general prescriptions were still more feudal than they were modern. The local opera house fitted well into the moral economy of this hierarchical status – rather than class conscious – and broadly reciprocal society, offering extensive opportunities to exhibit its general assumptions in concrete form and to rehearse their virtues on a face-to-face basis. Rosselli hints at this when he reminds us that the "theatre combined well-defined territorial rights with maximum display",[37] but we can go further to argue that since the very fabric of

FIGURE 10
Il Mondo Illustrato Cartoon.

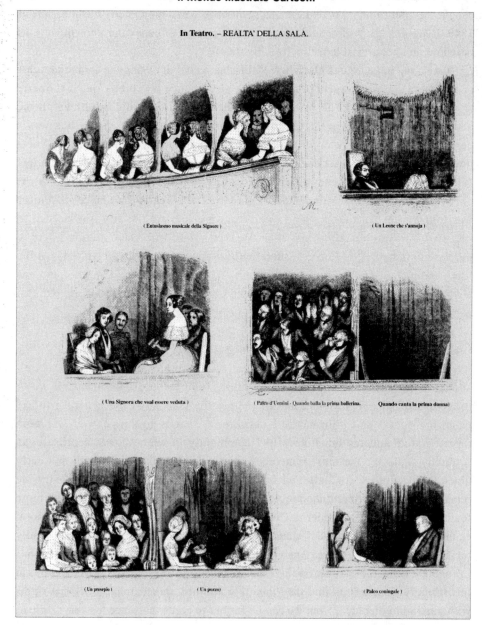

the theatre was dictated by local prescription, it offers us an unparalleled insight into that prescription's force and operation.

Such insights emerge most clearly if we consider, firstly, how theatre building was proposed and financed (for this was no minor undertaking) and, secondly, how its micro-geography worked on a more pragmatic level.

By the middle of the eighteenth century the construction of a theatre could be proposed on any number of bases and by all manner of people. Over time, emphasis tended to shift away from a single wealthy patron (typically a monarch or a duke or even a cardinal) towards a more concerted communal effort involving several – or sometimes all – of the local families of note. In some cases all of the citizens might be invited to subscribe, though more often the commune would take out several 'shares' on its citizenry's behalf, thereby giving the local councillors (particularly the mayor or *sindaco*) maximum voice in the construction at the minimum expense. These changes in financial arrangement tended to mirror the social diffusion of the opera more generally as it leaked out of the court and into the city, so that as opera became more insistently demotic, the house itself fell under more democratic control.

Contributors to the enterprise were, in effect, staking a claim to a place in the house and some influence in its running (for example the hiring of a particular season's impresario) through what was, in modern terms, a debenture system. This guaranteed to the individual (at various times in the year) a specific location in the array of boxes and to the general enterprise a level of capitalization sufficient to secure its completion (see Figure 11).

In some cases, the arrangement was much more formalized in that a set sum was established as a reasonable representation of the cost of building a single private box, to which was added a 'levy' representing an appropriate proportion of the costs of constructing the more 'communal' areas of the theatre. Though subject to further recurrent cost, these boxes then became in effect private fiefdoms over which the owner enjoyed exclusive rights of occupancy and sometimes of hire – a situation which in the smaller towns of Le Marche for example has continued until recent times.[38] In other words patrons paid for, and in effect constructed, their own private domain within the public shell of the theatre, just as they had done when constructing their *palazzi* in the landscape outside: here the social and spatial arrangements of the region were simply rolled up, dusted down and decanted into the theatre.

These different contractual arrangements clearly accorded to contributing individuals different levels of social control within the theatre, a fact which simultaneously served to heighten their profile outside it. In Naples, for example, where the theatre was financed directly by the monarchy, allocation of the San Carlo's

FIGURE 11

Sketch of the Distribution of Box Ownership in the 'Vecchio' Teatro, Camerino 1820 (Boxes 28 and 29 belonged to the Commune)

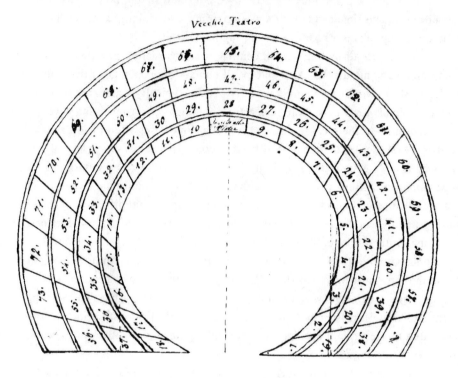

boxes lay exclusively with the King or Queen who, on an annual or seasonal basis, could dispense a political obligation, by offering a box in a favoured location, or banish a noble to a more distant tier, where some disfavour and demotion was implied.

Once built, the theatre required management both as an enterprise and as a civic asset, and though the individual or committee responsible for the building of the theatre sometimes ran it,[39] it was far more common to lease the theatre (together with the aforementioned gambling concession) to a commercial impresario – a class of men which had emerged with some rapidity in the late eighteenth century. Occasionally such men rose to greatness in both a commercial and social sense,[40] but more often they operated on a shoestring and spent every season hoping against both hope and past experience that this would be the one to establish their fortune.

In most theatres (especially in the larger cities), ownership of a box did not give automatic rights to free access, so that patrons were liable to pay both for a permit to enter the building (a modest *ingresso*) and a charge for the use of their own box. (In effect, this meant one charge for entering the building and another for accessing the auditorium – a small friction in the system which doubtless encouraged many to forego the entertainments of the latter and confine themselves to the delights of the anterior). These takings – together with the daily receipts from those without boxes, seeking entrance to the stalls instead – were used to pay the singers, orchestra and composer, indeed to finance the season as a whole. Accordingly, recurrent revenue normally went to the impresario, though there was much dispute when the owners of boxes who had paid their 'rent' for a season, privately hired them out to third parties on given nights. Since particular seasons and places in the theatre were cast in strictly hierarchical terms, the level of receipt as well as of liability varied from time to time and place to place. It was all very elaborate and frequently disputatious, but the general point is this: a more or less captive local audience was able to sustain a thirty- to forty-day season financially, and barring disaster (a failed opera, an indifferent tenor, a wooden soprano or a poor gambling take) the impresario could live to fight another day.[41]

Though the impresario and his (never her) financial wheeler-dealing spoke of the intrusion of a more 'modern' and increasingly capitalist market into the cozy arrangements of the opera,[42] the local context in which they operated continued to assume an altogether more traditional state of affairs. Here too the internal arrangements of the theatre might be counted a miniature of the immediate social world outside. We have already seen how the privatized spaces of the box sustained an 'at home' culture within what was in essence a public arena and how, in consequence, the theatre gave expression to a set of interconnected social concerns. Equally paramount was the need to connect these private worlds in such a way that the balance of the community outside was retained and the status distinctions through which everyday life functioned were not compromised within the more claustrophobic and altogether more 'familiar' confines of the theatre. The need was for demarcation, but demarcation within an ordered, accepted and recognizable system and, as in so many matters feudal, hierarchy was the key.

In fact, the theatre was capable of hierarchical arrangement according to several different devices, permutations of which yielded the finest distinctions and the subtlest social positioning. Time and space were both pressed into service, so that status claims could be attached to the reputation of a particular opera house, the fashionability of a particular season, the nature of the operatic genre on offer, and (still most significant of all) the physical disposition of audience members within the house itself.

In Paris, the first of these was of the greatest importance since, characteristically, a more sectarian approach was taken to the various houses of the city, each of which claimed a different social stratum for its natural clientele. For this reason, choice of which theatre to attend (or, more accurately, access to which theatre could be achieved) was by its very nature something of a social statement. It is also true that particular houses specialized in different operatic genres so that distinctions between them were often based on a double perception of their place in the hierarchy and thus their *éclat* when it came to being spotted.[43] At the top of the tree in its various guises (as Académie de Musique etc.) stood the Opéra (a status it held throughout several regimes), supported by theatres such as the Théâtre Italien, Opéra Comique, Théâtre de Monsieur, Odéon, Colisée, Lyrique, Trianon Lyrique, Bouffes-Parisiens, Eden, Gaîtée Parisienne, Marigny, Châtelet, Lyrique de la Renaissance etc. (perhaps some twenty-two in all by the 1870s). The *cachet* of a particular theatre (especially below the top two or three) was rarely fixed for long, since operatic fashion changed quite rapidly and equally decisively. Still, it matters little for the present purpose, for the point is this: whatever the relative hierarchy, the operative distinction within it, was a broadly economic one which emphasized class (i.e. exclusivity) and was controlled by wealth (rather than character), personal connection and above all by ability to pay.[44]

In contrast, in most of the towns of Italy (except perhaps Rome, Milan and Venice) the *lirica* was a much broader church which almost all the citizenry would expect to attend.[45] And much like the church, distinction came, not from attendance as such, but from placement and recognition within: an essentially feudal mechanism which emphasized commonality (i.e. inclusivity) and was policed by matters of status, deference and natural right.

How then was such 'placement' signaled? How were appropriate distinctions made? The standing of a particular season was one (Carnival – from St Steven's Night to Lent – was of the highest status, Autumn one rung down etc.[46]) and genre was another (different types of opera were deemed more suitable for – though not the exclusive preserve of – particular social strata). However, these continued to be

FIGURE 12

Status in the Theatre

Theatre
Premier Rank
Second Rank
Third Rank

Season
Carnival*
Autumn*
Non Seasonal

Genre
Opera Seria
Opera Semi
Seria Opera
BuffaFarsa
Spoken Play
Balletto Pantomimico
Animal Shows

Location
Boxes Tier 2
Boxes Tiers 1 and 3
Parts of Stall [Locked Seats]
Boxes Tiers 4 + or Gallery
Parts of Stalls [Standing]
Outside Theatre

*status reversed in Bologna

deliberately crude sieves, so that the most visible – and, therefore, most effective – denominator remained physical location within the theatre (see Figure 12).

Two vectors were operative in this dispositional process: physical elevation (or level) – as in the medieval city more generally – and proximity to the noble centre.[47] The former provided the coarsest division into social types, the latter more subtle demarcation within a broadly co-equal social group.

We have already noted that the second tier of boxes, with the noble box at its apex, was the most elite of the levels. Next in sequence came the third and first tiers followed by the upper boxes, and parts of the stalls. Depending upon the size and prestige of the town, the objective status of the occupants of these areas could vary considerably, but typically, the nobility would occupy tiers 1-3, the middle class (*galantuomini e donne di garbo*) the upper boxes (later the gallery) and the *minuto populo* (menu people) those more favoured area of the stalls which contained lockable seats. Also present in the stalls (or pit as it was more usually called in Italy) would be the military, the servants of the rich (often, up until the 1820s allowed in free as part of their employer's deal with the theatre) and, closest to the *golfo mistico* (the as yet unsunken orchestra area), students and *afficionados* who actually wanted to hear the opera. We should not forget

FIGURE 13

Salle Ventadour, Paris illustrating the different positioning of the Noble Box close to the Stage.

that many, who could not afford entrance to the theatre, were to be found crowded outside, clutching at the window sills for any view they could get, or listening (probably more attentively than those inside) when a familiar aria arose.[48]

Within particular tiers perceived status – in Italy at least – normally declined equidistantly from the noble box, though it could increase again marginally as one neared the stage. In this respect it was quite different from the Parisian theatre of the same period (see Figure 13).[49] In the Italian house, these gradients had, of course, much to do with the physical representation of proximity to the centre of power, though it is hard to avoid the conclusion, given the importance of 'audience-watching' generally, that they were not also related to the proportion of the total audience which could be surveyed from (and which could in turn survey) particular locations. Not only might the cost of such boxes vary in construction, but also the manner of their hire (even when privately owned) which would vary according to their desirability from both these points of view (see Figure 14).

Typically first to third row boxes were subject to annual contracts, fourth and above to seasonal disposal, and the less regulated parts of the house to weekly or, more commonly, nightly admission. The capital required to make such commitments (particularly in advance) could be very considerable, but – as befitted their status and

FIGURE 14
Interior of the Teatro Costanzi, Rome.

communal responsibility – it was the major box owners on yearly or seasonal advances who contributed most to the underwriting of the operatic year.

This then was the classic and expected design of an Italian opera house by the late eighteenth century: a form best summed up by Rosselli, when he comments that "Opera was an industry. Yet, it was also a means of displaying the hierarchical structure of Italian society and the ascendancy within it of the upper classes".[50] Less a representational model then, it was more a social mechanism: even a heuristic device.

Stretta (or now we're really motoring)

Of necessity, the foregoing has been concerned with the originating and somewhat static presumptions concerning the theatre and its role in community life. It would be wrong, however, as in any natural history, to overlook the ways in which this ecology evolved, both through competition and through natural selection. Indeed many of the most significant readings of the theatre come from recognizing the degree to which the assumptions it had idealized and made concrete in the eighteenth century were subject to challenge and systematic change in the nineteenth. By 1820, the writing was already on the wall and by 1840, the era of the social and 'gentlemanly' house was all but over. A new politics and a new class was now beginning to write its own chapter in the theatre's history and, as in its previous incarnation, the physicality of the house would prove a remarkable litmus of such alteration as its interior fabric continued to bear witness to whatever went on in the world outside.

In what was to become Italy entire, three changes were in the air after 1820. Firstly, commercial development was proceeding apace and as the economy generally advanced, so did the economics of opera: so that a new and rather more hard nosed capitalism entered into the business of singing, the business of composing and the business of production, taking a craft industry and fashioning from it, by the late nineteenth century, a fully fledged export-based manufacture. Secondly, Italian society and its aspirations were changing and in common with other parts of Europe, the rise of a more affluent and socially mobile middle class coincided with the stirrings of a nationalist sentiment which would eventually unite the country (Rome excepted) under a single monarchist regime. Whilst unification would never obliterate the regions or homogenize their distinctive cultures, it would certainly compromise the umbilical bond which, via the opera house, had connected people to community and community to region. A nation was on the move, and the static presumption of the old feudal theatre was amongst the first casualties. Finally, (within the world of the opera) autonomy was being wrested from the enabling nobility and bestowed upon the artist-composer who gave voice to the wider aspirations considered above and who began to mould from the medium of opera a cultural force which would give expression to the broadest and highest political ideals. Just as individual operas would become texts, so the theatre would become their reading room: a place where the performed work mattered and the audience fell silent as the curtain rose. In other words, as the business of opera ('the Italian art' as it became known) was subject to mounting international economic force, the natural focus of its composers and audience increasingly centred upon the nation state itself. Soon *Nabucco* and *Macbeth*, *Ernani* and *La Battaglia di Legnano* would be picked over and lauded for their (variably overt) nationalist sentiments. And each would stir the blood of a politicizing citizenry from Piedmont to Calabria, from Lombardy to the Veneto, and from Naples even to Rome.[51]

Within the theatre several developments signalled and nurtured these changes. The first brings us back to where we began: the destruction of private boxes and their replacement by a public gallery of open seats. Typically involving the removal of the sixth, fifth or fourth tier boxes, this change was more significant and had more wide-ranging consequences than might, at first, be imagined. It indicated and made possible not just a different division of space, or a more democratic theatre (important as these were), but rather heralded a 'modern' world: for not the least of its demands was the ceding of private feudal interests to a public (broadly capitalist) good. Without this, no alteration could take place. In practice, it ended (and equally importantly signaled the end) of the old relationship between master and men (which had once given access to the theatre to some, as an aristocratic concession), and put in its place a citizenry of increasingly equal rank (and gathering voice), which could demand its place in the theatre by right. Once begun the movement spread, both within particular theatres – as subsequent rows of boxes disappeared – and across the operatic landscape more generally, nicely reflecting the progress of precisely those changes from which it was born.[52]

Whilst this democratizing of the theatre's spaces marks a significant shift in the locus of its control, other alterations affected less the composition of its clientele and more the way in which the theatre was expected to work once the audience was present within it. In achieving this effect, they conspired towards a radicalizing of the theatre's form and an enhancing of the opera's power to arrest the public's attention and tie it to a cause. Together they made opera matter.

The first of these was the introduction of fixed seating throughout the stalls, something about which a good deal has been written from a broadly European perspective. This development has often been seen in a disciplinary context as a way of organizing audience behaviour, particularly amongst the lower ranks. Such theories have gained credence in the narrative history of, say, the English Music Hall, where the control of drinking (confining it to bars during the interval, rather than at tables throughout the performance) has been held to be the paramount objective. Alternatively, fixed – and particularly pre-bookable – seating has been viewed as a necessary corollary of the loss of the private box, since without it, no control could be exercised over who sat with who and in the company of which third party.[53] Almost certainly, we need to conflate these concerns in the Italian theatre, but to add to them an increasing desire on the part of audience and composer alike to reduce the peripatetic wanderings of the audience and fix their attention on the stage action directly ahead. The gentle raking of the auditorium bears witness to the same ideal: to make the stage as visible and as immediate as possible to the widest number of ordinary spectators (see Figure 15).

These trends were accelerated by a second development: the final removal of the curtains from those boxes of the first, second and third tier[54] together with the expropriation of their hitherto private anterooms for public use. (This created what we would later come to know as the often labyrinthine bars, refreshment and loitering

FIGURE 15
A Typical Small Italian Theatre: The Nuovo 'Marchetti', Camerino

areas of the theatre). Taken together, they constituted a further attempt to emphasize the hegemony of the stage. No longer was individual whim (be it temporary withdrawal behind the curtain or the desire for *ad hoc* refreshment in the box) deemed tolerable, and the evening was henceforth characterized by alternating periods of undisturbed concentration and compensating relaxation.

Next, came the sinking of the orchestra pit – the elaboration of the *golfo mistico* – which removed a major obstacle separating stage from audience, and contributed to the general impression that nothing now intruded between the individual and his or her direct theatrical experience. Only now did the third of the general relationships outlined initially (that between the stage and the audience, or the drama and the hearts and minds of the community at large) truly come into its own[55]. (And only now, were many of the celebrated physical and acoustical properties of the theatre exploited to their full capacity). Verdi again:

> *This arrangement for the orchestra is much more important than is usually believed, for the instrumental colouring, for the sonority, and for the effect. These small improvements will open the way to other innovations that will certainly come one day. One of them will be the removal of the spectators' boxes from the stage, thus enabling the curtain to come right up to the footlights. Another improvement would be to make the orchestra invisible. This idea is not mine but Wagner's, and it's a very good one. It's incredible nowadays that we should tolerate seeing horrid white ties and tails, for example, between us and the costumes of the Egyptians, Assyrians or Druids etc. etc. and, in addition, see the whole of the orchestra, which should be part of a fictitious world, almost in the middle of the stalls amongst the crowd as it hisses or applauds.*[56]

Finally came the revolution in theatre lighting (from candles, first to gas lamps and later to electric spot-lights): a truly modernist technical development which, alongside the institution of an audience blackout transformed the way in which opera was read. The former was largely responsible for increasing dramatically the palette of effects available to designers enabling them to enhance the realism and immediacy with which opera could be presented. The latter ensured that the old habit of audience watching was no longer an option and left little alternative to concentration on what was unfolding on stage. Taken together they helped mould the public into an audience and ensured that henceforth the theatre would be a place of intellectual and emotional engagement rather than of frivolous distraction and self-indulgent display.

Finale ultimo (or, much confusion: everyone on stage)

The premiere of Rossini's *Barber of Seville* took place at the Nobile Teatro di Torre Argentina (the Argentina) in Rome on 20 February 1816. Rossini had been offered a contract for it by the Duke Francesco Sforza Cesarini on 15th December 1815 – some 36 days before. The contract stipulated that the composer was to deliver the completed opera within a month, that he was to compose it to any libretto the Duke selected and "to adapt it to the voices of the singers (not then known) … and make all those changes which may be deemed necessary … for the singers' demands". He was required to be in Rome no later than the end of December, was to supervise all of the preparations, be present at such rehearsals as the impresario dictated and 'conduct' (from the cembalo as was customary) the first three performances. At the end of the third performance he would be paid 400 Roman *scudi* (in comparison to the prima donna and the distinguished baritone Luigi Zamboni who would be offered 500 and 700 Roman *scudi* respectively *for each performance*). The opera was a – to some extent pre-arranged – fiasco,[57] but little by little it reached all of the opera houses of Italy and was performed in all manner of ways: altered by singers where it suited them, truncated by conductors where they felt they could improve it, and butchered by impresarios where they sensed economies could be made.

In February 1868, Verdi wrote to Giulio Ricordi regarding rehearsals for *Don Carlos*, a work he had written for Paris and revised for its Italian premiere in Bologna in 1867. It was now attracting the attention of Italian theatres everywhere:[58]

> *(Don't tell me) that at Bologna 20 days sufficed (…) (because) at Bologna there were two rehearsals a day (…) In this way 20 days became 40; in addition the chorus had studied the opera for a month (prior) and the (principal) artists knew their parts. Despite this, you yourself saw that many things on stage, indicated and required by the music, were overlooked completely or badly performed (…). In D. Carlos there are seven scenes, five of them very complicated and of the greatest importance. I repeat once more, (…) 40 days are needed, with the entire personnel of the theatre free of other tasks.*[59]

Previously in 1844 he had written to the conductor Leone Herz regarding the Viennese premier of *Ernani*:

> *The tempos are all marked on the score with the (greatest) possible clarity. Enough that you pay attention to the dramatic situation and the text, (and only) with difficulty can you mistake a tempo. Only I caution (you that) I do not like slow tempos; it is better to err on the side of liveliness than to drag. Again I thank you for your attention, and because you want to perform Ernani correctly. On which account I ask that the parts be entrusted to those artists best received by the public, and that the performance be accurate…*
>
> *P.S. I ask that no cuts be allowed. There is nothing to remove and the smallest phrase cannot be taken away without damaging the whole.'*[60]

The contrast between Rossini's world and Verdi's could hardly be clearer. Even by the 1840s – and unquestionably by the 1860s – the 'jobbing' court servant had become the autonomous composer; the opera (formerly a vehicle for vocal display) had become a text; the experience of the opera house had become a vital matter of communicative drama and the public had become an audience.[61] Giusseppe and his like had taken control of the house that Gioacchino built and – together with an audience which increasingly gave such composers their wholehearted trust – they had subjected it to a major rethink.

In this essay I have sought to explore the ways in which a cultural institution was claimed, constructed and used by a public, together with the ways in which that use reflected its everyday preoccupations. As these preoccupations changed, so did the opera, both as a means of artistic expression and as an experience. The physical form of the house proved capable of accommodating and adapting to such needs, documenting in the process both its own and its community's natural history. As in all natural history, evolution and continuity were the keynotes. The theatre of Verdi's mature triumphs was very different from that of Rossini's early successes, let alone from the *sala grande* in which Monteverdi and later Scarlatti would have plied their trade. Yet they were lineally connected and organically related: recognisably from the same genetic pool. Much of the theatre's power came from its ability to adapt to circumstance and yet to retain its essential bond with its past: these gave it a history, a stability, an authenticity and a force. No composer – even in the febrile world of the nineteenth century – could be disrespectful of these resonances and remain successful.

At the start of the century the theatre had been a microcosm of local life. By its mid-point it was a microcosm still; but now, in addition, a macrocosm of national life: a perfect reflection of a world which many hoped to see and which, with cunning and determination, they believed might yet be. Composers did not seek to change, nor had they need to change, further a theatre which was by now responsive to their own and their public's demands. The most gifted continued to build upon a tradition and used it to fashion something entirely arresting, passionate and new. As Verdi marvellously reflected in old age: "torniamo all'antico: sarà un progresso" ("let us return to the past. That will be progress").[62] Even as it looked forward, the Italian theatre, like its greatest son, also looked back – and not least towards its own history: which was, after all, perfectly natural.

NOTES

1   The title of this essay is stolen – unashamedly – from Theodor Adorno's pioneering, and rather different essay: *The Natural History of the Theatre*. I am grateful to Professor James Burge of the University of Camerino for a number of helpful comments on an earlier draft.

2   Giuseppe Verdi to Giulio Ricordi quoted in G. Monaldi, *Le Opere di Giuseppe Verdi al Teatro La Scala* (Milan 1914) 226.

3   J. Rosselli, *The Opera Industry in Italy from Cimarosa to Verdi: the Role of the Impresario* (Cambridge 1984). Speaking of a similar conversion at an earlier time – that of the topmost boxes of the Teatro San Giovanni Gristostemo in Venice in 1819 – David Kimbell remarks: "The interesting point... is that it makes quite explicit the fact that such rebuilding was linked with an expansion of the popular audience for opera. It marks in fact the final refinement of the idea of the theatre as a microcosm of Italian society." D. Kimbell, *Italian Opera* (Cambridge 1991) 425.

4   M. Billinge, The musical elaboration of nationhood: form and function in nineteenth-century Italian opera *Geographical Review* (forthcoming).

5   Amongst historical geographers, no one has been more consistent in advocating this view than this volume's dedicatee, Alan Baker.

6   R. Williams, Culture is ordinary, in N. McKenzie (Ed.), *Convictions* (London 1958) reprinted in R. Williams, *Resources of Hope* (London 1989).

7   Quite what was internal and what external (what was local and what foreign) varied greatly throughout Italy in the politically turbulent *ottocento*. Foreign might at various times mean, for example, the Austrian authorities in Lombardy, the Bourbons in The Kingdom of the Two Sicilies or even the Pope in the less transient reaches of the Papal States. Napoleonic influences as always rather complicated matters as did Risorgimento politics so that 'foreign' was frequently defined by personal loyalty rather than geographical origin. Still, effective opera often asked of its audience precisely these questions: whose side are you really on? Where do you stand on the matter? In France, similar issues arose though far less explicitly in the text of the opéra as such. Here it was a question less of external authority than of internal loyalty and ideological persuasion; which particular regime controlled the opera and which did you favour? See Billinge, *op. cit.*, as well as R. Botti, *Donne nel Risorgimento Italiano* (Milan, 1966); W. Weaver (Ed.) *Verdi: A Documentary Study* (New York 1971) and G. Baldini, *The Story of Giuseppe Verdi* (Cambridge 1970), C. Osborne, *Verdi: A Life in the Theatre* (London 1987). Specifically political themes in Verdi's operas are also elaborated in A. Arblaster, *Viva la Libertà* (London 1992) Chapter 4; G. Martin, Verdi the Liberal Patriot in G. Martin, *Aspects of Verdi* (London 1989) Chapter 1 and O. Mula, *Giusseppe Verdi* (Bologna 1999) Chapter 5.

8   Take, for example, the region of Le Marche in mid south-eastern Italy (economically one of the most underdeveloped even of the comparatively 'backward' Papal States): its population by the mid-nineteenth century was perhaps a little less than 1 million, yet it had (conservatively) some 87 theatres. One of its small hilltop towns – Offida – (population *c.*1800 – 2,000) – had built a 400 seat theatre (Il Teatro Serpente Aureo) inside the town hall in the early eighteenth century and had been staging 'operatic' entertainment for its citizens almost from the genre's inception in the sixteenth century. The theatre remains to this day and has – like many of the Teatri Marchigiani – been extensively renovated of late. Its neighbouring communes were little different. A short distance across the mountains, Camerino built its theatre in the 1720s (when its population was 4,300), rebuilt it on a grander scale in the 1760s (through debentures raised by 72 local families plus 2 communal shares) and again in the 1850s. The level of, and enthusiasm for, theatre construction in the eighteenth and nineteenth centuries is quite unimaginable from today's perspective. See M. Vannicola, *Il Teatro Serpente Aureo e I pubblici spettacoli in Offida dal XVI al XX Secolo* (Offida 1999) and A. A. Bittarelli (Ed.) *Camerino: Teatro allo Specchio: Il Nuovo "Marchetti"* (Camerino 1990), and more generally, D. Cecchi, *Macerata e il Suo Territorio: La Storia* (Macerata 1979).

9   That the opera was a decidedly risky business financially is beyond doubt. It was impossible – certainly in the early nineteenth century – to break even (even with an opera declared an unambiguous success, and few were) – without other means of financial support – notably before the 1820s, the local gambling concession. See below and J. Rosselli, *op. cit.* Chapter 1 and J. Rosselli, *Music and Musicians in Nineteenth Century Italy* (London 1991).

10   For a context, see M. Vaussard, *Daily Life in Eighteenth Century Italy* (New York 1963).

11 The ways in which the building of theatres was financed is considered in greater detail later. Clearly it varied – in Ducal Parma, for example, it was often the Duke himself who was making such overt statements; in Calabria, the Monarchy; in Venice the ruling Doges, in the Papal States, the Pope or one of his Cardinals. In the larger cities either individual families or elements of the urban elite collectively dug deep in order to provide a facility of which they could be proud and, more importantly, which served their social purpose to perfection. I have noted above the close physical relationship of the opera house to the town hall in Le Marche where one was, effectively, an extension of the other. For the specific example quoted, E. Sori, *Il teatro nella Marche tra economia e societa*, in AA.VV *L'Architettura Teatrale nelle Marche* (Jesi 1988) as well as C. Baccili, *Il Teatro di Fermo* (Recanati 1886) and C. Ferrari, *Fermo. Teatro del-l'Aquila* (Fermo 1977).

12 Lady Morgan, *Italy* 2 vols (London 1821) 102.

13 Stendhal (M. H. Beyle) *Rome, Naples et Florence en 1817* (Paris 1817) edition V. del Litto (Lausanne 1960) 268-9. An early Neapolitan theatre (the Real) was completed by order of Charles III in 1737 and was the central act in a grand plan to revive and beautify the city in celebration of his accession in 1734. When Charles left to become King of Spain, his son Ferdinand I of the Two Sicilies continued the project, later ordering the rebuilding of the theatre after the destruction of the original in 1816. It re-opened as the San Carlo on 12 January 1817 i.e. Carnival, the significance of which is described below.

14 Quoted in P. Mioli, *Bellini: Tutti I Libretti d'Opera* (Rome 1997) 207. Bellini, who along with Donizetti and more particularly Verdi may be credited with enhancing the status of the composer and hence of the *lirica* itself in the early to mid *ottocento* trained in the capital of the Two Sicilies (Naples) with Zingarelli and made his career for the greater part in Milan. His future, interestingly, was planned for Paris, but he died indecently young. Unusually for a composer of the time (Rossini excepted) he was quite well off.

15 See G. Pannain, *Ottocento Musicale Italiano* (Milan 1952) especially Chapter 2. We should not forget that from the accession of Charles VI until the victory of the Risorgimento, Italy was substantially under Austrian 'occupation'. Milan was an Austrian city until 1859, Venice until 1866, and the theatres of La Scala and La Fenice were, in consequence, Austrian-controlled theatres. The Queen of Naples (Kingdom of the Two Sicilies) was Austrian, as were the Grand Dukes of Tuscany and of Parma. Like any occupying power, the Austrians were as obsessed with censorship and with the control of information as they were with the physical regulation of the ordinary population.

16 G. Piermarini (1734-1808). Piermarini was an architect who distinguished himself in every field available to him. His reputation certainly does not rest on his opera-house designs alone, though, had it done so, he would have had little to complain about.

17 Billinge, *op. cit.*

18 I suggest 'non-theatrical' only in the strictest sense of the word. In many theatres – and particularly in Paris this was the most important space of all – a place to see and be seen. Arguably – again in Paris – it was more theatrical than the interior, but then, in the Palais Garnier, it was all theatre from entrance to departure. See J. Fulcher, *The Nation's Image: French Grand Opera as Politics and Politicised Art* (Cambridge 1987).

19 Again, the term 'passive' should be read with care. An audience is only passive according to a particular school of theatrical semiotics which accounts it a non-participant observer. In fact, as this and other essays argue, the audience is – or at least should be – as active in the drama as the cast on stage. The true theatrical experience is a participant and shared one. The space of the auditorium is in this sense vital in fashioning an audience and shaping its sensibilities. See, for example, K. Elam, *The Semiotics of Theatre and Drama* (London 1980) and J. L. Styan, *Drama, Stage and Audience* (London, 1975). For the more specifically Parisian experience, see J. H. Johnson, *Listening in Paris* (London 1995).

20 Meyerbeer – the doyen and latterly the scapegoat of French grand opera – is credited with fashioning the epic five act (non) drama which characterised the Opéra from the 1830s onwards and particularly in the early years of La Belle Epoch. His themes were characteristically of the school which would later be dubbed the Cecile B de Mille: spectacular, busy and ultimately vacuous.

21   As is hopefully obvious by now, this essay in no way underestimates the importance of the relationship between the stage and the audience. Rather it reserves fuller consideration of it for another time.

22   Take for example, Lady Morgan: "The Roman theatres … are dark, dirty and paltry in their decoration; but what is infinitely worse, they are so offensive to the senses, so disgusting in the details of their arrangement, that to particularize would be impossible: suffice it to say, that the corridors of the Argentino exemplify the nastiness of Roman habits and manners more forcibly than volumes could describe. It is in this *immondezzaio* that one is taught to feel how closely purity in externals is connected with virtue in morals."

See also P. Cambiasi, *La Scala, Note Storiche Statistiche* (Milan 1888).

23   In Italy the provision of a modest amount of anterior space – particularly a saloon on the *piano nobile* – was a commercial as well as a functional necessity. Though relatively small and often notably plain, such rooms generated significant revenue by playing host to the town's gambling fraternity. Up until 1814 generally (1820 in Naples) the gambling concession – profits from which were used to underwrite the opera *per se* – was granted monopolistically for the duration of the season to the impresario who contracted the theatre's operas. Together with the revenue from galas, balls, lotteries and benefit nights, this cash injection was crucial and the loss of the gambling concession after the Restoration was a severe blow to many houses. It led Stendhal amongst others to predict their imminent doom. (see Kimball, *op. cit.*, 419). This rather intimate relationship between opera going and gambling continued outside Italy well into the twentieth century – indeed still does in, for example, Garnier's 'other' opera house in Monaco. In Paris, on the other hand, the anterior spaces needed little or no excuse for their existence beyond their ability to provide an appropriate backdrop for the social antics of the opera's favoured clientele. Being there and being visible was the essence of the enterprise. These prescriptions arguably impacted on Parisian opera in yet more significant ways: there are those who argue that the very form of French Grand Opera in the nineteenth century – five acts with a ballet in the middle – was constructed with the audience's social requirements in mind. A common pattern might be the provision of four generous intervals (some as long as the Acts themselves) and a ballet timed to appear at precisely the moment when the male section of the audience (always the most peripatetic) was present in the theatre between other social engagements. See Fulcher, *op. cit.* for the specifically Parisian resonances and L. Trezzini, *Due Secoli di Vita Musicale* (Bologna 1966) for the Italian case more generally.

24   The theatre in question was the Teatro San Cassiano. Originally a private theatre built by the Tron family at the beginning of the 16th century, it was destroyed by fire in 1629 and reopened as a fee-charging public theatre in 1637. The first opera performed at the re-opening was Mannelli's *Andromeda*. The precedent was rapidly followed and some sixteen other Venetian theatres variously came and went by the mid 17th century. Venice's most famous theatre La Fenice (The Phoenix) arose from the ashes (though not on the same site) of the Teatro San Benedetto destroyed by fire in 1774. The Teatro San Giovanni Grisostemo pictured above was built in 1678 as a private theatre on land owned by Marco Polo. See H. Rosenthall and J. Warrack *The Concise Oxford Dictionary of Opera* (Oxford 1978) 522. A more rarified (though equally plausible) candidate for the first 'horse-shoe' design is the Gran Teatro dei Farnese in the Palazzo della Pilotta in Parma. Inaugurated in 1628 (though built in 1618) for the marriage of Odoardo Farnese to Margherita de' Medici, the arena area below the seats was flooded to a depth of two feet to allow proper representation of the sea battles included in the specially commissioned opera (Monteverdi's now lost *Mercurio e Marte*). Intriguingly, such ancestry would speak to the auditorium's general shape as originating in the need for a not-quite-circular 'fish-tank'. See C. Plantamura, *The Opera Lover's Guide to Europe* (London 1996)

25   Some claim Piermarini invented the opera house's design, though it is clear that he elaborated a more or less traditional design. The Canobbiana actually *opened* a year after La Scala and was in many respects a 'lesser' version of it. Its audience was predominantly middle-class in comparison to the larger house's aristocratic clientele. This theme is explored later. Suffice it to say here that the Canobbiana experienced fluctuating fortunes and after a period of decline was transformed by the publisher Sonzogno (rival to Ricordi and champion of the *verismo* composers) into the Teatro Lirico. It was destroyed by fire in 1938 and quickly rebuilt in its present form.

26 For a detailed description and history of the magnificent theatre in Cremona see E. Santoro, *I Teatri di Cremona* (Cremona 1969-70).

27 It even survived transplantation into the 'democratic' society of late nineteenth-century New York. The Old Metropolitan Opera House (which opened on 22nd October 1883) would have been immediately intelligible to any mid-eighteenth-century Italian. Not only did it follow the general precepts of Piermarini's confection, it took the concept of a favoured second row and created from it 'a diamond horseshoe' of the wealthiest New York dynasties and beatified them all over again. See I. Kolodin, *The Metropolitan Opera House*, (New York 1966) and for a taste of its twentieth-century atmosphere (particularly its repertoire), P. Jackson, *Saturday Afternoons at the Met: The Metropolitan Opera Broadcasts 1931-1950* (Portland 1992).

28 For example, the Concertgebouw in Amsterdam, the Singverein in Vienna, the Conzerthous in Oslo. One notes, ruefully how experimentation with different designs have been notable failures – Avery Fisher Hall in New York, the Philharmonie in Berlin and our own contribution – The Barbican in London.

29 J. S. Mill is generally credited with the design. It has been a source of some fascination to geographers, but it would be too tedious to elaborate.

30 Some seem positively Stanislawskian by eighteenth- and nineteenth-century standards.

31 Quoted in Trezzini, *op. cit.,* 132.

32 At the San Carlo in Naples several of the boxes were fitted with mirrors on the rear wall, so that those who chose to play cards with their backs to the auditorium could still keep in touch with the action from time to time. It should not be imagined, however, that this meant that everything in the theatre was plush. See R. Ajello, *Il Teatro di San Carlo* (Naples 1987). As Antonio Ghislanzoni (later Verdi's librettist for Aida) reported on affairs at La Scala in 1832: "In the boxes of La Scala, during the opera performance, they played tarots and at times had supper. In the great theatre the benches in the stalls were covered with a heavy, yellowish canvass; the stairs were naked of carpets; the stage gloomily illuminated." Quoted in Weaver, *Golden Age*, 111.

33 The boxes depicted illustrate (top row) 'Ladies musical enthusiasm' and 'A bored lion'; (middle row) 'A lady who wants to be seen' and 'Men's box when the prima ballerina is dancing', 'The same when the prima donna is singing'; (bottom row) 'A crèche', 'A well (as in learning)', and 'A conjugal box'.

34 Billinge, *op. cit.*

35 See Ajello, *op. cit.,* 99-103.

36 Quoted in Weaver, *Golden Age*, 11.

37 Rosselli, *Opera Industry*, 42.

38 When the small theatre of Offida was recently restored, progress was considerably impaired by the need to trace and to contact all of the families who still owned individual boxes to seek both their permission and their financial support for the venture. Archivist of the Commune of Offida, *pers. com.* (July, 1999).

39 Control over all aspects of the theatre, from building through administration to censorship of individual works (the last regrettably common in nineteenth-century Italy) was particularly commonplace in the Papal States – see D. Cecchi, *Lo Stato Pontificio nella seconda Restaurazione* (Macerata 1980).

40 For example Barbaja. Domenico Barbaja (or Barbaia) (1778-1841) was born to a humble family in Milan. He began life as a waiter in a coffee/wine shop and later became – under the name Giuseppe Rovani – a novelist. In 1808 he gained the gambling concession at La Scala and subsequently secured the position of impresario at both La Scala and the Teatro alla Canobbiana. By 1809 he was running the San Carlo in Naples to which he lured Rossini whose international career blossomed thereafter. In the 1820s Barbaja extended his financial interests by gaining more or less monopolistic control of the Italian Theatre throughout the Austrian Empire. His mistress was the singer Isabella Colbran – perhaps the most celebrated of all

Rossinian sopranos. On a more general note, in Italy the more successful impresarios often referred to themselves as *commercianti* or *negozianti* (emphasising their role as tradesmen), whilst in Paris, as befitted its more advanced capitalist economy, their equivalent frequently chose the appellation *industriels*. See Berlioz, *Mémoires* (Paris 1870) 378.

41   The changing fortunes of the impresario can be best gauged, by documenting the growing power of the composer. On the whole what was good for the latter was bad for the former. For a measure of the very different contractual arrangements that could be extracted from composers (about which there is a brief note at the end of this paper) see: (for Rossini's contracts) A. Kendall *Giacchino Rossini: Reluctant Hero* (London 1992) 68; C. Osborne *The Bel Canto Operas* (London 1994) 52-61; and especially Rosselli, *op. cit.*, and J. Rosselli, *Singers of Italian Opera* (Cambridge 1992); and (for Verdi's contracts) M. Jane Phillips-Matz, *Verdi* (Oxford 1993) and B. Cagli, Verdi and the business of writing operas, in W. Weaver and M. Chusid (Eds), *The Verdi Companion* (London 1979) 106-120.

42   The internationalising of the market in singers' fees, for example, was a startling feature of the mid nineteenth century. It developed quickly, dramatically increased costs, and stretched the technical resources of the smaller scale impresario to breaking point. It was quickly 'identified' as the real source of the decline of opera as a ubiquitous commodity in Italy in the third quarter of the nineteenth century. See Rosselli, *Music and Musicians* and Rosselli, *Singers*.

43   Though Paris is generally held to be the crucible of *grand opera* – with its epic themes and even more epic proportions – it is interesting that the composition of opera in Paris was, before Bizet, a most un-French affair. Cherubini, Spontini, Paer, Meyerbeer [later Rossini, Donizetti and Verdi] each, in their own way, demonstrated both their mastery of the preferred Parisian idiom and the dependence of the Opéra on foreign imports. Evidently the taste for a more home-grown product only manifest itself at the end of the nineteenth century – coincidentally with the emergence of the national schools in many European countries – with Gounod, Saint-Saëns and Massenet.

44   For a general picture see Fulcher, *op. cit.*, and Heroic and lyric operas in Paris 1776-1875, in C. Headington, R. Westbrook and T. Barfoot, *Opera: A History* (London 1987); J. Harding, Paris: Opera reigns supreme, and J. Pasler, Paris: conflicting notions of progress, in J. Samson (Ed.), *Man and Music: The Late Romantic Era* (London and Basingstoke 1991) 99-123 and 389-416 respectively; P. Bloom, *Music in Paris in the 1830s*, (Quebec 1984); M. Carlson, *The French Stage in the Nineteenth Century* (New York 1972); W. Croston, *French Grand Opera: An Art and a Business* (New York 1948); F. W. J. Hemmings, *Culture and Society in France 1848-1896* (New York 1971) and A. Hervey, *French Music in the Nineteenth Century* (London 1903). F. Brown's, *Theatre and Revolution: The Culture of the French Stage* (New York 1980) is more concerned with drama than opera, but makes a number of relevant observations. For individual theatre histories see: R. Turnbull, *The Opera Gazeteer* (London 1988); O. Meslin, *L'Opéra de Paris* (Paris 1975); and T. J. Walsh, *Second Empire Opera: the Théâtre Lyrique, Paris 1851-70* (London 1981).

45   Calculation of the number of performances and levels of attendance at the Teatro Regio in Parma for the 1843 Carnival season (which witnessed the city's premiere of Verdi's *Nabucco*) suggests that something more than the total population of the city attended (the theatre holds *c*.1500, the population was less than 40,000 and the opera was given 30 times). Allowing for the very young and the very aged who did not attend and, of course, for the fact that many in the audience would have visited the theatre multiple times in the season, it still suggests that – rather like the cinema in the middle years of the last century – the majority of people would have gone to see Verdi's latest – and thus far most popular – offering. See M. Corradi-Cervi, *Il Teatro Reggio* (Parma 1962) 99; and, M. Cornati, Verdi e il Teatro di Parma in *Omaggio al Regio nel 150 Anniversario dell'apertura* (Parma 1979) and for a later production, Saggio di cronologia delle prime rapprazentazioni di Rigoletto, *ISV Bollettino*, (1992) Vol 3: 9.

46   With the single – puzzling – exception of Bologna where the two were reversed. The seasonal aspect of this hierarchy still exists in Italy today with the different *stagioni* [and within a *stagione* different *turni*] charging different admissions prices. Various nights continue to be designated '*popolare*'.

47   There is a significant congruence here between the organisational principles of the theatre and the medieval cityscape as envisioned by J. E. Vance. Certainly, elevation was more important than spatial positioning in the first instance and the occupation of a particular tier granted the same status as occupation of – say – grand apartments on the first floor of an urban house, or above a commercial ground floor in a mixed-use building. Once status was so established, only then did 'geographical' position – within the right 'quarter' as it were – matter.

48   The Opera House in Ascoli Piceno has what at first glance seem curiously immovable stains extending down from the sills of the lower windows (at a height of about seven feet). They are the remains of the grease which was regularly painted on them to prevent spectators clinging to the building and thereby enjoying a free view of the theatre's interior during performance. I am grateful to Dr James Burge of the University of Camerino for this insight. See also A. Mordenti, *Teatro e Societa Nella Storia delle Marche,* in AA.VV., *Il Teatri della Marche* (Ancona 1989).

49   Herein lay a major difference between Italy and France. In many Parisian theatres (particularly those with royal connection) the noblest box was placed not at the apex of the horseshoe, but next to – and often on – the stage (see Figure 13). The model was developed in the court theatre and exported quite widely (even to England). Explanation for this 'variant' lies in the evolution of the opera within the French court. Typically, seventeenth- and eighteenth-century sovereigns would expect to take part in court entertainment and would, naturally wish to be proximate to the performance to facilitate this. Though royal participation had become more vestigial by the late eighteenth century, it was still quite common for favoured members of the court to leave their stage-side boxes during performance, and to wander amongst the cast, admiring their costumes, checking out their looks and tee-ing up later 'entertainment'. Once it became less acceptable to interrupt the action in this way, the nobility still expected an opportunity to get up and dance at some point, hence French opera's continuing flirtation with ballet-masques etc and, in the later nineteenth century, (non-audience participatory) ballet interludes.

      Some Italian theatres also had boxes on stage (*barcaccia*), but they were nowhere near so prestigious as those in France, being most often allotted to musicans.

      See D. Charleton, The nineteenth century: France, in Roger Parker (Ed.), *The Oxford Illustrated History of Opera* (Oxford 1994); J. Drummond, *Opera in Perspective* (London 1980); and Headington, Westbrook and Barfoot, *op. cit.*, Chapter 5.

50   Rosselli, Opera Industry, *op. cit.,* 39.

51   J. Rosselli, 'Italy: the decline of a tradition' in Headington, Westbrook and Barfoot, *op. cit.* 126-150.

52   The date of box conversion varied greatly. Changes tended to take place first in the 'minor' provincial theatres and latest in those prestigious theatres where absolute authorities held control. In Palermo (the Carolino) it took place in the 1830s, in Milan (La Scala) first in the 1850s and later in the 1890s. La Fenice in Venice waited until 1878, despite the fact that a sister theatre, the more commercial San Giovanni Grisostemo had converted as early as 1819. For the last of these we can note, from the *Gazetta Priviligiata di Venezia* of 4 November 1819: "(The proprietors Giovanni Gallo and Luigi Facchini among them have undertaken)… the shrewd contrivance of transforming the topmost row of boxes into a gallery with a separate entrance, in order to facilitate access to the performances for the 'minuto popolo'." A further – and important – aspect of the gallery, apart from the fact that it often enjoyed the best acoustic, was the presence in it of the *claque*, the – sometimes paid – partisans who came to cheer one singer or another, and whose strength and behaviour could make or break an opera.

53   See, for example, W. Weber, *Music and the Middle Class: The Social Structure of Concert Life in London, Paris and Vienna* (London 1975).

54   Naturally this came to different theatres at different times, though the practice of drawing them during performance almost certainly disappeared before they were physically removed. As late as1887 at La Scala a special edition of the *Illustrazione Italiana* was published in celebration of the world premiere of Verdi's *Otello*. In it we read that:

"For any art lover, the sight of Verdi conducting a general rehearsal has something truly awe-inspiring about it. The eye can hardly make out the long rows of empty seats in the vast, dark and empty stalls. The silk curtains of the many boxes are drawn, thus increasing the general air of respectful mystery."

From U. Pesci, Le prove dell'Otello, in *Verdi e l'Otello*, special number of the *Illustrazione Italiana*, February 1887, 40.

55 See for example, B. Beckermann, *The Dynamics of Drama* (New York 1970).

56 The quotation comes from a letter Verdi had written to Giulio Ricordi during preparations for the Italian premiere of Aida in 1871. It follows typically detailed suggestions for various internal re-arrangements of the orchestra. From C. Osborne (Ed.), *Letters of Giusseppe Verdi* (London 1971) 178-9.

57 Anti Rossini – or rather pro-Paisiello factions – had determined that it would not replace the older composer's version of the same basic story and of the same name. See A. Kendall, *Gioacchino Rossini* (London 1992).

58 In Paris the opera, which was subject to several last minute revisions because of its length, received 270 rehearsals from August 1866 until the premiere on 11 March 1867. See J. Budden, *The Operas of Verdi* (London 1978) Vol 3 Chapter 1.

59 Quoted in M. Chusid, Verdi's own words, in W. Weaver and M. Chiusid, *op. cit.,* 150. See also F. Walker, *The Man Verdi* (Chicago 1982).

60 *Ibid,* 175-6. "Here (in Genoa) in the orchestra they have placed all the double basses in one mass, like sheep; and the result is deplorable beyond belief. I will put it this way, when the double basses encircle the entire orchestra, with their dark sound they cover, or at least smother in part, the piercing sonority of the brass and the bad intonation of the woodwinds. And the sonority in the loud (passages) comes out full and imposing. Like this (i.e. as in Genoa) it is piercing and empty. Further in the passages where the string section alone dominates, half the spectators hear only an indistinct buzzing, and the other half hears too much." To Giulio Ricordi in 1868 re the Genoa production of Don Carlos, *ibid.,* 153.

61 It is probably both unfair and inaccurate to characterise an Italian composer at the beginning of the *ottocento* or even the late *settocento* as a 'court' servant in the manner of say of Haydn at Esterhazy, or the young Mozart in Salzburg. He might be better described as a *libero professionista*, taking his commission at the start of the *ottocento* from a ruler (whose court might as easily be in Spain, Prussia or Russia as in Italy) and at its end from a commercial music publisher (typically the Casa Ricordi or Casa Sonzogno). One or two composers – exceptionally – achieved a higher status and, in consequence, enjoyed a more privileged (i.e. more independent) position. Rossini in Naples was one such, Bellini in Milan another. It was Rossini, in *Elisabetta Re d'Inglettera*, who (eventually) cut the wings of his singers and made them sing more or less what he wanted; Bellini's singers, several of them the same ones, also fell into line. It was left to Verdi, however, to wrest decisive artistic control over the production of his work from the hands of the singer/conductor/impressario. The secret in each case was a degree of independent or accumulated wealth.

62 To Francesco Florimo 4 January 1871, in Osborne, *op. cit.,* 167.

Chapter Eight

PROSTITUTIONAL SPACE IN THE NINETEENTH-CENTURY EUROPEAN CITY

PHILIP HOWELL

Introduction

Whilst historians, social scientists, social theorists, literary scholars, sex radicals and many others have come to place the relationship between cities and sex under close scrutiny, geographers have been remarkably reticent in this area until very recently.[1] And although a number of geographers, inspired in the main by feminism and queer theory, have begun the analysis of a series of geographies of sexuality, there is still a dearth of historical work on which to draw.[2] This is all the more surprising perhaps given the massive proliferation of work on the history of sexuality, much of which speaks to and through an analytics of space, most particularly in the urban context, and to which historical geographers might be expected to fruitfully contribute. It is towards establishing this kind of collaborative understanding of the historical geography of sexuality that this chapter is directed.

Specifically, I want here to develop a geographical understanding of the phenomenon of prostitution in the nineteenth-century European city, and then to speak to the construction of urban sexualities in the modern age more generally. I take the historian Alain Corbin's felicitous but opaque phrasing – "prostitutional space" – as a point of departure for this enquiry, and I proceed by examining what this characterisation might mean in the historical context under discussion.[3] The construction of geographies of commercial sexuality may then be used to inform our understanding of the historical geography of sexuality itself. Here, again, however, the absences in geographical work, and its limitations, must be frankly admitted: there has been in fact "a general silence on geographies of commercial sex-work in the urban West".[4] Given the marginality, vulnerability, and scapegoating of sex workers, it might be thought that geographies of prostitutional activity would figure prominently in attempts to understand the processes of social exclusion, but discussion by geographers has been largely limited to attempts to describe what we might think of as the *geography of prostitution*: that is, a mapping of prostitutional activity with little attempt to understand the complex spatialities in which prostitutional discourses and practices are embedded.[5] With honourable exceptions, research on the urban geography of prostitution remains notably undeveloped, all the more so given the longevity of misleading ecological understandings of urban 'vice areas' derived from the work of the Chicago School, and an uncritical acceptance of consumer models of sexual behaviour.[6]

I try here by contrast to develop a cultural geographical framework for understanding the meaning of prostitutional activity in the modern European city, by examining (with a low bow to Henri Lefebvre) what I will call 'the production of prostitutional space', a conception which may be used in contradistinction to any approach for which the spatialities of prostitution are taken to be merely incidental or secondary.[7] Here, just as we may say that the production of space is "an essential moment in the production and reproduction of social life", it is argued that the production of prostitutional space is a necessary element in the nature and meaning of commercial sexuality.[8] It is an argument which views the spatiality of prostitutional activity as essential both to its discursive definition and in the policies directed at the problems such activity is perceived to bring – policies which are summed up here by the key word 'regulation'. 'Regulation' is used in two ways: in a loose sense simply referring to the categorisation and control of 'deviant' sexuality; but in a specific sense, to the toleration of prostitutional activity and the strategies used to minimise the problems associated with it. This latter approach, which its supporters invariably characterised as modern, humane and tolerant, accepts the inevitability of prostitutional activity, and seeks, instead of repressing prostitution, to mitigate its most harmful aspects.[9] Its analyses led in the nineteenth century to the registration, medical inspection, and incarceration of female sex-workers, as well as to a system of officially tolerated, licensed, and inspected brothels. Space is critically implicated in the regulation of prostitution in both these senses, and we can recognise that prostitutional space is constructed as both precondition and product of the development of commercial sex work in the modern European city.

But this characterisation, like Lefebvre's general analysis of the production of space, is not without its problems, which are discussed below, in conjunction with similar problems involved in using a Foucauldian thematic. However, in a situation where the geography of sexuality is undertheorised, these problems may themselves be instructive, especially where historical contextualisation and periodisation is concerned. The familiar cliché has it that prostitution is the 'oldest profession' but in the policies directed to the problems such activity is thought to bring it has been understood as distinctly modern and urban; and I follow Carole Pateman and others in claiming the cultural and historical particularity of the modern prostitutional economy.[10] But the relationship between modernity and prostitutional space, the benefits of an historicist understanding notwithstanding, needs further scrutiny. And, ultimately, I want to insist on a more complex historical geography, dependent on a series of different spatialities.

The geography of prostitution

Discussion by geographers of phenomena associated with commercial sex work can with few exceptions be summed up in the phrase 'the geography of prostitution': contemporary and historical geographers have mapped the spaces of prostitutional activity, focusing mainly on street prostitution, and concentrating on the urban ecology of vice areas, red-light districts and toleration zones.[11] The more sophisticated discussions have insisted on the role of legislation and policing in producing the spatial patterns of urban sex work, seeing in the concentration of prostitutional activity in certain designated districts the geopolitics of regulation and containment.[12] And geographers have thus linked the production of deviant bodies, identities and sexualities with prostitutes' simultaneous visibility and marginalisation in the most socially-disadvantaged areas of Western cities. The dominant tropes remain, however, those of urban ecology and economic geography, with their somewhat under-theorised analytics of power. Particularly troubling in this regard is the dependence of much of this literature on a consumer-orientated model characteristic of mainstream economic geography. Symanski's discussion of Nevada's ranch-brothels, for instance, takes the entrepreneurial model of supply and demand as read, with the legal and semi-legal regulation of prostitution only contributing in a secondary sense to prostitutional geography.[13] Ashworth et al., similarly, interpret the red-light district, and the distribution of prostitutional activity in Western European cities in general, as the outcome of controls, namely accessibility, opportunity and constraint, without questioning the priority of the market function for sexual services.[14] Winchester and White have also attributed the concentration of street prostitutes in British inner cities to a localised, economically-marginal market for sexual services.[15] In effect, this literature, preoccupied as it is by locational analysis and urban ecology, employs a contractarian model of commercial sexual services, ignoring the fact that regulation articulates prostitution as marginalised sexuality and isolates it from the status of work, and leaving the relationships between state and society, space and sexuality almost entirely opaque.[16]

Generally lacking in this respect is a proper acknowledgement by studies of prostitution in the discipline of geography of the importance of the regulation of prostitution by both state *and* society. Whilst Ashworth *et al* do concede the "vast array of cultural, locational and institutional controls" on the location of areas of urban prostitution, and Symanski the importance of legal and semi-legal regulations, none insist on the role of state and society in the very constitution of prostitution and its perceived problems – ignoring the fact that law and police (and other agencies) may be mechanisms of sociocultural production as much as of repression.[17] Spatial regulation is in these analyses effectively a secondary element and the geography of prostitution limited to an understanding of how the spatial distribution of prostitutional activity is constrained by legal or quasi-legal ordinances. To give another example of this, we can cite Shumsky and Springer's historical analysis of San Francisco's zone of prostitution, in which whilst "the indisputable relationship between the changing spatial distribution of prostitution and legal development" is demonstrated, this is done by no more than mapping out the effects of rounds of regulatory activity on urban space.[18] Recent work has demonstrated the determining influence of police and legislative activity on the spatiality of sex-work, but there has yet been little attempt to integrate these findings within a wider problematic: there is little recognition for instance that the law is only one institution contributing to the spatiality of sex-work, or that its relationship to other institutions may be contradictory or subservient. As Philippa Levine has recently pointed out in a review of social historians' discussions of sex-work:

> *The law functioned as a powerful means of defining deviance and asserting control, but was enhanced by parallel assaults from its institutional kin, the medical profession, and the church, social work – whom we might usefully see as "filters" of the law. What they all shared was a perspective derived from implicit assumptions that prostitution though deplorable when practised publicly, was "inevitable" and thus an object requiring continual political governance.... Controlling prostitution meant controlling women, because women, defined by their sexuality, threatened disorder and unruliness.[19]*

These examples hardly exhaust the literature on the subject, but they will serve to indicate the largely uncritical acceptance of consumption and contractarian models in interpreting the distribution of prostitutional activity in the Western city. None properly theorise sex work, and none evidence the sophistication brought to the phenomenon of prostitution by researchers outside the discipline of geography. Historians of gender and sexuality, for instance, have understood the geography of prostitution in ways that go well beyond simple supply and demand models. American historians have demonstrated, for instance, that whilst the changing geography of prostitution in New York City in the nineteenth and early twentieth centuries was indeed related to the wholesale commercialization of the sex industry this cannot be abstracted from the commercial transformation of urban space and real estate, from the flourishing of a bachelor subculture, from the entrepreneurial agency of prostitute women themselves, and from ethnic and racial intermingling.[20] Others have discussed the dependence of the modern Western model of sexuality itself on a historically-particular consumerist paradigm, so that the sexual consumer himself cannot be essentialised and naturalised as a given.[21]

As Phil Hubbard has recently pointed out in criticism, the location of prostitutional activity "cannot be comprehended solely through an appreciation of supply and demand relationships, but requires a broader comprehension of how, as a criminalised activity at variance with the prevailing moral order, it is subject to specific legal and quasi-legal regulations which generally limit it to specific areas of (limited) tolerance".[22] It is vitally important to insist on the role of regulation, and this in a definition which goes beyond statute law and policing initiatives: and historians of gender and sexuality have linked the spaces of prostitutional activity to policies of regulation and tolerance in just this way. This spatial regulation extends not only to the official or unofficial toleration of prostitutional spaces, but also to the discursive definition of what is understood by prostitution itself. Regulation – and I use the word in its loosest sense here as the defining of deviant behaviour and the assertion of control – actively constructs the prostitute and prostitution, before proffering solutions to the problems they are perceived to foster. And this is a spatial regulation, both in the sense that prostitution is typically perceived as a public identity and a public problem, in the emphasis on streetwalking and soliciting, and in the policies directed at sex-work, such as the concentration of sex-work in tolerated zones and its domestication in regulated private spaces. Geography thus enters into both the definition of the problem and the policy solution: spatial regulation, in one sense, can act as a marker for both the discursive work of definition, and the specific policies addressed to the defined problem. Or, to invoke Lefebvre: "The state and each of its constituent institutions call for spaces – but spaces which they can then organize according to their specific requirements; so there is no sense in which space can be treated solely as an *a priori* condition of these institutions and the state which presides over them".[23]

The production of prostitutional space

Mapping the geography of prostitution, then, is not enough: such a project is unable to understand prostitution and sexuality in an historicist rather than an essentialist manner, or to appreciate fully the various ways in which regulatory regimes produce the geographies of sex-work, or to examine the interrelationships between commercial sexuality and social power. A rather different theoretical conception, better placed to accomplish these aims, may be taken from the work of Henri Lefebvre, and from his seminal work, *The Production of Space*.[24] What has appealed to geographers about Lefebvre's conception of space is its multi-dimensional, social constructionist, and historicist approach to spatial practices; and the surge of interest in Lefebvrian thematics in recent years has coincided with and contributed to a compellingly respatialized social theory.[25] Lefebvrian conceptions, for all their ambiguities and contradictions, have been a vital resource for a geography which has sought to combat the essentialising and naturalising of space: precisely the problem I think with much of the geographical work on sexuality and the city. I want to argue here, albeit briefly and sketchily, that Lefebvre's analytical distinctions help to make sense of the discursive and practical spatialities of prostitution, emphasising the historical and geographical nature of regulatory regimes, and tracing the interrelationships between commercial sexuality and the various forms of power operating within modern societies.

Lefebvre's understanding of the production of space operates via a now well-known triad of concepts, distinguishing between what he terms 'spatial practices', 'representations of space', and 'spaces of representation', these amounting to a spatialised dialectic with the capacity to trace the interaction between spatial arrangements and social order.[26] In the simplest terms, Lefebvre's first conception refers to the social practices, perceived through a "common-sense" form of understanding, which are "embodied in the modalities through which human beings live in space and produce and reproduce themselves within it": spatial practices involve the everyday routines of daily life and the spatially-differentiated urban environments we inhabit.[27] Such spatial practices would then encompass (though the interlinkages are not typically perceived) the reproduction of the social relations of production, including gender relations and the reproduction of the labour force.[28] The concept of 'representations of space' refers to the conceptions, knowledges, and ideologies of space that are linked to productive relations. Lefebvre is thinking here of the technocratically-conceptualized space of scientists, planners, urbanists and social engineers, as these are linked crucially to the work of ideology and the deployment of knowledge and power throughout society. This is conceived space, as opposed to the perceived space of spatial practices. The final element in this dialectic of spatial terms is 'spaces of representation', by which Lefebvre wishes to characterise the lived environments, symbolic and semiotic, through which space is actually experienced: characteristically, this lived space may contribute to the resistance and challenging of authority as much as coincide with the latter's interests. As Rob Shields points out, included in this last category are "clandestine and underground spatial practices, which suggest and prompt alternative (revolutionary) restructurings of institutionalised discourses of space and new modes of spatial *praxis*, such as that of squatters, illegal aliens, and Third World slum dwellers, who fashion a spatial presence and practice outside the norms of the prevailing (enforced) social spatialisation".[29]

It is not too difficult to see how the production of prostitutional space may be thought of in this way. Prostitutional space, in this sense, cannot be a distinct and unitary space, but should be taken to refer to: the spatial practices from which prostitutional activity is inseparable and through which it is perceived; the conceptual understanding and regulation of prostitutional activity by experts and social engineers; and the various forms of cultural mediation by and through which prostitution is represented and apprehended. The first understanding would necessarily be directed at the role of prostitutional activity within society, its relationship to the sanctioned procreativity of 'normal' sexuality and its role in the reproduction of the social relations of production. The strong, and critical, understanding of sex-work as a particular form of *labour*, within modes and regimes of productive activity, may be thought of in this way. The connections between productive bodies and capitalism, for instance, traceable at least as far as Engels, have long been a fruitful area of research. Most forcefully, perhaps, Luise White's analysis of prostitutional activity in colonial Nairobi has emphasised the role of colonial capitalism in promoting the proliferation of forms of sex-work.[30] And that this role is inseparable from spatial practices is made clear from White's insistence that the question of *where* prostitutes work is critical to its interpretation: simply put, "work performed one way in one place can have the opposite meaning in another place".[31] For White, in a persuasive and forceful argument, prostitutional activities are necessarily, not incidentally, spatial practices, and cannot be understood without a wider understanding of the contribution sex-work makes to the production and reproduction of labour power:

If prostitution is one of the forms domestic labor takes, then where it takes place merely describes the site of the reproduction of male labor power. Whether a woman is on the street or in her own room reflects her access to housing. The conduct of prostitution is determined by where the work takes place, not by a woman's personality, culture, or insecurities. The site of reproduction determines the form of a woman's prostitution.[32]

To jump to Lefebvre's third conception, 'spaces of representation', it is necessary to emphasise the cultural mediations through which the lived experience of space is embedded, and our attention may be directed to the ways in which prostitutional activity has been interpreted and mythologised as part of an aestheticised social imaginary. In nineteenth-century France, for example, prostitution and its spaces were metaphorically and metonymically linked to the worlds of art and literature, such that commercial sexuality could not but be apprehended through aesthetic and cultural filters.[33] But to underscore the equally important role of 'spaces of representation' in challenging orthodox and conventional representational work, Shannon Bell has recently discussed the role of prostitute performance artists in subverting the representations of prostitutes (and other sex-workers) and prostitutional space, contributing to what has been labelled 'prostitute space', or even, because of its metaphoric or metonymic connection with other stigmatized sexualities, 'pervert space'.[34] It should also be noted that "While forcing prostitutes into well-defined geographic areas has served as a public marker of their difference, it has also encouraged the proximity necessary for political organizing".[35]

But it is the second spatial term that is perhaps most resonant for the history of prostitutional space: for 'representations of space' which foreground the scientific, technocratic, and regulatory ambitions of modern society have an obvious and urgent applicability to the understanding of commercial sexuality. The meaning of 'prostitution' itself can hardly be divorced from the discursive power of systems of knowledge that have been directed at prostitutional activity and what are taken to be its distinctive problems, and from the practical policies that have followed from this ideological work. 'Regulation', or the official tolerance of prostitution, involving the registration, surveillance, and medical inspection of prostitutes, follows the contours of Lefebvre's 'representations of space' very closely, not surprisingly given that the dominant conception of prostitution throughout Europe was that of a pioneering social science aiming to establish its epistemological authority over what it would come to perceive as the 'social evil'. This conceptual form of prostitutional space is most famously associated with the work of the French theorist, social investigator, and 'enquêteur de terrain', Alexandre Parent-Duchâtelet – the Linnaeus of prostitution and the Newton of harlotry.[36]

Parent-Duchâtelet's great enquiry, *De la Prostitution dans la Ville de Paris* (1836) was the single most important, virtually definitive, text on prostitution in the nineteenth century, and exercised a continent-wide influence on social policy. Regulation or toleration of prostitution, the most distinctive disciplinary measure in Europe in the nineteenth century, takes its cue from Parent-Duchâtelet's pioneering analyses. Parent-Duchâtelet's concern with social hygiene and medical prophylaxis led him to treat prostitution as a necessary evil, "an indispensable excremental phenomenon that protects the social body from disease": something that could not be repressed, but which could be regulated in the service of state and society:

> *La prostitution existe et existera toujours dans les grandes villes, parce que, comme la mendicité, comme le jeu, c'est une industrie et une ressource contre la faim, on pourrait même dire contre le déshonneur; car à quel excès ne peut pas se livrer un individu privé de toute ressource et qui voit son existence compromise; cette ressource est, il est vrai, celle de la bassesse, mais elle n'en existe pas moins.*[37]

As many have now noted, regulation was most distinctively a spatial strategy, based on the creation of enclosed milieux which could be effectively supervised, to prevent the disturbing excesses of prostitutional activity (streetwalking, intrusive soliciting, disorderly behaviour, public obscenity and so on) and to control through regular medical inspection the terrible ravages of venereal disease.[38] As Corbin puts it, "The first task of regulation is to bring the prostitute out of the foul darkness and rescue her from the clandestine swarming of vice, in order to drive her back into an enclosed space, under the purifying light of power".[39] And reducing regulation to its essentials – the identification of prostitutes by compulsory registration with the authorities, medical inspection, and incarceration if unregistered, recalcitrant, or in a state of contagiousness – this strategy is recognisably a theory and practice of space, a veritable prophylactic geography. It meshes well in fact with the disciplinary ambitions of modernity described by Michel Foucault; but Lefebvre also insists on the ways in which the state uses space in this way for purposes of control, to produce "an administratively controlled and even policed space".[40] Dominating prostitution policy in nineteenth-century Europe, regulationism set in place a system by which the state sponsored definitions of normative patterns of gendered behaviour; and the link between the state and the control of prostitution has figured strongly in the historiography of modern regulation of prostitution. A Foucauldian interpretation of the historical geography of prostitution follows quite naturally: in discussing the Victorian Contagious Diseases Acts in England and Ireland, for instance, Judith

Walkowitz has pointed to the operation of both a technology of power and a structure of confinement that characterise Foucault's discussion of modern disciplinary processes.[41] This 'political geography of containment' is exemplified not just by the carceral institutions put in place by a range of authorities: the enclosed world of regulation refers too to the panoptic surveillance of registered prostitutes, and indeed, at a certain level, of all women's behaviour. In this sense we can see the production of prostitutional space in the service of the state and disciplinary society.[42]

But the secular, scientific, and 'pragmatic' stance adopted by proponents of regulation takes its cue from the epistemological violence effected by the original discourse on space: the ambition, as Corbin puts it, was "to enclose in order to observe, to observe in order to know, to know in order to supervise and control".[43] Such a dominant 'representation of space' was "so powerful, indeed, so often repeated that, in addition to distorting the vision of later researchers ... it probably determined to some extent the behavior of the prostitutes themselves".[44] Parent-Duchâtelet's emphasis on the location, visibility and spatial relationships of prostitutional activities is entirely characteristic of the truth about prostitution produced in the nineteenth-century enquiries: and Paris, the centre of French prostitutional space, is subject, emblematically, to a quite comprehensive spatial classification by Parent-Duchâtelet (Figure 1).[45]

The regulation of prostitution is therefore clearly identifiable as a classic example of Lefebvre's 'representations of space'. But, and it is worth emphasising Parent-Duchâtelet's historicism here, as well as Lefebvre's, this element of the production of space is taken in Lefebvre's work to be *historically* destined to become the dominant form of social space, as spatial practices and spaces of representation recede ever further in importance. Modern social space is occupied or colonized by what Lefebvre calls abstract space, which is, in fact, the distinctively modern form of '(social) space', appearing at about the time of the French Revolution.[46] Measurement, exchange, and calculation are foregrounded at the expense of the real, the corporeal, the immediate and the qualitative. This abstract space is excessively mediated by representations of space and insufficiently permeated by spaces of representation and spatial practice.[47] It is marked by the influence of commodification and bureaucratisation, and by geometric, optic, and phallic determinants. And it lends itself, via its contribution to norms and normalisation, and via its reformulation of the relationship between individuals and the modern state, to modern disciplinary power.[48]

Again, it is not hard to trace in the production of prostitutional space this historical spatialisation, especially when to modernity is added the inseparable sphere of the urban, and furthermore once Lefebvre's concern with masculinity,

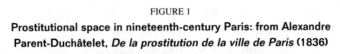

FIGURE 1

**Prostitutional space in nineteenth-century Paris: from Alexandre
Parent-Duchâtelet, *De la prostitution de la ville de Paris* (1836)**

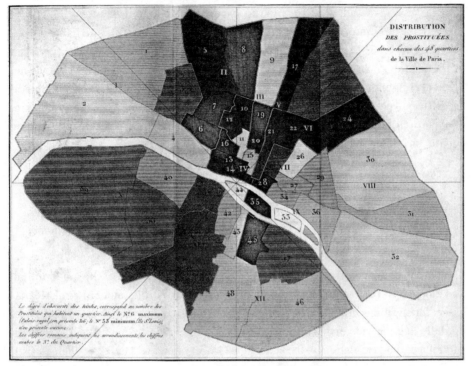

gender and sexuality are factored in. In the first place, the regulation of sexuality is
as apparently a modern phenomenon as the hegemony of abstract space. As Shannon
Bell argues,

> *Although different sexual populations have existed in all historical periods, it
> wasn't until the Victorian period that they were systematically marked and
> identified; mapped like a geographical terrain. Scientific knowledge produced
> sexual/social identities, such as the prostitute, through regulation, surveillance,
> and the labeling of human activity.*[49]

And the great concern with prostitution as a social problem stems from the modern
concern with productive and docile bodies, when sexual morality was yoked to the
economic destiny of nations.[50] Accordingly, regulationism, that most distinctive
response to dangerous sexualities, has been seen as a product of the nineteenth century,
fitting well with Lefebvre's chronology of abstract space.

Secondly, it is worth restating the direction of regulationism towards urban prostitutional activity. It is not simply that "The existence of prostitution as a social phenomenon was... confined to urban societies"; it is rather that the modern city acted as "an open-ended provocation to government", such that we can identify at the particular historical moment in question "a specifically urban 'will to government'".[51] The city demanded "the development, administration and enforcement of forms of quarantine and regulation", and the expertise both in social hygiene and medical regulation, so clearly conjoined in Parent-Duchâtelet's work, is undoubtedly an urban phenomenon.[52] The regulation of prostitution amounts to exactly this kind of expertise of the city, in which prostitutes, as characteristic urban subjects, become equally characteristic objects of urban governance:

> *Observations of these immoral subjects inscribed in a plethora of pamphlets, programmes, demands, solutions, tracts, scientific investigations, bureaucratic documentation, commissions of enquire, medical reports, and the like focused upon the dangers that life in towns posed the moral and physical constitution of subjects ... The city was a machine for the production of vile sensations.[53]*

Finally, the phallocentrism identified by Lefebvre in the regime of the modern finds its analogue in the regulation of commercial sex-work in the modern era. Abstract space, for one thing, eroticises leisure spaces and pleasure districts, such as the licensed bordello and the vice district, these at the same time coming under the "systematic surveillance and regulation by the state" that Gregory notes as a defining characteristic of abstract space.[54] Leisure and pleasure are of course masculinised, though, by a double standard in which male sexual license was endorsed as natural whilst women's dangerous sexuality was pathologised. And whilst the double standard is ancient, its nineteenth-century manifestation endorses a distinctively modern gender ideology grounded in the distinction between public and private spheres. Prostitutes, as 'public women', challenged the attempt to naturalise socio-sexual roles via the cult of separate spheres, forfeiting their rights to privacy because of their refusal to relinquish a public persona. And their ambiguous occupation of space encouraged and legitimated the modern interventionary state, as Levine has argued for Britain under the Contagious Diseases Acts:

> *Not only did the acts define dangerous districts through the mapping of scheduled jurisdictions (thus delimiting the geography of prostitution) and realize the threat of incarceration (in either hospital or jail), but they further signalled the acceptability of rendering a prostitute's actual body beyond her control. The literal penetration of the body – by client or by medical officer – acquired state*

sanction as did the penetration of her environment through scheduling and policing.[55]

If we follow Lefebvre's discussion of the production of space, then, we have not only the resources for understanding the spatialities of prostitution, but also their historical transformation. Lefebvre's analysis of abstract space in particular compellingly suggests the modernity of these European attempts to regulate prostitution and sexuality, the inseparability of urbanism from this historical geography, and the gendered determinants of this modernity.[56]

The historical geography of prostitutional space

So far I have suggested that Lefebvre's general analysis offers a useful foundation for understanding the geography of commercial sexuality: thinking about the production of prostitutional space alerts us to prostitution's historical spatialisation, its subordination to the spatial discourses and strategies of regulatory regimes, and its diffuse interpenetration with and superimposition on social space. There are, however, some clear and instructive failings with Lefebvre's analysis, with respect to the historical geography of commercial sexuality in modern Europe, and which are inseparable from the general difficulties that beset Lefebvre's work. It is certainly true, for instance, that Lefebvre's break with gendered analyses reliant on essentialised dichotomies of masculinity and femininity is incomplete: and in an area such as the geography of sexuality such a failing seriously vitiates his analysis.[57] And there must be difficulties too in differentiating between Lefebvre's taxonomic terms, especially given problems of overdetermination and abstraction. But I want to concentrate on one key failing here, which is the nature of Lefebvre's historicism. For whilst committed to an historical spatialisation, his history of space is rightly seen as deeply flawed: a linear periodisation of successive epochs, Lefebvre's analysis is Eurocentric, developmentalist, simplistic, and totalising. It does not amount to a very secure historical geography.

Lefebvre's historical typology certainly cannot serve as a straightforward guide to the historical geography of prostitutional space. For one thing, his paradoxical emphasis on chronology over geography must be treated with great caution. The trajectory of European regulation has for instance a distinctive geography as well as a history, and it is worth rehearsing this briefly here. The importance of France, the home country of regulationism, has already been fulsomely acknowledged. Parent-Duchâtelet's great achievement was to systematise an already existing toleration of prostitution, not to invent it. In France, the Revolution had abolished the ancient regulations relative to prostitution only for a new register of prostitutes, with physicians empowered to examine women, instituted in 1796; and under Napoleon prostitutes became a distinct caste under police control, located in a prescribed quarter of the city.[58] France was long understood as the home country of regulation, its most advanced and systematic proponent, and it was for a century or more at the forefront of the European approach to prostitution and its problems. This was an approach that in the second half of the nineteenth century spread to a number of cities in countries as diverse as Germany, Russia, Italy, and Switzerland: Europe followed it seems where France had shown the way.

In parts of Germany, such as the notable town of Hamburg, for instance, regulation of prostitution dated to the Napoleonic invasion; in some cases, however, regulation can be traced to the eighteenth century or earlier, Berlin having a system of regulation in 1792, under stricter control than in France.[59] Germany's regulation of prostitution traced a familiar European pattern of abolition and renewal, with licensed brothels closed in 1846, reopened in 1851, and closed again in 1856. This see-sawing between regulation and abolition was indeed common, but the commitment of virtually all the European regimes to some form of regulationism has nevertheless been well-established. In Italy, the Cavour government of the new Italian state instituted regulationist policies in 1860, as part of a self-consciously 'modern' strategy of governance, and although repealed in 1880 these were reinstituted in 1891 until its final demise, as in France, in the middle of the twentieth century.[60] And in Russia the Tsarist Ministry of Internal Affairs began to regulate commercial sex in the empire in 1843, once again revealing "the enduring power of the state" as the author and executor of regulation.[61] It is tempting therefore to posit a general regulationist movement, principally from France, through which the continent was converted, to a greater or lesser degree, to the toleration and regulation of prostitution. Most European cities adopted similar systems, and apart from Norway in 1890 no country followed the British repeal of prostitution ordinances in 1886. Britain stands out, in fact, from the European background, for the strength of its opposition to the philosophy and practice of regulation.[62] Apart from the brief reign and limited geography of the Contagious Diseases Acts (1864-1886), there is no real comparison to continental regulationism.

This is too simple a view of Europe's regulation of sexuality, however. For one thing, though France's claim to the title of home country of regulation is secure, it is necessary to establish that regulation was a policy deeply implicated in the *colonial* histories of European regimes. Britain's opposition to regulationism, for instance, looks rather shakier when we consider that the regulation of prostitution was in force in its colonial territories – such as India, Hong Kong, Malta, Gibraltar, and the Ionian Islands – long before the brief reign of the Contagious Diseases Acts.[63] The production of prostitutional space in Europe cannot therefore be delinked from racial and imperial spatialities, and Lefebvre's Eurocentric assumptions are clearly particularly unhelpful here. Historians have also shown how regulationist policies survived the demise of the Contagious Diseases Acts in 1886, not just in the colonies, but also at home, so that, as Philippa Levine rightly points out, we should not be too quick to assume that the Acts mark a significant historical watershed.[64] It is all too easy to make too much of this British commitment to liberalism at the expense of discipline, for quasi-regulationist policies existed outside the scheduled districts of the Contagious Diseases Acts and continued long after the repeal of the Acts in 1886.[65]

Nor, furthermore, should we be too quick to identify the regulation of prostitution with *modernity*. Even in France, as Jill Harsin points out, the broad outlines were established long before the 19th century.[66] And Parent-Dûchatelet himself noted that the principles of regulation might be traced to the era of Charlemagne, or to ancient Rome: "Ces notions historiques ... monstrent l'importance que l'on a de tout temps attaché a l'enregistrement des prostituées, et qu'on l'a toujours considéré comme le premier moyen d'arrêter le désordre inévitable de la prostitution".[67] The developmentalist tendencies of Lefebvre's historical typologies encourage us to understand the regulation of sexuality as a distinctively modern phenomenon, but the historical record shows us that the continuities with classical, medieval and early modern regimes are striking. Parent-Duchâtelet's metaphoric transposition of prostitutional and excremental hygiene is, for instance, as Corbin points out, in the purest Augustinian tradition: St Augustine's admonitions might readily be transposed with Parent-Duchâtelet's:

If you expel prostitutes from society, prostitution will spread everywhere ... the prostitutes in town are like sewers in a palace. If you take away the sewers, the whole palace will be filthy.[68]

These Christian apologetics fed the double standard just as surely in the middle ages as in the modern, with a system of municipally-owned or licensed brothels in a number of towns in Germany, France, Italy and Spain (Florence, Dijon, Nuremberg, Munich, Venice, Augsburg, Seville, for instance). Others (like Paris and Cologne) had a formally condoned prostitutional economy in certain geographical areas.[69] In England, in a quite striking parallel with the modern age, officially operated brothels were far less common, and except for three towns (Sandwich, Southampton, and Southwark) with local conditions – sailors in the first two towns, a tradition of brothels outside the jurisdiction of the city for the latter – "toleration tended to be unofficial and prostitution seems to have operated on a more casual basis".[70] Notwithstanding this, however, the general European tradition of toleration, with prostitutes simultaneously coded as central and marginal, survived into the early sixteenth century at which time the Reformation and Counterreformation ushered in a new era of intolerance.[71] We know far less about the intervening centuries, but the longevity, in a university town like Cambridge, say, of medieval and early modern regulationist statutes, so that the old systems could be revived from the beginning of the nineteenth century, suggests once more that the close association between regulation and modernity be at the least qualified.[72]

None of this invalidates an historicist approach to the geography of prostitution, of course, but it does suggest that we proceed by some other means than Lefebvre's historical typologies. Such difficulties are faced not only by theorists like Lefebvre, but also by Foucault, whose otherwise very useful theorisations are vulnerable to the same kinds of criticism. Foucault's occasionally overly schematic periodisations threaten to weaken his wider analytics of power. Laura Engelstein's salutary discussion of fin-de-siècle Russia, for instance, demonstrates how an awareness of that country's 'combined underdevelopment' complicates the schematic distinctions associated with Foucauldian analyses.[73] In pre-Revolutionary Russia the superimposition of the elements of law and sovereign power, the administrative policing of the *Polizeistaat*, and 'modern' disciplinary regimes, suggests that the temporalities identified by Foucault may be just as securely spatialisable, with all the complexities this suggests for the relationship of state to society.[74]

If we are to properly historicise the regulation of prostitution, therefore, or to put it another way to think through a dialectic of the history of prostitutional space, we would be best to readily accept its uneven geography and the dependence of regulatory regimes on particular political, social, economic and cultural developments. And the historical geography of this prostitutional space is something which clearly needs a great deal of further work. This is not the only area of our ignorance, it ought to be quickly admitted. We know too little about the regulation of sexuality by society rather than by the state, or by private agencies rather than public bodies.[75] Nor should repression and regulation be taken to be absolute polar opposites, for regulation and criminal sanctions could and did work hand in hand.[76] Nevertheless, as far as this chapter is concerned, it is the question of the spaces of prostitution that is crucial: and here the conclusions of Miles Ogborn's recent study of the spaces of modernity should be endorsed. That is, that whilst Lefebvre's commitment to understanding the production of space is salutary, his notion of abstract space is too broad to capture the differentiated and contextualised geographies of modernity. In the context of this essay, the production of prostitutional space needs to be understood geographically as well as historically, through complex and uneven spatialities, differentiated and heterotopic spaces, for which an overly schematic conception of modernity is inappropriate.[77]

Conclusion

I have argued in this chapter for a more aggressively spatialised understanding of the nature and meaning of commercial sexuality in modern Europe. Rather than simply map the geographies of prostitutional activity, even with a nod to the importance of legal and police regulation in producing that geography, I have advocated a focus on 'prostitutional space', and attempted to understand this in Lefebvrian terms. The production of prostitutional space can then be examined historically and geographically, and its relationship to the city and to modernity and to gender cultures can then be analysed. Here, the dominance of 'representations of space' that Lefebvre recognises as a hallmark of modernity and its promotion of 'abstract space' finds its analogue in the nineteenth-century hegemony of social scientific conceptions of prostitutional space and the associated spatial strategies of regulationist regimes. Both discursively and practically, prostitutional space was *produced*, in the service of an interventionist and disciplinary state: and these geographies of commercial sexuality may thus be linked to the wider thematics and mechanics of power in the modern European city. But, as I have cautioned here, the historical geography of the regulation of prostitution is more complex than Lefebvre's historicist typologies can account for, and the association of this regulation of sexuality with modernity is deceptively easy to make. It is better therefore to ground further enquiries on an understanding of the spaces of modernity and to note the complex spatialities and temporalities in which the regulation of sexuality is caught up.

NOTES

1   Some writing on the relationship between cities and sexuality: H. Bech, Citysex: representing lust in public, *Theory, Culture and Society* **15** (1998) 215-241; P. Califia, *Public Sex: The Culture of Radical Sex* (Pittsburgh 1982); L. Knopp, Sexuality and urban space, in D. Bell and G. Valentine (Eds), *Mapping Desire: Geographies of Sexualities* (London 1995); C. Stanley, Spaces and places of the limit: four strategies in the relationship between law and desire, *Economy and Society* **25** (1996) 36-63. For Bech, *op. cit*, 215, "the city is invariably and ubiquitously, inherently and inevitably, fundamentally and thoroughly, sexualized; ... modern sexuality is essentially urban". For Califia, *op. cit.*, 205, "the city is a map of the hierarchy of desire, from the valorized to the stigmatized. It is divided into zones dictated by the ways its citizens value or denigrate their needs. Separating the city into areas of specialization makes it possible to meet some needs more efficiently; it is also an attempt to reduce conflict between opposing sets of desires and the roles people adopt to try to fulfill these desires".

2   Recent writing on geographies of sexuality includes S. Best, Sexualizing space, in E. Grosz and E. Probyn (Eds), *Sexy Bodies: The Strange Carnalities of Feminism* (London 1995); Bell and Valentine, *op. cit.*; and N. Duncan (Ed.), *Bodyspace: Destabilizing Geographies of Gender and Sexuality* (London 1996).

3   See A. Corbin, *Women For Hire: Prostitution and Sexuality in France after 1850* (London 1990) 141-142.

4   P. Hubbard, Community action and the displacement of street prostitution: evidence from British cities, *Geoforum* **29** (1998) 269-286, 269

5   For social exclusion see D. Sibley, *Geographies of Exclusion* (London 1995). For a critique of the geography of prostitution see P. Hubbard, Sexuality, immorality and the city: red-light districts and the marginalisation of female street prostitutes, *Gender, Place and Culture* **5** (1998) 55-72.

6   There *are* exceptions such as, in historical geography, the work of M. Ogborn, Love – state – ego: 'centres' and 'margins' in 19th-century Britain, *Environment and Planning D: Society and Space* **10** (1992) 287-305, and *idem*, Law and discipline in nineteenth century English state formation: the Contagious Diseases Acts of 1864, 1866 and 1869, *Journal of Historical Sociology* **6** (1993) 28-55. In contemporary geography see the work of P. Hubbard, Community action, *op. cit.*, *idem*, Sexuality, immorality and the city, *op. cit.*, *idem*, Red-light districts and toleration zones: geographies of female street prostitution in England and Wales, *Area* **29** (1997) 129-140 and *idem*, Researching female sex work: reflections on geographical exclusion, critical methodologies and 'useful' knowledge, *Area* **31** (1999) 229-237. See also Angie Hart's brief discussion of the 'social spatialisation' of a Spanish red-light district: A. Hart, (Re)constructing a Spanish red-light district: prostitution, space and power, in Bell and Valentine, *op.cit.*

7   H. Lefebvre, *The Production of Space* (Oxford 1991).

8   D. Gregory, *Geographical Imaginations* (Oxford 1994) 349.

9   For an extended definitional discussion see P. Howell, Prostitution and racialised sexuality: the regulation of prostitution in Britain and the British Empire before the Contagious Diseases Acts, *Environment and Planning D: Society and Space* (forthcoming).

10   C. Pateman, *The Sexual Contract* (Cambridge 1988).

11   See, for instance, G. J. Ashworth, P. E. White and H. P. M. Winchester, The red-light district in the West European city: a neglected aspect of the urban landscape, *Geoforum* **19** (1988) 201-212; N. L. Shumsky and L. M. Springer, San Francisco's zone of prostitution, 1880-1934, *Journal of Historical Geography* **7** (1981) 71-89; R. Symanski, Prostitution in Nevada, *Annals of the Association of American Geographers* **64** (1974) 357-377; H. P. M. Winchester and P. E. White, The location of marginalised groups in the inner city, *Environment and Planning D: Society and Space* **8** (1988) 37-54.

12   See for example J. Lowman, Police practices and crime rates in the lower world: prostitution in Vancouver, in D. J. Evans, N. R. Fyfe and D. T. Herbert (Eds), *Crime, Policing and Place: Essays in Environmental Criminology* (London 1992).

13   Symanski, *op. cit.*

14   Ashworth *et al*, *op. cit.*

15   Winchester and White, *op. cit.*

16   For an excellent recent discussion of some of these issues see N. D. Zatz, Sex work/sex act: law, labor, and desire in constructions of prostitution, *Signs* **22** (1997) 277-308.

17   Ashworth *et al*, *op. cit.*, 212; Symanski, *op. cit.*, 359.

18   Shumsky and Springer, *op. cit.*, 72.

19   P. Levine, Rough usage: prostitution, law and the social historian, in A. Wilson (Ed.), *Rethinking Social History: English Society 1570-1920 and its Interpretation* (Manchester 1993) 285.

20   Some examples of such historical work, with reconstructions and discussion of sexual geographies, for New York City *alone*: G. Chauncey, *Gay New York: the Making of the Gay Male World, 1890-1940* (London 1995); T. Gilfoyle, *City of Eros: New York City, Prostitution and the Commercialization of Sex, 1790-1920* (New York 1992); M. W. Hill, *Their Sisters' Keepers: Prostitution in New York City, 1830-1870* (Berkeley 1993); K. J. Mumford, *Interzones: Black/White Sex Districts in Chicago and New York in the Early Twentieth Century* (New York 1997).

21   L. Birken, *Consuming Desire: Sexual Science and the Emergence of a Culture of Abundance, 1871-1914* (Ithaca 1988).

22   Hubbard, Community action, *op. cit.*, 271.

23   Lefebvre, *op. cit.*, 85.

24   For this all too brief Lefebvrian incursion I am indebted to Gregory, *op. cit.*; E. Dimendberg, Henri Lefebvre on abstract space, in A. Light and J. M. Smith (Eds), *The Production of Public Space* (Lanham, MD 1998); M. Poovey, *Making a Social Body: British Cultural Formation 1830-1864* (Chicago 1995); and R. Shields, *Lefebvre, Love and Struggle: Spatial Dialectics* (London 1999).

25   See E. Soja, *Postmodern Geographies: the Reassertion of Space in Critical Social Theory* (London 1989).

26   Like most commentators, I prefer 'spaces of representation' to the translator's 'representational spaces' in Lefebvre, *op. cit.*

27   Dimendberg, *op. cit.*, 20.

28   Lefebvre, however, does not convincingly break with gendered analyses of public and private: see V. Blum and H. Nast, Where's the difference? The heterosexualization of alterity in Henri Lefebvre and Jacques Lacan, *Environment and Planning D: Society and Space* **14** (1996) 559-580.

29   Shields, *op. cit.*, 164.

30   L. White, *The Comforts of Home: Prostitution in Colonial Nairobi* (Chicago 1990).

31   *Ibid.*, 20.

32   *Ibid.*, 12-13.

33   Easily the most interesting work in this regard is for France: see C. Bernheimer, *Figures of Ill Repute: Representing Prostitution in Nineteenth-Century France* (Cambridge 1989); C. Hollis, *Painted Love: Prostitution in French Art of the Impressionist Era* (New Haven 1991); J. Matlock, *Scenes of Seduction: Prostitution, Hysteria, and Reading Difference in Nineteenth-Century France* (New York 1994). For England, see L. Nead, *Myths of Sexuality: Representations of Women in Victorian Britain* (Oxford 1988). Critically influential fictions of prostitutes and fallen women, for regulationists and abolitionists, include Zola's *Nana*, Heymann's *Diary of a Lost Girl*, Gaskell's *Ruth*, and many others.

34   S. Bell, *Reading, Writing and Rewriting the Prostitute Body* (Bloomington 1994) 92. For this, admittedly contentious linkage to dissident sexualities, see G. Rubin, Thinking sex: notes for a radical theory of the politics of sexuality, in C. S. Vance (Ed.), *Pleasure and Danger: Exploring Female Sexuality* (London 1984), and J. Weeks, *Sex, Politics and Society: the Regulation of Sexuality since 1800* (London 1989).

35   Zatz, *op. cit.*, 303.

36   A. J. B. Parent-Duchâtelet, *De la Prostitution dans la Ville de Paris* (Paris 1836) 21; see also J. Harsin, *Policing Prostitution in Nineteenth-Century Paris* (Princeton 1985). 'Linnaeus of prostitution' is Corbin's phrase, *op. cit.*, 6.

37   Corbin, *op. cit.*, 4; Parent-Duchâtelet, *op. cit.*, Volume 2, 515.

38   A useful complement to Corbin's work, on Geneva, and stressing the organisation of space, is: A. Cairoli, G. Chiaberto and S. Engel, *Le Déclin des Maisons Closes: La Prostitution à Genève à la fin du XIXᵉ siècle* (Geneva 1987).

39   Corbin, *op. cit.*, 215.

40   Quoted in Shields, *op. cit.*, 169.

41   J. R. Walkowitz, *Prostitution and Victorian Society: Women, Class, and the State* (Cambridge 1980). See also F. Mort, *Dangerous Sexualities: Medico-Moral Politics in England Since 1830* (London 1987).

42   P. Levine, Consistent contradictions: prostitution and protective labour legislation in nineteenth-century England, *Social History* **19** (1994) 17-35, 29. For discipline and panoptic surveillance, both within and without the subjected districts of the British Contagious Diseases Acts, see L. Mahood, *The Magdalenes: Prostitution in the Nineteenth Century* (London 1990); M. Spongberg, *Feminizing Venereal Disease: The Body of the Prostitute in Nineteenth-Century Medical Discourse* (New York 1997); N. Wood, Prostitution and feminism in nineteenth-century Britain, *M/F: A Feminist Journal* **7** (1982) 61-77.

43   Corbin, *op. cit.*, 16.

44   Harsin, *op. cit.*, 102; Corbin, *op. cit.*, 7.

45   For purposes of comparison the geography of prostitution in eighteenth-century Paris is well described in E.-M. Benabou, *La Prostitution et la Police des Moeurs au XVIIIᵉ siècle* (Paris 1987) 195-209.

46   Note though that Lefebvre's historicism, or perhaps the status of his historicism, though attested to by Gregory, *op. cit.*, and Shields, *op. cit.*, is questioned by others such as Dimendberg, *op. cit.*, 47.

47   Dimendberg, *op. cit.*, 32.

48   Noted by Poovey, *op. cit.*, 31.

49   Bell, *op. cit.*, 13.

50   See, for instance: J. Donzelot, *The Policing of Families* (New York 1979); M. Foucault, *The History of Sexuality, Volume I: An Introduction* (New York 1980); T. W. Laqueur, Sexual desire and the market economy during the industrial revolution, in D. Stanton (Ed.) *Discourses of Sexuality: From Aristotle to AIDS* (Ann Arbor 1992); D. Levine, Punctuated equilibrium: the modernization of the proletarian family in the age of ascendant capitalism, *International Labor and Working-Class History* **39** (1991) 3-20.

51   R. J. Evans, Prostitution, state and society in imperial Germany, *Past and Present* **70** (1976) 106-129, 107; T. Osborne and N. Rose, Governing cities: notes on the spatialisation of virtue, *Environment and Planning D: Society and Space* **17**(1999) 737-760, 759, 738.

52   Shields, *op. cit.*, 148; Levine, Rough usage, *op. cit.*, 282: "The city itself posed a significant threat as a symbol of autonomy, anonymity and independence"; Poovey, *op. cit.*, 41: "In the city, signs of disease took the form of clogged drains and overcrowded tenements; these problems also forecast social disorder, because, in an analysis that conflated physical with moral 'debility', environmental factors were thought capable of eroding self-discipline and moral rectitude: insalubrious living conditions, in short, could breed prostitution, trade unionism, and revolutionary politics."

53   Osborne and Rose, *op. cit.*, 743.

54   Gregory, *op. cit.*, 401, quoted in Dimendberg, *op. cit.*, 18.

55   Levine, Consistent contradictions, *op. cit.*, 28-9. For reflections on the blurring of the boundary between individual people – especially women, arguably – and the spaces they occupied, see Poovey, *op. cit.*, 37, and Best, *op. cit.*

56 See also R. Felski, *The Gender of Modernity* (Cambridge, MA 1995).

57 Blum and Nast, *op. cit.*

58 See V. Bullough and B. Bullough, *Women and Prostitution: A Social History* (Buffalo 1987); Harsin, *op. cit.*

59 Evans, *op. cit.*, 109; and R. J. Evans, *Tales from the German Underworld: Crime and Punishment in the Nineteenth Century* (New Haven 1998); also see, in a pioneering work on the neglected eighteenth century, I. V. Hull, *Sexuality, State, and Civil Society in Germany, 1700-1815* (Ithaca 1996).

60 M. Gibson, *Prostitution and the State in Italy, 1860-1915* (New Brunswick 1986); Prostitution laws after Italian unification: the role of 'regulationist' and 'abolitionist' elites, *Criminal Justice History* **11** (1990) 105-117.

61 L. Bernstein, *Sonia's Daughters: Prostitutes and their Regulation in Imperial Russia* (Berkeley 1995) 9.

62 Walkowitz, *op. cit.*

63 Howell, *op. cit.* There is a growing literature on imperialism and sexuality, for which the following is a good review: L. Bryder, Sex, race, and colonialism: an historiographical review, *International History Review* **20** (1998) 791-822

64 Levine, Rough usage, 284.

65 See Mahood, *op. cit.*; L. Bland, 'Guardians of the race', or 'vampires upon the nation's health'?: female sexuality and its regulation in early twentieth-century Britain, in E. Whitelegg *et al* (Eds), *The Changing Experience of Women* (Oxford 1982); *idem*, In the name of protection: the policing of women in the First World War, in J. Brophy and C. Smart (Eds), *Women-In-Law: Explorations in Law, Family and Sexuality* (London 1985).

66 Harsin, *op. cit.*

67 Parent-Duchâtelet, *op. cit.*, Vol I, 370. This kind of historicism is glaringly paradoxical but something of a commonplace in regulationist apologetics.

68 Saint Augustine, quoted by S. Shahar, *The Fourth Estate: A History of Women in the Middle Ages* (London 1990) 206; see Corbin, *op. cit.*, 4.

69 For medieval and early modern prostitution and its regulation see: S. K. Cohn, *Women in the Streets: Essays on Sex and Power in Renaissance Italy* (Baltimore 1996); R. M. Karras, *Common Women: Prostitution and Sexuality in Medieval England* (New York 1996); L. L. Otis, *Prostitution in Medieval Society: The History of an Urban Institution in Languedoc* (Chicago 1985); L. Roper, *The Holy Household: Women and Morals, in Reformation Augsburg* (Oxford 1989); J. Rossiaud, *Medieval Prostitution* (Oxford 1995); R. Trexler, Florentine prostitution in the fifteenth century: patrons and clients, in *Dependence in Context in Renaissance Florence* (Binghampton, NY 1994).

70 Karras, *op. cit.*, 34.

71 Otis, *op. cit.*, 45: "In this new Christian society, which was to adumbrate its paradisaical successor, there was no longer any room for the role of social stabilizer granted to the prostitute in late medieval times. And prostitution ceases at this point to be in the domain of institutional history, but rather becomes a part of the history of criminality and marginality in the early modern period".

72 P. Howell, A private Contagious Diseases Act: prostitution and public space in Victorian Cambridge, *Journal of Historical Geography* **26** (2000) 376-402.

73 See L. Engelstein, Combined underdevelopment: discipline and the law in imperial and Soviet Russia, *American Historical Review* **98** (1993) 338-353.

74   Engelstein also points to an interesting dialogue between tradition and modernity, between town and country: see L. Engelstein, *The Keys to Happiness: Sex and the Search for Modernity in Fin-de-Siècle Russia* (Ithaca 1992) and *idem*, Syphilis, historical and actual: cultural geography of a disease, *Reviews of Infectious Diseases* **8** (1986) 1036-1048.

75   See the useful critical commentary of P. W. Werth, Through the prism of prostitution: state, society and power, *Social History* **19** (1994) 1-15. Hull, *op. cit.*, rightly portrays the 'sexual system' that immediately preceded the nineteenth century as a function of both state and society, suggesting that regulation was created out of the state/civil society distinction: this basic relinquishing of the absolutist state's moral responsibility to that of civil society by the end of the eighteenth century paving the way for the public/private distinction of the succeeding century.

76   B. Hobson, Prostitution, in M. K. Cayton, E. J. Gorn and P. W. Williams (Eds), *Encyclopedia of American Social History*, volume III (New York 1993).

77   M. Ogborn, *Spaces of Modernity: London's Geographies, 1680-1780* (London 1998) 21. Similar, but much less effective arguments can be found in K. Hetherington, *The Badlands of Modernity: Heterotopia and Social Ordering* (London 1997).

Chapter Nine

THE POLITICS OF HISTORICAL GEOGRAPHY

French Intellectuals and the Question of Alsace-Lorraine, 1914-1918

MICHAEL HEFFERNAN

Studies in historical geography must ... embrace ideologies as well as being themselves explicitly ideological.[1]

Introduction

There are many lessons to be learnt from Alan Baker's investigations into the rural life of Loir-et-Cher, that section of the middle Loire valley that has been the focus of his inquisitive attention for the last four decades. Baker's careful reading of hitherto unexamined documents from the deepest archival vaults in Blois has greatly enriched our understanding of French rural society in the century from the end of the Napoleonic wars to the outbreak of World War One.[2] His analysis of peasant voluntary associations, the building blocks of the local community, re-affirms how an historical and a geographical imagination can be brought together to create an historical geography of ideas, ideologies and political sentiments. In Baker's writings, history and geography are considered not as external, independent variables determining social action but as active elements in the intellectual conflicts that generate political change, whether gradual or revolutionary.

Alan Baker's historical geography represents an intriguing and fruitful hybrid of two national traditions. On the one hand, there is a very British concern with empirical rigour and painstaking archival work, a legacy of Baker's training under Sir Clifford Darby. On the other hand, there is a very French preoccupation with the deeper structural shifts and continuities in economy, society and politics. This latter perspective owes a great deal to the inter-disciplinary research undertaken during the inter-war years by that remarkable group of economic and social historians, the so-called *Annales* school, who gathered together at the newly reconstituted French Université de Strasbourg under Marc Bloch and Lucien Febvre.[3]

As Baker has himself noted, the *Annales* School can be seen as an extension of the regional geographical work of Paul Vidal de la Blache and his many students in the decades before World War One.[4] Indeed, it is possible to argue that the tragic years from 1914 to 1918 were pivotal in the development of this distinctively French geo-historical imagination, the bedrock of the *Annales* School. This essay, offered as a modest tribute on the occasion of Alan Baker's retirement, provides a commentary on the rise and political significance of French historical geography in this troubled era.

My particular focus is the remarkable outpouring of French historical and geographical research about Alsace-Lorraine, that fiercely disputed border zone including the major cities of Strasbourg, Mulhouse and Metz ceded to the new German Empire under the terms of the Treaty of Frankfurt (10 May 1871) after the Franco-Prussian War only to be restored to France following the Treaty of Versailles at the end of World War One. In considering this literature, most of it written and published in Paris, my starting point is the short quotation from Baker cited at the beginning of this essay. I want to demonstrate how the emerging hybrid discipline of historical geography was, even at its inception, a profoundly ideological project, perceived as such not only by its founding practitioners but also by those government officials who sponsored research in this field and who saw historical geography as a "sternly practical" pursuit with important political implications for the definition of national territories and national identities.[5]

From Alsace and Lorraine to Elsaß-Lothringen

'Alsace-Lorraine' is a rather misleading term from a French perspective. The ancient provinces of Alsace and Lorraine had no administrative significance on the eve of the Franco-Prussian war and were certainly not regarded as a single, distinctive region. The hyphenated 'unity' Alsace-Lorraine acquired in the French geographical imagination after 1871 was largely a consequence of the German annexation of this area and the fact that it was considered as a separate administrative territory within the German Empire: the *Reichsland* of Elsaß-Lothringen.[6] This area, well over 13,000 square kilometres with a population of *c*.1.6 million, cut across the limits of the former French *départements*. It included most of the predominantly German and Alsatian speaking *départements* of the Bas-Rhin and the Haut-Rhin, centred on Strasbourg and Colmar, though the fortress town of Belfort, and its immediate environs in the south of the former Haut-Rhin, remained in French hands. Also transferred were the more German-speaking sections of the otherwise mainly French-speaking province of Lorraine, including most of the former French *département* of the Moselle, centred on Metz, and a significant portion of the former French *département* of the Meurthe, an area that would subsequently be described as *Deutsche-Lothringen*. A small eastern enclave from the former French *département* of the Vosges was also transferred to Germany (see Figure 1).

The new Franco-German border, hastily devised in late 1870 by the German military authorities in Strasbourg based on French and German censuses, statistical digests and assorted archival material, gave the German Empire complete control of the middle Rhine and possession of Strasbourg, the major port in that sector of the river.[7] Germany also controlled the whole of the Saar coal field, a substantial sector of the iron-ore field to the east of the Moselle (Mosel) river, the extensive and still under-developed potash reserves north of Mulhouse (an acquisition which meant a world monopoly in this resource) as well as the valuable textile industries in the same area.

The loss of these lands, together with the extremely harsh terms of the Treaty of Frankfurt, unleashed an outburst of nationalist anger in France. This gradually subsided into a simmering, embittered sense of injustice but the wound was never to heal. The desire to recover from the humiliating *débâcle* of 1870-1, either directly by restoring French rule in *les provinces perdues* or indirectly by acquiring compensatory colonial territories beyond Europe, was arguably the dominant motivation of France's political leadership in the decades before World War One, even though this most sensitive of issues was rarely openly debated. As Léon Gambetta famously remarked of Alsace-Lorraine: "pensons-y toujours, n'en parlons jamais".[8]

The question of Alsace-Lorraine was no less important in French intellectual life, although it was often subliminal. Some of the more persistent and visceral disputes between French and German savants can be connected to their very different interpretations of 1870-1. This was especially clear of French and German theories of the nation-state. While the former sought to rationalise defeat and territorial loss, the latter sought to legitimise victory and territorial gain. The ideas of Ernest Renan represent an eloquent statement of the French position. In his famous Sorbonne lecture

FIGURE 1
The Borders of Alsace-Lorraine, 1814-1919

Note: After 1871, the remnants of the former French *départements* of the Moselle and the Meurthe became a new, single *département*, the Meurthe-et-Moselle, the *chef lieu* of which was Nancy. After 1918, the pre-1870 *départements* were re-established

of March 1882, *Qu'est-ce qu'une nation?*, Renan developed a theory of the modern nation-state that stood in direct and conscious opposition to the prevailing social Darwinian perspective invoked by many German intellectuals, particularly the ultra-nationalist historian Heinrich Treitschke who deployed a biological rationale to explain and justify German expansionism.[9] Dispensing in turn with the racial, linguistic, religious, economic and strategic geographical factors so often discussed by German writers, Renan insisted that a nation meant something far more than any of these crude measures could possibly convey. "Une nation", he asserted, "est une âme, un principe spirituel". It depended on "la possession en commun d'un riche legs de souvenirs" and also "le consentement actuel, le désir de vivre ensemble, la volonté de continuer à faire valoir l'héritage qu'on a reçu indivis". Nationalism was ultimately about love and "On aime en proportion des sacrifices qu'on a consentis, des maux qu'on a soufferts". Defeat in 1870 thus bound together the French population more closely than ever because "la souffrance en commun unit plus que la joie ... [et] ... les deuils valent mieux que les triomphes, car ils imposent des devoirs, ils commandent l'effort en commun". A nation was not, nor could it ever be, simply a racial, ethnic or linguistic community as so many German theorists claimed. Nor should it be seen as a living organism, as these same theorists also insisted, an entity greater than the sum of its parts that was propelled by dark Darwinian forces beyond the control of individual citizens. A nation, in Renan's view, was the outcome of collective political will and daily action: "L'existence d'une nation est ... un plébiscite de tous les jours".[10]

The politics of economic calculation: Alsace-Lorraine, 1914-1915

The outbreak of World War One brought these simmering political and intellectual conflicts to boiling point. The question of Alsace-Lorraine became the focus of immediate concern. The French government, in a joint statement with its Russian allies, made it clear as early as 5 August 1914 that the German invasion invalidated the Treaty of Frankfurt. The official French position was that hostilities should continue until Alsace-Lorraine was returned to France.[11] This surprised no-one, of course, least of all the German General Staff Alfred Graf von Schlieffen's famous preparations for a massive 'wheeling' invasion of northern France through Belgium, based on the plausible and, as it turned out, correct assumption that French military strategists, transfixed by the dream of recovering Alsace-Lorraine and committed to the principle of all-out offensive warfare (*la guerre à outrance*), would respond to a German invasion in the north with an immediate counter-attack in the south in an attempt to seize as much of the 'lost provinces' as possible. Schlieffen and his successors calculated that the French counter-attack in Alsace would merely hasten the advance of German troops in the north, leading to the virtual encirclement of the French forces in eastern France.

The Schlieffen Plan, and France's Plan XVIII to reclaim Alsace-Lorraine, were both modified before and during the opening days of the war but this deadly game of thrust and counter-thrust was more or less what transpired before the trench lines were dug in after the German advance collapsed on the River Marne in the autumn of 1914. German troops now occupied a great swath of French territory in the north (an area that had been producing, *inter alia*, nearly three-quarters of France's coal and two-thirds of its steel). French forces, on the other hand, had at least reclaimed a small sector of Alsace, an area populated by around 100,000 people including the town of Thann.

The French claim to the whole of Alsace-Lorraine was henceforth regarded as officially non-negotiable. Peace was inconceivable until the region was safely back in French hands. However, the staggering number of French casualties during the early weeks of the war had already weakened political resolve in respect of Alsace-Lorraine and complicated the apparently simple geopolitical objective of restoring France's 1870 frontiers. Early in 1915, the pacifist left within and beyond France began to argue that the future of Alsace-Lorraine should be settled by a plebiscite. Following intense and often heated internal debate, the *Section Française de l'Internationale Ouvrière* (SFIO), France's powerful socialist party, called openly for a plebiscite in the region following the anticipated restoration of Alsace-Lorraine to French control. The coalition war cabinet of Prime Minister René Viviani, himself a moderate socialist, firmly rejected this idea but the left's insistence on the need for a plebiscite revealed the fragility of the *union sacrée* between the political parties and demonstrated that the question of Alsace-Lorraine was less clear cut than had previously been assumed.[12]

Conservative and revanchist politicians who sought a definitive restoration of French rule in Alsace-Lorraine as part of a punitive peace settlement with Germany now realised that their geopolitical objectives needed to be carefully justified if French public opinion, not to mention the French cabinet, were to remain firmly behind the war and if politicians in allied and neutral countries were to be convinced by the French position. An early opportunity to strengthen cabinet resolve on the question of Alsace-Lorraine came in mid-February 1915 when a small *ad-hoc* committee was established in the *Ministère des affaires étrangères*, subsequently called the *Conférence d'Alsace-Lorraine*, under the chairmanship of Louis Barthou and with André Tardieu and Louis Marin as senior members. Barthou, Tardieu and Marin were to be intimately involved in the war-time campaign to secure French rule in Alsace-Lorraine. All three were experienced, widely-respected conservatives close to, but at that time not actually members of, the French cabinet.[13] Unfortunately for Barthou and his associates, the *Conférence* met infrequently and did not survive beyond the summer of 1916. It also had a relatively narrow brief and focused mainly on the legal questions associated with the introduction of a new French administration in Alsace-Lorraine.[14]

Frustrated by this experience and increasingly alarmed at the persistent calls from the SFIO for a plebiscite in Alsace-Lorraine, a number of conservative politicians decided to launch their own unofficial campaigns to steel public opinion and strengthen government determination. This constituency was concerned less with 'secondary' questions such as the administrative regime that might be introduced in a newly-restored Alsace-Lorraine. Rather, these men wanted to clarify precisely what constituted Alsace and Lorraine in the changed circumstances of 1915. In April of that year, Marin, a native of Lorraine, launched the *Groupe lorrain* with the active support of fellow *députés* François de Wendel (a powerful Lorraine industrialist and a champion of far-right causes) and Maurice Barrès (also a native of Lorraine, the president of the *Ligue des patriotes* and the dominant French theorist of the radical right).[15]

Barthou, for his part, served as one of several vice-presidents alongside Barrès on yet another private pressure group, the *Comité d'études économiques et administratives relatives à l'Alsace-Lorraine* (CEAL), established by Jules Siegfried, the energetic industrialist, former minister, Senator, mayor of Le Havre and founder of the *Musée Social*.[16] The *Comité Siegfried*, as it became known, proved especially productive, assembling on 38 occasions from February 1915 to June 1919 to debate no fewer than 33 detailed reports by assorted academics, politicians and businessmen on a range of economic and legal questions raised by the resumption of French control in Alsace-Lorraine, all of which concluded with specific recommendations that were duly passed to the principal cabinet ministers and their advisers.[17]

One of the more important resolutions adopted by Siegfried's committee was the idea that France should reclaim not only the territory ceded to Germany in 1871 but also the whole of the Saar coal field that straddled this earlier border (see Figure 1). This argument was based on a detailed study of the changes that had taken place in the economy of Alsace-Lorraine under German rule. French analysts calculated that, due to the region's rapid industrialisation since 1871, the 'lost provinces' were consuming 12 million tonnes of coal per year on the eve of the war. Much of this had come from mines on the adjacent Saar coalfield. These produced 17.5 million tonnes in 1913. Only four million tonnes of this total production came from the smaller number of mines located on the southern Saarland, within the area France had ceded to Germany in 1871. If France claimed only the area acquired by Germany in 1871, and if the Lorraine iron and steel mills were to function at full capacity, the already excessive French dependency on imported coal would need to *increase* from 23 to *c*.31 million tonnes per annum.

The *Comité Siegfried* concluded that without the Saar coal reserves, a post-war France would be unable to maintain industrial production levels in a restored Alsace-Lorraine and the region's economy would be plunged into a serious crisis. The *Comité* therefore sought to demonstrate that the Saarland had become economically integral to Alsace-Lorraine as a result of the preceding era of industrial development under German control. Only if the whole of this region were returned to France could the country reduce a potentially crippling coal deficit and maintain levels of industrial production and employment. Assuming that the industrial infrastructure remained relatively undamaged on both sides of the 1914 border, however, a favourably modified frontier would, in theory, increase French annual iron production from 5.2 to 10.5 million tonnes and annual steel production from 4.7 to 9.1 million tonnes. The corresponding German annual production figures for iron and steel would, by contrast, fall from 11.5 to 6.2 million tonnes and from 12.3 to 7.9 million tonnes respectively.[18] By the end of 1915, the campaign by conservative politicians to counter the prospect of a post-war plebiscite in Alsace-Lorraine (the result of which was by no means assured) had produced an entirely new set of economic arguments that effectively re-defined the area France might claim in the event of an Allied victory.[19]

Jeux avec frontières: Alsace-Lorraine, 1916

The economic case for a 'greater' French Alsace-Lorraine, including the Saarland, was unlikely to convince politicians in Allied and neutral countries, many of whom were attracted to the idea of a post-war plebiscite and openly suspicious of French claims. In London, only Sir Edward Grey was known to be personally sympathetic to a return to the 1870 borders. To the dismay of French politicians and diplomats, successive war-time British governments refused to make an unequivocal commitment on the subject of Alsace-Lorraine. If anything, the British position seemed to grow more sceptical about French arguments with the passage of time. In Washington, the American administration was even more reticent, both before and after the US declaration of war against Germany in April 1917.[20]

In these discouraging circumstances, it became clear that French claims to a 'greater' Alsace-Lorraine would need to be couched in a less obviously self-interested economic language. The indefatigable Marin, an anthropologist of some renown and an enthusiastic supporter of geography, decided that new arguments for a 'greater'

Alsace-Lorraine should be developed as part of a much wider French geopolitical programme that would consider the whole of post-war Europe and the colonial world. An active member of several scientific societies, Marin also decided that the *Société de Géographie de Paris* (SGP), the oldest geographical society in the world with an impressive building in central Paris and its own extensive map library, was the ideal forum for a more ambitious private *démarche*. Having secured tacit support for his plans from a few members of Prime Minister Aristide Briand's cabinet and following brief discussions in early February 1916, the SGP's council established four *sous-commissions*, each comprising senior members of the Society plus assorted academics and politicians, many of them veterans of earlier committees. The objective was to consider the full range of questions raised by possible geopolitical changes in four regions – Alsace-Lorraine, central Europe, Africa and Asia-Oceania – and submit a series of reasoned recommendations in respect of each area to the government.[21] The wildly varying scale of the 'regions' considered by these four *sous-commissions* is itself a telling commentary on French geopolitical priorities.

The *sous-commission* on Alsace-Lorraine comprised 25 permanent members including Marin, several leading geographers such as Jean Brunhes from the *Collège de France* and Lucien Gallois from the Sorbonne. It assembled on six occasions between 16 February and 10 July 1916 before merging the following October with the smaller 20-man Central European *sous-commission* (which had assembled on only three occasions over the same period) for a final, unsuccessful attempt to devise a wider, pan-European policy for submission to the French cabinet. The minutes of the Alsace-Lorraine *sous-commission* provide a revealing commentary on the changing nature of the Alsace-Lorraine question through 1916 and the growing tensions between liberal and conservative viewpoints.[22] The economic arguments for the restoration of a 'greater' Alsace-Lorraine, including the Saarland, were examined and endorsed once again during discussion of new reports submitted by representatives of the *Comité Siegfried* and the *Comité des forges de France* (the powerful association of French iron and steel manufacturers that had established its own peace conference committee in August 1915).[23]

The most extreme revanchist position was expressed in a concise report, written by François de Wendel and submitted to the *sous-commission*'s final meeting on 1 July 1916. In this, de Wendel considered three possible Franco-German borders (see Figure 1):

1) the 1870 border, a line that dated from the second Treaty of Paris (20 November 1815) following the Battle of Waterloo and the final collapse of the Napoleonic era at the end of the 'Hundred Days';

2) a version of the short-lived 1814 border, the line negotiated by Tallerand at the first Treaty of Paris (30 May 1914) following Napoleon's initial abdication and before his return from exile, though extended to include the whole of the Saar coalfield as well as the environs of Landau to the east;

3) an entirely new border that would follow the Rhine as far north as the Dutch border, encircling Luxembourg and Belgium with an enormous northward expansion of 'French' territory into the German Rhineland.

De Wendel dismissed the first option out of hand, citing the familiar economic arguments outlined above. The second option, though preferable as an economic settlement, was also deemed unsatisfactory in terms of France's future military security. According to de Wendel, the only really effective solution in economic and military terms was the permanent annexation of the entire west bank of the Rhine envisioned in his third option. Only this arrangement would provide the necessary "zone de couverture pour protéger l'Alsace-Lorraine".[24]

This was a remarkable proposal but de Wendel was by no means alone in advocating this solution. The vehemently anti-German former Foreign Minister Théophile Delcassé, supported by senior soldiers in the French General Staff, had been arguing for some time that a defeated Germany should be divided into nine independent states, with the Rhineland annexed permanently to France.[25] A victorious France would thus claim sovereignty over several German cities arrayed on the west bank of the Rhine from Speyer in the south to Krefeld in the north, including Ludwigshafen, Worms, Mainz, Koblenz, Bonn and Köln.[26] The argument that the Allies should insist on a demilitarised German Rhineland, policed initially by French troops, was not new and had been consistently advocated by senior figures in the French army, and by their political allies, since the beginning of the war. But de Wendel's report went far beyond this, arguing for the permanent political incorporation of this huge area and its entirely German population.[27]

The liberal academics on the *sous-commission* were aghast at this suggestion, pointing out the enormous economic, social, political and legal difficulties involved in re-establishing French control in the pre-1870 Alsace-Lorraine following 45 years of German rule, let alone seeking the annexation of a comparable area to the north with a much larger, entirely German population.[28] De Wendel's report airily dismissed such faint-hearted reservations. The Rhineland had been French under the Napoleonic First Empire, albeit briefly, and

Si les circonstances faisaient qu'à la guerre actuelle succédait une période de paix aussi prolongée que celle qui s'est écoulée depuis 1870, et si l'on sait respecter suffisamment les coutumes et surtout les croyances des populations, il

n'est pas douteux que ces populations du Rhin qui, sous le Premier Empire, avaient très facilement accepté la domination française, seraient assimilées avant la fin de cette période.[29]

Such astonishing proposals served only to underline the growing differences between liberal and conservative opinion about France's future in the post-war era. In these circumstances, it is scarcely surprising that the SGP initiative on Alsace-Lorraine fizzled out in the autumn of 1916 without producing the kind of clear and comprehensive report Marin had anticipated.

Mobilising the academics: Alsace-Lorraine, 1917

By early 1917, the various conservative attempts to counter the intensifying calls for a negotiated peace had produced only confusion and dissent. The strength of the French position was also weakened by much larger political and military set-backs. The collapse of Tsarist Russia in February 1917 removed a regime that had been (paradoxically, given its diametrically opposing ideology) France's most reliable ally. The catastrophic failure of Général Nivelle's offensive along the Chemin des Dames the following April came perilously close to breaking the French army, which would henceforth adopt a largely defensive posture until the summer of 1918. Faced with food shortages and declining real incomes at home, a wave of strikes swept the country with pacifist and revolutionary slogans much in evidence. The American declaration of war in April 1917 came as an enormous relief but even this welcome development was not without its difficulties. US military involvement inevitably meant that American political solutions to European problems would now carry far greater weight. On the question of Alsace-Lorraine, officials in Washington had already shown themselves to be decidedly cool about French territorial demands.

Aristide Briand, Prime Minister since October 1915, was still clinging to power in the early months of 1917 in the face of mounting attacks from both right and left. Although he supported Nivelle's disastrously over-optimistic plans, Briand seems to have decided that a military break-through was no longer possible. A former socialist now despised on the left for his strike-breaking tactics before the war, Briand had concluded that the failure to end the war was partly due to a general unwillingness to specify clear geopolitical objectives.[30] The earlier unofficial commissions of inquiry on the Franco-German border and Alsace-Lorraine had failed to produce credible recommendations, Briand believed, because they had been established by revanchist conservative politicians, many with personal interests in Lorraine, who were motivated by a desire to discredit pacifist calls for a negotiated settlement (which would inevitably have cast doubt on French claims to Alsace-Lorraine) rather than a genuine interest in establishing consensus around a series of reasoned geopolitical objectives. Excessive weight had been placed on economic and military considerations and this had produced unrealistic territorial demands that were clearly unacceptable in London and Washington.

Briand decided that all questions relating to the Franco-German border, Alsace-Lorraine and the rest of Europe should be considered afresh by yet another commission, this time with full official backing. Rather than rely on politicians, businessmen and military commanders, he decided that the new commission should comprise hand-picked, internationally renowned liberal academics. Like many French politicians, Briand admired intellectuals and enjoyed the company of scientists whom he saw as the guardians of France's cherished ideals of reason, logic and objectivity. To reinforce the desired impression of rational neutrality, he suggested that the proposed commission should not work towards a single, definitive solution to the problem of Alsace-Lorraine but should rather consider a range of options, more and less favourable to France, and provide evidence for and against each alternative.[31] The new commission's first duty would be to revisit, in these new and tragic circumstances, the age-old geopolitical question that had preoccupied generations of statesmen, soldiers and intellectuals from the seventeenth century to the First Napoleonic Empire: where were France's 'limites naturelles'?[32]

But which disciplines and which individuals should take part in this renewed quest? Briand turned for inspiration to his friend and supporter Charles Benoist, *député* for the Seine and a distinguished historian from the *École Libre des Sciences Politiques* in Paris.[33] Benoist was an authority on Machiavelli and a left-of-centre advocate of electoral reform who had been *doyen* of the *Faculté des Lettres* in Nancy during the turbulent years following the Franco-Prussian war. Nancy, a sleepy provincial town in 1870, became an important frontier city virtually overnight following the German annexation of Alsace-Lorraine. A mere 15 kilometres from the new border, the city's population virtually doubled between 1871 and 1873 due to the huge influx of French-speaking refugees from the former French territories to the east. The incoming population included staff and students from the former French Université de Strasbourg, now in German hands. The new republican authorities in Paris had identified educational reform, including a re-organised university system, as the key to national revival after the disasters of 1870-1 and Benoist and his fellow academics in Nancy were given generous financial assistance to transform their city into an important French intellectual centre, a rival to Strasbourg and the other German university cities on the Rhine. As Louis Maggiolo, the *Recteur* of the *Académie* de Nancy, expressed it in July 1871: "Le développement de l'enseignement supérieur à

Nancy sera tout à la fois un bienfait public, un progrès et surtout une manifestation nationale en face de l'Allemagne".[34] The new education minister, Jules Simon, instructed Benoist to place particular emphasis on history and geography, subjects already identified as having special significance in a reformed civic educational system.[35] Simon's reasoning was simple: the coming generations of French Lorraine must never be allowed to forget their historical and geographical affinities with their brothers and sisters beyond the new German border. In Benoist's words:

> *Nous devons nous occuper dans cette région de constituer un centre scientifique de la France. Une lutte inévitable doit s'établir entre les universités allemandes et, en particulier, entre celle que la politique prussienne veut doter si richement à Strasbourg avec nos dépouilles ... C'est moins que jamais l'heure du désarmement intellectuel ... C'est une grande cause nationale que Nancy doit à sa position géographique de réprésenter aujourd'hui ... L'enseignement inauguré depuis deux ans à Nancy devrait faire un des principaux objets d'un second cours d'histoire et de géographie.*[36]

Benoist's experience in Nancy convinced him that French arguments for a restored Alsace-Lorraine were best formulated in historical and geographical terms.[37] He therefore suggested that the President and Vice-President of the new commission should be the country's leading historian and geographer respectively. In Benoist's considered opinion, France's pre-eminent historian was undoubtedly his friend and political ally Ernest Lavisse, director of the *École Normale Supérieure*. Lavisse's star had shone with undiminished brilliance since the latter years of Second Empire when he served as secretary to Victor Duruy, Napoléon III's liberal education minister. Lavisse was, in Benoist's view, the ideal figure to direct the proposed commission: a patriotic Frenchmen, to be sure, but also a liberal republican with a long-standing and sympathetic interest in German history and the author of outstanding volumes on Frederick the Great and the Prussian monarchy. Lavisse was, in short, the very antithesis of French revanchism – a Germanophile French intellectual, widely respected by German scholars and a man who had sought to learn from Germany's intellectual and academic success. Another of his many books, on Wilhelm von Humboldt and the origins of the University of Berlin (the exemplary modern university in Lavisse's view), had directly influenced the attempts to reform the French university system.[38]

Benoist was equally certain about the identity of the country's leading geographer. Paul Vidal de la Blache had established, more or less single-handed, France's distinguished school of regional geography.[39] Although retired from his chair at the

Sorbonne, Vidal was still teaching and researching alongside Benoist at the *École Libre des Sciences Politiques* in Paris. The close collaboration between Benoist and Vidal had a long history: it was the youthful Vidal who had been recruited by Benoist to the new chair in history and geography at the *Faculté des Lettres* in Nancy in 1872.[40] Vidal had remained in Lorraine until his appointment at the *École Normale Supérieure* in Paris in 1877 and had been much influenced by this experience.[41] Like Lavisse, Vidal admired German thought, particularly the geographical writings of Alexander von Humboldt and Karl Ritter. Encouraged by Benoist, he had worked hard to establish personal contacts with leading geographers in the major German universities during his tenure in Nancy in accordance with the institution's policy of 'learning from the enemy'.[42]

Lavisse and Vidal shared far more than a common academic interest in German thought and German educational practices. The two men had been students together in Paris during the 1860s and were close personal friends.[43] Politically and intellectually, they were cut from the same liberal, republican cloth. They also shared a profound conviction that France's identity and, by implication, its territorial extent, were the result of a long historical interaction between people and nature. This was, to be sure, a perspective that owed a great deal to the idea of the nation developed by Ernest Renan in 1882. This conviction directly informed the structure and organisation of Lavisse's greatest editorial achievement, the monumental, multi-volume *Histoire de la France* which he was still overseeing when war broke.[44] Lavisse believed the nation's history could only be narrated once its environments and landscapes had been fully explicated. As he memorably expressed it in another context: "la France existe avant la France".[45] The first volume of his mammoth work, published in 1903, was accordingly Vidal's widely-praised *Tableau de la géographie de la France*.

These four men – Briand, Benoist, Lavisse and Vidal – held at least one preliminary discussion in January 1917. They decided that the new commission should be called the *Comité d'Études* and that its activities should be divided into two consecutive projects. A relatively small group of experts should immediately begin work on Alsace-Lorraine and the Franco-German border. Once this group had reported, a larger selection of experts would then be assembled (including some, but not necessarily all, of the first group) to prepare a comparable report on the wider European questions.[46] Aside from Lavisse, Vidal and Benoist, the initial Alsace-Lorraine group (formally announced on 17 February 1917) was as follows:

1. Alphonse Aulard, the leading historian of the French Revolution and founder of the journal *La Révolution Française* (based at the Sorbonne);[47]

2. Ernest Babelon, France's leading numismatist and archaeologist (based at the *Collège de France* and the *Bibliothèque Nationale* where he was director of the *Cabinet des Médailles*);

3. Émile Bourgeois, the biographer of Voltaire, an historian of 'secret' diplomacy in the eighteenth century and a leading advocate of educational reform (based at the Sorbonne and at the *École libre des sciences politiques*);[48]

4. Général Bourgeois, the Chief of the *Service Géographique de l'Armée* (SGA), the agency within the *Ministère de la Guerre* that was responsible for the production of French military maps;[49]

5. Arthur Chuquet, an historian of Napoleonic France and modern Germany and the founder of the *Revue d'Histoire Littéraire de la France* (based at the *Collège de France*);[50]

6. Ernest Denis, an historian of the Slavic world and of modern Germany (based at the Sorbonne);[51]

7. Lucien Gallois, a Sorbonne geographer and an authority on German geographical thought;[52]

8. Camille Jullian, a prolific historian of ancient, medieval and modern France (based at the *Collège de France*);[53]

9. Emmanuel de Martonne, a Sorbonne geographer and an authority on south-central Europe;[54]

10. Christian Pfister, an ecclesiastical and political historian of medieval and modern France, with particular reference to Alsace and Lorraine, and the editor of the *Revue Historique* (based at the Sorbonne);[55]

11. Christian Schéfer, a political historian from the *École libre des sciences politiques*;

12. Charles Seignobos, the leading historian of modern French politics and foreign relations (based at the Sorbonne).[56]

These men were the cream of the nation's historians and geographers. Conspicuous by their absence were specialists from the contemporary social sciences (economics or sociology) or representatives of other disciplines in the humanities (philosophy or languages). The leading figures in these 'missing' disciplines had been no less involved in the nation's war effort prior to 1917. It would appear, therefore, that their undoubted expertise was deemed inappropriate for the task in hand.[57] The composition of the *Comité d'Études* implies that Briand had decided that French claims to Alsace-Lorraine should be made by reference to 'objective' and relatively stable geographical and historical evidence rather than endlessly changing economic and military considerations or social and linguistic factors that often favoured Germany rather than France.[58]

With the exception of Général Bourgeois, those invited to join the *Comité* were all drawn from prestigious Parisian institutions of higher learning and would certainly have known each other well.[59] Only Gallois and Schéfer had served on the earlier SGP Alsace-Lorraine commission, though many of their new colleagues had spent the preceding months pondering various geopolitical questions.[60] The *Comité*'s inaugural meeting took place on 23 February 1917 in the Sorbonne's *Institut de Géographie*. Lavisse was formally elected President, Vidal Vice-President and de Martonne was nominated as Secretary. A further 15 meetings took place on 28 February; 19 and 26 March; 23 and 30 April; 7, 14 and 21 May; 4, 11, 18 and 25 June; 2 July; and 12 and 19 November. Some 27 detailed reports were prepared and discussed at these meetings, including three submitted by co-opted experts: Maurice Alfassa (a mining engineer), Lucien Romer (an economist) and Phillippe Sagnac (an economic and political historian of the Rhine from the University of Lille). The map collections and cartographers of the *Institut de Géographie*, the SGP and the SGA helped with the supply and preparation of maps.

The historians, the French Revolution and Alsace-Lorraine, 1917-1918

Drafts of the *Comité*'s 22 reports on Alsace-Lorraine became available at various dates from mid-1917 to early-1918 and were circulated to the war cabinet and to senior officials in the principal ministries. These were impressively detailed works of historical geography, each supported by dozens of scholarly footnotes, additional notes, appendices and newly-drawn maps.[61] While they contained their fair share of emotive, anti-German rhetoric (descriptions of Alsace and Lorraine as "enfants perdus" yearning for reconciliation with "la mère patrie" proliferated, as did corporeal metaphors about amputation or the mutilation of the French body politic), these reports were easily the most comprehensive and thoroughly researched statements of the French position on Alsace-Lorraine yet produced. Unlike earlier forms of French geopolitical propaganda, they were based on fresh investigations of newly-assembled published and unpublished evidence from censuses, trade digests, military reports, topographic maps and archival materials. Most importantly, all sections of the text, including those devoted to economic and strategic considerations, consistently deployed historical evidence and historical precedent to underscore the political and cultural connections between France and the area ceded to Germany in 1871 and, equally significantly, to problematise the converse relationships between this area and the post-1871 German Empire. Historical scholarship was also used to question the legitimacy of German claims to the disputed regions bordering Alsace-Lorraine, particularly the Saarland but also the west bank of the Rhine.

These were difficult arguments to sustain, not least because the majority of the population of Alsace-Lorraine spoke German. For the French savants on the *Comité*, the case for Alsace-Lorraine had to be advanced in such a way that language was reduced to a mere epiphenomenon, a superficial and mutable factor that did not seriously affect the vaunted enthusiasm of Alsatians and Lorrainers for French culture and civilisation. In their introductory statement, Lavisse and Pfister stated the argument in terms which clearly echoed those of Ernest Renan a generation earlier: "il faut finir avec le sophisme qui fait de la langue le facteur essentiel de la patrie. La patrie, ce sont les souvenirs communs, les joies et les misères éprouvées ensemble, l'affection récriproque des ancêtres se continuant dans l'affection réciproque des descendants, les sentiments identiques des cœurs".[62]

But what exactly were these "souvenirs communs", these collectively recalled "joies" and "misères" ? Which historical experiences could be mobilised to bind an overwhelmingly German-speaking region to France? The answer, repeated with equal insistence throughout the volume, was simple: the French Revolution and the republican tradition. According to the report, the entirely distinct historical experiences of Alsace and Lorraine prior to 1870 made their forced administrative unification within Germany after 1871 all the more unjust and inappropriate. Neither region had any genuine cultural meaning before the Revolution. Prior to 1789, Alsace and Lorraine were no more than "expressions géographiques", collections of overlapping fiefdoms plagued by religious strife and chronically underdeveloped. The events of 1789 swept away the final vestiges of feudalism from the region, destroyed for ever these pernicious internal divisions and created not only a sense of republican unity within Alsace and Lorraine but also between these two regions and the rest of revolutionary France.

A complex range of evidence was mobilised to demonstrate the popularity of revolutionary republicanism in Alsace and Lorraine in the immediate aftermath of 1789. The argument hinged on the idea that these provinces had marked the geographical frontier of the new revolutionary state and had, as a result, been gripped by a particularly intense commitment to republicanism. As Lavisse and Pfister remarked, travellers crossing the eastern frontier of the new Republic in the early 1790s would have passed newly-planted liberty trees marking the border, each festooned with red, white and blue ribbons, *tricolore* flags and a familiar placard annnoucing: "Ici commence le pays de la liberté". It was in Strasbourg, moreover, that Rouget de l'Isle's anthem to the French republic, subsequently (and misleadingly) entitled *La Marseillaise*, was composed and first performed on

26 April 1792.[63] The region's commitment to French republicanism had endured through the nineteenth century, the report insisted, and had survived even the long years of German rule.

The *Comité*'s case often emphasised the earlier unity of Alsace, Lorraine and pre-1789 France but it ultimately rested on a repeated assertion that the 'lost provinces' had shown a deep and persistent commitment to the idea of France as the wellspring of modern European republicanism, the home of the revolutionary ideals of liberty, equality and fraternity. This tradition had admittedly been overwhelmed during successive monarchist and Napoleonic interludes but, according to the historians on the *Comité*, these were mere diversions from France's true republican destiny. The Third Republic established in 1870 had survived and the revolutionary tradition it reflected was now beyond challenge. The cruel irony of history was that this same Republic had been forced to cede Alsace and most of Lorraine to Germany as a result of the imperial excesses of the preceding Napoleonic era, thus depriving *la mère patrie* of a major republican heartland. German aggression in 1914 had destroyed for ever its claim to this region and, after 47 years, it was now time to restore these cherished lands to their natural ideological home.

The French claim to Alsace and Lorraine, as developed by the members of the *Comité d'Études*, had nothing to do with economic or strategic considerations, nor did it rely on 'mutable' and 'superficial' cultural factors such as language. It rested, rather, on an insistence that there existed a fundamental historical and political affinity between republican France and the revolutionary values that still burned brightly amongst the people of Alsace and Lorraine despite the long years of oppressive German imperial rule, an affinity born of this region's defining geographical role in the pivotal era of French and European history. As Lavisse and Pfister concluded:

> *elle [la France] est soutenue par sa volonté de libérer et de rappeler au 'foyer' les enfants qu'elle a perdus, il y a quarante-six ans. Elle ne fait pas une guerre de conquête ... Elle ne cherche pas un intérêt matériel. Notre peuple ne songe même pas à la richesse du sol d'Alsace et de Lorraine, aux produits de son agriculture, de son vignoble, de ses mines; il ne se préoccupe ni de minerai de fer, ni de pétrole, ni de potasse. Il veut que la patrie recouvre cette population qui lui appartenait, qui était la chair de sa chair et le sang de son sang. Il sait que cette volonté est fondée en droit et en justice. N'est-ce pas lui, notre peuple, qui a proclamé les droits de l'homme, et aussi les droits des peuples?[64]*

The *Comité*'s version of French history was, therefore, uncompromisingly republican and placed primary importance on 1789 as the defining moment in the nation's development. The 'true' France was the nation that had conceived the Declaration of the Rights of Man and of the Citizen, the France that came fleetingly but gloriously into existence in the early 1790s, before war, counter-revolutionary violence, terror and the rise of Napoleonic imperialism shattered the infant Republic's idealism. This was the moment when all those who yearned for freedom and justice, including the people of Alsace and Lorraine, looked to France for inspiration and support.

The geographers, the French Revolution and Alsace-Lorraine, 1917-1918

This staunchly republican version of French history implied a comparable republican vision of France's political geography. According to the report's succinct analysis of the nation's changing frontiers from 1789 onwards, written by Lucien Gallois, the shape of the 'true France' was reflected neither by the borders of 1871 to 1914 nor by those of 1815 to 1870. Both these arrangements had been imposed on a defeated nation following disastrous episodes of Napoleonic imperialism. Modern, democratic and republican France, a nation fighting for its very survival against a ruthless enemy that had violated the eastern portion of its national space, demanded and required a border that would not only secure the nation in the future but would also reflect the values of those who had established the first Republic after the Revolution of 1789.

But which borders best represented France's foundational republican sentiments? The actual frontiers in the years after 1789 were problematic for a variety of reasons. The 1789 borders reflected the politics of the *Ancien Régime* rather than the Revolution while the frontiers of the early 1790s were both chronically unstable and included 'enclaves' of French territory surrounded by land held by rival states. For Gallois, the imagined geographies of revolutionary France provided a most useful guide, particularly Danton's famous observation of 1793 about the Republic's 'natural' borders. According to this, France was limited by obvious sea and ocean coastlines to the north, west and south-east (the English Channel, the Atlantic, and the Mediterranean) and by equally imposing mountain ranges to the south-west and south-east (the Pyrenees and the Alps). The remaining eastern sector of the frontier should be delimited, according to Danton, by another natural feature: the Rhine.

As Gallois noted, this geopolitical arrangement was secured after the Treaty of Lunéville in 1801, following the rise of Napoleon, and for the next fourteen years this entire area had formed a single *mère patrie* with a common administrative system. If this expanded France was no longer acceptable, Gallois further argued, then surely some compromise was possible between these expansive 1801 borders and the diminished frontiers imposed on France in 1815. The obvious solution, Gallois implied, was the 1814 border, negotiated so brilliantly by Talleyrand after the initial abdication of Napoleon and before the Hundred Days (see Figure 1). This would give France Saarlouis and Saarbrücken, together with most of the Saar coal field, as well as Landau and its environs. This should be France's baseline negotiating position at any future peace conference.[65]

Not everyone on the *Comité* agreed with Gallois, however, and it must be emphasised that despite the attempts by Lavisse and Vidal to recruit like-minded scholars, the *Comité*'s membership displayed many of the divisions that had hampered earlier commissions of inquiry. While the idea of a permanent annexation of the Rhineland (the extreme revanchist position previously articulated by de Wendel and his supporters) enjoyed no support, at least one member of the *Comité*, Général Bourgeois, made a powerful case for a permanent French annexation of the Saar coal field coupled with a long-term military occupation of the west bank of the Rhine. For Bourgeois, France should seek not a single, definitive line of demarcation but at least two different borders with Germany: a political border (to include Alsace-Lorraine and the Saarland) and a military border corresponding with the River Rhine.[66] This argument was reinforced by the long final section of the report, co-written by Bourgeois, Jullian, Pfister, Sagnac and Denis, on the history and current political sentiment of the west bank of the Rhine. These carefully researched pages sought to underline the cultural distinctiveness of this region from the rest of imperial Germany.[67]

But the Général's position was a minority viewpoint. Most members of the *Comité*, particularly Lavisse, Vidal, Aulard, Gallois and Seignobos, felt that a French military presence in the Rhineland would be unsustainable even in the medium term and would inevitably store up resentment against occupying troops. These individuals also calculated, probably correctly, that liberal opinion within and beyond France would not readily accept territorial revisions that could only be sustained by force. French claims needed to be convincing in political and cultural terms. A return to the 1870 border was a realistic prospect but further territorial claims should be kept to a minimum. In two of the more convincing chapters in the report, Vidal and Gallois hinted that a treaty guaranteeing French access to the Saar coal reserves would be preferable to the annexation of the entire coalfield.[68] Likewise, Émile Bourgeois, de Martonne and Gallois provided an impressive analysis of the economic and political history of the Rhine trade, complete with complex thematic maps showing the volume of commerce in different periods by country of origin and commodity. This culminated with a renewed plea for improved international regulations governing the neutrality and freedom of navigation on the river, an argument that challenged the need for a French military presence in the area.[69]

The *Comité*'s relatively moderate stance was confirmed at the *séance de clôture* on 19 November 1917. The brief summation, written by Charles Seignobos, was the very model of restraint. Revanchist territorial claims represented the discredited diplomacy of the past, Seignobos insisted, and punitive peace treaties maintained by force were in no-one's interests. French policy should be guided by three principles: *restitutions*; *réparations*; *garanties*. These principles translated into the following specific objectives:

1) German aggression invalidated the Treaty of Frankfurt and, as a result, the area ceded to Germany in 1871 should be returned to France without the need for a plebiscite;

2) Germany must accept its responsibility for the war and agree to compensate France for the cost it had been forced to bear;

3) Future relations between France, Germany and the other European states, both existing and potential, should henceforth be guaranteed by internationally recognised legal treaties rather than the secret diplomacy of the past.

These were, in some respects, surprising conclusions. The first proposal simply ignored all the complex arguments about the Saarland and the west bank of the Rhine. The second and third proposals emerged from nowhere as neither had received any sustained comment in the preceding reports. But these remarks were aimed at an international, especially an Anglo-American, audience as well as senior French politicians. Although there was no explicit mention of the League of Nations, Seignobos's language was deliberately internationalist. The message was clear: France would not be able to dictate peace terms with Germany on a unilateral basis and the peace process would inevitably require international agreement. Excessive claims threatened to undermine international support for the French case and endanger even the most fundamental geopolitical objectives. Modest claims were most likely to maintain allied unity. Once this was achieved, further concessions could be proposed during the negotiations themselves.[70]

The political and intellectual legacies

The political impact of the *Comité* is difficult to assess. The influence of its various reports on France's political leadership was initially modest. Aristide Briand, the *Comité*'s patron, fell from power in March 1917, soon after work began, and his successors, Alexandre Ribot and Georges Clemenceau, initially displayed little faith in the persuasive powers of French intellectuals, though they continued to support the *Comité*'s work. Senior politicians probably had no time to consider the subtleties and nuances of the *Comité*'s detailed findings before the end of the war. According to

Charles Benoist, only President Raymond Poincaré habitually read the documents produced by the *Comité* prior to their eventual publication in late 1918. As a native of Lorraine and an arch advocate of a punitive peace settlement with Germany, Poincaré would probably have been unconvinced by his late night reading.[71]

However, the announcement of President Woodrow Wilson's Fourteen Points on 8 January 1918 underscored the importance of developing intellectually coherent claims with respect to Alsace-Lorraine. Clemenceau, by then in power, had no choice but to accept Wilson's strongly internationalist programme as the basis of a future peace conference even though he was privately dismayed by the vague wording adopted by the Americans in respect of Alsace-Lorraine.[72] The subsequent success of the Allied counter-attack after the last-ditch German offensive on the Western Front in the summer of 1918 further intensified interest in the preparations for the peace discussions.

From August onwards, Clemenceau organised regular briefings with senior figures from the *Comité d'Études*, some of whom were still working on reports about the wider European questions. Like most French politicians of his generation, Clemenceau was obsessed with Alsace-Lorraine and the Rhine and most of these meetings concerned these matters. It is unlikely these encounters changed the attitude of the French Premier but they may have played some part in convincing him to adopt a cautious tone on the question of Alsace-Lorraine when the German armistice request was finally published. While Poincaré and senior army officers wanted to continue the war into German territory, Clemenceau insisted only on a provisional occupation of the pre-1870 Alsace-Lorraine following the ceasefire.[73]

In the interlude between the armistice of November 1918 and the beginning of the Peace Conferences in February 1919, a host of new objectives and programmes were brought into play. Maréchal Foch, flushed with his success as Commander-in-Chief of the Allied armies, intervened decisively to reinforce the case for an Allied occupation of the Rhineland and proposed his own version of Bourgeois's defensible military frontier, a strategic border enclosing the whole of the Saar coal field as well as a German population of around one million (see Figure 1).[74]

Objectives shifted again as the negotiations got underway. Although several members of the *Comité* were involved in the Peace Conferences as expert academic advisers,[75] the major decisions concerning policies and negotiating tactics were obviously made by Clemenceau and his closest aides, notably André Tardieu whose interventions on the Franco-German border proved decisive.[76] The articles eventually included in the Treaty of Versailles (signed on 28 June 1919) about Alsace-Lorraine, the Saarland and the Rhine represented a hard-fought compromise between a revanchist French perspective and the moderate position advocated by the *Comité d'Études*. The re-establishment of the 1870 border was certainly consistent with the *Comité*'s conclusions and the transfer to France of the Saar coal mines, although passed over in silence in Seignobos's summation, probably reflected the view of most *Comité* members. Revealingly, the implications of the new arrangement were hastily re-considered in a revised and expanded 1919 version of the earlier reports by Vidal and Gallois.[77] The fact that the Saar basin was to be placed under neutral League of Nations control (it was finally returned to Germany following a plebiscite fifteen years later) also corresponded with the *Comité*'s conviction that Franco-German relations should be set within an agreed international framework.[78] But the enforced German demilitarisation of both the east and west banks of the Rhine reflected more traditional fears and anxieties and with the arguments previously developed by the revanchist conservative right and the French army.[79]

The arguments developed by the *Comité d'Études* and the other commissions that campaigned for a French Alsace-Lorraine were often extremely presumptuous and reflected attitudes that would intensify anti-French feeling in the region through the 1920s and 1930s. Although the largely French-speaking urban bourgeoisie of Strasbourg, Metz and the other cities were plainly delighted by the restoration of what they saw as liberal, republican rule, the German and Alsatian-speaking workers and peasants were understandably alarmed to discover they now lived in a highly centralised state renowned for its intolerance of regionally distinct cultures. These divergent class reactions to the new regime were complicated by local factors, notably religious differences between Catholics, Protestants and Jews. French war-time proclamations about the commitment of Alsace and Lorraine to the ideals of liberty, equality and fraternity must have seemed rather hollow when it was revealed that the authorities had interned as enemy aliens all those people resident in France who were born in German Elsaß-Lothringen after 1871 or who had opted to stay in the region after 1872. Not surprisingly, perhaps, many Alsatians turned their backs on both Germany and France during the inter-war years and sought solace in various forms of regionalist and autonomist politics.[80]

It is no less difficult to assess the wider intellectual influence of the *Comité*'s findings and perspectives. The published report, on Alsace-Lorraine and on the larger European questions, enjoyed a surprisingly wide readership in the immediate aftermath of the war but the relevance and interest of its findings quickly faded. Individual members of the *Comité* clearly drew extensively on their war-time experiences in their subsequent research, not least Vidal himself whose remarkable final work, *La France de l'Est*, published in 1917 a few months before his death, extended many of the arguments he and his co-workers developed during their work on the *Comité*.[81] As was mentioned in the introduction, the resumption of French rule in Alsace-Lorraine after 1918 and the re-establishment of a French Université de Strasbourg on the Rhine produced a new flowering of French historical and geographical scholarship in the region under the auspices of the *Annales* school, and this owed a great deal to the preceding work of the liberal republican scholars who served on the *Comité*. Works such as Demangeon and Febvre's *Le Rhin*, published in 1935, reflect both the continuity of the French geo-historical method as well as the persistence of the geopolitical concerns and anxieties that had inspired its development during World War One.[82] Throughout the 1920s and 1930s, French historians and geographers were acutely aware that the political and intellectual battle for legitimacy in Alsace and eastern Lorraine was by no means finished. Inter-war writings on the region remained, therefore, deeply controversial.[83]

Conclusion

The campaign to restore French rule in Alsace-Lorraine during World War One produced a mountain of published and unpublished literature on every conceivable aspect of the region's past, present and future. Several different perspectives were advanced, some more realistic than others, based on economic and military considerations. The *Comité d'Études* represented a distinctive aspect of this wider campaign. It developed a relatively moderate line, in contrast to the more draconian measures proposed by revanchist businessmen, politicians and senior army officers. It sought to identify realistic options that could command support across the political spectrum. The intention was to convince sceptics in France and elsewhere that the country was not seeking territorial aggrandisement but merely a just re-arrangement of the national space.

This is not to say that the evidence assembled by the *Comité* about Alsace-Lorraine was more 'accurate' than that compiled in other, more obviously partisan forms of French geo-propaganda. Nor, of course, were the *Comité*'s arguments more 'objective' than the corresponding German war-time claims about this region. The *Comité* constructed a common historical narrative for France and for Alsace-Lorraine, pivoting around the Revolution of 1789, and sought to associate this with a particular idealised geography. Its remarkable reports were exercises in applied historical geography, attempts to legitimise territorial claims by reference to newly assembled historical and geographical evidence expressed textually, cartographically and statistically by internationally renowned academics. The work of the *Comité d'Études* demonstrates that historical geography was (and arguably still is in many parts of the world) a powerful form of political rhetoric as well as a disinterested academic endeavour.

Acknowledgements

This essay is based on research carried out with the assistance of various grants from the British Academy and the Arts and Humanities Research Board in the UK and from the Alexander von Humboldt Foundation in Germany. It was written while I was Alexander von Humboldt Research Fellow at the Geographisches Institut at Ruprecht-Karls-Universität Heidelberg. I would like to thank Professor Dr Peter Meusburger and the other Heidelberg geographers for their hospitality as well as Professor Robert J. Young, from the Department of History at the University of Winnipeg, for an enlightening discussion about the political career of Louis Barthou.

NOTES

1   A. R. H. Baker, On ideology and historical geography, in A. R. H. Baker and M. Billinge (Eds), *Period and Place: Research Methods in Historical Geography* (Cambridge 1982) 233-243, quotation on p. 235.

2   A. R. H. Baker, *Fraternity among the French Peasantry: Sociability and Voluntary Associations in the Loire Valley, 1815-1914* (Cambridge 1999) lists many of the author's earlier publications.

3   The literature on the *Annales* school is huge, but see: S. Clark (Ed.), *The Annales School* (London 1999); P. Burke, *The French Historical Revolution: The Annales School, 1929-1989* (Cambridge 1990); C. Fink, *Marc Bloch: A Life* (Cambridge 1989); E. Weber, About Marc Bloch, in *idem, My France: Politics, Culture, Myth* (Cambridge, MA 1991) 244-258. This tradition was brilliantly exemplified in the post-1945 era by Fernand Braudel. See, for example, F. Braudel, *The Mediterranean and the Mediterranean World in the Age of Philip II* (Berkeley and Los Angeles 1995 [1949]); *idem, Civilisation and Capitalism, 15th-18th Centuries* (3 vols, London 1979); and *idem, The Identity of France* (2 vols, London 1989-1991). Baker's work can also be read as a sustained engagement by a geographer with ideas developed by a more recent generation of historians, notably Eugen Weber whose *Peasants into Frenchmen: The Modernization of Rural France, 1870-1914* (London 1979) has inspired admiration and criticism in equal measure. See A. R. H. Baker, Military service and migration in nineteenth-century France: some evidence from Loir-et-Cher, *Transactions of the Institute of British Geographers* **23** (1998) 193-206.

4   The relationship between the *Annales* school and geography is discussed in S. W. Friedman, *Marc Bloch, Sociology and Geography: Encountering Disciplines* (Cambridge 1996). For Baker's own thoughts, see A R.H. Baker, Reflections on the relations of historical geography and the *Annales* school of history, in A. R. H. Baker and D. Gregory (Eds), *Explorations in Historical Geography* (Cambridge 1984) 1-24.

5   This term is borrowed from D. N. Livingstone, *The Geographical Tradition: Episodes in the History of a Contested Enterprise* (Oxford 1992), 215-259.

6   On various aspects of German rule in Alsace-Lorraine after 1871, see F. von Aretin, Die Reichsländische schulpolitik während des Kulturkampfes 1872-1873, *Archiv für Sozialgeschichte* **32** (1992) 181-205; C. Baechler, *Le Parti Catholique Alsacien 1890-1939: du Reichsland à la République Jacobine* (Paris 1982); J. E. Craig, *Scholarship and Nation-Building: The Universities of Strasbourg and Alsatian Society, 1870-1939* (Chicago 1984); S. Harp, *Learning to be German: Primary Schooling in Alsace-Lorraine,*

1870-1918 (Unpublished PhD thesis, Indiana University, 1993); J.-M. Mayeur, *Autonomie et Politique en Alsace: la Constitution de 1911* (Paris 1970); F. Roth, Das Reichsland Elsaß-Lothringen: formation, histoire et perceptions, in M. Grunewald (Ed.), *Le Problème de l'Alsace-Lorraine vu par les Périodiques (1871-1914) /Die Elsaß-Lothringische Frage im Spiegel der Zeitschriften (1871-1914)* (Berne 1998), 13-36; D. P. Silverman, *Reluctant Union: Alsace-Lorraine and Imperial Germany, 1871-1918* (University Park, PA 1972); A. Wahl, La question des courants annexionnistes en Allemagne et 'l'Alsace-Lorraine', in F. L'Huillier, *L'Alsace en 1870-1871* (Gap 1971) 185-210; *idem, L'Option et l'Émigration des Alsaciens-Lorrains (1871-1872)* (Paris 1974); A. Wahl and J.-C. Richez, *L'Alsace entre la France et l'Allemagne 1850-1950* (Paris 1993); H. U. Wehler, Elsaß-Lothringen: Das 'Reichsland' als politische-staatsrechtliches Problem des zweiten deutschen Kaiserreichs, *Zeitschrift für die Geschichte der Oberrheins* **109** (1961) 133-199; P. Zind, *Elsaß-Lothringen, Alsace-Lorraine: une nation interdite, 1870-1940* (Paris 1979).

7   The German decision about where the new border should lie was more or less clear by September 1870 when the *Geographische und Statischische Abteilung* of the German General Staff published a new map in Berlin showing its recommendation. The modifications to this original map (including the agreement that France should retain Belfort and its environs in exchange for small concessions in the former French *département* of the Moselle) can be found in E. Hertslet, *The Map of Europe by Treaty; Showing the Various Political and Territorial Changes Which Have Taken Place Since the General Peace of 1814* (Vol. III, London 1875), 1913-4 and 1954-1973.

8   On this, see J.-M. Mayeur, Une mémoire-frontière: l'Alsace, in P. Nora (Ed.), *Les Lieux de Mémoire: Vol. 2 – La Nation* (Paris 1986) 62-95.

9   On Treitschke, see A. Dorpalen, *Heinrich von Treitschke* (New Haven 1957) and, more generally, J. Breuilly, The national idea in modern German history, in *idem* (Ed.), *The State in Germany: The National Idea in the Making, Unmaking and Remaking of a Modern Nation-State* (London 1992) 1-28.

10   E. Renan, Qu'est-ce qu'une nation?, in *idem, Œuvres Complètes* (10 Vols, Paris 1947-1961) I (1947), 887-906, quotations on pp. 905-6. Renan's remarks on the futility of racial theories of the nation included his most direct attack on Germany: "La vérité est qu'il n'y a pas de race pure et que faire reposer la politique sur l'analyse ethnographique, c'est de faire porter sur une chimère. Les plus noble pays, l'Angleterre, la France, l'Italie, sont ceux où le sang est le plus mêlé. L'Allemagne fait-elle à cet égard une exception? Est-elle un pays germanique pur? Quelle illusion!" (p. 902). For a recent English translation, see E. Renan, What is a nation?, in H. K. Bhabha (Ed.), *Nation and Narration* (London 1990), 8-21.

11   D. Stevenson, *French War Aims Against Germany, 1914-1919* (Oxford 1982) 11-2 though see also P. Renouvin, Les buts de guerre du gouvernement français, 1914-1918, *Revue Historique* **135** (1966) 1-38.

12   The cabinet was by no means united on this, however, and the socialist Interior Minister, Louis Malvy, remained convinced of the need for a negotiated peace settlement. See Stevenson, *op. cit.*, 15-18.

13   Barthou, a biographer of Victor Hugo, was the most senior of these three and had served in several pre-war cabinets and was briefly Prime Minister in the summer of 1913. In 1934, when Foreign Minister, he was assassinated by a Croatian nationalist along with King Alexander of Yugoslavia in Marseilles. See R. J. Young, *Power and Pleasure: Louis Barthou and the Third French Republic* (Montreal and Kingston 1991). Tardieu, a right-wing journalist, was elected to Parliament in 1914 and was a leading negotiator at the Paris Peace Conferences. He became minister for the *régions libérées* (Alsace-Lorraine) after 1919 and was Prime Minister on three separate occasions in the late 1920s and early 1930s. See F. Monnet, *Refaire la République: André Tardieu – une Dérive Réactionnaire (1876-1945)* (Paris 1993). Marin's political career as a long-serving *député* for the Meurthe-et-Moselle (the *département* established in 1871 from the remnants of the two older *départements* of the Meurthe and the Moselle – see Figure 1), sometime cabinet minister and leader of the far-right *Fédération Républicaine* in the late 1920s and 1930s was combined with his work as an anthropologist and geographer. See H. Lebovics, *True France: The Wars Over Cultural Identity, 1900-1945* (Ithaca 1992) 12-50.

14 Stevenson, *op. cit.*, 23.

15 Stevenson, *op. cit.*, 23. On de Wendel, see J.-N. Jeanneney, *François de Wendel en République: l'Argent et le Pouvoir, 1914-1940* (Paris 1976). The literary and political career of Maurice Barrès provides one of the best commentaries on the shifting nature of French right-wing thinking in the Third Republic. See R. Soucy, *Fascism in France: The Case of Maurice Barrès* (Berkeley and Los Angeles 1972) and E. Weber, Inheritance, dilettantism, and the politics of Maurice Barrès, in *Idem, My France: Politics, Culture, Myth* (Cambridge, MA 1991) 226-43. On Alsace-Lorraine as a focus of right-wing French nationalism. See M. Burns, Families and fatherlands: the lost provinces and the case of Captain Dreyfus, in R. Tombs (Ed.), *Nationhood and Nationalism in France from Boulangism to the Great War 1889-1912* (London 1991) 50-62 and W. Serman, The nationalists of Meurthe-et-Moselle, 1888-1912, in *ibid.*, 121-135.

16 On Siegfried and the *Musée Social*, established in 1895 as a focus for moralising social research aimed at improving the lot of workers while preserving the economic system under which they laboured, see S. Elwitt, *The Third Republic Defended: Bourgeois Reform in France, 1880-1914* (Baton Rouge 1986) 155-69. Jules Siegfried was the father of André, the prolific political and economic geographer and the author of several memoirs about his father's life and work, notably A. Siegfried, *Jules Siegfried, 1837-1922* (Paris 1942).

17 Twelve of the *Comité's séances* took place in 1915, seven in 1916, three in 1917, nine in 1918 and two in 1919. Most of these reports were published and can be consulted on microfilm in the *Bibliothèque de France* (BF-M-18062). A summary of the *Comité's* work and a full list of its publications, also available in BF-M-18062, can be found in CEAL, *Rapport d'ensemble sur les travaux du Comité, par M. Roger Merlin (adopté en séance du Comité du 14 juin 1919)* (Paris 1919) while the significant impact of the *Comité's* resolutions in shaping the French negotiating stance at the Paris Peace Conferences can be deduced from CEAL, *Rapport comparatif sur les clauses du traité de paix avec l'Allemagne concernant l'Alsace-Lorraine et les vœux précédemment émis par le Comité, par Roger Merlin (adopté en séance du Comité du 14 juin 1919)* (Paris 1919).

18 Some 41 million tonnes of iron ore were mined in Lorraine in 1913, 21 million on the German side of the border (c. 75 per cent of the total German production) and 20 million on the French side (c. 90 per cent of the total French production). These figures are discussed in Stevenson, *op. cit.*, 216-8.

19 This position was developed and extended in numerous official memoranda circulating in different government ministeries, notably that drafted in late 1916 as a directive for French discussions with Allied countries by Paul and Jules Cambon (the diplomat brothers who were serving as Ambassadors in London and Berlin respectively when the war broke out). See Stevenson, *op. cit.*, 42-3.

20 Stevenson, *op. cit.*, 25-6, 62, 78-9, 83, 99-103, and 251. On French concerns about American attitudes before and after the US entry into the war, see D. Stevenson, French war aims and the American challenge, 1914-1918, *Historical Journal* **32** (1979) 877-894.

21 Marin was also behind an earlier private project (which was still on-going when he approached the SGP) to develop a much wider economic programme within which to advance French claims to Alsace-Lorraine. In December 1915, he persuaded his fellow members on the council of the *Société de Géographie Commerciale de Paris*, the more overtly political of the two geographical societies in the French capital, to organise a *Commission d'Études Économiques*, under the presidency of former Commerce Minister Raoul Peret, with a view to developing a general economic plan to allow France to wage the war more effectively and enhance its post-war economic performance. See M. Heffernan, The spoils of war: the *Société de Géographie de Paris* and the French empire, 1914-1919, in M. Bell, R. Butlin and M. Heffernan (Eds), *Geography and Imperialism, 1820-1940* (Manchester 1995) 221-64, esp. 259-60.

22 Archives of the *Société de Géographie de Paris* colis 9, dossiers 2284-2287 (SGP 9/2284-7).

23 Stevenson, *op cit*, 23, 38-9; SGP 9/2285 and 2287. To underscore the huge importance of the Lorraine iron and steel industry, one of these reports made the startling claim that had the French army held the frontier in Lorraine in 1914 and then pushed back the German armies seven kilometres over a 15-kilometre front, the Germany war effort would already have collapsed for want of iron and steel.

24   On the development of this argument through the war, see W. Kern, *Die Rheintheorie in der Historisch-Politischen Literatur Frankreichs im ersten Weltkrieg* (Sarrebrück 1973).

25   Stevenson, *op. cit.,* 43.

26   SGP 9/2286.

27   The sole military representative on the *sous-commission*, Général Lacroix, had also argued for a French military occupation of the Rhineland on 23 February but only after warning against excessive territorial ambitions which he felt would only provoke "des idées de revanche et feraient naitre dans les pays annexés des sentiments analogues à ceux qui nourissent des Alsaciens-Lorraines à l'égard de l'Allemagne". Lacroix's scheme was limited by the Rhine and the Moselle rivers, in which the northernmost point of French claims would be the city at the confluence of these two rivers, Koblenz. SGP 9/2284. For a thoughtful analysis of the army's role in the formulation of French territorial objectives in the early phase of the war, see R. A. Prete, French military war aims, 1914-1916, *Historical Journal* **28** (1985) 887-899.

28   See the various comments by Gallois and Brunhes in SGP 9/2284 and by Christian Schefer, from the *École des Sciences Politiques*, in SGP 9/2285.

29   SGP 9/2286. Supporters of this position, together with those who argued the less extreme case of a demilitarised Rhineland policed by French and/or Allied troops, formed their own committee in February 1917, the *Comité de la rive gauche du Rhin*, under the chairmanship of the historian Édouard Driault. This proved to be one of the more successful lobbies before and during the Peace Conferences. See Stevenson, *op. cit.,* 37, 150 and, for Driault's own perspective, E. Driault, *Pas de Paix Durable sans la Barrière du Rhin* (Paris 1917).

30   Despite repeated maulings from Georges Clemenceau, Briand refused to sack Louis Malvy, his socialist Interior Minister, who was widely known to favour a negotiated peace settlement and generally believed to have dragged his heels in the pursuit and prosecution of French pacifists. Malvy actually survived Briand as Interior Minister but was forced from office at the end of August 1917 following revelations that *Le Bonnet Rouge*, a pacifist left-wing newspaper he had allowed to continue publication, was being secretly funded by the German government. Malvy was subsequently tried for treason (which would have meant the death penalty) but was convicted on the lesser charge of culpable negligence and exiled for five years. Briand's passionate advocacy of the League of Nation and the cause of international peace after 1918 (he was awarded the Nobel Peace Prize in 1926) reflects the very painful lessons he learned during World War I. See G. Suarez, *Briand: sa Vie, son Œuvre avec Jon journal et de Nombreux Documents Inédits. Vol. IV – Le Pilote dans la Tourmente, 1916-1918* (Paris 1940).

31   Suarez, *op. cit.,* 130.

32   Pioneering studies, see R. Dion, *Les Frontières de la France* (Paris 1947); N. J. G. Pounds, The origins of the idea of natural frontiers in France, *Annals of the Association of American Geographers* **41** (1951) 146-157; *idem*, France and 'les limites naturelles' from the seventeenth to the twentieth centuries', *Annals of the Association of American Geographers* **44** (1954) 51-62; N. Smith, The idea of the French hexagon, *French Historical Studies* **3** (1969) 139-155. More recent statements include M. Sahlins, *Boundaries: The Making of France and Spain in the Pyrenees* (Berkeley and Los Angeles 1989); *idem*, Natural frontiers revisited: France's boundaries since the seventeenth century, *American Historical Review* **95** (1990) 1423-1451; and E. Weber, In search of the hexagon, in *idem, My France: Politics, Culture, Myth* (Cambridge, MA. 1991) 57-71.

33   C. Benoist, *Souvenirs* Vol. 3: *1902-1933 – Vie Parlementaire, Vie Diplomatique* (Paris 1934), 324-9. Benoist subsequently served as French ambassador to The Hague.

34   Quoted in A. Sanguin, *Vidal de la Blache: un Génie de la Géographie* (Paris 1993) 106. On Maggiolo's one-man campaign to promote educational reform (which involved the collection of politically incriminating statistics on French literacy rates from the *Ancien Régime* to the 1870s to demonstrate the

costly neglect of education in the past) see F. Furet and J. Ozouf, *Reading and Writing: Literacy in France from Calvin to Jules Ferry* (Cambridge 1982).

35   In July 1871, Simon charged Émile Levasseur, professor of geography, history and economic statistics at the *Collège de France*, and Louis Himly, the sole professor of geography at the Sorbonne though, like Levasseur, an historian by training, to investigate how the teaching of history and geography might be improved. On their inquiry and recommendations, which continued until 1875, long after Simon's fall from power, see H. Andrews, A French view of geography teaching in Britain in 1871, *Geographical Journal* **152** (1986) 179-182; N. Broc, Histoire de la géographie et nationalisme en France sous la IIIe République (1870-1890), *L'Information Historique* **32** (1970) 21-26; *idem*, L'établissement de la géographie en France: diffusion, institutions, projets (1870-1890), *Annales de Géographie* **83** (1974) 545-568.

36   Quoted in Sanguin, *op. cit.,* 106.

37   For a general discussion of this strategy, see A. B. Murphy, Historical justifications of territorial claims, *Annals of the Association of American Geographers* **80** (1990) 531-548.

38   On Lavisse, see P. Nora, Lavisse, instituteur national, in *idem, Les Lieux de Mémoire*: Vol. I – *La République* (Paris 1984).

39   V. Berdoulay, *La Formation de l'École Française de Géographie* (Paris 1981); A. Buttimer, *Society and Milieu in the French Geographic Tradition* (Chicago 1971).

40   Vidal's post at Nancy was originally designated in history and geography and was intended to replace the Strasbourg chair of history, previously occupied by Numa Denis Fustel de Coulanges. Vidal was not awarded a full professorship until his thirtieth birthday in 1875, by which time he had persuaded the authorities to re-designate the post as geography only. See Sanguin, *op. cit.,* 99-118.

41   See H. Andrews, Les premiers cours de géographie de Paul Vidal de la Blache à Nancy (1873-1877), *Annales de Géographie* **95** (1986) 341-361; J.-C. Bonnefont, La Lorraine dans l'œuvre de Paul Vidal de la Blache, in P. Claval (Ed.), *Autour de Vidal de la Blache: la Formation de l'École Française de Géographie* (Paris 1993) 81-88.

42   In 1873, Vidal applied to the *Ministère de l'Instruction Publique* for financial assistance to support a fact-finding tour of German universities, a trip that involved meetings with Friedrich von Richthofen in Berlin and the Oscar Peschel in Leipzig. Archives Nationales F[17] 3013 (Ministère de l'Instruction Publique: Missions scientifiques et littéraires. Dossiers individuels: XIXe siècle – Paul Vidal de la Blache, 1873-4).

43   On Vidal's youth, see H. Andrews, The early life of Paul Vidal de la Blache and the making of modern geography, *Transactions of the Institute of British Geographers* **11** (1986) 174-182.

44   The *Histoire* was planned at the end of the nineteenth century and the 27th and final volume appeared in 1922, the year Lavisse died.

45   Quoted in Saguin, *op. cit.,* 198.

46   On the wider European aspects of the *Comité d'Études*, see M. Heffernan, La géographie de l'histoire: French visions of Europe, 1914-1920, *Political Geography*, (forthcoming).

47   See, for example, A. Aulard, *Études et Leçons sur la Révolution Française* (9 Vols, Paris 1893-1924).

48   See, for example, E. Bourgeois, *La Diplomatie Secrète au XVIIIe Siècle* (2 Vols, Paris 1909-10).

49   On Général Bourgeois, see A. Lévy, *Les Coulisses de la Guerre: le Service Géographique de l'Armée 1914-1918* (Paris 1926).

50   See, for example, A. Chuquet, *La Jeunesse de Napoléon* (3 Vols, Paris 1897-9).

51 See, for example, E. Denis, *Fin de l'Indépendence Bohême* (2 Vols, Paris 1890) and his three-volume, variously titled study on the history of Germany from 1789 to 1871.

52 See, for example, L. Gallois, *Les Géographes Allemandes de la Renaissance* (Paris 1890).

53 See, example, C. Jullian, *Histoire de la Gaule* (8 Vols, Paris 1908-1926).

54 See, for example, E. de Martonne, *La Valachia: Essai de Monographie Géographique* (Paris 1902).

55 See, for example, C. Pfister, *Histoire de Nancy* (3 vols, Paris 1902-09) and his work on the language geography of the region in *idem, La Limite de la Langue Française et de la Langue Allemande en Alsace-Lorraine* (Paris 1890).

56 See, for example, C. Seignobos, *Histoire Politique de l'Europe Contemporaine* (Paris 1897).

57 A powerful case could certainly have been made to include Émile Durkheim on the *Comité*. He was, after all, the son of a prominent Jewish rabbi from Lorraine who had worked tirelessly earlier in the war on various committees preparing publications to be despatched to neutral countries to counter German propaganda. Although he was to die unexpectedly aged only 59 in November 1917, Durkheim was at the height of his powers in the early part of that year, despite his grief at the death of his only son the preceding year. However, Durkheim's sociological method was fundamentally at odds with the historico-geographical perspective championed by de la Blache, with whom Durkehim had conducted a bitter 'turf war' at the Sorbonne. His relationship with his native province was also somewhat coloured by the anti-semitism he had experienced as a young man. See H. Andrews, The Durkheimians and human geography: some contextual problems in the sociology of knowledge, *Transactions of the Institute of British Geographers* **9** (1984) 315-336; V. Berdoulay, The Vidal-Durkheim debate, in D. Ley and M. Samuels (Eds), *Humanistic Geography: Prospects and Problems* (London 1978) 77-90. On Durkheim's bitterness at the continuing anti-semitism of Alsatians and Lorrainers, see his contribution to H. Dagan, *Enquête sur l'Antisémitisme* (Paris 1899) 60.

58 For a useful wider analysis of French historical research during World War I, see J. Fernique, *L'Histoire au Combat: les Historiens Français Pendant la Grande Guerre* (unpublished Mémoire de Maîtrise, Université de Strasbourg II, 1985).

59 Gallois and de Martonne were both devoted students of de la Blache. De Martonne was also his mentor's son-in-law. Émile Bourgeois's friendship with de la Blache is revealed by the historian's *éloge* in honour of the geographer before the *Académie des sciences morales et politiques* in the *Institut de France* on 27 November 1920 following de la Blache's death in 1918. See E. Bourgeois, *Notice sur la Vie et les Travaux de M. Paul Vidal de la Blache* (Paris 1920).

60 Émile Bourgeois and his colleagues at the *École Libre des Sciences Politiques*, including de la Blache, had organised a series of round-table discussions about the origins and economic implications of the war through 1915 and 1916 while Seignobos had organised an important seminar on the nationalities question in south-central Europe at the *École des Hautes Études Sociales*. See É. Bourgeois et al., *Les Origines de la Guerre* (Paris 1915); *idem, La Guerre et la Vie Économique* (Paris 1916); C. Seignobos, *Les Aspirations Autonomistes en Europe: Leçons faites à l'École des Hautes Études Sociales* (Paris 1913). Gallois, de Martonne and de la Blache had also been involved on the *Commission de Géographie*, established by Général Bourgeois in the SGA in late 1914 to prepare geographical handbooks on the various theatres of war, including nine detailed surveys of the front-line French *départements*. See Heffernan, The spoils, 234-5, 259.

61 The complete version of the report, divided into six sections and 22 single or joint-authored chapters, was not published until after the armistice in November 1918, when the work on the wider European questions was also finished. See Comité d'Études, *Travaux du Comité d'Études. Tome Premier: L'Alsace-Lorraine et la frontière du Nord-Est* (Paris 1918) [hereafter *TCE*]. This first volume ran to 450 pages and was accompanied by an atlas containing 22 new thematic maps and facsimile reproductions of five documents discovered in national and local archives. The second volume, on *Questions Européennes*, was nearly 900 pages in length and was accompanied by an atlas containing 21 maps.

62 While forced to concede the overwhelming numerical dominance of German speakers in Alsace-Lorraine, Lavisse and Pfister nevertheless insisted that, insofar as a language frontier could ever be identified with precision, it lay far to the west of German claims in 1870-1. French speaking was also much more widespread than was popularly recognised, they claimed, particularly amongst the social and intellectual elite. During the eighteenth century, "[l]a noblesse et la bourgeoisie alsaciennes s'initièrent aux manières français ... [et] ... parlaient correctement le français" while during the nineteenth century, "[l]e français devint de la sorte la langue de la bourgeoisie et des familles aisées de la campagne. Parler français fut un signe de culture et de bonne éducation et comme un titre de noblesse ...". E. Lavisse and C. Pfister, La formation de l'Alsace-Lorraine, in *TCE*, 3-40, quotations on pp. 23, 26-7 and 31.

63 E. Weber, Who sang the *Marseillaise?*, in *idem*, *My France: Politics, Culture, Myth* (Cambridge, MA 1991) 92-102.

64 *Ibid.*, 36.

65 L. Gallois, Les variations de la frontière française du Nord et du Nord-Est depuis 1789, in *TCE*, 41-56.

66 Section on Questions stratégiques, in *TCE*, 305-339. The idea that France might insist on a separate 'economic frontier', distinct from both a 'military frontier' on the Rhine and a 'political frontier' corresponding with the 1870 line, was discussed by Schéfer in La frontière économique du Nord-Est: rapport préliminaire, in *TCE*, 193-206.

67 Section on Les populations rhénanes, in *TCE*, 341-443.

68 This would have involved establishing a French government-backed company that would acquire and operate the larger Saar mines on both sides of a re-drawn border. See P. Vidal de la Blache, La frontière de la Sarre, in TCE, 77-101 and L. Gallois, Le bassin houiller de Sarrebruck: étude économique et politique, in *TCE*, 104-140.

69 Section on Le Rhin: fleuve international, in *TCE*, 243-304.

70 Lavisse endorsed these conclusions though he noted that not everyone on the *Comité* agreed with them. See *TCE*, 445-53.

71 Benoist, *op. cit.*, 324-9.

72 Wilson's Eighth Point stated vaguely that: "All French territories should be freed and the invaded portions restored, and the wrong done to France by Prussia in 1871 in the matter of Alsace-Lorraine ... should be righted in order that peace may once more be made secure in the interest of all". See R. Henig, *Versailles and After, 1919-1933* (London 1995), 75-6; Stevenson, *op. cit.*, 101, 132, 251.

73 Stevenson, *op. cit.*, 118-9.

74 *Ibid.*, 145.

75 Général Bourgeois, de Martonne and Gallois all served as members of the *Service Géographique Français* that advised the French negotiating team on basic geographical questions. The geographers Albert Demangeon and Jean Brunhes, who had worked on the larger European questions considered by the *Comité*, also worked for the *Service* during the Peace Conferences. For a French geographical analysis of the new political landscape after World War I, the very title of which reflects the arguments developed in this chapter, see J. Brunhes and C. Vallaux, *La Géographie de l'Histoire: Géographie de la Paix et de la Guerre sur Terre et Mer* (Paris 1921).

76 Stevenson, *op. cit.*, 152-60, 177-80. See also A. Tardieu, *La Paix* (Paris 1921).

77 P. Vidal de la Blache and L. Gallois, *Le Bassin de la Sarre: Clauses du Traité de Versailles – Étude Historique et Économique* (Paris 1919).

78 For an definitive study of the Saar question at the Peace Conferences, see H. Hirsch, *Die Saar in Versailles: Die Saarfrage auf der Friedenskonferenz von 1919* (Bonn 1952).

79   See R. McCrum, French Rhineland policy and the Paris Peace Conference, 1919, *Historical Journal* **31** (1978) 623-648.

80   See, for example, M. Anderson, Regional identity and political change: the case of Alsace from the Third to the Fifth Republic, *Political Studies* **20** (1987) 17-30; S. H. Goodfellow, From Germany to France? Interwar Alsatian national identity, *French History* **7** (1993) 450-471; *idem, Between the Swastika and the Cross of Lorraine: Fascisms in Interwar Alsace* (Dekalb, Ill. 1999); W. D. Smith, From the Reich to the Republic: Alsace, 1918-1925, in M. Kelly and R. Böck (Eds), *France: Nation and Regions* (Southampton 1993) 182-9; Zind, *op. cit.*

81   For a brilliant analysis of this remarkable text, see Yves Lacoste's long introductory essay to his 1994 edition of the book in P. Vidal de la Blache, *La France de l'Est (Lorraine-Alsace) 1917: un Livre de Géopolitique passé sous Silence depuis Soixante Ans* (Paris 1994) i-xxxviii.

82   A. Demangeon and L. Febvre, *Le Rhin: Problèmes d'Histoire et d'Économie* (Paris 1935). Febvre's section of this work has recently been re-issued as L. Febvre, *Le Rhin: Histoire, Mythes et Réalités* (Paris 1995) with an outstanding introductory essay by P. Schöttler, Lucien Febvre ou la démystification de l'histoire rhénane, 11-56. For the wider political context within which this work was produced, see W. A. MacDougall, *France's Rhineland Diplomacy, 1914-1924: The Last Bid for a Balance of Power in Europe* (Princeton 1978).

83   P. Schöttler, The Rhine as an object of historical controversy in the inter-war years: towards a history of frontier mentalities, *History Workshop Journal* **39** (1995) 1-21.

Chapter Ten

RETOUR À LA TERRE

Peasantist Discourse
in Rural France c.1930-1950

MARK CLEARY

Introduction

The diverse ways in which the peasantry has sought to either organise itself – or be organised by others – has been an important theme in research on the French peasantry in the nineteenth and twentieth centuries. Indeed, the nature of peasant organisations or, more widely, organisations in the peasant world, has been central to much of Alan Baker's work. As his recent *Fraternity among the French Peasantry* demonstrated, the sheer range and diversity of such organisations – the *syndicat* and *mutuelle*, the co-operative, fire-fighting fraternities or musical societies – makes historical arguments about the innate individualism of the peasantry difficult to sustain. The processes which contributed to individual and community activities in peasant society are arguably too complex and too differentiated by region, class, religion and politics to permit easy generalisation.

A second theme in much of Alan's work has been a critical and contextualised analysis of the connections between changing rural *mentalités* and the organisations set up to represent, channel or exploit those views. As he notes, "the idea of fraternity was complex, its practical possibilities were multiple. It came to be incorporated into the traditional, paternalistic, social order envisaged by the Catholic Church as well as into the new visions of social order presented by republicans, socialists and nationalists".[1] Thus the agricultural innovator sought support from the local *syndicat* in testing particular products, machinery or techniques. The co-operative was created to provide a degree of protection from unscrupulous fertiliser or seed companies as well as security for the small wine or dairy producer seeking to improve returns. An array of cultural organisations from village brass bands, to reading clubs and village libraries offered physical and social space for those seeking the comfort of group activity or the desire to widen horizons. Political and social groupings – from Church to republican *confrérie* likewise solicited peasant support for a variety of motives. Such organisations help to provide an illuminating window into peasant life in particular and rural life generally. Their origins, activity, membership and ideologies reveal much about the fabric of daily life in rural France and of the connections between *pays* and *paysan*.

Change in the fabric of peasant life in the nineteenth and twentieth centuries has been a constant. It is difficult to privilege one historical period over another in the process of transformation. For Weber, the transformation of peasants into Frenchmen was a product of the years between about 1870 and 1914; for Mendras, 'la fin des paysans' occurred primarily in the 1950s and early-1960s; others point to the changes of the 1970s as marking the final death knell of the peasantry.[2] Whether one identifies technical change, the cultural transformation of the peasantry through education and military service, the role of producer and processing co-operatives, or the impact of European and global agricultural trade on French farming, determines in large measure the significance attached to particular periods of change. Similarly, the varied geographical patterns of change impose their own significance. The dynamic north-east, the backwardness of the Massif Central, the economically and culturally enclosed interior of Brittany, or the precocious *sociabilité méridionale* of Provence can be seen as emblematic of the conflicts and contradictions of rural change.

This essay, rather than focusing strictly on a particular period and place, seeks to examine the importance of a singular and remarkably persistent discourse about peasant communities and the place of the peasantry. 'Retour à la terre', literally, 'back to the land', was one of the mainsprings of peasantist ideology in France. It had deep roots. The notion that a return to rural and agricultural origins might provide both economic and indeed moral benefits to the nation had been encapsulated in the writings of academics, writers, politicians and policy-analysts from at least the late-eighteenth century. At the heart of this powerful discourse was the notion that a strong, numerically and economically important agricultural sector was fundamental to the health of French society. Thus, the land and its peoples were the mainspring of wealth, it was argued, and the peasantry itself was the repository of a range of supposedly eternal values (love of *pays* and nation, adherence to the Catholic faith, respect for the established order) that urban and industrial growth could only threaten. As Lavergne wrote, "avec le progrès agricole, tout grandit ... l'intérêt agricole, ce n'est rien moins que l'intérêt national à sa haute puissance".[3] The peasant then, represented both the economic base of the nation and its moral ballast. The peasant family – fecund, hard-working, loyal and church-abiding assumed for many observers an almost iconic status.

Peasantist discourse, however, was not limited to the symbolism of poet and painter or the plot of novelist and playwright. That discourse embraced a range of complex economic, social and political analyses. Thus the corporatist philosophy which was to be of immense significance in the 1930's, drew on and elaborated a number of peasantist doctrines. In the economic and political field arguments about self-regulation for the farming sector coalesced with a political philosophy which saw the salvation of France in the Vichy period (1940-44) in a return to peasant values and *mores*. The link with corporatism was a very important feature of this period and, in practical terms was to lead to the creation of a wide network of agricultural syndicates and co-operatives. At a time when economic crisis, rural out-migration and growing industrial and urban expansion were fashioning new environments and communities in France, corporatist doctrines came to take on a particular resonance.[4] Their powerful appeal to regionalism, to notions of economic and social autonomy, to social Catholic philosophies and to political doctrines of the Right meant that in the inter-war years corporatism had a profound impact on both attitudes and actions in the peasant community.

Inter-war rural France

The myth of a peasant France was perhaps at its strongest in the inter-war years. Some eight million people, over a third of the working population, could be classed as peasant around 1930. Numerically preponderant in many regions, the 36,000 *monuments aux morts* in village and small town through the country, served to reinforce the virtues of sacrifice and salvation in the rural community. The notion that the peasantry represented the backbone and saviour of the nation was deeply embedded in the years after the Great War.[5]

The persistence of that peasant myth defied statistical and economic reality. Workers in the industrial and service sectors far outstripped those working the land in both numbers and, more particularly, economic contribution and, furthermore, their numbers were growing apace with the rural exodus. The economic contribution of agriculture was, at best, mixed. Comparison of the technical state of French farming with neighbouring countries produced a far from flattering portrait. Yields of wheat, for example, were barely half the levels of neighbouring Belgium or the Low Countries and lagged behind Italy and Germany by the end of the 1930s. For a range of other products – rye, maize or potatoes, for example, the gap between French and European averages remained marked. Fertiliser consumption in the 1930s barely reached one-quarter of the German or Belgian levels; five times as much potassium found its way onto German and Belgian fields than onto their French neighbours. Subsistence farming persisted far longer in France that in many of its north European neighbours. In Franklin's phrase farming objectives were overwhelmingly genealogical rather than economic – to secure the farm and family livelihood and to pass on the farm to its successors.[7]

Archaic techniques, a degree of *auto-consommation* at odds with the demands of a market economy, and poor living conditions marked out the peasant sector. Whilst electrification of the countryside began to accelerate in these years, vast numbers of small farms lacked power and proper running water. Local roads were poor and remained impassable in winter periods. The reality of life for the mass of peasant farmers remained some considerable distance from the bucolic portraits of peasantist writers and artists. The notion of peasant pre-eminence was also belied by the nature of property units in the countryside. Large farms (in general over 50 hectares although the threshold size inevitably varied from region to region) covered more that half of the agricultural area in 11 *départements* of France in the 1930s and constituted more than 30% of the area in some 37 other *départements*. A nation of small peasant-farmers? Hardly, when, in terms of production and productivity, considerable parts of the country were dominated by the larger, technically advanced farm/entrepreneur. In many such areas renting of land and the employment of salaried labour, rather than the archetypal peasant family, characterised the enterprise.

If in economic terms the notion of France as a peasant Republic is hard to sustain, in political and social terms the epithet is perhaps more appropriate. Peasant society, whether it voted on the left or right, was innately conservative in terms of a *genre de vie* which required frugality and the minimising of risk in farming practice and techniques. Attitudes and social structure were predominantly paternalist in character and dominated in many regions by the *notables* who ranged from the traditional landed aristocracy to the local squire, doctor, lawyer and merchant. There was thus a considerable diversity of occupations in the countryside although that diversity was being reduced through the steady disappearance of many of the artisans who serviced the needs of the agricultural sector. Catholicism was almost universal in the French countryside – much of western France and the Massif Central were bastions of the faith providing the religious orders and the priesthood with a steady supply of recruits, and swelling both the pews and coffers of the Church.[8]

This picture of a peasant France – anchored to routine, conservative, and Catholic – was geographically nuanced. Western France – especially Brittany – was a peasant fortress. Almost one-quarter of what might be termed the peasant population was to be found in 14 *départements* of western France.[9] A large population of small peasant farmers, low levels of productivity, large families and poor material conditions typified much of interior Brittany and the west. The rural exodus was late in these regions which maintained a traditional, hierarchical social structure longer than in many other parts of France. Further south, the south-west had experienced a rather earlier rural exodus and rural densities were markedly lower than in western France. Practices such as share-cropping dominated in some areas and a low level of farming technique and returns meant that overall yields were well below even a modest national average. Large areas of the Massif Central could be characterised in much the same way. Whilst the rythms of the rural exodus sharply differentiated certain parts of the region, in general much of the Massif shared the characteristics of western France – Catholic, conservative, and slow to adapt to the changed economic environment.

Eastern France and Burgundy offered rather different characteristics. In Lorraine, industrial growth had led to a rapid decline in the rural population whilst Alsace and Burgundy remained characterised by high rural populations and strongly paternalistic social relations dominated, as in western France, by the *notabilité*. Southern France offered a range of economic and social contrasts between the extensive viticultural areas of Languedoc, the pine forests and dune landscapes of the Landes, and the small, polycultural farmers of inland Provence. Contrasts in economic situation, in the precocity or otherwise of the rural exodus, and in the power of the Church and the landed elite were at the heart of these regional differences which makes generalisation about the nature and effects of peasantist discourse difficult.

The peasantist philosophy

For Gordon Wright, one of the most striking features of the inter-war years was "the rediscovery of corporatist theory by some of the peasantists".[10] The comment is apposite in at least two respects. First it emphasises that the development of corporatism in this period was built on a strong historical tradition of corporatist theories which can be traced back to the last decades of the nineteenth century. Secondly, Wright's comment reminds us of the distinctions between peasantist and corporatist theory in these years. For peasantists, corporatism was one strand, a technocratic strand, in a much wider discourse about peasants and rural society generally. That discourse was rooted in at least three elements.

At the outset, the impact of social Catholic ideas on the arguments of the peasantists is evident. The peasant sector was traditionally the mainstay of Catholic support in France. Whilst nominally professing obedience to the Church in huge numbers, the French population might usefully be divided between an increasingly apathetic, if not hostile, urban population (especially in the larger towns and cities) and a largely loyal, unquestioning rural population. Areas such as Brittany, Alsace, much of the Massif Central and the Alps were bastions of Catholicism. They attended Church in the greatest numbers, were loyal to the hierarchy, and the peasantry remained largely subservient to the social paternalism of the Church. Only in a few areas (parts of the south-west, for example, or the northern fringes of the Massif Central) had the peasantry had become distanced from the Church and espoused more radical, republican ideals. Threats to the numerical and moral force of traditional peasant society were viewed as threats to the continued power and influence of the Church itself. The plough and the Cross had long proved powerful allies.[11]

Social Catholic theories, boosted by the publication of the papal encyclical, *Rerum Novarum* in 1891, argued for both a strengthened and constructive dialogue between the Church and emergent industrial-urban society, and for a more direct relationship between the peasantry and the Church that it supported. The Separation of Church and State in 1906, accompanied as it was by a degree of social unrest and violence, further strengthened the relevance of such doctrines.[12] As a consequence, social Catholics, epitomised by the aristocratic Albert de Mun and René de la Tour du Pin, sought to embed church influence through a range of new agricultural associations – syndicates, co-operatives and mutual-insurance groups. By improving rural living conditions Church activists hoped to secure a strong, fecund and Catholic peasantry. In those areas where the Church was weak, Republican activists were equally assiduous in developing their networks of organisations. For social Catholics, "the syndicates (were) a marvellous instrument to maintain the religious fervour of our peasants, to improve their living conditions and to prevent the iniquitous spread of socialism into our tranquil villages".[13] In strongly Catholic parts of France – and, by and large, that meant most of rural France – the *maison sociale* of farming was built on foundations laid in large part by the Church. The most powerful unions and cooperatives in the inter-war years – the Plateau Central in central-southern France, the Office Central in Brittany – were imbued with the socially conservative and paternalist ethos of social Catholicism.[14]

A second, defining element of peasantist discourse was a mistrust, not to say disdain, for the role of the state. The roots of this disdain certainly went deep in

French rural society – a legacy, perhaps, of the Revolutionary period – but a political hardening of attitudes at the time of the Church/State separation undoubtedly took place. That was one of the reasons why the right was so anxious to avoid any state control of the syndical and co-operative movement at the beginning of the twentieth century, leading to a split between the republican/Left movement (known as the Bd St Germain after its Paris headquarters) and the conservative/Right (the rue d'Athènes).[15] For peasantists, self-help and, crucially, self-regulation (albeit through a panoply of largely aristocratically-controlled co-operatives, syndicates and mutualist organisations) was the key to the transformation of rural conditions. The role of the state was viewed with distrust – 'la profession agricole' itself was regarded as the best body to govern its own affairs. At a time when pressures for state intervention were growing as a consequence of the economic depression in the 1930s, such a view was likely to conflict with state policy itself.

That view was to become a powerful element in peasantist doctrines in the 1930s. With the economic crisis, a collapse in agricultural prices had prompted a range of government initiatives (Figure 1). The election of the Popular Front government in 1936 led to greater intervention in agricultural affairs – most notably through the *Office du Blé* – which was heralded by one opponent as "the handsomest Marxist monument known to legislation anywhere".[16] But its passage presaged growing state intervention in farm affairs. Legislation on accident and unemployment insurance, on paid holidays, on the reform of sharecropping were promised by the new government in its drive to extend hard-won reforms in industrial labour conditions to the countryside. For many peasantists, such ideas were alarming and led to a quickening of the anti-collectivist pulse. State control over price and production decisions, even at a time of acute financial crisis in many parts of the countryside, was for many the harbinger of socialism.

A third thread in this fabric was a strong regionalist tradition. Peasantist groups were rooted in the development of very powerful regional unions and cooperatives such as the *Office Central* at Landernau in Finistère, the *Plateau Central* in the Massif Central and the *Union du Sud-Est*. Disseminating both faith and fertilisers such groups were the bedrock of the rural Right and frequently embraced a range of regionalist themes. The maintenance of regional folklore and language were often part and parcel of their activities, fostering in the diversity of rural France a bulwark against the increasing dominance of urban-industrial society. In their *foires* and *manifestations* many such groups integrated their modernising role with a social ethos which eulogised the conjunction of *pays* and *paysan*.[17] That conjunction accorded well with the conservative and traditionalist ethos of many peasantist

FIGURE I

Text of a poster advertising a series of protest movements about the collapse
of agricultural prices in late-1935. Such protests formed part of a wider discontent which
fuelled the growth of both right and left-wing movements.

LA MISÈRE DES PAYSANS
RUINE LE PAYS !

Les prix des **PRODUITS AGRICOLES** sont tombés à moitié
de leur valeur d'avant-guerre.

	1934	1935
LE BLÉ	27.00	14.00
L'AVOINE	20.00	8.00
LA VIANDE DE PORC	0.95	0.80
LA VIANDE DE BOEUF	1.30	0.50
LE LAIT	0.20	0.15
LE VIN	25.00	11.00
LES POMMES DE TERRE	10.00	4.00
LA LAINE	1.70	0.70

**LE POUVOIR D'ACHAT DU PAYSAN EST
RÉDUIT À RIEN!**

**Résultat: 20 millions de consommateurs agricoles
ne peuvent plus acheter les produits de l'industrie...**

C'est l'usine qui ferme
C'est le commerce qui fait faillite
C'est l'accroissement du CHÔMAGE
C'est l'artisan rural qu'on ne peut plus payer

**Conclusion: Dans l'intérêt de toutes les
forces vives du pays: UNE POLITIQUE
AGRICOLE TOTALE ET COORDONNÉE
POUR POBTENIR UNE HAUSSE DES
PRIX AGRICOLES**

*L'union Régionale des Syndicats Agricoles du Plateau Central
La Société Centrale d'Agriculture de l'Aveyron*

groups. Artistic and folkloric expressions of regional identity were heavily imbued with eulogies of 'timeless rural France', a rural France which was built on the strength of its regional traditions.

Anchored in these wider inventions and reinventions of peasant tradition were the more focused and technocratic arguments of the corporatists. Corporatist theory argued that the profession itself should organise its own affairs without state intervention. The mixed, agricultural syndicate, an association embracing the whole gamut of groups in the countryside, from landowner to small farmer, sharecropper to agricultural labourer, was to control and regulate the affairs of the profession. The very concept of classes and, heaven forfend, class conflict was scrupulously eschewed. Thus questions of production, stockage and pricing, precisely the questions the new *Office du Blé* was seeking to tackle in the arable sector, were to be delegated to regional and local syndicates. Agricultural education, technical trials, advice and other regulatory activities were to be placed fair and square in the hands of a hierarchical syndical structure. That the 'profession' could best be represented through the syndicate was, of course, taken as read. Those members of the rural community outside these syndicates (members, for example, of republican syndicates, or class-based syndicates) were ignored. A single, unitary syndical movement, allied to a powerful cooperative sector were to be the vanguards in the struggle against the supposed socialist excesses of the Popular Front government elected in 1936.

Peasantist philosophies, then, embraced dual, often contradictory dimensions. Alongside the romantic idealisations of peasant society – a romanticism represented in art, literature and folkloric output – was a more realistic and hard-headed assessment of the place of agriculture in the modern economy. Attitudes towards the growing rural exodus exemplified this. By the early 1930s a group of agricultural theorists had begun to distance themselves from the traditional, conservative agricultural unionism of the rue d'Athènes to develop a more modernist focus to agricultural policy. Acting through a new organisation – the *Union Nationale des Syndicats Agricoles* (UNSA), theorists such as Jacques le Roy Ladurie and Louis Salleron, increasingly recognised the necessity and value of the rural exodus, advocated a more market-oriented approach to farm production, and vigorously pressed for the modernisation of the countryside. Electrification programmes, the improvement of rural communications, the dissemination of modern agricultural methods and the professionalisation of the farm community were essential elements in this new programme.[18]

Though stemming from the same roots, such policies undoubtedly contrasted with traditional peasantist views. The vision of the large, self-sufficient peasant family, ensconced in bucolic bliss in deepest France, was replaced by that of the agricultural entrepreneur keen to embrace technical change and wedded to new forms of production and marketing. That contrast, slow to manifest itself in the early-1930s, had by the end of the decade, effectively created two distinct strands of peasantist thought. Those two contradictory strands, initially blended together in the agricultural institutions of the Vichy years, ultimately led to the demise of peasantism with the collapse of Vichy itself.

Organising the peasant

The economic crisis and collapse in agricultural prices, coupled with increased hostility to the perceived urban-industrial bias of the state, prompted a series of peasantist movements in France through the thirties which was to lead, perhaps inexorably, to the creation of the *Corporation Paysanne* under Vichy. Those movements were of two major types. Peasant political movements were best exemplified by the *Défense Paysanne* of Henri Dorgères, a journalist with a taste for demagoguery, for dressing his supporters in Greenshirts and for small-scale thuggery. His party drew on the deep well of suspicion amongst many sections of the peasantry and the rural élite that state policies were systematically ignoring the difficult conditions in the countryside. Leaving aside the more extreme manifestations in the movement they were at least, unlike traditional farm unions, led and largely controlled by peasant farmers at regional and local level. Together with a number of other, similar movements – the colourful *Parti Agraire*, for example – they reflected an important stage in what Wright was to term the rural revolution. The defensive reflex of such groups, notes Houée, "opposed to both State and the town and lacking doctrinal clarity or political astuteness, was nonetheless the first major peasant explosion of the industrial era".[19] They were widely developed in rural France in the inter-war years reflecting the degree of unrest in peasant France (Figure 2).

The conjunction of peasantist ideologies and peasant organisation was not limited to movements of the Right. For communists and socialists, an appeal to the peasant population was equally anchored on the distinctiveness of the rural way of life. Traditional Trotskyite policies of 'entryism' into bourgeois unions were often suspended in order to create powerful unions on the Left. An appeal to the small peasantry, arguments for the reform of tenancy agreements to provide more security for tenant farmers, and a general anti-urban ideology characterised such alternative groups as the *Confédération Nationale Paysanne*, active in the south-west.[20]

It is evident that well before the establishment of the Vichy regime in 1940, avowedly corporatist bodies had been set up in many of the traditional heartlands of

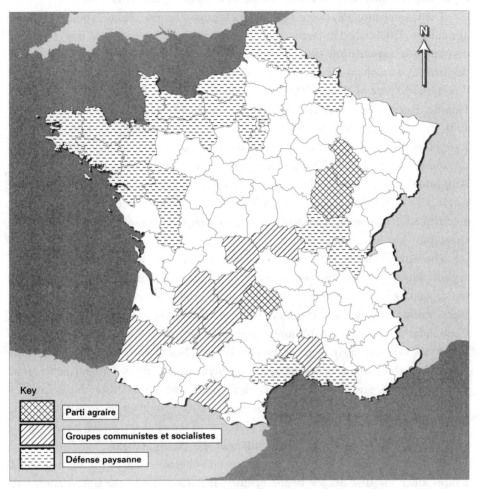

FIGURE 2

The major agricultural protest movements in the 1930s were concentrated in western France (especially Brittany and Normandy) and the flanks of the Massif Central.

Key

Parti agraire	
Groupes communistes et socialistes	
Défense paysanne	

the peasantist Right – the Massif Central, Brittany, Normandy and parts of the north-east. But, as noted earlier, two sometimes contradictory strands animated the life of such groupings. On the one hand was a strong technocratic strand, characterised by the writing of Salleron and Le Roy Ladurie which sought, not a return to 'l'ordre éternel des champs' but rather a recognition of the need to transform agriculture into a modern and dynamic enterprise, based, as before, on a model of family farming, but one that had the capacity (technical and financial) to modernise. Clear policies on co-operation, on agricultural credit and agricultural education characterised this group. By contrast, the notion of a 'return' to a France based on 'sound' rural moral qualities was an equally powerful strand in the peasantist argument which was to be especially resonant in the ideology of the new Vichy regime after 1940.

The *Corporation Paysanne* was the lynch-pin of the new régime's policy towards agriculture. Established in December 1940, the pre-war diversity (and it was argued, disunity) of agricultural unions was abolished. A single network of local and departmental unions was put in place with the national *Corporation* determining the direction and pace of change. The doctrinal tenets of the new Vichy regime ('Travail, Famille, Patrie') accorded well with the new peasantist leaders in the *Corporation*. Both strands of peasantist thought co-existed uneasily in the organisation; alongside a series of mythical and mystical pronouncements of the importance of the peasant sat sometimes radical and far-reaching proposals to modernise the farm sector.[21] Alongside sometimes execrable novels, poems and paintings extolling what Richard Cobb called a dreadful *nostalgie de la boue* were proposals on cooperatives, on rural electrification and on farm modernisation that were to prove influential in helping to shape post-war agricultural policy.[22]

The establishment of the *Corporation* was generally swift especially in those regions which, pre-war, had been dominated by peasantist organisations. As Cépède has argued, only where communist or left-wing groups were previously strong, was there serious opposition to the establishment of these new groups.[23] In the Massif Central, for example, the establishment of the *Corporation* had been largely prefigured in the new syndical movements of the late-1930s. Thus in Aveyron, Cantal and Tarn, a new Union had been established by 1937 which was largely indistinguishable from the corporatist organisation to be set up three years later.[24] Its membership document (Figure 3) laid out the importance of peasantist doctrines (unity of all country-dwellers, the moral values of peasant France, the fostering of regionalism) which were to be so important in the 'new' France of which Pétain was the figurehead.

In Aveyron, Cantal and Tarn, *départements* characterised by strong peasantist unions since the first decade of the century, the transition to the Corporation was smooth and largely unchallenged. The *Union des Associations Agricoles du Plateau Central* which had dominated the agricultural affairs of the region for three decades was swiftly incorporated into the new corporative organisations. An emphasis on 'traditional' values coupled with strong, conservative leadership characterised the new organisations, characterised as much by what Mesliand called "l'éxpression d'une fidelité à un ordre de choses du passé" as by a forward-looking modernising drive for farming.[25] In those areas of France characterised by strong pre-war peasantist movements, the transition was swift. In Brittany the powerful *Office Central* at

FIGURE 3

**Text of a membership document for a union in the southern
Massif Central in late1940. The emphasis on the unity of all country-dwellers, on the
importance of regional 'peasant' traditions and on the moral and social qualities of the
peasantry accorded well with the precepts of the new Vichy regime under Pétain.**

EXPOSÉ DES MOTIFS

Le syndicat corporatif d'action et de défense paysanne ou syndicat paysan de.............. a
été fondé le .... à la suite d'une visite par M. le Docteur Ayrignac, Délégué de
l'Union Départementale des Syndicats paysans du Rouergue.

Il a pour but de grouper les familles paysannes de .... (commune)

Il est affilié à l'Union Départementale des Syndicats paysans du Rouergue. Ce mouvement
a pour but de maintenir et de rétablir l'une des puissances organiques françaises que
constitue la paysannerie rouergate, en organisant la défense des intérêts moraux et matériels
de la famille, de la profession terrienne, et de l'état paysan.

Indépendants à l'égard des partis politiques et des hommes politiques. à l'égard des affaires
et des journaux, les syndicats paysans s'informent des besoins moraux et matériels de
leurs adhérents, soutiennent les revendications justifiées de la profession et de la famille
paysanne, étudient les amélioration de la production, des débouchés, règlent les rapports
des paysans syndiqués avec les autres organismes professionnels qui constituent, à côté du
paysannat, l'économie nationale.

Les syndicats de l'Union Départementale, développent, en outre, ou font renaître le
sentiment régional, par le maintien de la langue rouergate, des tradition de la race terrienne
du Rouergue: éducation, vertus sociales, coutumes familiales, chants et danses populaires.

À ce programme qui est celui des dirigeants de l'U.D.S.P.R. depuis 35 ans, s'ajoute, dans
les circonstances présentes, la déclaration de la plus sincère adhésion des Syndicats de
l'Union Départementale à l'oeuvre de redressement français entreprise par le Maréchal
PÉTAIN, estimant que c'est la dernière occasion de la restauration française, après cette
guerre que les dirigeants de l'U.D.S.P.R. ont tous fait pour éviter et après la défaite, les
syndicats entendent servir la France en informant le gouvernement du Maréchal sur les
besoins vitaux de la paysannerie, base de la France, et en informant les paysans sur les
sacrifices qu'ils doivent consentir, les disciplines et le labeur qu'ils doivent s'imposer pour
aider leur partie à renaître.

Le Président des Syndicats Paysans

Landernau in Finistère adopted the new regime with some enthusiasm. In other areas-Normandy, north-eastern France, parts of the Loire valley the transition was also relatively smooth. Elsewhere, however, the process was more difficult. The northern flanks of the Massif, parts of Languedoc and south-western France all saw considerable difficulties in making the transition to the new *Corporation*, reflecting the nuances of political and economic change.

By early 1943 the *Corporation* could be regarded as constituted throughout France but, by then, any real impact it might have had in improving farming conditions or methods was dissipated by a series of internal conflicts. First, manpower shortages and food supply were exacerbated by the scale of German requisitions (an estimated 15 per cent of all agricultural produce was sequestered by the Germans) which meant that the role of the *Corporation* was increasingly to facilitate these requisitions.[26] The problems of *ravitaillement général* were to dog the *Corporation* throughout its short life. Secondly, there were clear and chronic conflicts of interest between the *Corporation* and the Ministry of Agriculture. For a *Corporation* whose avowed aim was supposed political independence this was a serious issue. By 1943 a flood of regulations – ranging from rationing to the deeply unpopular *Service du travail obligatoire (STO)* in Germany – were *de facto* being implemented at local and regional level through the offices of the Corporation. The Vichy state and the *Corporation* were by then inextricably linked.

Retour à la Terre – policy and practice

The Vichy period was to mark the triumph of the peasantist pholosophies of the Right although in reality, as Boussard has emphasised, those philosophies had both deep roots and, indeed, continued to resonate well beyond the fall of Vichy and the Liberation. There had been a long debate in agricultural circles about the problems of rural depopulation, and the acceleration of rates of rural exodus in the inter-war period heightened these concerns. For Michel Augé-Laribé (an authority on the agricultural economy and by no means on the peasantist Right) rural depopulation and the harsh living conditions in the countryside were of a piece: "comme nous sommes loin de la légende qui faisait des paysans les protecteurs de notre société! Une race qui va mourir, voilà ce que nous montrent les médecins".[27] Whilst the rural exodus was producing acknowledged benefits in terms of an increase in average farm sizes, both Augé-Laribé and Louis Salleron (the major theorist of corporatism in farming), regarded a large, fertile, small peasant population as the fundamental economic, social and, above all moral ballast of the nation. The rural exodus threatened that stability, it was argued: for Victor Boret, "nous comparerons l'exode rural à une fièvre qui se manifeste lorsqu'un organisme est déjà malade. C'est le signe avertisseur que quelque chose ne va plus normalement dans le jeu naturel des forces économiques et agricoles".[28]

The contradictory elements we noted early in peasantist philosophies between a romantic and technocratic element continued to animate discussions as to the 'appropriate' level of manpower in the countryside. In his seminal *Une Solution au Problème Agraire: La Terre à la Famille Paysanne* (1919), Pierre Caziot had argued that, notwithstanding the advances of mechanisation in the countryside, a large rural population was essential to the economic health and wealth of the nation. It was a theme picked up by Henri Queuille at the end of the 1930s in a series of presentations arguing for much more focus on improving rural living conditions (electrification, water, transport and agrricultural credits) in order to encourage as large a population as possible to remain on the land. The fundamental question: how large an agricultural population does France need? remained at the heart of such debates. For Queuille, the hope in 1938 was that "en décongestionnant les grandes cités, on combattre l'exode des campagnes qui affaiblit l'économie de notre pays".[29] Events after May 1940 were, sadly, to fulfil at least the first of these hopes as the cities emptied in front of the German advance. The arguments in favour of a 'retour à la terre' were not solely political or moral in nature; strong economic arguments were also made by some observers. Thus Louis Chevalier, writing during the Occupation, made a distinction between the 'normal' pattern of population shift from country to town and the 'abnormal' rural exodus which threatened the very survival of the peasantry.[30] For Mallet, "the economic necessity of a return to the land is fundamental to both France and to the other nations of the world".[31]

For the Vichy regime, the notion of a return to 'peasant values' was a fundamental part of its moral programme to 'rebuild' France. The rural exodus, the decline in peasant numbers, the abandonment of farms in some parts of France was for many traditionalists in charge of the *Corporation Paysanne*, especially at regional and local level, symptomatic of the political and moral collapse of the Third Republic. It is not suprising, then, that this traditionalist wing of peasantist philosophies lost little time in establishing a programme to encourage town-dwellers to return to work in the countryside. Marshall Pétain's exhortation to rediscover peasant values underpinned this programme: "la terre ne ment pas. Elle demande votre secours ... une champ qui tombe en friche, c'est un portion de la France qui meurt. Une jachère de nouveau emblavée, c'est une portion de la France qui renaît".[32]

Legislation to encourage and support the programme of encouraging a return to farming was not new. On the statute books since 1924, the legislation was greatly expanded under Vichy and the *Corporation Paysanne*, together with the departmental

Direction des Services Agricoles (DSA) were given responsibility for implementing the new policy. What impact then did this back to the land policy have locally? The example of the Massif Central gives some clues at to the success, or otherwise, of the policy.

The economic and demographic experience of the Massif Central was diverse, but, along with regions such as south-western France, Brittany and Normandy, the rural exodus had had a major impact since the late nineteenth century. The northern flanks of the Massif had experienced rural depopulation since the 1850s; elsewhere the exodus began a little later but was no less fierce. *Départements* such as Aveyron, Cantal, Lozère and Tarn had their highest rates of rural depopulation in the inter-war periods. Much of the *retour à la terre* programme between 1941 and 1944 met with little success and both the *Corporation Paysanne* and the DSA were preoccupied with problems of regional food supply and the difficulties of coping with problems of shortages of equipment, petrol and (as a consequence of compulsory work orders) manpower.[33]

From mid-1941 the *Corporation* and DSA began to undertake a survey of vacant or 'poorly-farmed' land in the region. Using the 1924 legislation as a base, the regional DSA's, together with officers of the Corporation, sought to draw up a list of farms which might be re-allocated to new families under the revamped programme. Such a procedure caused some difficulties and had the potential to reignite old animosities in the countryside. The dossiers in Aveyron, for example, bulged with letters and documents in which farmers were denounced for either abandoning or failing to farm their lands properly. The very act of drawing up a list of farms to be transferred proved extremeley difficult. Numerous cases of neighbours casting covetous eyes on each others land were recorded. A 25 hectare farm at Moyrazes, for example, was, according to one neighbour, poorly farmed because of the laziness and incapacity of the present farmers. After demanding that the land be ceded to him, the author of the latter respectfully requested the authorities to destroy the letter. For another farmer at Estaing in the Lot Valley, the site of a neighbouring farm being inadequately cultivated was too much to bear. Writing to the DSA he asked that, as the father of five children with only a tiny farm, the land be ceded to him at once. Following an apparently acrimonious divorce, one woman argued that her husband's farm should be appropriated because it was not being properly farmed. In one of many similar cases, the mayor of Ste Hippolyte argued that one landowner, out of sheer greed, refused to develop the farm and employ farm workers and should therefore lose his land.[34]

Despite this plethora of complaints, the final list drawn up by the DSA in Aveyron (a *département* with some 40,000 farms) contained only some 30 farms which might be deemed suitable for the *retour à la terre* programme. Equally uninspiring was the demand for such farms. The majority of the applications submitted to the DSA in the Aveyron were from French colonies rather than the mainland and, to judge by the marginal comments in these applications, most were quite unsuitable for farming in the region. The lack of success of the programme in the region seems to reflect the national picture. There were fewer than 600 successful applications for 'abandoned' farms in France as a whole, a paltry figure which, noted Gervais, perhaps reflected the anachronistic message of the programme.[35]

Conclusion

The particular conditions of wartime France, most notably food shortages and the difficulties of urban life under the Occupation, lent some support to the notion that France should maintain a strong, numerous agricultural sector to ensure security of food supply. Such arguments continued to be strongly expressed in the post-war period; hardly suprising given that most of the local and regional leaders of the *Corporation Paysanne* continued to hold office in post-war agricultural organisations. As Wright comments, "the Liberation did not magically produce a new set of leaders" and both the personnel and ideas which were part of the *Corporation Paysanne* remained powerful despite the political turmoil of the immediate post-Liberation period.[36]

In the immediate post-war period, there were few threats to the primacy of the peasantist arguments. If the political expression of such views was thoroughly discredited by the experience of Vichy, many of the technical and economic arguments advanced by peasantists remained strong. Post-war economic reconstruction, driven by the Monnet plans, continued to envisage a large agricultural population, albeit at a much higher technical level than in pre-war decades. However, the debate surrounding the work of agricultural economists such as Colson or Dumont suggested a review of the notion that the rural exodus inevitably posed huge dangers for the nation.[37] Both suggested that rural France was overpopulated and that the necessary technical modernisation of farming could only take place if the farming population fell and if average farm sizes rose. Departing radically from the orthodox view that the rural exodus was inevitably damaging, such arguments sowed the seeds for the radical shifts in farm policy in the late-1950s and early-1960s.

The 'rural revolution' of those years, a revolution in farm structures, farm policy and the attitudes of farm union leaders was to mark a radical break with the peasantist traditions which had dominated agricultural France for some four decades. The accelerating rural exodus, the emergence of 'Une France sans Paysans' or 'La Fin des Paysans' marked a final break with a peasantist tradition which harked back to a populous, family-based farming system based on a conservative social, political and economic culture. The advent of the Common Agricultural Policy and the global restructuring of farming has, it would appear, finally laid peasantist philosophies to rest. Or has it? Is it not possible that in the revival of regional farming traditions (reflected, for example, in the widespread search for new *appellation contrôlée* for a whole range of products), the almost exponential increase in demand for organically-farmed food, the drive to divest farming systems from the control of global capital, there are hints of the peasantist philosophies of the inter-war years? It may be that in our expressed fears of the consequences of 'La France du Vide' are submerged vestiges of a rural philosophy once thought laid to rest in the ashes of Vichy France.

NOTES

1   A. R. H. Baker, *Fraternity among the French Peasantry. Sociability and Voluntary Associations in the Loire Valley 1815-1914* (Cambridge 1999), 63.

2   R. Béteille, Survivance et résistance des paysans, *Revue des Deux Mondes*, (1994) 19-39; H. Mendras, *La Fin des Paysans* (Paris 1967); E. Weber, *Peasants into Frenchmen. The Modernization of Rural France 1870-1914* (London 1977).

3   L. Lavergne, *L'Agriculture et la Population*, (Paris 1857) 52.

4   M. C. Cleary *Peasants, Politicians and Producers. The Organisation of Agriculture in France since 1918* (Cambridge 1989) 71-91.

5   M. Augé-Laribé, *Le Paysan Français après la Guerre* (Paris 1923); T. Kemp, *The French Economy 1913-1939* (London 1972).

6   A. Sauvy (Ed.), *Histoire Économique de la France Entre les Deux Guerres. Vol. III* (Paris 1972) 55-73; W. Ogburn and W.Jaffé, *The Economic Development of Post War France. A Survey of Production* (New York 1929) 470-517.

7   S. Franklin, *The European Peasantry. The Final Phase* (London 1969) 48.

8   See *inter alia*: F. Boulard, *Problèmes Missionnaires de la France Rurale* (Paris 1945); G. Le Bras, *Études de Sociologie Religieuse* (Paris 1955); F. Isambert and J-P Terre-noire, *Atlas de la Pratique Religieuse des Catholiques en France* (Paris 1980); P. Mercator, *La Fin des Paroisses* (Paris 1997).

9   Sauvy (1972) *op. cit.*, 72.

10   G. Wright, *Rural Revolution in France* (Stanford 1964) 86.

11   P. Barral, *Les Agrariens Français de Méline à Pisani* (Paris 1968); F.Boulard (1945) *op. cit.;* M. Cleary, Priest, squire and peasant: the development of agricultural syndicates in south-west France 1900-1914, *European History Quarterly* **17** (1987) 145-63.

12   J. McManners, *Church and State in France, 1870-1914* (Paris 1972).

13   *Bulletin de l'Union Catholique Aveyronnaise* **10** (1911).

14   See *inter alia*: M. Augé-Laribé, *Syndicats et Coopératives Agricoles* (Paris 1926); S. Berger, *Peasants Against Politics:Rural Organisation in Brittany* (Cambridge, Mass. 1972); G. Garrier, L'Union du Sud-est

des syndicats agricoles avant 1914, *Le Mouvement Social* **67** (1969) 30-42; R. Hubscher, *L'Agriculture et la Société Rurale dans le Département du Pas-de-Calais du Milieu du XIXe siècle à 1914* (Paris 1979) 614-635.

15   Barral (1968) *op. cit.;* Cleary (1989) *op. cit.,* 33-47.

16   Quoted in Wright (1964) *op. cit.,* 62.

17   M. Cleary, Pays and paysan in Western France: regional traditions in the historical geography of agricultural associations, in J. Soumagne (Ed.) *Les Nouveaux Espaces Ruraux de l'Europe Atlantique* (Poitiers 2000) 62-73.

18   L. Salleron, *Naissance de l'État Corporatif: Dix Ans de Syndicalisme Paysan* (Paris 1942); Union Nationale des Syndicats Agricoles, *Vers la Corporation Agricole* (Paris 1934); Union Nationale des Syndicats Agricoles, *Congrès Syndical Paysan* (Caen 1937).

19   P. Ory, Le Dorgérisme: institution et discours d'une colère paysanne (1929-39), *Revue d'Histoire Moderne et Contemporaine* **XXII** (1975) 168-190; G. Wright (1964) *op. cit.,;* P. Houée, *Les Étapes du Développement Rural* (Paris 1972), 141.

20   For a good summary of such groups see P. Gratton, *Les Luttes de Classes dans les Campagnes, 1870-1921* (Paris 1971); *ibid., Les Paysans Français contre les Agrariens* (Paris 1972). See also: M. Cleary, The French peasantry as class or community? The development of agricultural syndicalism in the *département* of Landes 1920-1936, *Journal of Historical Geography* **16** 1 **(1990)** 140-150.

21   I. Boussard, *Vichy et la Corporation Paysanne* (Paris 1980); M. Cépède, *Agriculture et Alimentation en France durant la IIe Guerre Mondiale* (Paris 1961).

22   Richard Cobb, *Promenades* (Oxford 1986) 45-51.

23   Cépède (1961) *op. cit.,* 76.

24   *Archives Départementales (A. D.) Aveyron* 35 M 5; 7 M 34; *A. D. Tarn* 6 M 33.

25   C. Mesliand, Le Syndicat Agricole Vauclusien, *Le Mouvement Social* 67 (1969) 59.

26   See Cépède, *op. cit. ;* R. Milward, *The New Order and the French Economy* (Oxford 1970).

27   M. Augé-Laribé, *L'Évolution de la France Agricole* (Paris 1912) 282.

28   V. Boret, *Pour ou Contre la Terre* (Paris 1929) 133.

29   Quoted in Boussard, I (1980) *op. cit.,* 227.

30   L. Chevalier, *Les Paysans. Étude d'Histoire et d'Économie Rurale* (Paris 1947) 101.

31   R. Mallet, *Nécessités d'un Retour à la Terre. Étude d'Économie Comparée* (Paris 1941).

32   Quoted in J. Gazave, *La Terre ne Ment Pas – Introduction à une Physiocratie Nouvelle* (Villefranche 1940).

33   *AD Aveyron:* 36 M 1 (4) 1941-42; *AD Tarn:* 16 M (1942); *Rouergue-Paysan* March 1941-Oct 1944.

34   *AD Aveyron:* 36 M *Retour à la Terre* (1924-1944).

35   G. Duby et A.Wallon (Eds), *Histoire de la France Rurale* 4, 566.

36   G. Wright (1964) *op. cit.,* 98.

37   R. Colson, *Un Paysan Face à l'Avenir Rural* (Paris reprint 1976); R. Dumont, *Voyages en France d'un Agronome* (Paris 1956).

Chapter Eleven

COLONIAL CONNECTIONS

Capital Investment, Technology Transfer and the Building of Victoria Bridge, Montreal 1850-1860

IAIN S. BLACK

Obeying, no doubt, some inscrutable law of commerce, the grand enterprise,– "perhaps the grandest when you consider the amount of territory manipulated, which has ever opened itself before the eyes of a great commercial people,"... had swung itself across [to] London, turning itself to the centre of the commercial world as the needle turns to the pole.[1]

Introduction

Though Trollope, writing in *The Way We Live Now*, was referring to the fictional South Central Pacific and Mexican Railway, he could easily have been referring to the Grand Trunk Railway of Canada. In the 1850s the Grand Trunk was the largest railway project in the world. This essay is concerned with the design, financing and construction of the pivotal section of this immense railway project: the Victoria Bridge erected to carry the railway across the mighty St. Lawrence River at Montreal. Although the examination of great civil engineering projects has not generally been a fashionable research area in historical geography, I will argue here that their study provides an important perspective upon the evolution of political, economic and technological relations between societies, as part of what David Harvey calls 'the historical geography of capitalism'.[2] In the case of the Grand Trunk, of course, such relations were irredeemably imperial too.

Prior to 1850 there was relatively little railway development in Canada.[3] The 1830s and 1840s had seen a number of extensive improvements to river transport, including the building of canals. Given the large capital and long duration involved in canal building schemes, the coming of rail was seen by many as a competitive threat. Also, the nature of goods traffic in the 1840s, chiefly timber and wheat, was well suited to water borne transport. Such concerns served to delay the widespread adoption of the new technology. In fact, the propaganda surrounding most projections for new railways drew attention to sources of demand outside the country. A dominant recurring theme was the control of the commercial traffic of the United States. The logic for this claim lay in the geographical location of the colonies between Europe and the mid-western states of the North American continent. It was argued that it was only natural that the commodity trade of the rapidly growing mid-west would gravitate to a direct route along the St. Lawrence. Such superficially convincing, though as yet unproven, claims persisted through the decades of extensive railway building in the second-half of the nineteenth century. The projection of the Grand Trunk Railway provides a classic example of such nationalistic commercial rhetoric.

The company was launched in 1853 to build a railway trunk line between the Great Lakes and the eastern seaboard, uniting the commerce and trading interests of both Upper and Lower Canada along a route of more than 1100 miles (see Figure 1). The line was to run from Sarnia, at the foot of Lake Huron, through Toronto and Kingston to Montreal. Here it was proposed to bridge the St. Lawrence River: first, to connect with the St. Lawrence and Atlantic Railway already close to completion between Montreal and Portland (Maine) and, second, to continue along the southern side of the St. Lawrence to Trois Pistoles. The Appendix to the Company's Prospectus indulged in some unrestrained commercial boosterism:

> The Grand Trunk Railway of Canada, it will be therefore seen, commencing at the debouchure of the three largest lakes in the world, pours the accumulating traffic in one unbroken line throughout the entire length of Canada into the St. Lawrence at Montreal and Quebec, on which it rests at the north, while on the south it reaches the magnificent harbours of Portland and St. John's on the open ocean. The whole future traffic between the western regions and the east, including Lower Canada, parts of the states of Vermont and New Hampshire, the whole of the states of Maine, and the provinces of New Brunswick, Nova Scotia, Prince Edward's Island, and Newfoundland, must therefore pass over the Grand Trunk Railway.[4]

FIGURE 1
Projected route of the Grand Trunk Railway of Canada, 1853.

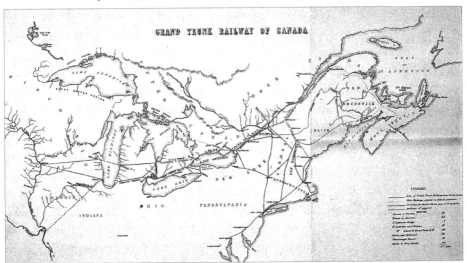

Source: The Baring Archive, London.

It is clear from Figure 1 that though the proposed railway was an immense undertaking it was, in fact, predicated upon the absorption of existing and projected lines, in addition to new construction.[5] The technical and business history of the Grand Trunk Railway has been told many times, most comprehensively by A.W. Currie.[6] My purpose is not to rehearse these well-worn arguments in detail here, but rather to examine the building of the Victoria Bridge at Montreal, exploring the ways in which this immense engineering project became a classic example of the diffusion of British technological innovation consequent upon the growth of British imperial interests between 1850 and 1914.

Study of the economic and financial relationships that were central to the construction and maintenance of British imperial power has recently been enlivened by Cain and Hopkins' wide-ranging two-volume historiography entitled *British Imperialism*.[7] In particular, Cain and Hopkins break new ground by placing the City of London, and its associated class of 'gentlemanly capitalists', at the centre of their explanation of the political economy of the British Empire. Dumett, reflecting upon volume one of *British Imperialism*, which centres on the nineteenth and early-twentieth centuries, claims to identify an "analytical tripod" within what he calls "the Cain/Hopkins paradigm":

The first leg consists of the underlying economic structures – financial, commercial and industrial – of modern Britain which laid the base of imperial power. The second leg in the study is the English socio-political ruling elite, which, Cain and Hopkins argue, evolved from a synthesis between the older landed elite (aristocracy and gentry) and the nouveaux riches of the City of London controlling what they label 'the service sector' of the economy. The third leg of the tripod represents the 'periphery' of the imperial and quasi-imperial structures – the outer regions of political control and commercial penetration which Cain and Hopkins dub 'the wider world'.[8]

This essay explores the nature of one particular set of imperial relationships, stretching between Britain and Canada, which linked the three 'legs' of the tripod identified by Dumett. Central to the success of the Victoria Bridge, and indeed the railway more generally, was the support of two of the City of London's leading merchant banks, whose evolving relationship with the emerging Canadian nation was a primary factor linking the financial and commercial power of the City, via the activities of its 'gentlemanly capitalists', to the colony.

British merchant banks and Canada

Between the 1830s and the 1890s the financial affairs of successive governments of Canada were entrusted to two leading merchant banks in the City of London: Baring Brothers & Co. and Glyn, Mills & Co.[9] The connection began with Barings, who were approached by the Province of Upper Canada in 1830 and 1833, with requests to raise funds for public works.[10] On both occasions the bank refused, largely on the grounds that security was inadequate and potential returns did not warrant the inherent risk. In 1835, following yet another request by Upper Canada for finance, Barings finally agreed to do business and tendered for a £400,000 loan. The fact that money was plentiful in London no doubt encouraged the partners yet, according to Ziegler, the bank was still hesitant and "were glad to split the loan with the rival bidders, Thomas Wilson and Co."[11] The management of the loan was uneventful at first, the debt being used to develop the infrastructure of Upper Canada through the building of canals and the improvement of river navigations.

However, in 1837 an economic and financial crisis hit the United States which led to serious disturbances in the Canadian economy too. Wilson and Co. collapsed and Barings themselves were under strain.[12] The collapse of Wilson's threatened the emerging financial connections between London and the colony as they held one-half of the financial agency for Upper Canada, together with Barings, and were the London agents for the Bank of Upper Canada, established in 1822. In fact, Fulford argues that the bank knew Wilson's was in serious danger and "decided before the collapse ... to transfer the London agency to Glyn".[13] This opened the way for Glyn, Mills & Co. to embark upon their first substantial venture in imperial finance. Glyn's were not granted a share of the financial agency immediately however. According to Fulford, the Receiver-General of Canada "arrived to find that one half of the Canadian financial structure had been engulfed but that the other half (Baring's) was steady. He accordingly made a provisional arrangement with Baring's to take over the sole agency".[14] But on attending the Colonial Office to report this decision, he learned that Glyn's had agreed to take over Wilson's share of the original 1835 loan, some £200,000. Presented with effectively a *fait accompli*, the Receiver-General agreed to continue the divided agency, taking Glyn's in place of Wilson.[15] This division of responsibility between Barings and Glyn's in the management of the Canadian financial agency was to last until 1893, surviving the unification of Upper and Lower Canada in 1840 and Confederation with the Maritime Provinces in 1867.[16] Only in 1848 did the Canadian government again suggest a sole agency relationship to Barings. They refused.[17] The agency was eventually transferred to the Bank of Montreal in 1893, reflecting the maturing of the Canadian economy and the increasing independence of the new nation in political and economic affairs.[18]

The work of the two merchant banks for the provincial government involved the management of large capital issues in the London market. Orbell describes their business in the 1850s, when:

> Barings became deeply enmeshed in the finance of the Canadian Government whose external borrowings were largely made through Barings and Glyns so that much greater control could be exercised over the market than in the case of United States securities. The two houses continued to sell government 'debentures' as and when the market allowed and to make advances to cover dividend payments when money was tight. There were occasional major issues to meet extraordinary needs, as in 1859-60 when £2.8 million was issued to pay off local debt at a higher rate of interest.[19]

Despite the success of such major issues as that in 1859-60, managing the Canadian finances was frequently problematic. On several occasions both Barings and Glyn's were drawn in to such an extent that only by using their own resources could the necessary credit be found. Fulford argues that to successive Canadian Finance Ministers the two banks "stood in much the same relation as did the Bank of England to the British Chancellor of the Exchequer".[20] Aside from government finance *per se*, Barings and Glyn's were heavily involved from the outset in railway finance in the colony. The first call came in connection with the St. Lawrence and Atlantic Railway, projected between Montreal and Portland on the New England coast. £400,000 was needed, to be raised by 6 per cent debentures.[21] Both Barings and Glyn's agreed that placing the bonds would be extremely difficult and the inevitable low price would alarm those holding existing classes of Canadian Bonds. In a joint letter the banks wrote:

> We are most desirous not only to prevent such an occurrence but to aid to the utmost of our power in the advancement of every work likely to promote the prosperity of the Province ... We see no other mode therefore than to purchase a portion ourselves and by that means to try to give confidence to others, as well as to meet your immediate wants, and though not anxious to buy a security for which we as yet see no chance of a re-sale, we consent ... to buy debentures to the extent of £100,000 nominal capital.[22]

This letter indicates the lengths to which the two banks went to aid the development of a remote and financially precarious colony holding little interest for the mainstream British investor. As infrastructure development proceeded, most notably with the projection and construction of large-scale railway trunk lines across the Province, Barings and Glyn's were drawn deeper and deeper into the financial affairs of both the provincial government and the railway companies themselves.[23] With the Grand Trunk Railway this relationship was stretched almost to breaking point.

Whatever the long-term strategic importance of the line in providing a vital link between the separate Canadian provinces leading up to Confederation in 1867, as a business venture the railway was widely recognised as a commercial disaster.[24] Responsibility for financing the line fell heavily on Barings and Glyn's. The Company's prospectus had confidently predicted the costs of construction at £9.5 million. By 1865, *The Economist* calculated that costs had escalated to £19 million for the 1,150 miles of track then completed.[25] Problems of raising capital were evident from the outset, with only three-quarters of the first issue of £3,623,000 taken up within the first year.[26] Canadian interest and participation in the project, as far as private capital investment was concerned, remained way below initial expectations. Most of the £622,700 of shares reserved for Canadian investors in the first issue either suffered default or were rapidly resold in London at reduced prices. Indeed, Canada's overall contribution was limited to a public investment totalling some £3,111,500, in government debentures advanced to the Grand Trunk and sold in England.[27] With the second debenture issue proving a failure, the whole Grand Trunk project was only kept afloat by the efforts of Barings and Glyn's, as Platt and Adelman explain:

The public would lend no more, and the construction of the railway could not have been continued without heavy advances and loans from both London houses, a large and semi-permanent commitment in shares, and a substantial part of Thomas Baring's own private fortune. In the summer of 1858, the house of Baring itself (irrespective of the private holdings of its partners) had £361,500 tied up in Grand Trunk shares and debentures, together with company debts in current account of a further £125,000. The amount was considerably increased when Barings and Glyn's had to take up the greater part of the second Preference issue of £3,111,500 in 1859 ... In 1860, when the company was on the verge of bankruptcy, Barings' and Glyn's advances, quite apart from their holding of shares and debentures, amounted to £635,355 sterling.[28]

The commitment on the part of Barings and Glyn's to effectively underwrite the Grand Trunk Railway project applied, *de facto*, to the Victoria Bridge too. Although the bridge was the pivotal link in the whole Grand Trunk line, projected costs of construction were exceedingly high and a constant worry to the Company, its shareholders and its bankers. It needed the continued financial intervention of the London merchant bankers to ensure that the bridge was finally completed and the whole of the Grand Trunk opened up to through traffic.

The Victoria Bridge

The scale of the challenge to bridge the St. Lawrence at Montreal, a distance of more than two miles, was unprecedented in the experience of the world's railway builders. The great importance of the bridge was highlighted in the Appendix to the Company's Prospectus of 1853:

A work of this stupendous character, required to span a navigable river of two miles in width, can only be undertaken by a large combined capital, and is justified by its paramount importance. The site selected is at the sole point on the river St. Lawrence, from the Great Lakes to its mouth, where a bridge can be placed without interfering with the navigation. And also at that point no less than 1,595 miles of continuous railway, now in operation ... from New York, Boston, Portland, and Quebec, arrive on the south shore of the river, opposite to Montreal ... On the northern shore, the railway either in progress or completed, including the western section of the Grand Trunk, number already 967 miles, exclusive of projected lines. The completion of this link is essential to the satisfactory and economical working of the Grand Trunk Railway; and it has therefore been incorporated with the entire line.[29]

The Victoria Bridge was, therefore, the vital link in the chain which would give the projected railway a significant advantage over other lines and, indeed, over any other competing modes of transport. The report noted further that: "it will be constructed according to the plans and under the superintendence of Robert Stephenson, Esq., C. E. ... and Alexander McKenzie Ross, Esq., C. E.; and the structure will be of that substantial character which a work of such magnitude requires. For the bridge an ample allowance of capital is made, and the work has been provisionally contracted for with Messrs. Peto, Brassey, Betts, and Jackson".[30] Peto, Brassey & Co., an eminent firm of English contractors experienced in railway building, were the main contractors for most of the new lines comprising the Grand Trunk project. The bridge required the sanction of the Canadian Parliament and an act was duly passed in 1853.[31]

The huge scale of the project, the obvious technical difficulties involved and, above all, the immense cost of the new bridge, continued to worry shareholders. Directors' Reports constantly sought to reassure investors in the company's early years. Following Robert Stephenson's visit to Canada in the autumn of 1853, the directors circulated his report which, though drawing attention to the design challenges and large costs involved, stressed the necessity of it for the success of the whole Grand Trunk Scheme.[32] Stephenson asserted that the Grand Trunk did not intend to compete directly with the St. Lawrence River, but sought to provide a year-round line of communication for its staple commodity exports via a "direct and easy connexion with all the ports on the East Coast of the Atlantic, from Halifax to Boston, and even New York", and consequently to Europe.[33] But the St. Lawrence provided a formidable barrier to such direct connection between the Canadian Provinces and the ice-free ports of the Atlantic coast. Therefore, continued Stephenson, "if the line of Railway communication be permitted to remain severed by the St. Lawrence, it is obvious that the benefits which the system is calculated to confer upon Canada must remain in a great extent nugatory, and of a local character".[34] Worse still this would open the door for American competition to capture the growing trade from western Canada in natural resources and agricultural products, moving them to the coast along American railways via Niagara and Buffalo. Stephenson ended his report by arguing for the building of Victoria Bridge in the strongest terms:

> *I cannot conceive anything so fatal to the satisfactory development of your Railway as the postponement of the bridge across the river at Montreal ... looking at the enormous extent of rich and prosperous country which your system intersects, and at the amount of capital which has been already, or is in the progress or prospect of being expended, there is in my mind no room for questions as to the*

expediency – indeed, the absolute necessity of the completion of this bridge, upon which, I am persuaded, the successful issue of your great undertaking mainly depends.'[35]

Though clearly not a disinterested perspective his report nonetheless reflected the view of most commentators on the new railway project: the Victoria Bridge was the single most important link in the whole scheme, providing a connection of great economic and political importance, and vital to the commercial success of the Grand Trunk Railway.[36]

Design sources for the Victoria Bridge

The Victoria Bridge was a classic example of technology transfer in the mid-nineteenth century.[37] The choice of Robert Stephenson to design the new bridge was no doubt stimulated directly by his recent success in designing the Britannia Bridge across the Menai Straits for the Chester and Holyhead Railway.[38] The Britannia Bridge was a pioneering solution to a new and pressing design problem, brought about by the rapid expansion of railway building in Britain. It was, according to Petroski, "the most significant construction project underway in the British Isles, if not the world, in the late 1840s".[39] The need for a crossing of the Menai Strait resulted from the choice by the government of Holyhead, in Anglesey, as the port for a London to Dublin rail and ship connection. Though the direct responsibility for its construction fell to the Chester and Holyhead Company, it was the official recognition of the need for a rapid, regular and secure route for the exchange of mail between London and Dublin that lay behind the scheme.[40] The challenge facing Stephenson, of carrying a railway across a substantial natural water passage, was unprecedented.

Various initial schemes were discussed, including a proposal to adapt Telford's existing road suspension bridge to rail use, though this was quickly rejected as being insufficiently strong and lacking in the necessary stiffness to carry fully loaded trains.[41] A further complicating factor was the crucial importance of the Menai Straits to the British Admiralty, who rejected any proposals that involved placing obstructions in the channel, even those temporarily needed for construction. These factors precluded any designs based on existing technology, such as the use of iron arch construction or even traditional solid masonry. These difficulties led Stephenson to reconsider using a suspension bridge design, though the lack of detailed technical knowledge required to calculate stresses and strains accurately led him to reject this idea too. Indeed, not long after, Stephenson declared himself emphatically against the use of the suspension technique with regard to bridges for railways, largely due to the celebrated failure of the Tees Bridge at Stockton designed by Samuel Brown.[42] Addressing a Parliamentary

Commission in 1848, Stephenson stated that: "I do not think that a railway bridge could be made on suspension principles; we have one at Stockton, which I replaced by one of these iron girder bridges, and it was fearful when the engine went on to it ... when the engine and train went over the first time ... there was a wave before the engine of something like 2 feet, just like a carpet".[43]

Given these constraints a novel design solution was required. For Stephenson, the key conceptual leap was to envisage his bridge as effectively a tube through which trains could pass, rather than providing a structure over which they would run. It was for this reason that the term 'tubular bridges' was coined. Such tubes would have to be immensely strong, to support both themselves and the weight of locomotives and carriages passing through them. The tubes were to be constructed from iron girders of unprecedented size, as shown in the cross-section in Figure 2. As Petroski notes, "not only their form but also the manner of erection of the tubes would involve untried and thus unproven technology".[44] Due to the need to develop these new technological solutions, Stephenson and his collaborators used scale models and conducted numerous tests to find the strongest configuration of tube design and construction.[45] However, despite such efforts the only sure way to fully test the tubes was to build the bridge and proof test what was, of course, a unique structure. The Britannia Bridge was completed in 1850, with the first tube opened in March and the second in October of that year (see Figure 3).[46]

Stephenson's understandable preoccupation with preventing failure led to a continuing curiosity of the final achieved design. Stephenson had thought to use supporting chains, in the manner of suspension bridges, to aid the placing of the tubes onto the towers. They could also provide supplementary support during use. However, such chains were found to be unnecessary and, according to Petroski "the towers would remain confusingly tall and be found aesthetically objectionable by some structural critics".[47] In fact, the great tubes were incredibly robust and, in purely structural terms, the success of the tubular concept was total. However, evaluating Stephenson's new bridge design in broader economic and environmental terms raised many questions about its heavy use of basic materials, its extraordinary weight, its high unit cost and, finally, its suitability for conveying passengers through enclosed tubes over considerable distances. But these were questions for the future. In the immediate aftermath of the opening of the bridge, Stephenson's work was seen as a tremendous success. Samuel Smiles, in a near contemporary comment, remarked how "the Britannia Bridge is one of the most remarkable monuments of the enterprise and skill of the present century. Robert Stephenson was the master spirit of the undertaking. To him belongs the merit of first seizing the ideal

FIGURE 2

Cross section of the Britannia Tubular Bridge, *c.* 1849

Fig. 344. CROSS SECTION OF ONE OF THE TUBES.

Source: Science Museum, London.

FIGURE 3

The Britannia Tubular Bridge, March 1850

Source: Science Museum, London.

conception of the structure best adapted to meet the necessities of the case; and of selecting the best men to work out his idea ... carrying his magnificent original conception to a successful practical issue".[48] Within the space of three years, Stephenson was called upon to apply the innovative techniques developed on the Britannia Bridge to an enterprise of much greater magnitude when asked to design the Victoria Bridge for the Grand Trunk Railway at Montreal.

Building the Victoria Bridge

Construction of the Victoria Bridge began on 24 May 1854, when the first floating dam was towed up the St. Lawrence from the Lachine Canal and moored near the site of the bridge's north abutment. [49] Prior to this date, the contractors had been engaged in early preparations for the great building project, including locating stone quarries on a scale sufficient to meet the huge demand for stone. Quarries were initially opened at Point Clarie, sixteen miles west from Montreal, to supply work commencing from the north bank of the river. To transport the stone to the point of construction, a mile-long tramway was laid to Lake St. Louis, from where boats could take it the rest of the way by river. Later, once the Grand Trunk rail line along the north shore of the

St. Lawrence was completed, passing within half-a-mile of the quarries, stone was moved by rail too.[50]

Throughout the building of the bridge, the overwhelming difficulty facing the contractors was the rigour of the local climate. In particular, the regular formation of ice in the St. Lawrence dictated the rhythm of construction and posed an ever-present danger to the emerging structure of the bridge. Each year ice began to form in the St. Lawrence about the beginning of December and only began to clear around the middle of the following May. In the early stages of building this limited the construction season to approximately six months in the summer and autumn of each year. Once construction had become more established and the need to complete the structure became ever more pressing, work was extended into the winter months too. However, at certain times of the year the ice in the St. Lawrence became very unstable, resulting in large-scale movements known locally as 'shovings'. Hodges, in his classic account of the engineering of the bridge, describes the process thus:

> *The surface ice, arrested in its progress, packs into all sorts of imaginable shapes; and, if the cold is very intense, a crust is soon formed, and the river becomes frozen over till many square miles extent of surface-packed ice is formed. As the water rises, the jamb against which this field rests, if not of sufficient strength to hold it in place, gives way; when the whole river, after it is thus frozen into one immense sheet, moves 'en masse' down stream, causing the "shovings" so much dreaded by the people of Montreal. The edges of the huge field moving irresistibly onwards, plough into the banks of the river, in some instances to a depth of several feet, carrying away everything within reach. In places the ice packs to a height of twenty or thirty feet, and goes grinding and crushing onwards till another jamb takes place, which, aided by the grounded masses of packed ice upon the shoals and shores, offers sufficient resistance to arrest in its progress the partially broken up field.*[51]

Clearly, the immense power of the ice moving under such pressure would pose a significant threat to any structure placed across the river to carry a railway, both in the early stages of its construction and once fixed in place. It was therefore decided to build the Victoria Bridge with heavy stone piers, widely spaced across the two-mile span of the St. Lawrence. Each pier, "being of the most substantial character, and having a large wedge-shaped cut-water of stonework inclined against the current, and presenting an angle to the ice sufficient to separate and fracture it as it rose against the piers".[52] Figure 4 shows how, in addition to supporting the tubes carrying the railway across the river, the piers also acted as ice-breakers countering the pressure of the ice.

At the point where the bridge was projected to cross the St. Lawrence the water had a depth, in summer, of between five and fifteen feet and its bed comprised limestone rock, strewn with large boulders. With the additional hazard of fast flowing currents, the engineers decided upon the use of floating dams to enable the masonry towers to be fixed upon the river bed (see Figure 4). Hodges describes these floating dams as consisting of "a framework of timber, forming a large caisson of proper shape and dimensions to encircle a pier, with sufficient space for piling, puddle chamber, and for the workmen engaged in the construction of the masonry".[53] Once a dam was in place, water was pumped out of the structure for a number of hours until the river bed came into view, and subsequently became dry, providing for the workforce the curious sight of "the waters of the St. Lawrence rush[ing] frantically past, while, inside the dam, the bare rock was visible, with the piles simply resting upon it".[54]

The north abutment was the first section of the bridge to be undertaken (see Figure 5a). The site for the construction was some 1200 feet from the north shore of the river, which presented severe difficulties of access. In consequence, a tramway was erected upon a skeleton frame of cribwork leading out from the shore to the dam.[55] The masonry for the north abutment commenced on 28 August 1854, the stone brought through the Lachine Canal by barge before being transferred to trucks running along the tramway out into the river. During this first summer of work some 85,428 cubic feet of stone was laid, the abutment rising to approximately six feet above summer water level.[56] Despite this initial success however, Hodges remarked that "the first working season at the Victoria Bridge was a period of disaster, difficulty, and trouble".[57] The climate and the terrain surrounding the site of the new bridge presented clear difficulties to the contractors, as has already been mentioned. In addition, the project suffered from the outset from a pervasive labour shortage. The problem here was twofold: firstly, there was a severe lack of labour with the requisite skills and experience in large-scale construction work of this type and the contractors had to arrange for a substantial number of immigrant workers to be sent from Britain; secondly, with many large-scale infrastructure projects being undertaken in the United States and Canada at this time, labour was prone to strike frequently and, if demands were not met, to move on to other projects paying higher wages. Thus the retention of labour posed an ongoing problem. Finally, the summer of 1854 saw a severe outbreak of cholera, which further depleted the workforce.

By early December, when the onset of the cold season effectively stopped work, progress had been disappointing. The north abutment was largely in place, though unfinished and still retaining its dam. No. 1 pier was finished and No. 2 nearly so, though both were still encircled by their respective floating dams. The intention had

FIGURE 4
Victoria Bridge, Montreal: works seen from Pier No.6 in 1858

Source: Institution of Civil Engineers, London.

been to remove the dams to a safe harbour through the winter and being left in place exposed them to the danger of destruction from the ice 'shovings' experienced each winter season. So it proved. Hodges takes up the story:

> *The whole of the river and La Prairie Basin was one mass of packed ice, which, being held up by the jamb below, had been accumulating and rising for four days. At last some slight symptoms of motion were visible. The universal stillness which prevailed was interrupted by an occasional creaking, and every one breathlessly awaited the result ... the uncertainty lasted but a short period, for in a few minutes the uproar arising from the rushing waters, the cracking, grinding, and shoving of the fields of ice, burst on our ears. The sight of twenty square miles (over 124,000,000 tons) of packed ice ... all in motion, presented a scene grand beyond description. The traveller-frames and No. 2 dam glided for a distance of some hundred yards without having a joint of their framework broken.*

FIGURE 5

Progress of the Victoria Bridge Montreal: (a) to 1 December 1857 (b) to 20 September 1859

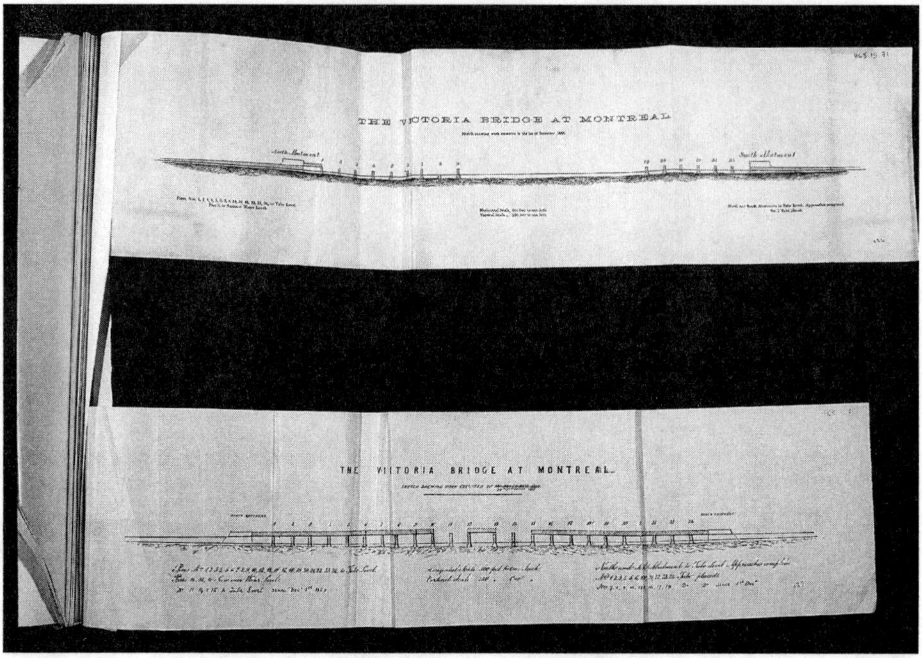

Source: The Baring Archive, London.

But as the movement of the ice became more rapid, and the fearful noises increased, these tall frameworks appeared to become animate, and, after performing some three or four evolutions like huge giants in a waltz, they were swallowed up, and reduced to a shapeless mass of crushed fragments.[58]

In 1855 very little progress was made on the bridge, largely because of the continuing and deepening financial problems of the company, which found increasing problems raising finance as the London money market tightened during the Crimean War. The first task was to survey the damage to the works resulting from the massive ice shoving described above. Luckily, the damage was limited to the temporary works, such as the dams and timber scaffolding surrounding the construction sites. The masonry of the piers and the north abutment was found to be sound. The construction season, beginning in early May, was again disrupted by strikes. Nonetheless, despite these difficulties work commenced on the south abutment about the middle of May. Conditions nearer the south shore were far more benign than in the northern reaches, the river being shallow and slow moving. A cribwork tramway was constructed out to the dam at the site of the south abutment to carry the stone necessary for its construction. The dam was finished and pumped clear by 26 July and the masonry commenced on 27 August. The stone for this abutment, as well as for some of the southern bridge piers was obtained from quarries on La Motte Island, in Lake Champlain. These quarries were more distant than those serving the northern side of the construction works and the stone travelled some forty miles by barge to St. John's whence it was carried a further nineteen miles to the works by the Champlain Railway. By the end of the 1855 season the following works had been completed: first, the north abutment was made up to the winter water level and the embanked approach to it repaired; second, piers No. 1 and 2 were finished; third, No. 5 pier was completed to two feet two inches above summer water level; finally, the south abutment was made up to two feet six inches above summer water level (see Figure 5a).

It was in the season of 1855, when the financial state of the company was severely strained and with little prospect of relief in sight, that the Directors of the Grand Trunk were forced to consider alternative and cheaper ways to bridge the St. Lawrence.[59] On 9 August 1855 Robert McCalmont, a director of the railway, wrote to an independent civil engineer Mr Charles Liddell indicating he had "been requested by the Grand Trunk Board to ask you to submit to them a Report of your opinion as to the most economical mode of constructing a permanent and substantial Railway Bridge across the Saint Lawrence, at Montreal".[60] On 22 September Liddell replied with his report, in which he claimed after due consideration of all the issues, that "my estimate for the superstructure, on the plan I have recommended, is £123,000, and for the piers £220,000; and the total estimate for the bridge, with an allowance of 10 per cent. for contingencies, amounts to £377,000".[61] The difference between this estimate and the original projected cost of £1,400,000 was so great that the Board felt compelled to ask Stephenson and his associates to respond. By 12 December 1855 Stephenson, I. K. Brunel, Edwin Clark and Alexander Ross had all provided detailed reports to Liddell effectively refuting his proposals for any alterations to the original design and maintaining the necessity for the huge capital cost of £1.4 million.[62] Liddell claimed that the original cost projection, which all the reports defended, "has no true relation to the work to be done, and in none of the Reports is there any attempt to show that it has such relation".[63] Yet, despite reiterating his view that a bridge could be erected "for less than £400,000 sterling", the Board were not convinced.[64] On 30 April 1856 McCalmont wrote to shareholders tendering his resignation. McCalmont felt betrayed by the Board's lack of co-operation and, in a parting shot, urged shareholders to press for a full inquiry into "the reckless manner in which the Company are being heretofore led on blindfold in regard to this Bridge".[65]

His injunction went unheeded as the Board reaffirmed their faith in the merits of the original scheme.[66]

Following a winter of unusual severity, the new season's works began towards the end of April 1856.[67] Piers were now advancing across the river from both shores and between May and November piers number 4, 5 and 7 were completed from the north shore and numbers 24 and 23 from the south. In addition, the south abutment was finished up to the tube level. Hodges again complained about the shortness of the working season, which comprised no more than six months at the outside. The early season was, he claimed, "taken up in preparing for the setting of masonry", and it was very unusual for the setting of stone to begin before mid-August.[68] Indeed, he continued, 'it was quite certain that all work must cease by the end of November. *Sixteen weeks*, therefore, constituted the whole of the working season for the pier masonry".[69]

Early in 1857 the contractors were again plagued by uncertainty over whether the Company would be able to continue financing the work and it was not until the end of June that definite instructions were received to proceed. The delay meant that precious time early in the season had been lost. Figure 5a shows the work completed on the bridge by the end of the 1857 season. Despite some discrepancies with Hodges's account it is useful to help visualise the building programme.[70] Piers number 22, 21, 20 and 19 were built from the south shore, No. 19 being the last that could be reached by the temporary tramway extending from the south abutment for carrying stone to the construction sites. No. 18 was also commenced early in the season and was completed by 6 November. From the north shore work began on piers 8 and 9 and both were partially completed before the weather forced a closure of operations early in December. Figure 5a shows that the first of the twenty-five tubes that would eventually carry the railway across the St. Lawrence had been completed between the north abutment and pier No. 1.

The tubes were built between the piers with the help of additional support known as staging. The staging was constructed using scows, or unpowered barges, some 60 feet by 20 feet, which were "moored in position, scuttled, and kept in place by piles sliding in grooves".[71] Once the piles were fitted to the rock bed of the river, they were "bolted to the sides of the scows, and the tops levelled to receive the sills upon which the framing carrying the truss and platform was erected".[72] This gave a level surface upon which to place rails for trucks to bring the necessary iron to the point of construction and also to facilitate the travellers used in the erection of the tubes (see Figure 6). The tubes were erected from the bottom up, with the floor riveted together first, followed by the erection of the side plates working progressively from the centre of each side of a tube. Once the sides were completed, the top was plated

FIGURE 6

Work on the centre tube of the Victoria Bridge, Montreal, 1859.

Source: Institution of Civil Engineers, London.

into position as soon as possible, giving a structural integrity to the whole. Hodges provides further details on the building process:

> The tubes of the bridge, although erected separately, as if for independent beams, were afterwards united in pairs, and were firmly bolted to the masonry of the piers over which they were so united, so that no movement could possibly take place. This pier was always called the "resting pier". The other ends of the tube were placed on rollers so arranged upon the adjoining piers that they might expand or contract from the resting piers as the temperature varied; a space sufficient for this purpose being left between each pair of tubes.[73]

The staging for tube No. 25, between the south abutment and pier No. 24 (see Figure 5a), was put up during the summer of 1857 too, using as an experiment a temporary cribwork pier in place of scows. Following this, according to Hodges "the truss forming the platform upon which the tube was to be erected was completed before the winter

273

set in, but no ironwork was commenced".[74] Once the ice bridge formed across the river, work on erecting the tube was to begin with the aim of completing it before the spring thaw. If this worked it would demonstrate the possibility of extending the working season through the winter months and provide a means of erecting the centre tube without affecting seriously the river navigation at that point.

Considerations of allowing river traffic to pass through the bridge continued into 1858 when it was determined that No. 11 pier should not be built until the large central span – 330 feet as opposed to 242 feet for the other twenty-four spans – was put in place.[75] The plan was to build piers Nos. 12 and 13 in the summer season of 1858 and put up the large centre tube during the following winter (see Figure 5b). To help achieve this ambitious pace of construction, it was agreed to place cribwork at the site of the centre tube during the winter of 1857-58 and hope any spring shoving would not move it. Cribwork to form dams for the subsequent building of piers 14, 15 and 16 was also placed during the winter though, unfortunately, this work did not survive the spring shoving. That surrounding the sites for piers 12 and 13 was somewhat displaced, but not destroyed, and needed repairing before the summer work could commence. Pier No. 13 was finished by 26 November and No. 12 by 3 December 1858. Pier No. 17 was also completed, in the very rapid time of six weeks between the laying of the first stone on 23 July and 3 September. After the wreckage of the cribwork originally placed for piers 14, 15 and 16 had been removed, work commenced on these piers too, with No. 16 being finished on 23 November.

In June 1858, according to Hodges "anxious deliberations took place as to the possibility of getting the bridge finished and ready for opening by the end of 1859".[76] The question was pushed hard by the Grand Trunk's Directors as they continued to believe that opening this vital link in the 1100-mile chain of railway was the true key to lasting commercial success for the railway. After some consideration, the contractors answered that the bridge could indeed be finished and a new urgency was injected into the construction works. As they pushed on with the work, No. 10 pier was begun on 7 October and completed on 30 November, an extraordinary feat. No. 8 pier, held over from December 1857 was also finished by 21 October 1858. With the embanked approach on the south side of the river begun and finished up to its winter water level, it is clear that great progress was made during 1858.[77] According to Hodges "at the close of this season there was only No. 11 pier to be founded, Nos. 14 and 15 to be carried up from summer water level, and the abutment walls to finish".[78] In addition, during the 1858 season no less than eleven tubes were erected.

The manufacture, shipment and subsequent erection of these tubes was a major feat of engineering skill and organisational excellence, as Hodges explains:

FIGURE 7

Staging for the centre tube of the Victoria Bridge, Montreal, 1859.

Source: Science Museum, London.

The whole of the iron-work for the tubes was prepared at the Canada Works, Birkenhead, where a plan or map of each tube was made, upon which was shown every plate, T bar, angle iron, keelson, and cover plate, in the tube, the position of each being stamped and marked upon it by a distinctive figure, letter, or character. As the work progressed at Birkenhead, every piece of iron, as it was punched and finished for shipment, was stamped with the identical mark corresponding with that on the plan; so that, when being erected in Canada, although each tube was composed of 4926 pieces, or 9852 for a pair, the workmen, being provided with a plan of the work, were enabled to lay down piece by piece with unerring certainty till the tube was complete.[79]

The centre piers, Nos. 12 and 13, were finished in time for the erection of the large centre tube over the winter months and two temporary piers were placed in the centre opening to support the necessary cribwork for staging (see Figure 7). Work had to stop as the river began to freeze over, thus preventing river craft from attending to the works. As soon as the ice bridge formed across the St. Lawrence work could then resume, as gangs of labourers worked to form roads across the ice to convey materials for building the centre tube. Plating of the bottom of the tube began on 31 January 1859. The work was arduous, with extremely cold temperatures presenting the constant threat of frostbite. On 12 February, work began on placing the side plates for the tube, brought to the site across the ice in sleighs. Work progressed quickly and by 21 March the whole of the plating was complete and needed only a further 18,000 rivets to finish the tube. But conditions were becoming more precarious as the ice began to move.

On the 25 March it became evident that "the whole of the ice in the La Prairie Basin, of some twenty miles area, was in motion".[80] Understandably, tension rose sharply amongst the workmen, caught between a desire to flee to the shore, approximately one-mile distant, or remain upon the tube. Fortunately, temperatures soon dropped and made the ice more stable again and the work continued. Despite such anxiety, "the general opinion was, that unless this was accomplished it would in all probability either fall into the river or be so crippled that it would be necessary to take it to pieces and reconstruct it".[81] Following the thaw and the opening of the river to traffic the staging for the centre tube was rapidly removed to clear obstructions from the navigation.

Construction of No. 11 pier, the final one needed to complete the bridge, proved a difficult exercise. The channel into which it was placed was the only one now available for steamboats and rafts to pass the bridge and the building of a dam here was continually threatened by collision. Indeed the first dam erected was destroyed by an Indian raft which struck it head on, with considerable loss of life. At the second attempt, the foundation stone of this final pier was laid on 12 August and the whole completed by 26 September 1859. To complete the bridge required the construction of further temporary staging to allow the erection of the remaining tubes. By 18 May the centre span was finally cleared for navigation, reducing the danger of collision between the temporary staging and river traffic, though the occasional raft that had drifted off course still posed a threat.

Simultaneously with the erection of further tubes, the contractors began to clear away the dams and cribwork now no longer needed. This work was completed before the season closed, as well as the removal of cribwork for the tubes, excepting some remnants at Nos. 12 and 14. The cribwork here was left to its fate from the ice shoving and was, in fact, cleared away by the ice on 17 December 1859, the day chosen for the first passage of trains through the bridge.[82] This circumstance, clearing the bridge

FIGURE 8

The official opening of the Victoria Bridge, Montreal, 25 August 1860. The Prince of Wales laying the last stone.

Source: Guildhall Library, Corporation of London.

of its entire temporary works on its day of opening, greatly "added to the *éclat* of the day's proceedings" noted Hodges.[83] The working season had also seen the finishing of the embanked approaches to the bridge and the placing of roofing materials of wood, covered with tin, across the top of the tubes. The first train crossed the bridge on 17 December 1859. Eight months later, on the 25 August 1860, the Prince of Wales (see Figure 8) officially opened the bridge.[84]

Financing the Victoria Bridge

As noted, the Victoria Bridge was always seen as an integral part of the overall Grand Trunk scheme. For this reason, the projected costs associated with building the bridge were notionally fixed at the outset. The contract struck in 1853 with Messrs. Jackson, Peto, Brassey and Betts for building the new bridge, specified a sum of £1.4 million.[85] This projected figure proved, in fact, remarkably accurate.[86] The Report of the London Directors of the Company, dated 12 July 1861, showed total expenditure on the bridge to 31 December 1860 at £1,356,020, within the context of total expenditure on the railway as a whole at that date of £11,443,158.[87] In otherwords, the building of the bridge had absorbed almost 12 percent of the total capital sunk in the railway between 1853 and 1860, showing just how capital intensive that two-mile stretch of track had been.

What these bare figures mask, of course, was the impact of the very great financial difficulties afflicting the Grand Trunk Railway for most of the period of its construction. These have been discussed for the railway as a whole above. The financing of the Victoria Bridge was no exception. Indeed, in the final year of construction, financial difficulties threatened to halt the entire building process. Once again, it was only through the intervention of Barings and Glyn's, acting jointly as the company's bankers, that the funds were finally forthcoming to complete the bridge. A handwritten memorandum by Thomas Baring remarked:

> *That Messrs Baring Brothers &c. and Messrs Glyn Mills &c. having consented in consideration of the depressed prices of the securities and the exhausted state of the credit of the Grand Trunk Railway Company of Canada to lend temporally to the said Company Provincial Government Bonds of Canada... of five hundred thousand pounds capital for the express purpose of aiding the completion of the unfinished works of the Victoria Bridge.[88]*

For the bridge, as for the railway, it was the continued willingness of the London merchant banks to continue advancing credit which allowed construction work to proceed long after the solvency of the company had been called into question.

Colonial connections

The completion of the Victoria Bridge was a tremendous engineering achievement (see Figure 9), allowing for the first time a fixed railway link from the interior of Western Canada to the Atlantic coast, bringing together the diverse communities of the emerging Canadian nation (Appendix 1 provides the full technical specification of the bridge, together with details of the labour force and motive power employed in its construction). In purely commercial terms, however, the putative benefits of the opening of the Grand Trunk for through traffic never really materialised. According to Platt and Adelman, "it failed to draw enough cargo from Western Canadian farmers and it fared even less well in securing return cargo; Canadian and American-bound cargo followed United States routes. Like the canals before it, Canada's Grand Trunk could not compete with the American lines".[89] In addition, despite the sheer scale of the building project and the extraordinary difficulties overcome in its construction, the Victoria Bridge was seen in retrospect as a design failure. Its cost, at nearly £1.4

FIGURE 9

A general view of the Victoria Bridge and Montreal, *c*. 1860

Source: Institution of Civil Engineers, London.

million, was never wholly justified by the engineers and contractors. Despite the fact that open web girders had become widely used prior to the planning of the bridge, offering a far cheaper solution, Rapley argues that "Stephenson was never reconciled to the trussed girder, something he had never used and of which he had no experience, and in this matter the quality of his advice to the GTR was questionable".[90] The extreme length of the tube through which the trains passed, at 6,588 ft, presented continuing problems. Despite learning from the smoke-filled carriages of the Britannia Bridge, by providing generous ventilation for the Victoria's tubes, the bridge continued to be dogged by smoke problems. Stephenson's tubular design was to last thirty-eight years, before the bridge was reconstructed using trussed girders.[91] The piers, though, were an undoubted success and remain in service to this day.[92]

But the bridge was always more than simply a piece of magisterial civil engineering. It provided a vital *colonial connection* within the emerging Canadian national space, as well as being itself constituted within a web of *colonial connections* centred on London. By establishing a permanent link across the St. Lawrence it provided a regular, reliable and year-long routeway for the circulation of people, goods, capital and information between Upper and Lower Canada, with links to the Maritime Provinces and New England. It was still a European-centred vision, of course, in that the whole of the Grand Trunk was conceived as a great conduit for the exchange of Canadian primary products for largely British manufactures. That said, the project received strong Provincial Government support precisely because it promised to enhance local economic prospects whilst reinforcing Canadian independence from American trade routes. The vision was one of Canadian integration as much as British penetration. Though the railway struggled to achieve its economic goals in the mid-nineteenth century, McIlwraith suggests that the bridge played an important wider role in Canadian history, by providing "a critical element in the achievement of Confederation in 1867".[93] The political importance of the railway as a tool of national unity was taken to its logical conclusion with the building of the Canadian Pacific in the later nineteenth century.[94]

The building of Victoria Bridge also provides a window on the evolving imperial relationship between Britain and Canada in the mid-nineteenth century. This relationship has been subject to varying interpretation in the literature. The principal thrust of Cain and Hopkins' arguments concerning the British Empire in general, and Canada in particular, centre on minimising theories of colonial autonomy.[95] In otherwords, their perspective is heavily focused upon the activities of metropolitan dominated flows of finance capital and commercial information in shaping the political and economic fortunes of Britain's dependent territories. According to Kubicek, "they also stress that the machinations of financial capital have more explanatory power than the needs of industrial capital" in understanding the nature of colonial relationships.[96] Yet with regard to the building of Victoria Bridge and, indeed, the whole Grand Trunk project, the engineers and contractors, as representatives of British industrial capital, were primary driving forces in ensuring that the line went ahead. As Currie notes, "the Grand Trunk was the outcome of three sets of forces: residents of the St. Lawrence Lowlands wished for greater prosperity and stronger political ties with Great Britain; *a prominent firm of British contractors wanted to make money*; and Portland, Maine, was ambitious to capture the trade of Boston and New York".[97] Peto and Co. were already a pre-eminent firm of railway builders well before the Grand Trunk scheme was mooted, having built several lines in Britain and France. Expansion into the British Empire was an obvious route to commercial expansion and the firm went on to build in Australia and India as well as Canada, together with the completion of projects in regions of informal British commercial interest such as Russia.[98] Industrial capital was never simply the handmaiden to the financial interests of the City in these large-scale infrastructure projects.

Indeed, the 'machinations of financial capital' are not mentioned by Currie, though Cain and Hopkins regard them as central to their interpretation of the Grand Trunk scheme, going so far as to argue that without the help of London's merchant bankers "the Grand Trunk might never have been completed".[99] The latter claim seems valid, and is backed up by the detailed work of Platt and Adelman on financing the railway.[100] Yet surely the ambitions of the railway builders have a place in the story too? It was the dovetailing of *both financial and industrial capital* that drove the Grand Trunk project forward and which locates the great engineering project of bridging the St. Lawrence firmly within the web of colonial interdependencies stretched between Britain and Canada. Those colonial interests were not solely limited to the City of London, despite Magill's bold claim that "it was not the Fathers of Confederation but Lombard Street which built the canals, the railways, financed the lumber and grain trades, the mines and the industries without which Canadian provinces would now be states in the American union".[101] Much of the track, locomotive and rolling stock, as well as the entire ironwork for the Victoria Bridge, was manufactured at the contractors' Canada Works in Birkenhead, before being shipped out to Canada piece by piece. The British railway builders were instrumental in creating a space in the Canadian colony for the expanded reproduction of *their* commercial empire.[102]

In sum, perhaps the building of Victoria Bridge was less a paradigm of British technological diffusion into the periphery of the world economy, than a complex and highly personalised story that challenges the neat divisions of larger-scale theories of the political economy of empire. It was projected, and eventually completed, through a complex fusion of British engineering enterprise, migrant and colonial labour, and overwhelmingly British capital. Yet its design was the result of the stubborn genius of one man, Robert Stephenson, whose towering reputation at home allowed him to impose an engineering solution at Montreal that was later judged to be almost entirely inappropriate to the conditions of a developing nation in a new continent.

Acknowledgements

Many individuals and institutions have helped me with the research upon which this paper is based. First, I am very grateful to ING Baring Holdings Limited for permission to consult The Baring Archive. In particular, the help, advice and support of Dr John Orbell and Ms Jane Waller, Archivist and Deputy Archivist respectively, has been much appreciated. Second, I would like to thank the Royal Bank of Scotland PLC, for permission to consult the records of Messrs. Glyn, Mills & Co. The help of Mr Philip Winterbottom, Archivist, is gratefully acknowledged. Third, the help and advice of Ms Carol Morgan, Archivist of the Institution of Civil Engineers, was invaluable in understanding the work of both Robert Stephenson and James Hodges. Both Dr Orbell and Professor Robin Butlin read an earlier draft of this paper, for which I am very grateful. Figures 1 and 5 are reproduced with permission from ING Baring Holdings Limited; Figures 2, 3 and 7 with permission from the Science and Society

Picture Library of the Science Museum; Figures 4, 6 and 9 with permission from the Institution of Civil Engineers; Figure 8 with permission from the Guildhall Library, Corporation of London. Finally, I would like to take this opportunity to acknowledge a personal debt to Alan Baker for his kindness, friendship, advice and support over the last fifteen years.

Appendix 1

Dates:

- North abutment coffer-dam towed into place 24th May, 1854.
- First stone of bridge laid 20th July, 1854.
- First train passed over the bridge 17th December, 1859.

Dimensions and Weights:

- Total length of tubes, 6592 feet.
- Total length of bridge, 9144 feet.
- Height of bottom of centre tube above surface of water, 60 feet.
- Height of bottom tubes at abutment, 36 feet.
- Rise of tubes to centre, 1 in 130.
- Weight of iron in tubes, 9044 tons.
- Number of rivets in tubes, 1,540,000.
- Painting – number of coats, 4; number of acres in each coat, 32. Total acres, 128.
- Number of piers, 24.
- Number of spans, 25; twenty-four from 242 to 247 feet each; one, 330 feet.
- Quantity of masonry in piers and abutments, 2,713,095 cubic feet.
- Greatest depth of water, 22 feet.
- Average rate of current, seven miles an hour.
- Quantity of timber in temporary works, 2,280,000 cubic feet.
- Quantity of clay puddle used in dams, 146,000 cubic yards.

Force Employed in Construction:

- Number of men employed, 3040.
- Number of horses, 144.
- Locomotive engines, 4.
- Number of steam-boats, 6.
- Number of barges, 75.
- Tonnage of barges, 12,000.
- Power of steamers, 450 H.P.

Source: J. Hodges, *Construction of the Great Victoria Bridge in Canada* (London 1860) p. 82

NOTES

1 A. Trollope, *The Way We Live Now* (Oxford 1982) 324.

2 But see S. Oliver, The Thames Embankment and the disciplining of nature in modernity, *Geographical Journal* **166** (2000) 227-238. For a theoretical outline of the 'historical geography of capitalism' see D. Harvey, *The Limits to Capital* (Oxford 1982) 373-445.

3 See G. P. de T. Glazebrook, *A History of Transportation in Canada* (Toronto 1938).

4 The Baring Archive (hereafter B. A.), at the ING Baring Group, London HC 5.15.5: *Prospectus of the Grand Trunk Railway Co. of Canada*, London, 1853, Appendix, 1.

5 B. A. HC 5.15.5: *Prospectus of the Grand Trunk Railway Co. of Canada*, London, 1853, notes that "Acts of the Canadian Parliament have also been passed authorising the amalgamation of all the Companies whose railways intersect or join the Main Trunk Railway with the Grand Trunk Railway Company, so as to form one Company, under the name of the 'Grand Trunk Railway Company of Canada'. Arrangements are accordingly in progress for a fusion of the Grand Trunk Railway Company of Canada East, the Quebec and Richmond Railway Company, the St. Lawrence and Atlantic Railway Company, the Grand Junction Railway Company, and the Toronto and Guelph Railway Company, with The Grand Trunk Railway Company of Canada".

6 A. W. Currie, *The Grand Trunk Railway of Canada* (Toronto 1957). See also Glazebrook, *op. cit.*, 167-187 and H. A. Lovett, *Canada and the Grand Trunk* (Montreal 1924).

7 P. J. Cain and A. G. Hopkins, *British Imperialism: Innovation and Expansion 1688-1914* (London 1993) and P. J. Cain and A. G. Hopkins, *British Imperialism: Crisis and Deconstruction 1914-1990* (London 1993).

8 R. E. Dumett, Exploring the Cain/Hopkins paradigm: issues for debate; critique and topics for new research, in R. E. Dumett (Ed.), *Gentlemanly Capitalism and British Imperialism: The New Debate on Empire* (London 1999) 4-5.

9 P. Ziegler, *The Sixth Great Power: Barings, 1762-1929* (London 1988); J. Orbell, *Baring Brothers & Co., Limited. A History to 1939* (Privately printed, London 1985); R. Fulford, *Glyn's 1753-1953: Six Generations in Lombard Street* (London 1953). See also R. T. Naylor, *The History of Canadian Business 1867-1914. Volume One: The Banks and Finance Capital* (Toronto 1975) 20-30.

10 Orbell, *op. cit.*, 33.

11 Ziegler, *op. cit.*, 156.

12 Fulford, *op. cit.*, 144.

13 *Ibid.*, 145.

14 *Ibid.*, 146.

15 *Ibid.*, 147. The establishment of the financial agency of Upper Canada has been subject to varied interpretation. I have followed the evidence and arguments put forward in the business histories of the two key banks involved: Glyn, Mills and Co. and Baring Brothers & Co., quoted above (note 9). For a different interpretation, see M. L. Magill, John H. Dunn and the bankers, in J. K. Johnson (Ed.), *Historical Essays on Upper Canada* (Toronto 1975) 194-215. Magill argues that it was only after the American crisis of 1837 that John H. Dunn, the Receiver-General of Canada sought the appointment of an official financial agent for the province. Moreover, he claims that Glyn's were chosen as the sole agent, apparently with the acquiescence of Barings, as "their private relations had always been close and the fact that Glyn Mills & Co. was the official agent made no difference to them as far as the province was concerned". See Magill, *op. cit.*, 211-212.

16   On political developments in Canada, see G. Martin, Canada from 1815, in A. Porter (Ed.), *The Oxford History of the British Empire. Volume III: The Nineteenth Century* (Oxford 1999) 522-45.

17   Ziegler, *op. cit.*, 157. Ziegler's account is at variance with that of Fulford, *op. cit.*, 148, where he claims Barings were "mortified" by Glyn's appointment as joint agents and that in 1848 they wrote to the Inspector-General of Canadian finances "complaining that in 1837 the Canadian Government had declined to make their House sole financial agents for the Province".

18   Orbell, *op. cit.*, 65.

19   *Ibid.*, 41.

20   Fulford, *op. cit.*, 150.

21   *Ibid.*, 152.

22   Quoted in *ibid.*, 152.

23   These issues are discussed in some detail in D. C. M. Platt and J. Adelman, London merchant bankers in the first phase of heavy borrowing: the Grand Trunk Railway of Canada, *Journal of Imperial and Commonwealth History* **18** (1990) 208-227.

24   *Ibid.* See also L. H. Jencks, *The Migration of British Capital to 1875* (London 1938) 198-206.

25   Platt and Adelman, *op. cit.*, 220.

26   *Ibid.*, 219.

27   *Ibid.*, 219-220.

28   *Ibid.*, 220.

29   B. A. HC 5.15.5: *Prospectus of the Grand Trunk Railway Co. of Canada*, London, 1853, Appendix, 2.

30   *Ibid.*

31   *Construction of Victoria Bridge*, 16 Vict. c. 75 (1852-53).

32   Royal Bank of Scotland Archives (hereafter R.B.S.A.) GM/94: *To the Shareholders of the Grand Trunk Railway Company of Canada*, London, 6 May 1854.

33   *Ibid.*

34   *Ibid.*

35   *Ibid.* This view was reiterated the following year by the Company's Directors. See B.A. HC 5.15.11: *Grand Trunk Railway of Canada. Report of the First Meeting of Shareholders,* Quebec, 27 July 1854 (Reported by the London Board, August 1854), wherein the directors remarked that the bridge's necessity "became daily more apparent ... viewed in relation to its commercial importance [they] are more than ever impressed that, without it the large and comprehensive traffic system involved in the construction of the Railway, could only be partially and by comparison ineffectually carried out at a very great cost".

36   A contrary view was, however, put forward by Anthony Trollope during his travels in North America. See A. Trollope, *North America.* Volume 1 (London 1986; first edition 1862) 59, where he remarks that "probably it might be easy now to show that the road might have been made with sufficient accommodation for ordinary purposes without some of the more costly details. The great tubular bridge on which was expended 1,300,000*l.* might, I should think, have been dispensed with".

37   See N. Rosenberg and W. G. Vincenti, *The Britannia Bridge: The Generation and Diffusion of Technological Knowledge* (Cambridge, Mass. 1978)

38 Not surprisingly, there is a large literature on Stephenson and the Britannia Bridge. For the classic contemporary accounts, see E. Clark, *The Britannia and Conway Tubular Bridges, with General Inquiries on Beams and on the Properties of Materials used in Construction* (London 1850) and W. Fairbairn, *An Account of the Construction of the Britannia and Conway Tubular Bridges* (London 1849). A useful account can also be found in Smiles's biography of the Stephensons, see S. Smiles, *The Story of the Life of George Stephenson; Including a Memoir of his Son Robert Stephenson* (London 1873) 320-340. See also L. T. C. Rolt, *George and Robert Stephenson: The Railway Revolution* (London 1960). More recent accounts include H. Petroski, The Britannia Tubular Bridge: a paradigm of failure-driven design, *Structural Engineering Review* **5** (1994) 259-270 and J. Rapley, *The Britannia Bridge 1845-1850: A Sesquicentennial Celebration* (London: Institute of Civil Engineers 1999).

39 Petroski, *op. cit.*, 259.

40 Rosenberg and Vincenti, *op. cit.*, 5.

41 Petroski, *op. cit.*, 263.

42 See D. Smith, The use of models in nineteenth-century British suspension bridge design, *History of Technology* **2** (1977) 169-214.

43 *Ibid.*, 194.

44 Petroski, *op. cit.*, 264.

45 His principal collaborators were William Fairbairn and Eaton Hodgkinson.

46 Rosenberg and Vincenti, *op. cit.*, 82, n. 9.

47 Petroski, *op. cit.*, 265.

48 Smiles, *op. cit.*, 339-340. The first edition of Smiles's work was published in 1857.

49 J. Hodges, *Construction of the Great Victoria Bridge in Canada* (London 1860) 19.

50 *Ibid.*, 11.

51 *Ibid.*, 7.

52 *Ibid.*, 8.

53 *Ibid.*, 13.

54 *Ibid.*, 23-24.

55 Cribwork was a construction technique widely used in Canada and the United States, though quite unknown in Britain. It effectively overcame the need for expensive piling techniques by utilising the skill, technology and materials available to builders in the new continent. The use of the axe was far more widespread in North America and supplies of rough-hewn timber were very plentiful as a building material. Techniques therefore evolved which allowed the construction of skeletal structures of timber at great speed in the most arduous of conditions. Hodges, *op. cit.*, 21 notes how in North America "the wharves, and even the foundations for bridges in deep water [were] almost entirely of this 'cribwork'. It is formed simply by laying timber along the whole of the outer edge of the work, and at intervals of from five to ten feet, parallel therewith throughout the whole of the breadth, connected by means of transverse timbers firmly trenailed and notched into them ... as soon as one course of work is thus formed, another is laid upon the top of it, and the two are firmly trenailed together. An axe and an auger are the only tools used. The flatted pine ... and a piece of freely splitting hard wood for trenails, are, with the stone required for sinking, the only materials employed ... the timber work below the water line, not being subject to worms, never decays; and as in the Canadian lakes and rivers the rise of the water is not great, the major part of such work is imperishable, and a stranger cannot fail to be astonished at the rapidity with which work of this description is executed, and with its stability when finished".

56   *Ibid.*, 23.

57   *Ibid.*, 26.

58   *Ibid.*, 29-30.

59   B. A. HC 5.15.12: *Grand Trunk Railway of Canada. Statement of the London Board of Directors*, London, July 1855. The directors noted, with characteristic understatement, that "the diminished rate of progress of the works on the Victoria Bridge is in accordance with a desire very generally expressed, and by concentrating the energies and resources of the contractors upon other parts of the undertaking, will expedite the completion of the Main Line of Railway. It also affords an opportunity for consideration whether some plan of construction may not be devised, whereby all the advantages to be derived from completing this important link in the great chain of communication may be obtained at a less charge upon the undertaking".

60   B.A. HC 5.15.70: *Grand Trunk Railway Company of Canada. Victoria Bridge. Letters and Reports on the Best and Cheapest Mode of Bridging the St. Lawrence at Montreal*, London, 1856, vii.

61   *Ibid.*, xi.

62   *Ibid.* The reports were immensely detailed, reaching 77 pages of closely argued text, interspersed with detailed replies by Liddell to each point raised.

63   *Ibid.*, v.

64   *Ibid.*

65   *Ibid.*, ii.

66   B.A. HC 5.15.13: *Grand Trunk Railway of Canada. Statement of the London Board of Directors*, London, June 1856. Referring to the reports by Stephenson, Brunel, Ross and Clark, the directors claimed that "having due regard to the solidity and permanence of this structure, no material reduction in the outlay can be effected. At the same time, certain modifications have been recommended by which some saving may be obtained in the masonry and the approaches".

67   Hodges, *op. cit.*, 35, where he notes that "the snow storms of the winter of 1855-6 were far more formidable than any before remembered in Canada".

68   Hodges, *op. cit.*, 42.

69   *Ibid.* Emphasis in original.

70   The outline of the building programme has also been cross-checked in the company's relevant Annual Reports. See B. A. HC 5.15.17: *Grand Trunk Railway of Canada. Statement of the London Board of Directors*, London, April 1858, which notes that "the progress of the works of the Victoria Bridge continues to be very satisfactory:- fourteen piers out of twenty-four are completed; the construction of all but two will be finished during this and the next year. The two abutments are up to tube level; the approaches to each are completed; one tube is fixed and finished, and either eight or nine will be fixed in their places before the termination of the present year. The Expenditure, to the present time, has been £712,192 out of the £1,250,000, the price at which the Bridge is to be completed under the last agreement entered into with Messrs. Peto, Brassey, and Co.".

71   Hodges, *op. cit.*, 42.

72   *Ibid.*

73   *Ibid.*, 44.

74   *Ibid.*, 45.

75   These dimensions are taken from Smiles, *op. cit.*, 358.

76   Hodges, *op. cit.*, 52.

77   B. A. HC 5.15.18: *Grand Trunk Railway of Canada. Proceedings of the Fifth Annual General Meeting*, Toronto, 15 December 1858 (Reported by the London Board, January 1859), wherein the directors "congratulate the Shareholders upon the very satisfactory progress which has this season been made at the Victoria Bridge [it being] fully anticipated the bridge will be opened for traffic in time for the fall business of next year, at which period, the Directors trust to have a continuous line of railway from the upper lakes, and the vast producing regions of the West to the Atlantic seaboard ... the Directors entertain no doubt that with the advantages which this route affords over all other competing lines to the Atlantic coast, time alone is required to accomplish the success of the enterprise".

78   Hodges, *op. cit.,* 53.

79   *Ibid.*, 54-55.

80   *Ibid.*, 60.

81   *Ibid.*, 61.

82   *Ibid.*, 71.

83   *Ibid.*, 72.

84   *Illustrated London News* 25 August 1860, 188.

85   R.B.S.A. GM/96: Grand Trunk Railway of Canada: Contracts Book of William Jackson, 1853.

86   Though note that the original contract specified above was, in fact, renegotiated in 1856. See B. A. HC 5.15.13: *Grand Trunk Railway of Canada. Statement of the London Board of Directors*, London, June 1856, Appendix C, which states that on 20 August 1856 "the contract for the Victoria Bridge, originally fixed at £1,400,000, with a power of increase, for contingencies, to £1,500,000, to be reduced to £1,250,000 in consideration of payments to the extent of £650,000 being made in cash, instead of in B bonds and shares".

87   B. A. HC 5.15.23: *Grand Trunk Railway of Canada. Statement of the London Directors*, London, July 1861.

88   B. A. HC 5.15.72: Memorandum in the hand of Thomas Baring. Resolution of Barings and Glyn's to make a temporary loan for the completion of Victoria Bridge, *c*. November 1859.

89   Platt and Adelman, *op. cit.*, 223. Though note that bulk cargo was not the only business targeted by the new railway. The Grand Trunk also expected to capture a significant share of the flow of immigrants from Europe to the new continent. See B.A. HC 5.15.101: Memorandum on Working of Through Traffic Office from 1857 to 1860, March 1860. Its purpose was explicitly stated thus: "The Through Traffic Office was established at the beginning of the year 1857, for the purpose of disseminating throughout Great Britain and Ireland, and the continent of Europe, reliable information on the subject of Canada and the Grand Trunk Route, with a view to setting forth the advantages of the former as a field for the employment of capital and labour, and of the latter as a carrying route to and from Canada, &. Through it, to and from the Great producing Districts of the Western States".

90   Rapley, *op. cit.*, 61.

91   See J. E. Vance, *The North American Railroad: Its Origin, Evolution, and Geography* (Baltimore 1995) 252, where commenting on the Victoria Bridge he notes that "in 1898 the tubular spans at Montreal were replaced by trusses when this structure was reconstructed using the original piers as the Royal Jubilee Bridge".

92   Rapley, *op. cit.*, 61.

93   T. F. McIlwraith, The railway age, 1834-1891, in R. L. Gentilcore (Ed.), *Historical Atlas of Canada. Volume II: The Land Transformed 1800-1891* (Toronto 1993) plate 26.

94 Vance, *op. cit.*, 253-278. Barings were heavily involved in the financing of the Canadian Pacific railway too. Orbell, *op. cit.*, 51 and 56 remarks that "in 1885 the house [Barings] joined with Glyns to become financial agents in London for the Canadian Pacific Railway Co. [and] in 1886 £4,191,500 Canadian Pacific Railway Co. stock was underwritten by a syndicate of 13 houses. Barings took a £2,306,500 underwriting participation and then had 'to support the market' by purchasing £325,000 stock".

95 Cain and Hopkins, British Imperialism: Innovation and Expansion *op. cit.*, 258-273.

96 See R. Kubicek, Economic power at the periphery: Canada, Australia and South Africa, 1850-1914, in R. E. Dumett (Ed.), *Gentlemanly Capitalism and British Imperialism: The New Debate on Empire* (London 1999) 113.

97 Currie, *op. cit.*, 3.

98 *Ibid.*, 5.

99 Cain and Hopkins, British Imperialism: Innovation and Expansion *op. cit.*, 263. Indeed, in their admittedly much broader interpretative summary of Canadian development between 1850 and 1914 they do not mention the railway's contractors once.

100 Platt and Adelman, *op. cit.*

101 Magill, *op. cit.*, 214.

102 See Currie, *op. cit.*, 6, where he notes that "the Peto firm was on the lookout for larger business opportunities. Railway construction in Britain was becoming less profitable because of over-building and competition among contractors. The firm was about to complete some work in France and unless it could get more business elsewhere, it would have idle equipment on its hands".

Chapter Twelve

THE COLONIAL DREAM

Empire, Quebec and Colonial Discourse in the Nineteenth Century

SERGE COURVILLE

Welcome to my shores, distressed European; bless the hour in which thou didst see my verdant fields, my fair navigable rivers, and my green mountains! – If thou wilt work, I have bread for thee; if thou wilt be honest, sober, and industrious, I have greater rewards to confer on thee – ease and independence[1].

Written by a Frenchman who established himself in Orange County, New York, after the British conquest of New France in 1760, these words remind us of the role played by the American dream in the settlement of the New World. In this imagery, America was portrayed as a land of hope and liberty, where all dreams could come true. Other places were similarly described. Among these were the British settlement colonies, which were also presented as unique places for success. In Quebec, even the Canadian Shield was portrayed as a land of happiness by the politico-religious elite of the late-nineteenth and early-twentieth centuries. Most scholars have interpreted this clerical discourse as only a response to local difficulties, full of French references and nostalgia about the past. Recently this view has been challenged by authors who detail the economic conditions of colonisation, as well as the influence of the American dream and the impact of Victorian science and morals.[2]

However, there has been little attempt to compare this French-Canadian discourse with the propaganda brochures used in the British Empire to attract immigrants to the colonies. Such a comparative approach shows that there was a colonial version of the American dream that was diffused throughout the British colonies, one whose themes and rhetoric were integral to the Quebec colonisation discourse that was developed during the nineteenth century. To understand that connection, one needs to adopt a broad geographical and historical perspective, as well as to compare and contrast the content of the brochures between different places and times. In this paper, we will first recall the general context of the time, and analyse the propaganda material used in the settler colonies of the British Empire to promote immigration. Then, we will compare their content with the brochures used by Quebec political and clerical leaders to promote their own projects of colonisation.

The age of immigration

Seen as the age of liberalism and democratic ideals, the nineteenth century was also the age of exploitation and morality, which echoed the rise of pauperism and missionary zeal. It was additionally the age of migration and settlement, where some 30 to 35 million people were driven into exile between 1815 and 1911. Of this number, more than 19 million left from the British Isles, including 5 million from Ireland during these years. In Britain, emigration was the question of the hour and was seen as a safety valve for the cyclic problems of the economy and the rise of poverty, both of which were considered a threat to social and political order.[3] Emigration was also perceived as an important bulwark in the defence of the colonies and, along with the new free-trade policy of the 1840s, as a way to build a 'Greater Britain'. By peopling the colonies and offering them the hope and the means of becoming true commercial partners, it was thought that the integrity of the Empire would be assured.[4]

Science played an important role in these issues by discussing problems related to slavery, climate and natural resources, as well as by furnishing tools for the expansionist movement.[5] Science also nourished the hope in the colonies for material progress and industrialisation, in the manner of Great Britain and the United States; this was notably the case in Canada.[6] However, despite the efforts to support 'scientific' emigration[7], movement to the British colonies actually declined during the nineteenth century, as more migrants went to the United States (Figure 1).

In response to this growing emigration to the United States, numerous brochures and pamphlets were produced in Britain and her colonies, which constructed the basis of a real 'colonial' dream. Successful at first, the British colonies eventually lost their advantage. Even Canada became only a place of transit to the United States.

FIGURE 1
Emigrants from the British Isles, 1815-1911.

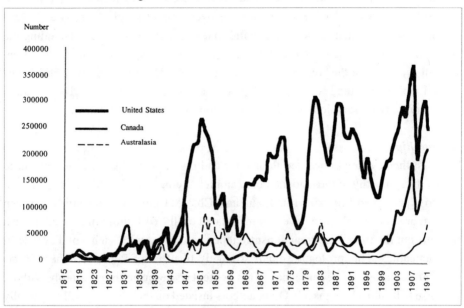

Source: Stanley C. Johnson, 1913; Helen I. Cowan, 1961.

Nonetheless, although it failed to attract more migrants to the British colonies, the colonial dream did greatly influence the rhetoric of migration in the colonies, even in the French part of Canada, which was a focus of attempts to promote colonisation within their own territories.

Shaping the dream

As with the American dream[8], the colonial dream had its origins in mythical constructions about the Western Hemisphere that had existed in Europe since the fifteenth century and that had made the New World into a veritable 'Promised Land'. It consisted of a series of propositions that were inspired by the 'American dream' and, like it, fed from the contrasting images of garden and desert, civilisation and savagery, settlement and nomadic life. However, contrary to the American dream, the colonial dream was mainly an institutional discourse, one that appeared after the American Revolution to support and protect what was now seen as a menaced Empire. In this sense it lacked the popular spirit of the American version.

The dimensions of this colonial dream can be reconstructed from the propaganda material encapsulated in pamphlets, brochures and leaflets written to attract immigrants to the settlement colonies of Canada, Australia, New Zealand, and South Africa[9]. Filled with simplistic views and ideas, these writings focused on a range of themes that, as we shall see, changed little over time. Though their style evolved through time, they maintained their moral tone. As a context for understanding the connection between the British and the French-Canadian discourses on colonisation, we will first analyse the content of the literature that was written for the English part of the Empire, including some of the English speaking parts of Canada. The literature was commonly divided into a series of key themes, as discussed below.

Authorship

The first theme often concerned the author and his/her credentials. It was meant to attract the sympathy of the readers. For example: "Being only a matter-of-fact person, and no experienced author", wrote Lieutenant Charles Rubidge[10], "it would have been much more congenial … to have communicated orally with those interested in such matters, but the time, labour, and insufficiency connected with such a plan, render it impracticable". This prologue sounds strangely like that of Pierre Boucher[11] in his 1664 presentation of New France: "I am content to describe things simply without recourse to beautiful language". Other authors insisted on their honesty: "Being totally unconnected with any speculation either in land or commerce, I cannot be suspected of having any sinister motives for lauding one part of America or depreciating another".[12] As for those who tried to convince the readers of their sincerity, they referred to disinterested 'witnesses' or to official documents, such as extracts of laws, maps, official plans, political addresses, or census data that would demonstrate the soundness of their proposal and encourage prospective colonists to come and discover the truth for themselves.

Colonial advantages

The next theme described the advantages of the land and compared it to other places. Sometimes this was limited to a simple passing comment, such as "you will find there the best soil in the country", but it could also be more elaborate when, for example, the author compared the advantages of the colony with some other countries. The proximity of Canada was frequently emphasised. Why suffer the discomfort and dangers of a long voyage to distant colonies, claimed many Canadian agents, when it is so easy to go to Canada? The land was not only closer to England, but more easily reached. Such logic was certainly forceful, especially in relation to Australia and its 'emptiness'[13] (Figure 2). However it was also used for the American Mid-West: "By the time that the Illinois emigrant has arrived at the place of his destination", affirmed

FIGURE 2
An example of competing visions of Canada and Australia.

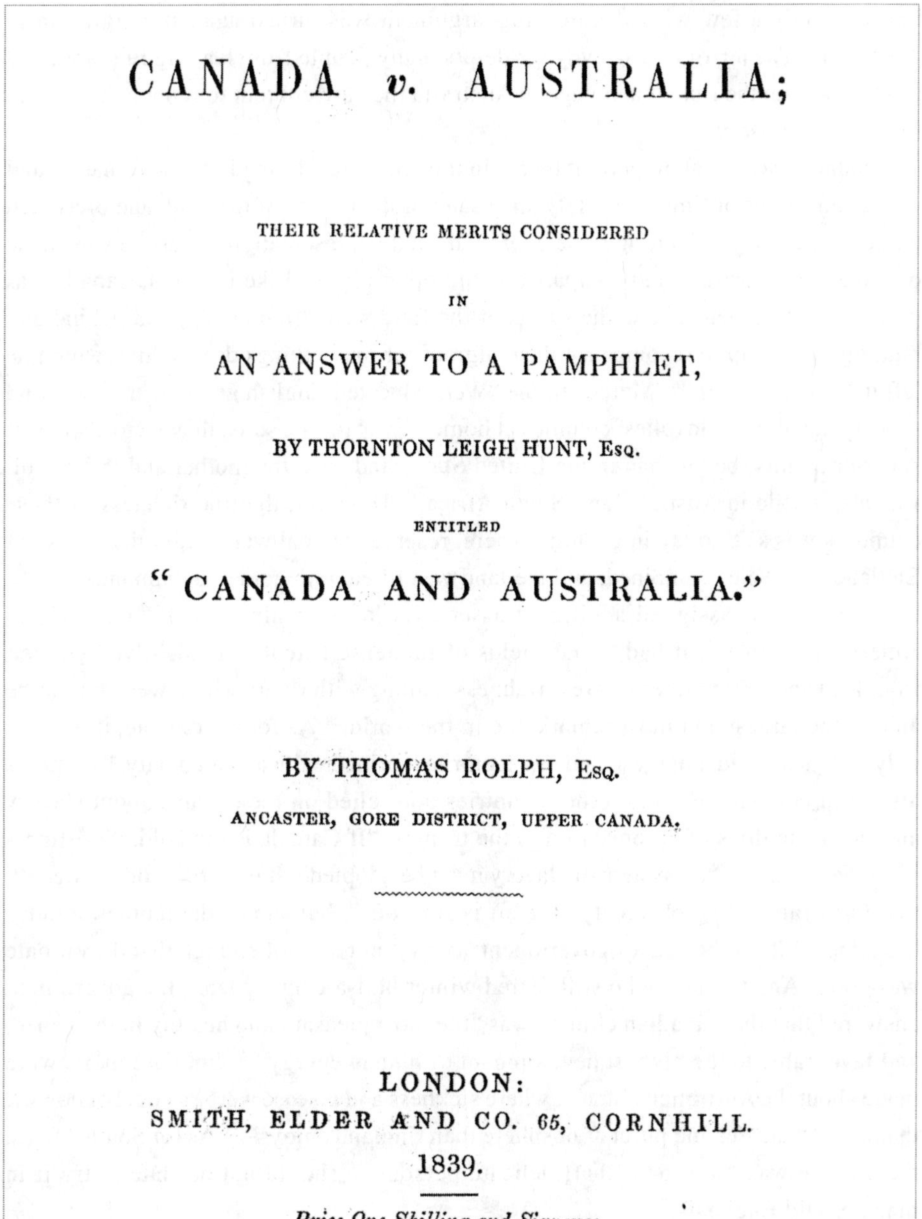

CANADA *v.* AUSTRALIA;

THEIR RELATIVE MERITS CONSIDERED

IN

AN ANSWER TO A PAMPHLET,

BY THORNTON LEIGH HUNT, Esq.

ENTITLED

" CANADA AND AUSTRALIA."

BY THOMAS ROLPH, Esq.

ANCASTER, GORE DISTRICT, UPPER CANADA.

LONDON:
SMITH, ELDER AND CO. 65, CORNHILL.

1839.

Price One Shilling and Sixpence.

Source: Commonwealth Library, Cambridge.

Charles Grece[14], "the Canadian emigrant might be comfortably seated by his own fire-side, resting from the fatigues of his voyage", as if it was possible to build a house in only a few weeks! Later, this argument was turned against emigration to Australia: "The terror of a sea voyage deters many people from leaving England, and rather than run the risk of a voyage to Australia they are content to remain at home in the greatest misery".[15]

Nature also was an important theme in the brochures. Using both the romantic and utilitarian values of English society, they sang of the beauty of the land, and presented nature as capital just waiting to be exploited. In this presentation, great use was made of rhetorical flourishes and comparison with other places. Like England, Canada was proclaimed a garden. There, the sports of the field were "free to all", and fishing and hunting "will help to recompense the emigrant for many things dear to him, which he left in his native land"[16]. Moreover, the "Well-educated English gentlemen ... will find scenery equal to the loveliest counties at home".[17] As for the soils, they were always of superior quality, better than in the United States and even the motherland.[18] The soil was also fertile in Australia and South Africa.[19] However, the true richness of these countries was said to lay in geology. There, reserves of coal were larger than those of England and Wales combined, and the land was filled with gold and diamonds.

Canada was assigned additional assets. As large as almost half of the North American continent, it had "Coal Fields of immense extent ... gold, silver, copper, iron, lead and other mines of great richness", along with rivers which were said to be among the largest and most remarkable in the world.[20] As for the climate, it was not only well described, but presented as a factor favouring health and longevity. Brochures also used comparisons with other countries and relied on the debates about slavery and the difficulties of colonisation in the tropics. "If Canada is too cold, the Illinois is too hot". There, "the system of slavery must be adopted". It was true, added Grece[21], that in the area of Quebec City "the air is rigorous", but since "the mother country has adopted it for the seat of government", was it not a proof enough that the climate was good? And to those who still feared winter half-a-century later, the government answered that the Canadian climate was "the most pleasant and healthy in the world, and favourable to the highest development of human energy".[22] Similar reports were made about the Australian climate, where sickness and disease were "scarcely known", thanks to "a clearer and purer atmosphere than England enjoys".[23] As for South Africa, the climate was "so grand [that] delicate persons ... should not hesitate to try it in place of Old England".[24]

All the colonies at one time or another faced political difficulties. Thus, it was necessary to reassure immigrants about the security of the new home country. In

Canada, for example, the Rebellion was now "happily terminated"; as for the Indians, "there never was a more harmless or kind race of people", who were receiving from the missionaries "a plain English education".[25] The country offered a "greater degree of security than can be enjoyed in any other British colony".[26] And when later brochures spoke of the transcontinental railway, they used the example of India, then threatened by Russia, to affirm: "How the danger and difficulty will disappear on the opening of the Canadian Pacific Railway, by which troops and stores could be conveyed through our own territory without let or hindrance!".[27] Further, too, "the railway makes settlements".[28] In Australia peace was also at hand.[29] As for South Africa where war had caused desolation for too many years, the future was said to be surely "a rosy one!".[30] The strongest argument for stability within the colonial dream lay in British moral and institutional order. This was especially the case for Canada, where a peace was said to reign that was not found in the United States, thanks to "the mild and equal sway of firmly executed British laws, which secures every man in his religion, person and property".[31] This order also guaranteed the security of the country and proved the "civilised" nature of the country, where many "well-educated gentlemen and officers" were now settling.[32]

In the first half of the nineteenth century, many British colonies were still in the early stages of development. Nevertheless, they were described with great enthusiasm. This was the case, for example, with the townships situated to the south of Montreal. There, "bridges are built, and roads are cut, villages and settlements are rising in all directions under its care, and four years have made a change in this part of Canada, which, under other circumstances, could hardly have taken place in a hundred".[33] In Upper Canada, "every comfort, and almost every luxury, may now be procured".[34] Furthermore, in Canada: "The advantages of civilisation may be enjoyed, without enduring many of those annoyances and grievances so common amongst the other nations of Europe".[35] The same rhetoric was used for Western Australia, which was said to be "in a high state of civilisation"[36], and for South Africa, which had plenty of accommodations and activities that the "English ladies" could enjoy in their leisure time: "Races, dances, theatres ... not to mention the chapels, churches, public libraries, parks and useful institutions, as plentiful in proportion to the population as in England".[37] Such clear advantages were said to be beneficial for the immigrant, who would be able to find *in situ* all he needed at a good price.[38] As for capitalists, they also would find great opportunities, with the additional benefits of an advantageous fiscal regime. This was the case in Canada, where taxation was said to be five times less than in the United States[39] and "about 80 per cent less than in Great Britain, and more equally apportioned".[40]

Related to the prospects of material and moral advance outlined above, there was also the possibility for the immigrant to start a new life. All the brochures had promises of progress, success and happiness, not only for the immigrants but for their children. However, most of them insisted that such success was conditional. Many referred to the personal qualities cherished by capitalist entrepreneurs: perseverance, sobriety, and work. Others echoed Wakefield's principles of neighbourliness in Australia, by stressing the necessity for the immigrant to listen to the counsel of those who had experience in the country.[41] Even in Canada, the brochures adopted a moral tone: "By following something like the plan [I] laid down, the [newly arrived immigrant] will find himself in prosperous circumstances in the fourth or fifth year. Let it be understood, however, that I am supposing the party to be sober and industrious".[42] As for South Africa, where the discovery of gold and diamonds had caused the authors to adopt a language close to that of the American dream, immigrants were told the same. "We immigrate to make money" said Fred Darrell[43], but if one really wished to succeed, he had to avoid "alcohol and gambling", and to remain honest and polite. As for those who failed, the fault has been their own!

The colonial mission

The immigrants who established themselves in the colonies were said to be participating in a project that would be beneficial to both the local and the motherland's economy. This economic morality was inherited from liberal discourse as well as from the patriotism and the missionary idealism derived from British military and evangelical movements. In Canada, for example, where many authors denounced the trade with the United States, self-sufficiency was often presented as an issue of colonial security, even a question of loyalty: "if they are not for their country, they are against it", claimed Grece.[44] In the Eastern Townships, where the arrival of the French Canadians made it difficult to maintain a strong Protestant colony, an appeal was made "to all in the Old Country who take an interest in the spread of the Protestant religion, to back by their influence the efforts now being made, to save these Townships to their Faith".[45] As for England, it was hoped that its social and demographic weight would benefit from new markets: "The more you increase the number of consumers on the other side of the ocean, the larger becomes the necessary production at home".[46] Thus the motto during the celebrations of the Royal Jubilees in 1887 and 1897: "Men's eyes were opened to the glories of their Empire"![47]

Such a message held strong symbolic meaning. On the one hand, the immigrant was to become an inheritor of the country which he would help to build. On the other, he was to become a "Citizen of the Empire" or of "Greater Britain" for, as an eminent Cambridge professor noted at the time, the English colonies were England overseas, "Greater England, but England the same".[48] To ensure the success of such a project, however, it was necessary for the settlers to be relatively homogeneous, which is to say British or, at least, European in origin. If Canada serves as a good example in this respect (except for the Chinese on the West Coast), clearly this was not the case in Australia or South Africa, where Asiatic immigration was sharply resented and resulted in legislation to enforce a greater homogeneity.[49] This principle of exclusion also applied to poor people and criminals, and became clearly expressed in the brochures in the second half of the nineteenth century. If Canada was the "poor's man country", it was not for the "sluggard's", the "idler", or the "dissipated".[50] Even in Britain, views changed. Contrary to early opinions, in the late-nineteenth century, emigration was no longer seen as "the sending away of our paupers and criminals to the Colonies, for if we did so the Colonies would refuse them". Instead, it meant "the removal of suitable persons who, in spite of want of employment, have managed to keep out of the workhouse".[51]

Despite their efforts, the colonial propagandists were not able to divert immigrants from the United States. Moreover, within the colonies themselves, the imperial project was often left behind. Without renouncing British values and traditions, but shaped by the hopes and conditions of life in the new worlds, the colonial societies that resulted loosened their connections with the metropole, obtained representative government, and searched for an identity that was different to either England or the United States. Although Britain was still perceived as a parent, it came to be seen as a foreign entity. One of the reasons for the migrant's desire for increased independence was, of course, an economic one. Because of its natural resources and the strength of its development, the United States became a formidable place of settlement for all strata of society. Symbolised as a dream, its promises came to offer more than the colonial dream, which was too 'rational', a characteristic that was even stressed by immigration officials.

Like the programmes of immigration, the British discourse of colonisation was 'scientific'. It sought to provide a well-informed project, stripped "of any language calculated to work on the imagination, or to interfere with the calm and dispassionate exercise of their own judgement on the part of those whom you may address", as Lord Russell said to the commissioners charged with immigration in 1840. This was also the view of colonial governments and of those who requested the creation of an office in Britain, in order to make "a perfectly rational plan of emigration".[52] Contrary to the American dream, the colonial dream was not able to capture people's imaginations with wide-open spaces, and quickly made fortunes. Certainly, immigrants found a land of liberty and opportunity in the colonies, but they would also face a collection of laws, regulations and controls that would set limits on their initiatives. As for success, it was certainly possible, but only with perseverance and after many years of hard work that would often benefit only future generations. Few immigrants, in fact, paid attention to these promises and many may never have even read the brochures presenting them. Their attention was stimulated rather more by messages and rumours about the United States that came from parents, friends, the popular press, and various spectacles like circuses or cowboy shows. Nonetheless, the brochures strongly influenced those in the colonies who wanted to attract immigrants for their own internal colonisation projects. This was certainly the case in Quebec, where the French-Canadian elite adopted this model.

The dream transposed: the example of Quebec

Until the turn of the nineteenth century, British immigration to Quebec was relatively weak. Then, from 1830 to 1840, the number of English-speakers increased. The largest contingent came from Ireland. Taken under state and religious control, Irish immigrants were directed towards the backwoods of the *seigneuries* and the neighbouring townships, where land was still available for colonisation. By the mid-nineteenth century, foreigners represented almost 10 per cent of the population. Yet, the major phenomenon of the period was the emigration of French Canadians to the United States, which began in the early decades of the century and would reach an unprecedented volume by the early 1900s.[53] This emigration was seen as a veritable haemorrhage by Quebec's politico-religious elite. It stimulated their own colonisation propaganda and the adoption of a political agenda not only to support rural development, but to construct a national territory capable of assuring the survival of the French language and culture in North America, while protecting French-Canadian society from the excesses of American capitalism. This regeneration was to be accomplished through the promotion of agriculture, a familial-centred society, and religion, more than through industry and commerce, which were considered to be foreign to French-Canadian identity. Nonetheless, it was hoped that some of these enterprises would be integrated into the rural milieu and would help the colonisation process.[54]

Discourses on colonisation

In Quebec, each region produced its own propaganda literature. The best known examples were the brochures or pamphlets published by the provincial government and the societies of colonisation in order to attract French Canadians and colonisers from overseas to new areas of settlement. These brochures were numerous, and just a few examples can be discussed here, as exemplars.

The first example is representative of governmental propaganda. A brochure published by the Provincial Government of Quebec in 1870, addressed to European immigrants, noted how as in the rest of the Empire it meant to inform the reader about the advantages of the province in a manner that would "succinctly treat the matters referred to; and (from a purely practical point of view), not to fatigue the reader with theoretical notions".[55] The first theme presented the advantages of the country. They were said to rest in the "various resources" of the land, the "solidity" of the political institutions, the "rare perfection" of the laws, the "material prosperity" shared by the people, and the "peace, unity and good fellowship which reign between all classes".[56] Likewise, if immigrants chose to settle in Quebec, they were said to be able to " find [ease and comfort] in the cultivation of the soil, and in the pursuit of the different branches of industry". And since the province was opening new roads and building railways, it was to offer favourable advantages to those who were "without means, but in quest of labour". Within a short time, the immigrant might "amass sufficient to warrant him a domain of his own". [57]

The countryside gave witness to this promise of success in 'splendid farms' and 'princely residences'. To whom do these belong? "You will be surprised to find, in how many cases, their owners are men who, a short time ago, came here with absolutely nothing".[58] As to those who stated that Canada was still a wilderness, officials replied that the creation of European civilisation there had already been achieved thanks to the first French missionaries and pioneers, from whom civilisation had spread, along with the growth of population and education. And, "Since transatlantic communication has become more frequent, it may be safely said that Europe has transmitted to us its habits and tastes, and even its very luxuries", as shown by various statistics concerning the country.[59] Thus, immigrants to Quebec were asked to contribute less to the development of the Empire, as in other colonies, than to the expansion of European civilisation.

Yet, it is in the propaganda material written by the Catholic church, often through the societies of colonisation, that we find the clearest examples of the themes that had been developed elsewhere in the British Empire in order to promote colonisation (Figure 3). The one exception was the lack of need to establish authorial credibility. This was because the Catholic Church was the paramount moral authority in Quebec and was also at the very heart of these colonisation societies. As in Britain, the first issue of these brochures acknowledged the demographic problem and its related

FIGURE 3
An example of religious propaganda concerning colonisation

PAMPHLET

SUR

LA COLONISATION

DANS

LA VALLEE D'OTTAWA,

AU NORD DE MONTREAL,

ET

REGLEMENTS ET AVANTAGES

DE LA

SOCIÉTÉ DE COLONISATION DU DIOCÈSE DE MONTRÉAL,

PAR LE RÉVD A. LABELLE, PTRE,
CURÉ DE ST. JÉROME.

Montreal:
IMPRIMÉ PAR JOHN LOVELL & FILS,
1880.

Source: Commonwealth Library, Cambridge.

economic and social difficulties. In Quebec, this problem was mainly that of the St. Lawrence Valley, where all the land was said to be occupied, making it impossible to further divide the farms, which would result in a general impoverishment. The solution was seen to lie in immigration, especially to the Canadian Shield, an area as great as "an entire province" that had riches enough to provide life for "a million farmers". This was a theme that would later be used in Australia to promote settlement.[60] Why, then, asked French-Canadian colonisation pamphlets, "crowd one on top of the other like chickens under a hen when the wide open spaces beckon to us"[61], "Think of your children, see for yourselves".[62]

One of the first advantages of this northern country was its proximity to the St. Lawrence Valley. The most accessible area, the Laurentides, was close to the district of Montreal, where almost half of the population of the province was situated. Although it was also an area marked by glaciation, the promoters minimised the environmental constraints and converted them to advantages. "All the beauties of nature have been brought together here to provide a gay and charming appearance".[63] Although the mountains reached a height of fifty to three hundred feet, they gave an 'undulating' appearance to the countryside and favoured the drainage of the land. Good soil was everywhere and allowed everything to grow 'marvellously'. This was not to say that the region was a "garden", but evidently, a soil that had good trees was also excellent farm land. And, in order to reinforce such views, experts such as explorers and surveyors were cited, such as Joseph Bouchette, Jr., who wrote in 1859 that the land in the valleys of the Red River and La Lièvre were "not surpassed by any in Upper or Lower Canada".[64] The climate was described with the same optimistic logic. Again referring to an expert, Professor Macoun, it was argued that: "In the north country of the province the climate is not more rigorous than in other parts of Quebec".[65] Moreover, proximity to the mountains allowed "no epidemics to hinder birth".[66]

As for the potential of the region, it was described as enormous. There were multitudes of lakes and rivers, trout everywhere, and "countless" sites for waterpower. Such a profusion of natural resources was "perhaps without equal in the province" and offered many opportunities for the building of mills, tanneries, and manufactures of all sorts. The forests provided considerable resources for heating and lumbering, wood lots would quickly rise in value, and mineral wealth was at hand. And indeed, if one was to judge by the observations made in the Cornouailles, "a good silver vein always wears an iron cap". There was little doubt that the region could be proclaimed "a good one for metallic richness".[67]

Of course, settlement in the area was at first difficult, but the new settlers would be coming to an established and organised country, thanks to the alliance that was now uniting "as in a single beam, the religious, civil, commercial, and industrial interests".[68] The land could be bought at a good price, was protected from seizure, and the government was providing all that was needed for subsistence. In short, hopes were high for success! This was the land of dreams for the small farmers and the unemployed workers from the cities, who would find there another hope, another gift for work. And since there were fewer luxuries in the new townships than in the old, "girls will [be] content with dresses more modest and hats less decorated; comfort, then, was at hand, but only if the colonist persevered, stayed sober, and worked hard".[69]

As for the moral value of the project, it was confirmed in letters and extracts of laws included in the brochures. It was expected that immigration to the plateau would be "a pretty strong remedy for the cancer of emigration that is eating us up and scattering our people among the lands of strangers ... As Fénélon said long ago, it is the hardiness of the people and the abundance of food that provides the real strength and richness of a kingdom ... Let's differ from the Irish who flew away from misery by spreading all over the earth. Because God placed us here in the cherished country of Canada, in the British Empire, he made it our land to live in. Let us establish there and nowhere else!".[70] Or again, "In peopling the Laurentides, we will build a boulevard for the French-Canadian race in Canada ... Go to the North, then, French Canadians, the country is waiting for you".[71] Yet, there was only a lukewarm response to this appeal, as greater and greater waves of people were attracted to the United States and to factory work in the cities. Compared to the St. Lawrence Valley, the northern area offered too little, too late, to those who were already part of a modernising society. Certainly, there was a movement towards the plateau and large groups of people were established there, but the majority of the settlements were tentative and marked by failure, except in those areas where the geographic conditions were propitious. *Curé* Labelle had anticipated this problem when he wrote "all the territory that does not resemble the St. Lawrence Valley is seen as unfavourable to agriculture. This is an illusion. We live as well in the mountains as on the plains, which are only exceptions, since the globe is almost all covered with mountains".[72]

Colonial or American dream?

The similarity between the British and Quebec propaganda on colonisation illustrates the ideological proximity of Quebec to the rest of the Empire, despite the growing influence of French references among the French-Canadian elite.[73] Yet, because the rhetoric in use in the province was close to that of the American dream, some authors drew explicitly upon *that* dream in their search for immigrants to Quebec. This resulted in something of a paradox however, for at the same time as they were condemning

America as a destination, the French-Canadian elite drew admiring parallels with the achievements of the United States. "It is in the townships of the north where you find the true California for our young Canadians; each lot contains a treasure for them to discover".[74]

Other literary vehicles, such as novels, also tried to "Quebecise" American values, "grafting onto the old French ways the spirit of adventure associated with the Anglo-Saxons, the triumphant liberalism of the nineteenth century and the development of the New World". Such an argument was summarised by Robert Major in his work on Antoine Gérin-Lajoie's novel, *Jean Rivard*. Major challenged the views of those who saw only reactionary themes in the colonisation discourse, themes seen as aimed at the implantation of a feudal and theocratic society on the plateau, despite the rationality of the liberal and democratic ideologies of the time. Instead, Major suggested the subtle irony of a novel that was an early form of 'Americanness', filled with the same utopias that animated the American dream. We share this point of view, so abundantly demonstrated by Major. But rather than see *Jean Rivard* as just a simple transposing of the American dream, we can consider it a work of mediation, inspired by the colonial dream, but constructed around the themes of a dream with distinctly American qualities. Such a construction seems apparent for two reasons: first because the American dream held a widespread fascination for the popular classes and the elites, and second, because the traumas occasioned by the British Conquest and the failure of the Rebellions of 1837-1838 required such a mediation. Since the English were seen as the source of all the problems in Quebec, they could not be used as direct models, even if their achievements were admired. Thus the necessity for such a mediation, where British examples were essentially argued for *through* American images.

Yet this thesis is itself open to question, for the following reasons: first, there is the clear similarity between the Quebec and British discourse; second, there is the geopolitical situation of Quebec in Anglo-Saxon North America, which makes it different to either Canada or the United States; third, the fact that northern Quebec was seen as an internal colony of the St. Lawrence Valley, not only in respect to settlement, in the British sense of the term, but also as a colony of exploitation. It is there that the surplus population from the lowlands would go and from there that the supplies for the cities and the southern part of the province would come. Even Montreal would benefit from that area, and indeed this city could "be proud to have [as Quebec city] its Lake St. John".[75] However, unlike the colonies within the British Empire, the colonisation regions within Quebec never obtained responsible government!

Furthermore, one must also take into account the ideas of Gérin-Lajoie himself and those with whom he was in contact. They were acquired through his English courses at Nicolet and, even more so, through his father-in-law, the journalist Étienne Parent, a former participant in the 1837 Rebellion, who became a highly placed official in the government. Although Parent referred to the United States in his public conferences, he constantly proposed the English 'race' as a model to his listeners, this nation of shopkeepers who had created a large empire and succeeded against Napoléon. "The system that I propose for [the direction of society] in Quebec", he said, "is somewhat analogous to the results that have come from the wisdom of many generations in England. This merits reflection, because this English system provided order, stability, and internal liberty; external grandeur, strength and glory; and finally incredible industrial and commercial prosperity unknown elsewhere".[76] He implied that the best way to fight the English was to imitate them! The fact that the hero in Gérin-Lajoie's novel is American is of no importance. It is no more important that this author endorsed the same anti-British sentiment as other novelists of his generation. His basic reference is British, guided by British values. Is this not the essence of history, in terms of identity made of many fragments?[77]

Conclusion

Colonialism in the nineteenth century took different paths. One of its most powerful means of control was to project images and discourse on colonial societies in a way that would eventually lead local political and clerical leaders to adopt the same goals and the same rhetoric to promote their own projects of development. As the Comaroffs remind us, "the essence of colonization inheres less in political overrule than in seizing and transforming 'others'".[78] This was the case in Quebec, where a whole political and religious elite presented the northern plateau as the inner colony of the St. Lawrence Valley, a comparable relation with that between the British colonies and Britain.

Until recently, the discourse of the French-Canadian elite in the nineteenth century was seen only through an ethnocentric prism, as a local response to local difficulties, matched with a national and psychological dimension that disclosed the weakening character of marginality of the colonist in a constrained society. However, by comparing the content of their discourse with the propaganda material used in the British Empire to formulate the basis of the colonial dream and attract immigrants to the British colonies, one realises that they fed from the same ideas and rhetoric. As with their British counterparts, the French-Canadian elite condemned the great exodus to the United States and stressed the necessity of colonising their own possessions. They also shared the same vision about the role that the 'periphery' could play for the 'centre'. Nonetheless, although they admired British accomplishments, these elites could not directly use them as a model because of the exclusion they felt they suffered as a result of the British Conquest. Thus they formulated propositions that were based on the colonial dream, but which used images of the American dream as well as French references. As with the other British colonies, the Quebec dream was unable, over the longer-term, to successfully challenge the American competition, resulting in the somewhat fleeting success of their northern project of colonisation. This exploration of the historical geography of intellectual constructs within the nineteenth-century British Empire illustrates several important issues. First, that there was a British colonial dream. Secondly, that this dream was developed in part through an opposition to the American dream. And, thirdly, that the Quebec dream was a fusion of these two dreams and demonstrates the connections the elite of Quebec had with the outside world. This study reinforces, therefore, the need for new perspectives in the comparative study of intellectual connections between colonial elites and their impact on local populations.

Acknowledgements

This essay is the result of the research I performed at the Commonwealth Library at Cambridge, England, in February 1998. The research was made possible thanks to the scientific support of Dr Alan Baker and the financial aid of the British Academy and Emmanuel College. I wish to acknowledge their encouragement. I also express my gratitude to Mrs Teddy Barringer of the Commonwealth Library, whose valuable assistance helped me to find the necessary documents, Barry Rodrigue, a Ph.D. candidate at the CIEQ for his help in the translation of my paper, and Brian Osborne, who kindly accepted to read the final version of my presentation.

NOTES

1   J. H. St John de Crèvecoeur, *Letters from An American Farmer* (London 1783) 65-66.

2   Among these are N. Séguin, *Agriculture et Colonisation au Québec* (Montréal 1980); D. Owram, *Promise of Eden* (Toronto 1980); C. Berger, *Science, God and Nature in Victorian Canada* (Toronto 1983); S. Zeller, *Inventing Canada: Early Victorian Science and the Idea of a Transcontinental Nation* (Toronto 1987); R. G. Moyles and D. Owram, *Imperial Dreams and Colonial Realities: British Views of Canada, 1880-1914* (Toronto 1988); R. Major, *Jean Rivard ou l'Art de Réussir. Idéologies et Utopie dans l'Œuvre d'Antoine Gérin-Lajoie* (Sainte-Foy 1991); G. Bouchard, *Entre l'Ancien et le Nouveau Monde* (Ottawa 1996); and Y. Lamonde, Le lion, le coq et la fleur de lys: l'Angleterre et la France dans la culture politique du Québec (1760-1920), in G. Bouchard et Y. Lamonde, *La Nation dans tous ses États. Le Québec en Comparaison* (Montréal 1997) 161-182.

3   R. E. Cresswell, *Space for Everyman, Addressed to the Right Honourable Lord Ashley, MP*, (Lynn 1849).

4   W. B. Paton, *State-Aided Emigration* (London 1885).

5   S. F. Cronon, *Science in Culture* (New York 1978); B. Morris, *Social Change and Scientific Organisation* (Ithaca 1978); W. Cronon, *Changes in the Land* (New York 1983) and *Nature's Metropolis* (New York 1991); T. W. Heyck, *The Transformation of Intellectual Life in Victorian England*, (London 1982); D. Harvey, *The Condition of Postmodernity* (Cambridge and Oxford 1990); D. Livingstone, *The Geographical Tradition* (Cambridge and Oxford 1992).

6   Owram, *op. cit.*; Berger, *op. cit.*; Zeller, *op. cit.*; C. Gaffield and P. Gaffield, *Consuming Canada: Readings in Environmental History* (Toronto 1995).

7   Examples of these efforts can be found in the campaigns to promote emigration, selection of emigrants, subsidies for transportation and settlement, 'sufficient price' policy for land, Wakefield's cluster settlement policy, special programmes for women, boys and girls, etc. Most of these programmes, however, faded through the century. For debates surrounding these issues, see Mrs. Chisholm, *The A.B.C. of Colonisation, in a Series of Letters Addressed to the Gentlemen Forming the Committee of the Family Colonisation Loan Society* (London 1850); T. F. Elliot, *Progress of Emigration and Contrast of New Colonies With the Old* (1850); Paton, *op. cit.,*. For a presentation of British colonial policy and a definition of nineteenth-century capitalism and colonialism, see K. Bell and W. P. Morrell, *Select Documents on British Colonial Policy, 1830-1860* (Oxford 1928); P. Léon, *Histoire Économique et Sociale du Monde. La Domination du Capitalisme, 1840-1914* (Paris 1978); R. J. Johnston, D. Gregory and D. Smith, *The Dictionary of Human Geography* (Cambridge and Oxford 1994).

8   Robert Major provides a good account of the American dream: "America offered immense spaces, vast stretches of cheap land for establishing communities; it offered its isolation, without the corruption of old Europe; it offered the enormous agricultural and industrial possibilities of a young continent, as well as the promise of an exalted growth; finally it offered liberty, this is to say political liberty, liberty of conscience, freedom of association. America, this was the atmosphere of a new start, a new life, another life, the very definition of utopia ... And indeed, the 19th century was a grand century for utopia and America was its kingdom". R. Major, *op. cit.*, 217. See also R. C. Harris, The simplification of Europe overseas, *Annals of the Association of American Geographers* **67** (1977) 469-483; and R. Chodos and E. Hamovitch, *Quebec and the American Dream* (Toronto 1991).

9   The total volume of this print production was extremely high and extended throughout the century. In the early-nineteenth century, all the colonies were the object of attention. However, Canada became the principal focus from the 1830s until the start of the 1890s, after which attention was directed more towards the southern colonies and to Australia in particular. In spite of this change of focus in the later period, the brochures about Canada still make up half of the sample that I found in the Commonwealth Library collection. This sample is composed of around fifty documents, consisting of propaganda pamphlets and brochures on Canada, Australasia and South Africa, in addition to a dozen information leaflets and exposition catalogues, as well as photographic documents from the Fisher Collection. The two types of document discussed in this paper are the propaganda pamphlets and brochures. The pamphlets were largely addressed to public men in order to incite them to take an active part in the debates about immigration. The propaganda brochures and leaflets of information were addressed to potential immigrants through intermediaries (local politicians, Poor Offices, local societies of immigration and settlement, emigration agents, and others) in order to inform them of the advantages of the colonies and to provide them with useful information about means of travel and settlement. In contrast to the pamphlets, which served to debate political, economic and moral aspects of emigration in an emotive style, the brochures had a more clearly defined object, described in a straightforward style referring to ideas and debates then current in English and colonial societies, such as theories of ventilation, climate, hygiene, and security. As for their authors, they came mainly from societies of immigration, government agencies, local societies of colonisation, land companies, insurance companies, newspapers, benevolent societies, and others who were members, leaders or invited participants in these organisations.

10   C. R. N. Rubidge, *A Plain Statement of the Advantages Attending Emigration to Upper Canada* (London 1838) 18.

11   P. Boucher, *Histoire Véritable et Naturelle des Mœurs et Productions du Pays de la Nouvelle-France Vulgairement Dite le Canada* (Paris 1664) a.p.

12   W. G. Mack, *A Letter From the Eastern Townships of Lower Canada, Containing Hints to Intending Emigrants as to the Choice of Situation, etc., Accompanied with a Map* (Glasgow 1837) iv.

13   T. Rolph, *Canada v. Australia, Their Relative Merits Considered in an Answer to a Pamphlet by Thornton Leigh Hunt Esq. Entitled "Canada and Australia"* (London 1839).

14   C. F. Grece, *Facts and Observations Respecting Canada and the United States of America Apporting Comparative Views of the Inducements to Immigration Presented in Those Countries. To Which is Added An Appendix of Practical Instructions to Emigrant Settlers in the British Colonies* (Londres 1819) 5.

15   G. Potter, *The Australian Emigrant: Being a Valuable Descriptive Guide to Those About to Emigrate to New South Wales, Queensland, Tasmania, South Australia, Western Australia, Victoria. Also a Graphic Description of the Best Line of Steamers by Which to Reach the Various Colonies* (London 1883) 4.

16   Grece, *op. cit.*, xiii.

17   Rawson & de Chair, *The Advantages of the Eastern Townships for Emigrants of All Classes* (Sherbrooke 1864) 10.

18   Rubidge, *op. cit.*; Canadian News, *The Land of Hope for the Settlers and Artisan, the Small Capitalist, the Honest and Persevering, With a Description of the Climate, Free Grants of Land, Wages, and its General Advantage as a Field for Emigration, by the Editor of the Canadian News* (London 1857).

19   F. Pictet, *Land Settlement in New South Wales, Victoria, New Zeland, Tasmania* (London 1892).

20   Canada, *Information for Intending Emigrant* (Ottawa 1874) 10-11.

21   Grece, *op. cit.*, 9-11.

22   Canada, *op. cit.*, 11.

23   Potter, *op. cit.*, 3.

24   F. Darrell, *Should I Succeed in South Africa?, by a Successful Colonist* (London 1900) 100.

25   Rubidge, *op. cit.*, 33, 81.

26   *Canadian News, op. cit.*, 6.

27   F. Duncan, *Canada in 1871, or Our Empire to the West* (London 1872) 12.

28   *Ibid.*, 29.

29   Elliot, *op. cit.*, 9-10.

30   Darrell, *op. cit.*, 8.

31   Rubidge, *op. cit.*, 32.

32   R. Alling, in *Letters from Settlers in Upper Canada* (London 1833) 9.

33   Mack, *op. cit.*, 13.

34   Rubidge, *op. cit.*, 36-37.

35   *Canadian News , op. cit.*, 3, 6.

36   Potter, *op. cit.*, 14.

37   Darrell, *op. cit.*, 111.

38 W. F. Lynn, *Canada, Pamphlet for Working Men, on Emigration, Labour, Wages, and Free Grants of Lands* (London 1869).

39 Rubidge, *op. cit.*, 30.

40 Canadian News, *op. cit.*, 6.

41 K. Bell and W. P. Morrell, *op. cit.*

42 Rubidge, *op. cit.*, 4.

43 Darrell, *op. cit.*, 84, 113.

44 Grece, *op. cit.*, 9.

45 Rawson & de Chair, *op. cit.*, 4.

46 Paton, *op. cit.*, 4, 10.

47 H. E. Egerton and A. P. Newton, *A Short History of British Colonial Policy, 1606-1909* (London 1945) 10.

48 Sir John Seeley, 1883; cited in Egerton and Newton, *op. cit.*, 11.

49 F. Parsons, Australasian methods of dealing with immigration, *Annals of American Academy of Political and Social Sciences* **XXIV** (1904) 209-220.

50 Mack, *op. cit.*, 26.

51 Paton, *op. cit.*, 12-13.

52 *Ibid.*, 29, 34.

53 G. Paquet, L'émigration des Canadiens français vers la Nouvelle-Angleterre, 1870-1910 : prises de vue quantitatives, *Recherches Sociographiques* **V** (1964) 319-370; R. Vicero, *Immigration of French Canadians to New England, 1840-1900: A Geographical Analysis* (unpublished Ph.D. thesis, University of Wisconsin 1968); Y. Lavoie, *L'Émigration des Canadiens aux États-Unis avant 1930. Mesure du Phénomène* (Montréal 1972); Y. Roby, *Les Franco-Américains de la Nouvelle-Angleterre, 1776-1930* (Sillery 1990); B. Rodrigue, The Canada road frontier: from mythical reportage to analytical reconstruction, in S. Courville and B. Osborne (Eds), *Histoire Mythique et Paysage Symbolique / Mythical History and Symbolic Landscape: People in Time and Place* (Québec 1997) 61-62.

54 C. Morrissonneau, *La Terre Promise: le Mythe du Nord Québécois* (Montréal 1978); G. Dusseault, *Le Curé Labelle. Messianisme, Utopie et Colonisation au Québec, 1850-1900* (Montréal 1983); P. A. Linteau, R. Durocher, and J.-C. Robert, *Histoire du Québec Contemporain* (Montréal 1989); G. Sénécal, Les idéologies territoriales au Canada français, entre le continentalisme et l'idée du Québec, *Revue d'Études Canadiennes* **32** (1992).

55 Quebec, *The Province of Quebec and European Emigration* (Québec 1870) 1-2.

56 *Ibid.*, 1.

57 *Ibid.*, 2-3.

58 *Ibid.*, 3, 105.

59 *Ibid.*, 4.

60 Sociétés de colonisation des diocèses de Montréal et d'Ottawa, *Au Nord* (Saint-Jérôme 1883); Million Farms Campaign Association, *A Great National Purpose for Australia and How to Achieve it. A Million Farmers on a Million Farms* (Sidney 1922).

61 A. Labelle, *Pamphlet sur la Colonisation dans la Vallée d'Ottawa au Nord de Montréal, et Règlements et Avantages de la Société de Colonisation du Diocèse de Montréal* (Montréal 1880) 21.

62   Sociétés de colonisation des diocèses de Montréal et d'Ottawa, *op. cit.*, 12.

63   A. Labelle, *op. cit.*, 2.

64   Sociétés de colonisation des diocèses de Montréal et d'Ottawa, *op. cit.*, 5.

65   *Ibid.*, 6.

66   A. Labelle, *op. cit.*, 1.

67   *Ibid.*, 3-4, 9, 20.

68   *Ibid.*, 1, 20.

69   Sociétés de colonisation des diocèses de Montréal et d'Ottawa, *op. cit.*, 7-8.

70   A. Labelle, *op. cit.*, 18-19.

71   Sociétés de colonisation des diocèses de Montréal et d'Ottawa, *op. cit.*, 21.

72   A. Labelle, *op. cit.*, 21.

73   Lamonde, *op. cit.*, 159.

74   Sociétés de colonisation des diocèses de Montréal et d'Ottawa, *op. cit.*, 10.

75   A. Labelle, *op. cit.*, 2, 8.

76   Parent, cited in Major (1991) 47.

77   O'Hanlon, cited in D. Gregory, *Geographical Imaginations* (Cambridge and Oxford 1994) 188.

78   J. Cormaroff, and J. Cormaroff, *Of Revelation and Revolution: Christianity, Colonialism and Consciousness in South Africa*. Vol. 1 (Chicago 1991) 15.

Chapter Thirteen

WARSCAPES, LANDSCAPES, INSCAPES

France, War, and Canadian National Identity

BRIAN S. OSBORNE

It was always my ambition to make a collection of paintings of Canadian scenes and as fate would have it some of the landscapes with which the history of Canada will be bound up for generations are here in France.[1]

The Canadian artist, Mary Riter Hamilton, penned these provocative words in 1922 at a time of a vibrant Canadian nationalism. What did she mean by them? What were the fates that bound the landscapes of France with Canada? How did this come to be?[2]

That images of place are central to the project of nation-building has not gone unnoticed.[3] As Simon Schama put it, "national identity, to take just the most obvious example, would lose much of its ferocious enchantment without the mystique of a particular landscape tradition: its topography mapped, elaborated, and enriched as a homeland".[4] But the mental construction of a symbolic homeland is a complex business. The identification of people with place is seldom the simple product of long-standing association of a particular people with a particular setting. For Alan Baker, "People may ... be taken as a metaphor for place: a sketch of a landscape may capture or caricature its essence but it cannot be expected to reveal very much about its whole, complex, character".[5] But even if the complexity of people-in-place cannot be rendered solely by visual representation alone, collective memories, identities, and social cohesion are often grounded in 'inscapes'. That is, what Pierre Dansereau referred to as "the filtering inward from nature to man [sic], upward from the subconscious to the conscious, and from the perception to design and implementation".[6] Indeed, these shared mental constructions of place and time are then further constructed through the imagery of such interventions as anthems, flags, curricula, and state institutions. They demonstrate that nations are always narrations and the national chronicle is played out in storied locales that have been loaded with historically produced meanings.[7]

Yet such symbolically loaded landscapes need not always be associated with a 'homeland' that is spatially coterminous with the nation state. Agincourt, Waterloo, the Somme, Normandy all have a resonance for the complex emotional calculus of modern British identity. Consider the continued power of Gallipoli for nurturing Australian nation building and Vimy Ridge for Canada. It is not insignificant that these examples refer to bloodied places. According to Charles Tilly, nations make war, wars make nations.[8] Large-scale conflicts require that nation states mobilise internal social, economic, and political power.[9] But the power of war as an agent of nation-building transcends the logistics of the implementation of state-power. It is as if societies are hard-wired to always transform the grim realities of human sacrifice and suffering into collective psychic energy and a confirmation of putative national values. This is what Raphael Samuel means when he speaks of the "romanticization of war" as a "cultural universal" which "enters into the very marrow of the national idea."[10]

Paradoxically for a nation-state that prides itself on being a 'peaceable kingdom', this has certainly been true for Canada.[11] Despite the current 'blue-beret' fixation, a strong blood-red thread runs through the chronicle of Canadian national development. The act of establishing, controlling, and defending national territory has played a central role in the definition of Canadian identity. Thus, the American War of Independence, the 1812-14 War, and the Fenian raids of 1866 fortified the British connection and consolidated anti-Americanism in the Canadian psyche. The young state's reaction to the Riel rebellions of 1869-70 and 1885 served as a signal demonstration of Canada's own sense of a manifest destiny to defend the integrity of its Dominion. And Canadian participation in such imperial excursions as the Sudan Campaign of 1884-5 and the South African War did much to consolidate ideas of a Canadian state, albeit one tied to a British imperial global role.[12]

Emerging out of this progression of national militarist experience, the 'Great War' of 1914-1918 has played a particularly powerful role in the national imagination of self.[13] A young Canada rallied to the imperial cause, 619,636 Canadians participating in a conflict in which some 60,000 of them died. As elsewhere throughout the western world, Canada's reaction to the Great War was as ambivalent as it was profound. This was captured in the reflexive letters, poems, books, plays, and films that served as a post-war antidote to the manipulative jingoism of the war years.[14] The many artistic representations of the place of war were particularly evocative of the lived experience. Further, in Canada, these warscapes indirectly influenced the production of a category of iconic national landscapes that came to be such an important part of the national inscape. This is what underpins Mary Riter Hamilton's formulation that French landscapes played a role in the construction of Canadian history and national identity.

Memorializing the Great War in Canada

Throughout the nineteenth century, war-art shifted from panoramic views of the landscape of battle to the portraiture of group or individual heroism. Images of heroic deaths (Sir Philip Sydney, General Wolfe, or Horatio Nelson), glorious victories (Trafalgar and Waterloo) and even glorious defeats (Isandawalla) were intended to be both entertainments for the general public and also exemplars of what was required of a nation and its empire. Lady Butler's testosteronic heroes dominate our images of war as much as they do her canvases. The popular didactic role surged ahead with late-nineteenth century developments in lithography, mechanized printing, and the emergence of the genre of the illustrated magazine.[15]

As the Great War progressed, it soon became clear that the pictorial style of "Victorian high battle art," replete with "archaic and stale allegorical imagery" of its former excesses, was not suited to the new realities of combat.[16] As B. H. Liddell Hart observed first-hand on the first day of that apotheosis of the Great War, the Somme, the reality of modern mass war was not conducive to artistic rhetoric:

> During this reconnaissance I had a 'grandstand' view of a renewed attack that was launched by the 34th Division on the La Boiselle sector. It was strangely different from any picture sketched by war artists in the illustrated press. Instead of the dramatic charge of cheering troops which they depicted, one saw thin chains of khaki-clad dots plodding slowly forward, and becoming thinner under a hail of fire until they looked merely a few specks on the landscape.[17]

And what a landscape it was. The spatial and temporal scale of the strategy and tactics of that war did not lend themselves to the constraints of artistic synthesis and aesthetic norms. The realities of long periods of constant squalor syncopated by periodic outbursts of horrific slaughter could not be captured on imaginative canvas. The dystopian world of trenches and battle-torn terrain in which combatants lived and fought for so long challenged the standard pictorial conventions of both the heroic and the romantic. Warscapes defied the transformations of the picturesque and even the sublime.[18] The result was an impressionistic engagement with a very unheroic place that prompted some war artists to experiment with the innovative practices of impressionistic abstraction. Again, Wyndham Lewis commented on the opportune – if macabre – match between artistic styles and subject that was the outcome of war-art:

> War, and especially those miles of hideous desert known as 'the Line' in Flanders and France, presented me with a subject matter so consonant with the austerity of that 'abstract' vision I had developed, that it was an easy transition.[19]

The overall effect was what has been called the "Death of Landscape" in that the "Modernist method that before the war had seemed violent and distorting was seen to be realistic on the western front. Modernism had not changed, but reality had".[20] That is, the base realities of the Great War could not be accommodated by the usual technical, visual, and interpretative devices for recording the events and human experience of nations at war.[21] What did emerge was to prove to be a challenge for the national project of locating that war in the collective national memory.

Canada's reaction to the Great War is reflected in a whole range of individual, community, and governmental responses. As well as personal letters and journals, art, literature, and film, the form, scale, and iconography that memorialized the conflict are evocative of the public response.[22] From simple columns or statues throughout some 4,000 communities in Canada to the national monument at Vimy Ridge, war is rendered as an important part of the patriotic landscape.[23] In particular, Vimy has come to occupy a sacred place in Canada's mythic metanarrative of national development, symbolizing youthful sacrifice, national mourning, and the role of the Great War in nation building.[24]

However, other commemorative projects did not rely upon obelisks, crosses, and realistic renderings of valiant, albeit often suffering, heroic figures. Two in particular – the Canadian War Memorials Fund and the Gold Stripe Project – focused less on the personnel affected by the conflict than on the place and experience of conflict: that is, the landscapes of war. They were to prove to be important and pervasive agencies influencing the way in which Canada came to see itself.

The Canadian War Memorials Fund

Canada's entry into the Great War was prompt and massive.[25] The need to record the young nation's first major involvement in a major conflict was thought to be a pressing one. To this end, early in 1916, Sir Max Aitken (later Lord Beaverbrook) established the Canadian War Records Office in London in order to document and proselytize Canada's war-effort.[26] Visual representation of this role was considered vital to the nationalistic project. Accordingly, a war photographer, Captain H. E. Knobel, was appointed in May 1916, and a war cinematographer, Lieut. F. O. Boville, in July 1916. However, such were the contingencies of modern trench war and the limitations of photographic equipment that these pioneer war photographers resorted to technological devices (collages) and dramatic simulations (staged pieces) to communicate their message.[27]

A combination of dissatisfaction with faked or embellished action photographs, together with an appreciation of the interpretive and representational power of imaginative art, resulted in the establishment of the Canadian War Memorials Fund on 7 November 1916. Its purpose was to provide "suitable Memorials in the form of Tablets, Oil-Paintings etc., to the Canadian Heroes and Heroines in the War".[28] This programme was later expanded to cover such work on the home front as portraits, military camps, and factories and, eventually, more than half of the war-artists were employed in this area. Some were, however, directed to the front-line where they were to record the sacrifices and heroism of a glorious combat. The CWMF eventually produced over 900 works of art recording Canada's contribution to the Great War. Initial plans called for the construction of a 'Pantheon' to house the collection and to serve as a national monument.[29]

Initially staffed by British painters, there were some 'Canadians' among the 116 painters and sculptors who had represented the Western Front artistically.[30] In the early years of the war, traditional heroic conventions continued to prevail. Indeed, the very first piece commissioned by the CWMF was a 12 feet by 19 feet canvas "full of the worst excesses of Victorian high battle art," replete with heroic leader, sturdy defenders, and glorious dead and dying (see Figure 1).[31] But as the conflict became fixed in place and routine, the artists turned away from an externalized gaze of the heroic and the fabrication of myth. Instead, they rendered their own first-hand psychological and ideological reactions to the horror and drudgery of front-line combat. A.Y. Jackson commented on the essential challenge:

What to paint was a problem for the war artist. There was nothing to serve as a guide. War had gone underground, and there was little to see. The old heroics, the death and glory stuff were gone for ever; there was no more 'Thin Red Line' or 'Scotland For Ever". I had no interest in painting the horrors of war and I wasted a lot of canvas. The impressionistic technique I had adopted in painting was now ineffective, for visual impressions were not enough.[32]

FIGURE 1
Richard Jack [1918], *The Second Battle of Ypres, 22 April to 25 May 1915.*

Source: Canadian War Museum Collection.

David Milne was the most prolific of the CWMF artists, painting sixty-eight works. He was also, perhaps, the most eloquent in his written descriptions of the detritus of war:

> *The earth has been torn up and torn up and torn up again and from it at every step rifles and bayonets and twisted iron posts and wire projected. Shell hole merged with or overlapped shell hole, and everywhere was a litter of shell fragments, cartridges, shell cases and dud shells big and little, web equipment, helmets, German and British and even in some places French, water bottles of three nations, boots and uniforms, the boots often with socks and feet in them. Some shell holes even on top of the ridge had water in them and, over all, the sweet sickish, but not offensive, smell of death.*[33]

Fred Varley's reactions were equally shocking, his reportage of the devastation wreaked upon humanity and places, evoking an almost visual reconstruction:

> *You in Canada ... cannot realize at all what war is like. You must see it and live it. You must see the barren deserts war has made of once fertile country ... see the*

turned up graves, see the dead on the field, freakishly mutilated – Headless,
legless, stomachless, a perfect body and a passive face and a broken empty skull
– see your own countrymen, unidentified, thrown into a cart, their coats over
them, boys digging a grave in a land of yellow slimey mud and green pools of
water under a weeping sky. You must have heard the screeching shells and have
the shrapnel fall around you, whistling by you – Seen the results of it, seen scores
of horses, bits of horses laying around, in the open – in the street and soldiers
marching by these scenes as if they never knew of their presence – until you've
lived this little woman – you cannot know.[34]

These literary testaments of some of the CWMF artists' personal and professional engagement with the Great War demonstrate how they found themselves deflected from their task of generating 'suitable memorials' to 'Canadian Heroes and Heroines'. Rather, they struggled to comprehend the social and psychic meaning of the suffering and destruction as they attempted to communicate visually the essence of the place of war.

The Gold Stripe Project and Mary Riter Hamilton

Working with similar objectives, but outside the realm of the CWMF, Mary Riter Hamilton also made a significant contribution in memorializing the material contexts and consequences of the Great War. Indeed, in quantitative terms, her total oeuvre of over 300 battlefield landscapes exceeds that of any of the CWMF artists. Certainly, in qualitative terms, they are equally as evocative of the distinctive place produced by war. Perhaps more importantly, she presents a different perspective: a focus on the impact of the war on the former homes and communities that had been obliterated.[35]

Six months after the Armistice of 1918, Hamilton was assigned a 'special mission' by The War Amputations Club of British Columbia. She was to provide paintings of the battlefields of the Great War for publication in a veterans' magazine, *The Gold Stripe*.[36] Hamilton left in March 1919 and was in Arras by June, and immediately commenced her commission "to reproduce the battlefields in paint". She wanted to record the landscape before the process of reconstruction removed all "traces of war". She deliberately viewed the country around Vimy "under hard conditions," arguing that "I want to get the spirit of it ... I feel that is it fortunate that I arrive before it is too late to get a real impression".[37]

During her four years in France and Belgium (1919-22), Hamilton worked mostly in oils, but also charcoal, chalk, pastel, and pencil, on plywood, paper, canvas, and cardboard. Also, she finished her battlefield works on-site which accounts for the

FIGURE 2
F.H. Varley [1918], *Some Day the People Wulle Return.*

Source: Canadian War Museum Collection.

spontaneity which is thought to be lacking from that of other war artists. There was another difference. She too recorded the same desolate landscape and the iconography of war: "mine-craters, cemeteries, shell blasted trees, desolate roads going off into a distance of smoke and emptiness, destroyed tanks and pill boxes, and ruined buildings".[38] See Figure 2. The extent of the devastation of the conflict is evoked by the sombre colours and jagged edges of the aftermath of war:

> *In her depictions of cemeteries the dead have been buried and the flowers are beginning to grow. The only figures in her pictures are soldiers waiting to return home, women making homes in disused army huts and workers clearing the battlefields. With one exception, there are no images of those who died.*[39]

This is an important dimension of Hamilton's work. As she painted during the immediate aftermath of the conflict, she was also able to record the beginnings of the

FIGURE 3
Mary Riter Hamilton [n.d], *The Sadness of the Somme*.

Source: National Archives of Canada.

post-war reconstruction.[40] Thus, the pathetic realism of her *Sadness of the Somme* (Figure 3) and *Sanctuary Wood* has to be balanced against the first steps in the return to rural and urban recovery recorded in the *First Celebration at Zillebeke after the War* (Figure 4), *The First Boat to Arrive at Arras after the Armistice*, and *The New Home*.

Like the CWMF, from the outset, assessments of Hamilton's battle field project were couched in patriotic terms, referring to "her abiding love of her native land, of her admiration for the splendid men who went under arms across the sea to preserve the ideals of Empire". Like those of the CWMF, her paintings were also intended to be "fitting additions to the archives founded to preserve the history of the Dominions' part in the Great War"[41] and "an achievement of the greatest historical, as well as pictorial, importance".[42] But what dominates her pictorial record is a testimony of futile destruction and suffering – civilian as well as military.

FIGURE 4
Mary Riter Hamilton [1920],
First Celebration at Zillebeke after the War.

Source: National Archives of Canada.

Reaction

By the early 1920s, therefore, the CWMF and Mary Riter Hamilton's *Gold Stripe* project had presented Canada with over 1200 works of art intended to remember, memorialize, and commemorate Canada's role in the Great War. However, the original glorious and patriotic motives were dissonant with a major shift in the ideological climate of post-war Canada. The paintings proved to be an unwelcome reminder of an experience, if not to be forgotten, at least not to be indulged in. The words of one contemporary critic demonstrate how, by the end of the war, the CWMF project had taken on a new function:

> *The war memorials are not only national records, they are family records for*
> *most of us and as such they will have a sure interest handed down from generation*
> *to generation. We can feel certain of the pride of coming Canadians in these*

pictures. We may hope that they will read the moral in them truly, and so order the national affairs of their world that their youth may not need to be sacrificed to that monster of war which we allow to grow up on the earth.[43]

On 4 January 1919, the CWMF exhibited 400 paintings and sculptures representing the Canadian Expeditionary Force in the galleries of London's Royal Academy of Art at Burlington House. Later that year, the collection travelled to Canada where it was exhibited at the Canadian National Exhibition in Toronto, and the Art Association of Montreal.[44]

Similarly, Hamilton received considerable initial public acclaim. In 1920, some of her works were published in *The Gold Stripe*, others being exhibited in Vancouver and Victoria under auspices of the Imperial Order of the Daughters of Empire (IODE) and the Arts Council of British Columbia. In 1922, her battlefield paintings were displayed in the Foyer of the Paris Opera in conjunction with the showing of a proposed inter-allied monument, the 'Pantheon of the Somme'. They were also exhibited at the Société Nationale des Beaux-Arts, the Société des Artistes, and the Somme Memorial Exhibition held in Amiens. In 1923, over a hundred of her battlefield paintings were exhibited at the Simonson Galleries, Surrey House, London, in aid of a planned Somme Battlefield Memorial. In 1925, Hamilton returned to Canada for an exhibition in Winnipeg and several other receptions and displays of her work followed.[45]

Initially, the Canadian public evinced a considerable interest in war art, some 120,000 attending the 1919 exhibition of the CWMF work.[46] But after this enthusiastic reception, Canada's memorial warscapes soon disappeared from public view. Apart from a few jingoistic scenes and propaganda-motivated items, they had generally rendered a too didactic impression of the horrors and lessons of war.[47] Consider the reaction to F. H. Varley's, 'The Sunken Road – August 1918' which captured the 'ugly truth' of the monstrous landscape of war:

His cadaver picture, 'The Sunken Road', is an epic of the necrosis: men tangled and twisted like shattered trees, trunks and heads awry – a putrefying heap of mortality with vapours flitting over the dug-outs and the segment of an insolent, chuckling rain-bow at one corner. Any bard who would rise and sing 'They Shall Not Die' or to cite 'In Flanders' Fields' in front of that picture would be a master of satire.[48]

The following year saw a similar far from patriotic reaction to A.Y. Jackson's, 'A Copse, Evening' (1918):

Do the mothers and their wives think it is hard to know their men are dead? Let them look at this picture ... and know that it is lucky for them, but unfortunate for the living world, they do not know how and with what thoughts their men lived for some time before they escaped from a Copse, Evening. It was not death they dreaded. Sometimes that was welcomed. It was the mutilation of the mind.[49]

Such reactions to the verities of war, and especially the emotive renderings by artists, were part of a growing resistance to institionalised devices intended to remember it, whether as victory, patriotism, or sacrifice. For example, in the mid-1920s, the IODE's plan to circulate an exhibition of war art to schools across Canada to remind them of the "terrible wastage of war" had to be dropped because of public opposition. In April 1921, the CWMF collection was transferred to the Canadian government for storage. But Beaverbrooks's grand scheme of a Memorial Building-cum-Pantheon to house the collection never materialised.[50]

As for Mary Riter Hamilton, ever mindful of her original purpose, she gave some of her sketches and paintings to individual Vancouver war veterans. However, she also contacted the Dominion Archivist, A. G. Doughty, who had expressed interest in giving her work a prominent place in his national collection. Accordingly, in 1926, she presented 227 pieces to the Archives and in a letter to Doughty, her patriotic mission was again to the fore:

It is a great honour and privilege to know that the work amid the inexpressible desolation of No Man's Land has been considered worthy of a place among the Memorials of our Canadian men, the survivors and the fallen.[51]

Nevertheless, as with the CWMF project, Hamilton's work was also directed to archival storage rather than public galleries.

As society distanced itself from war time values, the works of the CWMF and Mary Riter Hamilton were confined to the vaults of the archives in a deliberate exercise of imposed amnesia. They no longer fitted the preferred collective memory of the Great War and the values of the new Canada.

From warscapes to landscapes and inscapes

But if the original mission of the CWMF and *The Gold Stripe* projects failed in terms of providing a collection of national memories, ironically, the national imagination benefited indirectly. At least this was true of the work of the CWMF artists. Mary Riter Hamilton never attained subsequent national acclaim as an artist, nor did her war works re-emerge into public view. Perhaps they were too preoccupied with the condition of the land and the people of France than with the heroism and sufferings of Canadians. But this was not the case with the CWMF artists. Several of them such as Maurice Cullen, A. Y. Jackson, David Milne, and F. H. Varley were to become influential Canadian artists. More particularly, Jackson and Varley were founder members of that group of impressionistic landscape artists and nationalist provocateurs, the 'Group of Seven'.[52]

While the origins of this Group must be sought in their pre-Great War experiences, the influence of the war on Jackson and Varley was profound, as was the influence of their work on those who saw it. As Maria Tippett has argued convincingly:

Nothing came to symbolize the war for the artist and the combatant as much as the land upon which it was fought ... No artist who visited the front could resist painting the landscape ... Pock marked with gaping water-filled craters, strewn with bones, metal, and all the refuse of modern warfare, the topography of the front line offered few familiar associations ... The machine had superseded God's handiwork; his landscape was being reshaped by man's instruments.[53]

Certainly, the apparent visual allusion to 'Hunswept' warscapes in the Group's artistic engagement with that other desolate landscape, the Canadian north was evident in the public reaction to F. T. Johnston's 'Fire-Swept Algoma, 1920' (Figure 5):

Two of [Johnston's] biggest, 'Fire-Swept' and 'Beaver Haunts' are tremendous hoardings of which the great Fire-Ranger of the eternal forest advertises Solitude for the Multitude. The 'Fire-Swept' is a gaunt and grim plateau of 'brule' like a Hunswept village in the foreground, a colossal trilogy of forested rock mounting a rough hill to a ribbon of sky.[54]

The similarity of composition, form, colour, and mood of French warscapes and the Canadian north demonstrated by A.Y. Jackson's 'A Copse, Evening' (1918) and his 'First Snow, Algoma' (1920) is startling (Figures 6 and 7). Broken trees, heaving land forms, and an air of desolation are common to both. It is hard to resist the causative connection between the artists' war time experience of the shell blasted landscapes and the new gaze they directed to the Canadian Shield and northern forests. To be sure, the subject of the 'north' had attracted Canadian artists before the Great War but their later representations reveal a fresh focus. For Tippett:

the stark, bleak, muddy-coloured landscape of the front, as experienced by those who had been there or as seen through the works of those artists who had been to

FIGURE 5

F. H. Johnston [1920], *Fire-swept Algoma.*

Source: National Gallery of Canada.

the front, had given ... a new appreciation for the irregular and barren wilderness
of northern Ontario ... the 'spirit' of painting in Canada, was thus associated
with a sense that this could best be done by employing methods and techniques
they and their colleagues had either seen used or themselves employed to paint
the war-torn landscape of the Old World.[55]

Certainly, on his return from France, A.Y. Jackson expressed a disinterest in painting
"serene" scenes and sought out "storms ... and things that had been smashed up".[56]

But surely, the Group of Seven must have been prompted by something more
than mere technique and mimesis? Is it not unreasonable to also see psychological,
aesthetic, and ideological motives in the new focus of their artistic gaze? Could it
have also reflected a turn to the wilderness as a rejection of civilization and its
discontents? Was it a broader based celebration of that which was native and pristine
and Canadian? Certainly, the discourses of the day suggest other possible influences

FIGURE 6
A. Y. Jackson [1918], *A Copse, Evening.*

Source: Canadian War Museum Collection.

in the development of a nativist focus.[57] Finally, there is no doubt that for many Canadian intellectuals of the day, their personal experience of the Great War caused them to rethink their personal identities and their definition of nationhood.

This point has been made forcefully in the biography of one significant Canadian, Brooke Claxton:

> *Claxton's nationalism was born of war. When the First World War began, he and other Canadians had responded as colonials; for him, as for many of the others, going to war had been a matter of duty to the empire; it was expected of a man of his class and station. At the front with his battery mates, the conflict became his war. Under fire, they were together as if a family. Under fire, they were not colonials; they lived, fought, existed for each other, not for some abstract concept such as duty or empire. For one thing, they were all Canadians.[58]*

FIGURE 7
A. Y. Jackson [1918], *First Snow Algoma*.

Source: MacMichael Canadian Art Collection.

Similarly, H. A. Innis' war experience had much to do with his nationalist introspection that was to establish him as one of Canada's leading historians.[59] It was while convalescing from his war-wounds that he wrote his Master's thesis, 'The Returned Soldier'. In it, he reflected on a national mission for national development:

> *Work, work of brain and of brawn, co-operation, organization and determination*
> *to heal the sores ... and to start again along the lines of sound national progress,*
> *is the hope of the Canadian people ... that she may take her place among the*
> *nations of the world for the privilege of which her best blood has been shed.*[60]

Men like Claxton and Innis were transformed by what they considered to be both a personal and national sacrifice. In the early 1920s, it prompted many of them to participate in what came to be known as 'the Canadian Movement', a broad array of similarly minded institutions such as the Association of Canadian Clubs, the Canadian

League, the Canadian Institute of International Affairs, and the League of Nations Society.[61]

Thus, the Great War should be seen as a formative period for many who had served in it. The standard argument is that, "Many of the men who had left Canada as proud British subjects returned with a sense of Canadian identity and a desire to develop a Canadian nation".[62] Certainly, this mission was to the fore when 'The Group of Seven' held their first exhibition at the Art Gallery of Ontario in Toronto on 7-17 May, 1920, within two years of the war's end. None could doubt their patriotic motives.[63] Their "Foreword" to their exhibition asserted their "like vision concerning Art in Canada" in several propositions: "an Art must grow and flower in the land before the country will be a real home for its people"; they encouraged artists native to Canada, "whose work is more distinctive, original and vital, and of greater value to the country"; and they supported "any form of Art expression that sincerely interprets the spirit of a nation's growth". Throughout the post-Great War period in Canada, the rhetoric and allusions of the Group and their supporters continued with the same theme.[64]

For J. E. H. MacDonald, "Only by fostering our own Canadian art shall we develop ourselves as a people".[65] For Arthur Lismer, the new idiom of landscape was "more in harmony with the energy and quality of our national character".[66] And for Lawren Harris, "It is only through the deep and vital experience of its total environment that a people identifies with its land and gradually a deep and satisfying awareness develops ... To us there was also the strange brooding sense of another nature fostering a new race and a new age".[67]

Unabashedly nativist, coloured by shades of nativism and environmentalism, these views nevertheless resonated with many contemporary Canadians in the years following the Great War.[68] Their work was but part of a surge in political, artistic, and literary nationalism that has been associated with a network of intellectuals preoccupied with making Canada a distinct and better place to live. It is in this political context that the emergence and public acceptance of the Group of Seven's particular image of Canada is best understood.

Abandoning individual isolation and becoming a 'group' may not have helped the artists to paint Canada better, but it did enable them to speak out more powerfully in the battles of the Canadian art world, and to transmit their nationalist vision to a wider audience.[69]

Conclusion

The cultivation of celebrated national landscapes has not been confined to Canada. Writing about landscape imagery and national identity, Stephen Daniels has argued:

National identities are co-ordinated, often largely defined, by 'legends and landscapes', by stories of golden ages, enduring traditions, heroic deeds and dramatic destinies located in ancient or promised home-lands with hallowed sites and scenery. The symbolic activation of time and space ... gives shape to the 'imagined community' of the nation. Landscapes, whether focusing on single monuments or framing stretches of scenery, provide visible shape; they picture the nation.[70]

Certainly, the project of imagining Canada has long been an important exercise. The oeuvres of Cornelius Kreighoff, Francis Hopkins, Lucius O'Brien, C. W. Jefferys, Maurice Cullen, and others have attempted to capture the essentials of a distinctively 'native' place and people. Taken together, they contributed much to the nurturing of a national geography, a national history, and a national culture.

Nevertheless, the work of the Group of Seven added a particular focus to a filtered gaze of the North, Nature, and 'wild places' that subsequently became transformed into a celebration of national identity. Why? As suggested above, post-Great War Canada was seething with cultural and political tensions. Their view of a distinctively Canadian geography offered a homeland that was common to all regions' experience, evoked memories of an encounter with a settlement history that had been common to many, and turned its back on trans-Atlantic imperialism and the continentalism across the 49th parallel. For some, however, it was a flawed representation: Quebecers favoured a more bucolic memory-place of 'les colons'; ruralites everywhere emphasized their pride and accomplishments in the 'middle landscapes' rather than in their former enemy, the wilderness; and urbanites, industrialists, and economic boosters favoured views of a vibrant, dynamic, modernizing nation-state. However, challenging the Group of Seven can be a risky business. One critic recently had the temerity to pose the question, "The Group of Seven – had enough yet?" He went on:

When it comes to Canadian icons, the Group of Seven painters are right up there with hockey and maple syrup. But they weren't very innovative and hardly anyone outside Canada knows them.[71]

The reaction was as immediate as it was predictable. Three correspondents rallied to the Group's defence in a collection of letters entitled, "Hands off the Group of Seven".[72] As one writer put it:

They were never part of the mainstream history of art. They were the eyes of a nation who [sic] wanted to be unique, who wanted to be Canadians. To us they are heroes, Canadian heroes. I have had enough of our damning our heroes, be they artists or war veterans.[72]

Of course, some of the Group were both – artists and war veterans. Ironically, while this debate on the appropriateness of the Group of Seven's work for a cosmopolitan and globalized Canada continues, the CWMF collection is receiving new attention. Funds have been allocated for the erection of Beaverbrook's Pantheon and plans drawn up for a permanent collection of the war-art that records Canada's martial role.[73] Further, many Canadians – and more importantly, many outsiders – continue to identify with an image of Canada rendered by the Group of Seven. And if this is the case, at least part of the explanation for their successful and long-standing evocation of a sense of this place must be found elsewhere: in their reflections on national identity that emerged from their engagement with the war scapes of France in the Great War.

NOTES

1   Mary Riter Hamilton, quoted in F. G. Falla, *Dauntless Canadian Woman Tells of Grim Experiences While Painting the Nightmare Land of the Somme* (New York 1922) n.p.

2   These questions also serve my purpose for this tribute to Alan Baker. Given his long-standing interests in both France and Canada, they allow me to link my own interest in the symbolic representation of Canada with Alan's preferred place of scholarship.

3   The concept of 'symbolic space' is central to national constructions: B. Anderson, *Imagined Communities: Reflections on the Origin and Spread of Nationalism* (London 1994) and also R. D. Sack, *Homo Geographicus: a Framework for Action, Awareness, and Moral Concern* (Baltimore 1997). Similarly, Lefebvre has critically discussed the nature of 'representational space': H. Lefebvre (trans. D. Nicholson-Smith), *The Production of Space* (Oxford 1991). For Daniels, nation-states are grounded in 'patriotic landscapes': S. Daniels, *Fields of Vision: Landscape Imagery and National Identity in England and the United States* (Princeton 1993). Sullivan has postulated the construction of 'landscapes of sovereignty': G. A. Sullivan, *The Drama of Landscape: Land, Property, and Social Relations on the Early Modern Stage* (Stanford 1998). For my own work on this see B. S. Osborne, The iconography of nationhood in Canadian art, in D. Cosgrove and S. Daniels (Eds), *The Iconography of Landscape* (Cambridge 1988) 162-78; Recording a nation's heritage: illustrators as fabricators of Canadian identity, in G. Norcliffe and P. Simpson-Housley (Eds), *A Few Acres of Snow: Literary and Artistic Images of Canada* (Toronto 1992) 28-47; Interpreting a nation's identity: artists as creators of national consciousness, in A. R. H. Baker and G. Biger (Eds), *Ideology and Landscape in Historical Perspective* (Cambridge 1992) 230-254; From space to place: images of nationhood, in H. J. Selwood and J. H. Lehr (Eds), *Reflections from the Prairies: Geographical Essays* (Winnipeg 1992) 1-13; Landscapes, inscapes, mythologies: some thoughts on new Canadian identities, in W. K. Davies (Ed.), *Canadian Transformations: Perspectives on a Changing Human Geography* (Swansea 1994) 49-55; Grounding national mythologies: the case of Canada, in S. Courville and N. Seguin (Eds), *Espace et culture* (Laval 1995) 265-274; Figuring space, marking time: contested identities in Canada, *International Journal of Heritage Studies* **2** (1996) 23-40; Establishing the centre, integrating the margins: an historical geographical approach to Canadian national identity, in C. Stadel (Ed.), *Salzburger Geographische Arbeiten* **34** (1999) 7-22.

4   S. Schama, *Landscapes and Memory* (New York 1995) 15.

5   A. R. H. Baker, Introduction: on ideology and landscape, in Baker and Biger, *op. cit.*, 1-14.

6   P. Dansereau, *Inscape and Landscape: The Human Perception of the Environment* (New York 1973) ii. The poet, Gerard Manley Hopkins (1844-1889), first used the term 'inscape' in 1868. He sought the quintessential aspects that produce distinctiveness, the uniqueness, the 'oneness' of things, or 'the outward reflection of the inner nature of a thing'. See W. H. Gardner (Ed.), *Poems and Prose of Gerard Manley Hopkins* (Harmondsworth 1976) xx.

7   H. K. Bhabha (Ed.), *The Nation as Narration* (London 1990).

8   C. Tilly, *Coercion, Capital, and European States, AD 990-1992* (Oxford 1992). See also M. Mann, *States, War and Capitalism* (Oxford 1988).

9   A. Giddens, *A Contemporary Critique of Historical Materialism. Volume Two: The Nation-State and Violence* (Berkeley 1987); M. Mann, *The Sources of Social Power: The Rise of Classes and Nation-States, 1760-1914* (Cambridge 1993).

10   R. Samuels, *Theatres of Memory, Volume II: Island Stories, Unravelling Britain* (London 1998) 8.

11   W. Kilbourne, *Canada: A Guide to the Peaceable Kingdom* (New York 1970); W. Kilbourne, The peaceable kingdom still, *Daedalus* **117** (1988) 1-29.

12   C. Miller, *Painting the Map Red: Canada and the South African War, 1892-1902* (Montreal-Kingston 1903).

13   I use the contemporary term, 'Great War' rather than World War I as its descriptor fits the symbolic argument being presented in this paper, as well as reminding me of my Uncle Tom's reference to it – even after the events of 1939-45.

14   P. Fussell, *The Great War and Modern Memory* (Oxford 1975); G. L. Mosse, *Fallen Soldiers: Reshaping the Memory of the World Wars* (Oxford 1990); J. Vance, *Death So Noble: Memory, Meaning, and the First World War* (Vancouver 1997); T. Wilson, *The Myriad Faces of War* (Cambridge 1986); J. Winter, *Sites of Memory, Sites of Mourning: The Great War in European Cultural History* (Cambridge 1995).

15   Popular enthusiasm for accounts of deeds of derring-do resulted in other vehicles for imperial reportage. Thus, *The City Press*, 9 November 1898 reports on an illustrated talk on "The Soudan Wars from 1881 to 1898" by Ex-Sergeant-Major W. Norman Morris, late of 10th Royal Hussars, in which he refers to the charge at the Battle of El-Teb: "The picture by the gallant artist, Major G. D. Giles (who took part in the charge) represents one of the most thrilling incidents of the day ...."

16   P. Gough, *Canada, Culture, and Commemorations*, Paper presented at Canadian Military Conference, Ottawa, May 2000.

17   Captain B. H. Liddell Hart, *Memoirs* (London 1967) Volume I, 20-3.

18   S. Glickman, *The Picturesque and the Sublime: A Poetics of Canadian Landscape* (Montreal and Kingston 1998).

19   S. Hynes, *A War Imagined: The First World War and English Culture* (London 1990) 195.

20   This is the title of a chapter in *ibid.*, 195.

21   The issue of the degree to which the Great War allowed the dissemination of Impressionism and Vorticism into the galleries dominated by traditional forms is another part of this story. See C. Hill, *The Group of Seven: Art for a Nation* (Ottawa 1995) 69-73.

22   For insights into the complexity of the problem of remembering see A. King, *Memorials of the Great War in Britain* (Oxford 1998), C. Moriarty, The absent dead and figurative in First World War memorials, *Transactions Ancient Monuments Society* **39** (1995) 7-40, and *idem.*, review article: the material culture of Great War remembrance, *Journal of Contemporary History* **34** (1999) 633-662. For particular studies see H. Clout, *Mémoires de Pierre: Les Monuments aux Morts de la Première Guerre Mondiale dans le*

Pas-de-Calais (Calais 1992); A. Gaffney, *Aftermath: Remembering the Great War in Wales* (Cardiff 1998); M. Heffernan, For ever England: the Western Front and the politics of remembrance in Britain, *Ecumene* **2** (1995) 293-324; K. S. Inglis, *Sacred Places: War Memorials in the Australian Landscape* (Melbourne 1998); N. Johnson, Cast in stone: monuments, geography, and nationalism, *Environment and Planning D: Society and Space* **13** (1995) 51-65; D. J. Sherman, *The Construction of Memory in Interwar France* (Chicago 2000); R. Shipley, *To Mark Our Place: A History of Canadian War Memorials* (Toronto 1987).

23 And the iconography of the Great War continues to be developed. On 24 May 2000, the remains of an unknown soldier were flown from France, lay in state in the Parliament Buildings until 28 May when they were buried with full military honours at the foot of the National War Monument in Confederation Square. This memorial to the 'Unknown Soldier/Le Soldat Inconnu' is to honour the 110,000 Canadians who died in the wars of the twentieth century, and the 27,000 who lie in unknown graves. The remains were interred with soil collected from Canada's ten provinces, three territories, and Vimy Ridge.

24 See J. Pierce, Constructing memory: the Vimy Memorial, *Canadian Military History* **1** (1992) 1-3. Ironically, the other place is Dieppe which plays the same role of memorializing colonial sacrifice, if in defeat, for World War II. Of course, as mentioned above, Gallipoli does the same for Australia.

25 'Ready, Aye, Ready!' was the rallying cry and, in 1915, a fleet of thirty liners conveyed the first contingent of 125,000 men.

26 J. Adell, *British First World War Art and The Group of Seven: The Relationship Between the War Art of A. Y. Jackson and Paul Nash and its Influence on the Art of Lawren Harris* (Unpublished M. A. Research Essay, Carleton University, Ottawa, 1984); S. Butlin, Landscape as memorial: A. Y. Jackson and the landscape of the Western Front, 1917-1918, *Canadian Military History* **5** (1996) 62-70; F. K. Stanzel, 'In Flanders fields the poppies blow': Canada and the Great War, in P. Easingwood, K. Gross and L. Hunter (Eds), *Difference and Community: Canadian and European Cultural Perspectives* (Amsterdam 1994) 213-226; M. Tippett, *Art at the Service of War* (Toronto 1984); M. Tippett, British and Canadian art and the Great War, in F. K. Stanzel and M. Loschnigg (Eds), *Intimate Enemies: English and German Literary Reactions to the Great War 1914-1918* (Heidelberg 1993).

27 Tippett, Art and the Service of War, *op. cit.*, 19-24.

28 *Ibid.*, 26. Tippett also informs us that the Germans had war artists in 1914, the Australians had some at Gallipoli in 1915, the French appointed two in 1916, and the British hired Muirhead Bone in 1916.

29 *Ibid.*, 23-35.

30 The term 'Canadian' does need some reflection. As pointed out by several scholars of the Great War, many of the troops were British born but were transformed into nationalist Canadians by their experiences. This issue is central to the role of the Great War in 'constructing' Canadian national identity. The list included Cyril Barraud, J.W. Beatty, Maurice Cullen, A.Y. Jackson, James Kerr-Lawson, James Morrice, David Milne, Charles W. Simpson, and F. H. Varley. Interestingly, several of these were familiar with landscapes of Europe having painted there prior to the war. Thus, Jackson had spent much time working in Europe. In June of 1912 he had rented a farmhouse at Trépied near Étaples in Picardy, France; see his 'Studio at Étaples' (1912). Similarly, Varley had painted in Belgium. It raises the question, did they ever comment on the contrast between the pre-war and war-time landscapes they painted?

31 Gough, *op. cit.*, Other examples include Edgar Bundy's "Landing of the First Canadian Division at Saint-Nazaire, 1915"; Alfred Munnings' "Charge of Flowerdale's Squadron."

32 A.Y. Jackson, *A Painter's Country: An Autobiography of A. Y. Jackson* (Toronto 1958) 47. Commenting on Jackson's war art, Arthur Lismer observed, "He saw things as an artist of sensitivity; not the struggle of men in action, but rather the sad and wistful aftermath. Some of his loveliest canvases were painted in the First World War, see: Art Gallery of Ontario, *A. Y. Jackson: Paintings, 1902-1953* (Toronto 1953) 6.

33 D. Silcox, *Painting Place: The Life and Work of David B. Milne* (Toronto 1996) 103.

34   Quoted in C. Varley, *F. H. Varley: A Centennial Exhibition* (Ottawa 1981) 38.

35   The best treatment of the impact of the Great War on France is the excellent study by H. Clout, *After the Ruins: Restoring the Countryside of Northern France after the Great War* (Exeter 1996).

36   A. E. Davis and S. M. Mckinnon, *No Man's Land: The Battlefield Paintings of Mary Riter Hamilton, 1919-1922* (Winnipeg 1992). In 1919, Vancouver publisher, H. F. Paton, began publishing *The Gold Stripe*, the proceeds of which were to go to 'The Amputation Club of British Columbia'. It published articles from veterans, stories, photographs, and memorabilia related to the war. After three issues, Paton produced a book, *The Gold Stripe*. There were several sub-titles: 'A Tribute to those who were killed, maimed and wounded in the Great War'; 'A Book, one of the many efforts to re-establish some back in civil life'; 'A Book of War, Peace and Reconstruction for Prosperity'.

37   M. R. Hamilton, An artist impressionist on the battlefields of France, *The Gold Stripe* **3** (1919) 11-12. She lived at first with a Canadian army contingent, then with Chinese workers hired to clear the battlefields; her place of work was made all the more hazardous in that the former battle-area was infested with criminals and deserters.

38   Davis and McKinnen, *op. cit.*, 22.

39   *Ibid.*, 24.

40   For more on the post-war reconstruction of France see Clout, *After the Ruins*.

41   J. E. M. Bruce, Mary Riter Hamilton, *The Gold Stripe* **2** May (1919) 23.

42   Hamilton, *op. cit.*, 11.

43   J. E. H. MacDonald, *The Toronto Globe*, 10 September, 1919.

44   Tippett, Art and the Service of War, *op. cit.*, 76-92.

45   Davis and McKinnon, *op. cit.*, 13.

46   Hill, *op. cit.*, 71.

47   For example, Derwent Wood's bronze, 'Canada's Golgotha', an image of a Canadian soldier purportedly crucified by the Germans, was thought to be too provocative to be shown. Indeed, it was later used by the Nazis as an example of Allied propaganda through lies. See Tippett, *op. cit.*, 81-7.

48   F. H. Varley's, 'The Sunken Road – August 1918', 1919, oil on canvas, Canadian War Museum Collection, Ottawa. A. Bridle, Are these new-Canadian painters crazy? *Canadian Courier*, 22 May 1920 6, 10, 20.

49   J. H. MacDonald, Mentioned in Dispatches, *The Rebel* **III** (1919) 205-207, quoted in Hill, *op. cit.*, 65.

50   Most of them were later transferred to the National War Museum. As Canada currently indulges itself in an enthusiastic search for monolithic metanarratives, military history is being celebrated and funds have been made available for an appropriate building to house the collection.

51   Davis and McKinnon, *op. cit.*, 6.

52   Frank Carmichael, Lawren Harris, A. Y. Jackson, Frank Johnston, Arthur Lismer, J. E. H. MacDonald, F. Horsman Varley. For the most recent and most comprehensive treatment of 'The Seven', see Hill, *op. cit.*

53   Tippett, Art and the Service of War, *op. cit.*, 58.

54   Bridle, *op. cit.*, 6, 10, 20.

55   Tippett, Art and the Service of War, *op. cit.*, 109.

56   Butlin, *op. cit.*, 68, quoting Tippett. It must be admitted, however, that for A.Y. Jackson at least, there were more prosaic reasons for his predilection for northern landscapes. Commenting on the collapse of

the Siberian expedition of which he was to be part, he noted that "All I got out of it was twenty tubes of white paint. It was probably the paint that was responsible for my becoming a snow painter as I had to find some use for it"!. See Jackson, *op. cit.*, 50.

57   Osborne, The iconography of nationhood, *op. cit.*

58   D. J. Bercuson, *True Patriot: The Life of Brooke Claxton, 1898-1960* (Toronto 1993) 59-60. In a letter to J. E. H. MacDonald on 6 April, 1918, A.Y. Jackson makes a similar observation: "You would be proud of the Canucks if you could see them. They have developed a wonderful army more Canadian and independent than it used to be" (Exhibition: *The Group of Seven: Art for a Nation* (Ottawa 1995). Similarly, when English-born F. H. Varley was lionized there after the war, he rejected the possibility of developing his career in England and pined for Canada in very nativist tones: "The boys here can't understand why I want to go to Canada again, but they haven't been there and they don't know there are a hundred more chances for progression out there than here. It's no use telling them." And he fantasized painting "a Canadian Indian summer with sunburnt humans in riotous dance – naked, sunbronzed, flying hair, trills of laughter, splashing water – golden pumpkins, purple grapes ..." (Both quotes from Varley, *op. cit.*, 46).

59   Following the Great War, Canadian historiography witnessed such national views as the Staples Thesis, the Laurentian School, and the Canadian Pioneer Frontiers Series. See C. Berger, *The Writing of Canadian History* (Toronto 1976).

60   Quoted in S. Gwyn, *Tapestry of War: A Private View of Canadians in the Great War* (Toronto 1992) 374.

61   Bercuson, *op. cit.*, 60. See also R. M. Bray, 'Fighting as an Ally': The English-Canadian patriotic response to the Great War, *Canadian Historical Review* **LXI** (1984) 141-168; R. Faris, *The Passionate Educators* (Toronto 1975); D. Owram, *The Government Generation: Canadian Intellectuals and the State* (Toronto 1986); M. Vipond, The nationalist network: English Canada's intellectuals and artists in the 1920s, *Canadian Review of Studies in Nationalism* **7** (1980) 32-52.

62   Faris, *op. cit.*, 1.

63   D. Reid, *A Reconstruction of the First Exhibition of the Group of Seven Organized by the National Gallery of Canada, Ottawa, with the Cooperation of the Art Gallery of Ontario, Toronto* (Ottawa 1970).

64   All of the following are taken from materials presented at the exhibition: *The Group of Seven: Art for a Nation* (Ottawa: National Gallery of Canada 1995).

65   J. E. H. MacDonald, A whack at Dutch Art, *The Rebel* **II** (1918) 256-60.

66   Arthur Lismer, from an address to the Canadian Club of Toronto, 13 December, 1926.

67   Lawren Harris, quoted in C. Berger, The true north strong and free, in P. Russell (Ed.) *Nationalism in Canada* (Toronto 1966) 3-26.

68   For a more critical discussion of the ideological underpinnings of these views see Osborne, The iconography of nationhood, *op. cit.*, and E. Mackey, *The House of Difference: Cultural Politics and National Identity in Canada* (London 1999), especially 40-49.

69   Vipond, *op. cit.*, 48.

70   Daniels, *op. cit.*, 5.

71   B. Gopnik, The Group of Seven – had enough yet?, *Toronto Globe and Mail*, 21 November 1998.

72   *Toronto Globe and Mail*, 28 November, 1998.

73   This initiative, together with the commemorations of D-Day and VE Day, and the dedication of a monument to the Unknown Soldier are signal demonstrations of the state's continuing awareness of Tilley's proposition that "nations make wars, wars make nations".

AFTERWORD

JOE M. POWELL

Like all too many Afterwords, this note scouts the problematical divide between impertinence and obligation. Hostage, as ever, to space and time, I was unable to attend the splendid gathering which produced this volume of essays, and therefore missed some of the ruminations which others may feel should now be addressed. That is a large handicap. On the positive side, isolation may lend perspectives that come untainted by propinquity's temptations, and if peripherality is for spectating more than participation, perhaps there is democratization of sorts from the view itself. Emmanuel's historic muster acknowledged a range of fine qualities. From my distant eyrie, I have fastened on one alone: it is Alan Baker's consistent contribution as insightful team-player that I have found most outstanding down the years. A marked divergence in our career itineraries diminishes, for some, a bracketing by year of birth: a small coincidence, admittedly, but its appurtenances underpin the following reflections.

My brief was to round off with a few comments from the Australasian-Asian-Pacific sector. Frankly, it would be sheer lunacy not to duck that enormous task, but in deference to the overriding objective I decided to try to go part of the way by essaying two academic neighbourhoods. This reliance on straightforward practicality offers a nod in Alan's direction: 'constructive' has surely been one of his commoner tags. The first section, deliberately and dangerously based on a recent, very limited exposure to Japan, may serve to demonstrate the folly of measuring any career, however prominent, against the full weight of received wisdom on subdisciplinary evolution. The next, on Australia and New Zealand, is similarly hedged, but also presents less speculative evidence of intellectual continuities and convergences, and a few mutual anxieties. Overall, the elementary premise is of course that well-attuned folk encourage us all to the song.

Japanese translations

The trajectories of historical geography in Japan necessarily reflect a formidably ancient heritage and an adroitly managed location between Asian and Western cultural realms and academic praxis. For our purposes it seems safer to point to fellow travellers, shared emphases or parallel developments and the like, than casually to project supposed external exemplars. Indeed, a reasonable case might be argued for Japanese singularities and anticipations. Nonetheless, given a debut in comparable hybridizations drawn from geology and history, and the stimulus of precocious initiative within a markedly hierarchical university system, the echoes of British and German experience do not exactly deceive.

Regarding the early generation of Japanese academic geography as a whole, Keiichi Takeuchi's invaluable overview insists on the recognition of a demanding milieu characterized by changing imperialistic, nationalistic, regional and local imperatives, and Kinda and others confirm the significance of similarly charged complexities in the introduction and elaboration of historical geography.[1] Until recently, thanks to a daunting language barrier, much of the absorbing background was not widely appreciated in the West. In this instance as in so many others, Japanese scholarship has assumed responsibility for most of the bridge-building, but Alan Baker's facilitative diplomatic presence, in the United Kingdom itself and globally, is warmly acknowledged. The long domination of the Imperial Universities of Kyoto and Tokyo, now far less pronounced, is relevant to our purposes insofar as the country's first specialist geographer, geology-trained Takuji Ogawa (1870-1941) was appointed in 1907 to Kyoto's history department, from whence he instigated historical-geographical analyses of China-Japan linkages and the evolution of rural and urban settlement patterns. This influential programme favoured a landscape emphasis from the outset, and well-tended expectations produced clarifications of the antecedents of current configurations. The same preferences were maintained by other prominent Kyoto researchers after Ogawa was transferred to the university's geology department. During the 1930s, J.Yonekura adapted Meitzen's morphological approach in his examinations of Japanese rural landscapes, established the seventh-century origins of the archetypal grid-based Japanese land system and pioneered a reconstructive analysis of a provincial capital. Saneshiga Komaki, initially a specialist in prehistoric and historical geography, served as Kyoto conduit for recent European developments, notably those of French geographers, and generally promoted a move towards a more systematic methodology by drawing upon the prestigious works of Hettner, Mackinder, Passarge and Schlüter. This search for greater systemization also persuaded Komaki to recommend a concentration on reconstructed cross-sections and, as in British historical geography, the strategy delivered improved subdisciplinary identity.

Takeuchi explains that Komaki's determined sieving was all too soon deflected into fanatical advocacy of Shintoist Japanese geopolitics: purged, with several of his colleagues, during the postwar occupation, he was reduced to running a second-hand bookshop in Kyoto.[2] Cross-sectionalization fared better. Kinda traces its definite 'thickening', with narrative interpolations and articulations, in the work of (Komaki-follower) K. Fujioka and his students in the mid-1950s, culminating two decades later in their multi-volume *General Historical Geography of Japan*. Over the same period, expansions of the interests of the powerful Kyoto coterie gradually accommodated medieval and early modern research, while upholding the familiar landscape tradition and intense regard for alert monitoring of Western trends.[3] It is principally in this amplified purview of the vigorous Kyoto school that one finds definite links with British interests, and specifically with the Bakerian outreach.

For expedience, let us imagine that, for our Japanese colleagues, the strongest resonances are probably most easily tracked through four critical nodes of Baker activity. Firstly, beginning in the early 1960s, there are timely commentaries on history, philosophy and practice – *the central resonance of declared vocation* – offered as solo or collaborative contributions. This series includes hands-on critiques in the fledgling *Progress in Human Geography*, a run of focussing volumes providing international updates, ruminative discussions on research methods, needs and opportunities, and a collection of exemplary pieces recommending some overdue interchange with resurgent political and cultural geography.[4] Secondly, there is the sustained individual research project, lit with rewarding topophilia: micro-analyses of medieval English field systems, with immediate import for many Japanese specialists; later an enduring affair with rural society, landscape and economy in nineteenth-century France, and its consummation in the Loire Valley. Resolute, here, on convenient characterization, I find the compelling *resonance of scholarly endeavour*.[5] Thirdly, there are frequent interwoven emphases on conjoint uses of documentary and physical evidence, practical notes on archival consultations, and a grasp of the need to address a reviving spectrum of interdependent constituencies – academic and lay audiences, global and local, intradisciplinary and interdisciplinary.

Perhaps the most pertinent indicators are judicious placements in a range of national and local historical journals and an evocative, not to say entrepreneurial volume co-edited with the late Brian Harley, *Man Made the Land*. If I put all of that down as the *resonance of profession* it is to acknowledge a self-conscious fidelity of purpose rather than mere territoriality.[6] Fourthly, there is a creative, painstaking involvement as mentor and advocate. Others are better placed to comment on Alan's approach to teaching and supervision. Here, I must add to the previously cited edited books a remarkable dedication to the production of almost 40 volumes, with a decidedly international scope, in the *Studies in Historical Geography* and *Cambridge Studies in Historical Geography* series. But that part of the profiling is incomplete without a listing of Alan's nurturing of the renowned Occasional Discussions in Historical Geography, foundation membership and indefatigable promotion of the *Journal of Historical Geography*, and of course his work as its editor in 1987-96, a period for which 'tumultuous' is more than usually apposite. To borrow from the ardent Loire attachment, this fourth category may be best recognized as *the resonance of fraternal association* – for the place-making it affords us all.[7]

This rough underlining of essentials which appear to have travelled remarkably well runs some risk of caricature, and 'resonance' demands more reciprocals than my recent overseas sojourn permits. At second-hand, as it were, my impression is that the firmest ground is to be found in the massive quantity of Japanese scholarship on ancient and medieval rural settlement, and especially in meticulously refined investigations of *jori* grid patterns. There are also many convincing instances of conjoint physical and documentary evidence – the Japanese experience seems rich in this regard – together with expert interrogations of startlingly dense cartographic materials, and an old-established civic impulse which is variously apparent in the involvement of historical geographers in co-operatively produced, multi-volume prefectural reference guides (reminiscent of Britain's *Victoria County Histories*, but larger) and in some highly successful popularizations of the country's exceptional map-making heritage.[8] Western stereotyping misses the thorough elaboration of traditional landscape approaches. Contrary to some notions, for example, reliance on the German concept of *Landschaft* was by no means exclusive, even in the early decades of this century, and postwar criticism of its restricted translation in Japan encouraged expansions into any number of cultural, ecological, economic, social and other considerations. These developments permitted an improved coverage of types of place-bonding sociability not unrelated to that noted in Alan Baker's *Fraternity Among the French Peasantry*; on the other hand, until recently the early modern and modern periods were comparatively under-researched, so the room for undisputed comparison is limited. In any event, the sheer amount and variety of historical-geographical enterprise in Japan inevitably mirrors nonpareil pasts and presents. The importance attached to singular local and regional cultures and power structures, the pervasive and still resilient influence of religion, some markedly East Asian urban emphases, and the complicated China-Japan-Korea nexus, all contrive to compose such a labyrinth that one simultaneously expects all manner of revised versions of Western approaches and their virtual submergence beneath a plethora of distinctive *in-situ* works.

Antipodean accommodation

Australian and New Zealand experiences are almost invariably telescoped, except in the respective local bailiwicks where that compulsory twinning is resented or ignored. In some lights, however, it is understandable that they are summed as a single antipodean with such direct immigrant linkages to Britain and Western Europe that the detection of lines of influence is thought to bring minimal threat or confusion, in comparison with the echoes found in the kind of parallel universe represented by Japan. Alas for some crucial differentiations – the recency of European settlement and its compression into an age of increasing technological sophistication and materialistic aspiration; stimulating kinship with North American scholarship; a postwar efflorescence of multi-ethnicity, alternately battling and blurring imported allegiances; the sizeable freight of unfamiliar environmental spheres; institutionalizations of mixed disciplinary milieux with which historical geography, like other inherited constructs, is required to transact; and not least the contingent existence of a perilously small number of specialist practitioners.

Much of that has been communicated in the landmark overviews commissioned for the earlier Baker surveys, notably *Progress in Historical Geography*, and in later statements also commissioned or endorsed by Alan.[9] Here, I shall summon an insider's abbreviated testimony as preface to the next slant on the task nominated for this Afterword. Rather than rehashing intricate details, consider first the punctuations along familism's crimson thread – Britain, Darby, University College, Cambridge – which recur in representative academic profiles in both communities. Trans-Tasman differences were not confined to the huge disparities of scale. Whereas the initial New Zealand connection regularly exhibited Darbyesque flourishes, from the 1960s our later-developing, more fluid Australian contexts welcomed the more influential American visitors, were romanced by a sudden boom in Australian history, edged towards causation and process at the expense of 'pattern', and *en route* explored the defining national and regional significance of the inter-related themes of environmental perception, environmental management and resource appraisal. Those trends became quite pronounced in the formation of academics who had completed major postgraduate theses in Australia. An inescapable osmotic accommodation promoted the transaction mentioned above, and its tangible results included a reasonably comfortable transition into complementary investigations of the antecedents of current issues. With apologies to Kiwi colleagues, those remarks begin to recommend a restriction of the main narration to my own country. The wider application of my quasi-findings may be disputed: in mitigation, I plead want of space (oddly enough, for an Australian ...).

Michael Williams' pioneering text, *The Making of the South Australian Landscape* (1974) effectively bridged the British, Australian and New Zealand approaches. Donald Meinig's *On the Margins of the Good Earth* (1962) was more swiftly taken up by a local historical profession which absorbed the American visitor's implicit endorsement of narrative skills, but then gradually conceded that Williams had in fact carefully sought the underlying dynamic linking snap-shot displays of a series of environmental transformations.[10] Both books became standards during an interdisciplinary pursuit of environmental lines which accelerated through Australian campuses in the 1980s. They appeared to confirm the superiority of state units as premier regional bases – the more so because South Australia's records and settlement experience were considered unrepresentatively 'orderly'. In the interim, Dennis Jeans had attempted a more inclusive introductory guide for our oldest unit, New South Wales, and Les Heathcote opted instead for what should have been a circuit-breaking ecological regionalization based on the management of the extensive interior grasslands.[11] Heathcote's account proposed a model of resource appraisal which resurrected and deciphered the nexus between 'official' and 'popular' resource evaluations. Others followed suit, adapting the model for interpenetrating ecological and socio-political formulations.[12]

In retrospect, this collective immigrant effort constitutes a form of direction-finding in which the most intense satisfaction was to be obtained from recovering and harnessing authentically Australian attributes and contexts. As it happens, Jeans and Heathcote were London contemporaries under Darby. The insertion of hazard studies and 'heritage' matters into their repertoires was accompanied – 'naturally', one is inclined to add – by interpretations of the roles of art and literature in the construction and expression of national and regional identities. They were not alone in this regard and, similarly motivated, others took the historiographical route, tracing the Australian roots of geographical thought through the biographical record. Then the strands promised to come together as a co-operative historical-geographical input to a swirling interdisciplinary project designed for the bicentennial of European settlement, in 1988. At that point some of the more parochial of our historians became late arrivals at the traditional site of exchange between historical geography and the *Annales* school. They exaggerated its apparent novelty and, although the multi-volume bicentennial production temporarily galvanized aspects of research management and enhanced the public image of Australian scholarship, the project experience ultimately disappointed those historical geographers who had naively envisaged wholesale 'paradigm shifts' and new curriculum constellations. The one marginal exception was the surprisingly tardy delivery of an Australian version of 'environmental history' – seeded in the midst of our 1980s extravaganzas, struggling to the surface in the 1990s.[13]

I dare not extend this too freely around the Pacific. New Zealand had its own challenges, but the counterparts comprised an environmental-historical shift and an interdisciplinary historical atlas. In both countries, historical geographers were also attracted by the resurgent, politicized field of cultural geography. Its assertive, multi-faceted analyses of the dispossession and maltreatment of indigenous communities, major ingredients in a trans-millennial revisiting of the stubborn national identity theme, relied quite heavily upon the recruitment of historical expertise; so too a related, continuing effort in interdisciplinary heritage studies. As several of these examples illustrate, the underlying trend was towards more co-operative scholarship, with commensurate stress on co-ordinated national programmes. But the lone writer-researcher still waved the boldest flags, and set the marks. For indomitable all-rounder Oskar Spate (a sometime rival of Darby), who had long been sustained by a profound distaste for academic boundary-riding, historical geography and cultural geography produced but a single silhouette. His prize-winning trilogy on the wider region, *The Pacific since Magellan*, was the fruit of an alleged retirement.[14] Spate's less confident successors seem reduced to hoarding each valiant exercise in synthesis, in hope of spontaneous multiplication – bean sprouts in a jar...

Now to re-introduce our lead character into my second Cook's tour. The Baker record to date is distinguished by a balance of emboldened synthesis, co-ordinator's zeal, guardian's cautions, champion's thrusts. The stimulating pull of internationalism has spiced that blend from the outset and more than anything else, perhaps, that explains the presence of palpable mediations – refreshing re-articulations, deft coaching, notices of new directions, all the reminders of shared goals and unfinished business. Our Australian and New Zealand interests in environmental perception and official-popular dichotomies found echoes and rejoinders in the edited surveys and in very familiar titles commencing 'Rhetoric and reality...', and our rediscoveries of the *Annales* school, together with those made by our history colleagues, were directly assisted by several of Alan's concise briefings.[15] The anxious or dutiful historiographical-biographical line, also signalled in the above paragraphs, can be tracked through much of his editorial commentary and in notes on Wheatley, Clark, Darby and others; that is also true of the intersections of popular culture and geographical writing.[16] In one location adaptive, antipodean re-awakening to the socio-political dynamic resonates with a notice on analyses of popular protest; in another our hand-wringing territorializations over environmental history are afforded ventilation in our flagship journal. Elsewhere, our rapprochement with social and cultural geography was assisted by a collection of essays under the co-editorship of Baker and Biger.[17]

In comparison with those welcomed cues and reassurances, the bulky file on the Loir-et-Cher peasantry seems a looming reproach: certainly where the culminating book is concerned there is no immediate parallel in our corner of the world.[18] It has already taken a prodigious feat from such a small company to reach the current stage, when – barring a prolongation of the chronic labour crisis – vaguely comparable regional analyses may soon be contemplated without losing sanity. Yet there is a drift to be caught from my tallying of robust concordances and I do not propose to block it here. For the lesson is not in the finely wrought superstructure which does indeed mock our wing-and-prayer panoramas, but in the Loir-et-Cher monograph's overarching bid for humanistic re-orientation, and in some of its constituent perspectives on the place-making contributed by taken-for-granted sociabilities and the impulse to voluntarism. The colonial translation of 'peasant' was 'yeoman' and it could be argued that elucidations of correlative, hardly dissimilar expenditures on 'fraternity' remain central to our addictive debates on national and regional identity.[19]

"the idea and the practice of association ..."[20]

Making due allowance for the specificities of context, what emerges from this quick inspection of remote and vastly differing cultures? Above all, I believe, the eccentric sampling points to a modern community of scholarship which has been built as much upon a host of acknowledged and unconsidered international influences as on local circumstances. Borrowing again from Loir-et-Cher, it appears to be in the nature of the academy that only a few individuals fully discern the need for wise and continuous investment in the construction of place-making *fraternité*. For almost four decades historical geography, our place, has been fortunate indeed in Alan Baker's yeomanlike ministrations.

NOTES

1   This section mainly draws upon K. Takeuchi, *Modern Japanese Geography: An Intellectual History* (Tokyo 2000), A. Kinda, Some traditions and methodologies of Japanese historical geography, *Journal of Historical Geography* **23** (1997) 62-75, and T. Mizoguchi, Studies in the historical geography of Japan, 1988-1995, *Geographical Review of Japan* **69** (1996) 21-41. See also G. J. Martin and P. E. James (Eds), *All Possible Worlds. A History of Geographical Ideas* (New York 1993) 291-301.

2   Takeuchi, *op. cit.*, 126-40.

3   Kinda, *op. cit.*

4   For examples (*seriatim*) A. R. H. Baker, Historical geography, *Progress in Human Geography* **1** (1977) 465-74; Historical geography: understanding and experiencing the past, *Progress in Human Geography* **2** (1978) 495-504; Historical geography: a new beginning? *Progress in Human Geography* **3** (1979) 560-70; A. R. H. Baker, J. D. Hamshere and J. Langton (Eds), *Geographical Interpretations of Historical Sources: Readings in Historical Geography* (Newton Abbot 1970); A. R. H. Baker (Ed.), *Progress in Historical Geography* (Newton Abbot 1972); A. R. H. Baker and M. Billinge (Eds), *Period and Place: Research Methods in Historical Geography* (Cambridge 1982); A. R. H. Baker and D. Gregory (Eds), *Explorations in Historical Geography: Interpretative Essays* (Cambridge 1984); A. R. H. Baker, Maps, models and Marxism: methodological mutation in British historical geography, *L'Espace Géographique* **4** (1985) 9-15, and The practice of historical geography, in J. R. Pitte (Ed.), *Géographique Historique et Culturelle de l'Europe* (Paris 1995) 31-49; on cultural geography see also A. R. H. Baker and G. Biger (Eds), *Ideology and Landscape in Historical Perspective* (Cambridge 1992). Relevant constituent essays in the above books are listed separately in the full bibliography included in the present volume.

5   *Seriatim*, the many studies of medieval field systems, especially for south-eastern England, listed later in this volume in a full bibliography; A. R. H. Baker and R. A. Butlin (Eds), *Studies of Field Systems in the British Isles* (Cambridge 1973); and A. R. H. Baker, *Fraternity Among the French Peasantry: Sociability and Voluntary Associations in the Loire Valley, 1815-1914* (Cambridge 1999).

6   The full bibliography shows support for the *Amateur Historian, Archaeologica Cantiana, Publications of the Bedfordshire Historical Record Society* and *Sussex Archaeological Collections*, for instance, as well as the *Economic History Review, Transactions of the Institute of British Geographers, Journal of Historical Geography* and *Agricultural History Review*: it will be noticed that my comment extends to *Mémoires de la Société des Sciences et Lettres de Loir-et Cher*. The book listed is A. R. H. Baker and J. B. Harley (Eds), *Man Made the Land. Essays in English Historical Geography* (Newton Abbot 1973).

7   For one international restrospect, see A. R. H. Baker, Cambridge Occasional Discussions in Historical Geography 1968-1988, *Historical Geography* **19** (1989) 7-12; by that time the series had produced 161 papers and accounted for over 1000 bottles of French wine.

8   Kinda, *op. cit.*, provides a convenient bibliography. See also the same author's recent books (in Japanese), *The Landscape of Ancient Japan: Ecology and Perception of the Grid Pattern Plan* (Tokyo 1993); *Manor Maps of the Ancient Period and the Landscapes* (Tokyo 1998) and *Ancient Japan Reconstructed from Ancient Maps* (Tokyo 1999). Japanese scholars Ukita, Senda and Tanioka made prominent contributions to sections of Baker and Billinge, *op. cit.* For astute comments on modern parallels in China, see A. R. H. Baker, Agendas for historical geography: reflections upon an international conference of historical geography, Beijing, P. R. China, 16-20 July 1996, *Journal of Historical Geography* **22** (1996) 479-83. Amongst its other useful observations, this paper reports an encounter with Prof. Renzhi Hou (one of Darby's postgraduate students at Liverpool in the early postwar years), on the maintenance of four distinct Chinese journals of historical geography, and on a (partly politically-stimulated) civic or applied emphasis.

9   For example Baker, *Progress, op. cit.*, 144-67; J. M. Powell, Past imperfect, future tense: 'civic' conjugations in Australia and New Zealand', *Journal of Historical Geography* **23** (1997) 389-92, introducing our special antipodean issue.

10 M. Williams, *The Making of the South Australian Landscape: A Study in the Historical Geography of Australia* (London 1974); D. W. Meinig, *On the Margins of the Good Earth: The South Australian Wheat Frontier, 1869-1884* (Chicago 1962).

11 D. N. Jeans, *An Historical Geography of New South Wales to 1901* (Sydney 1972); R. L. Heathcote, *Back of Bourke. A Study of Land Appraisal and Settlement in Semi-Arid Australia* (Melbourne 1965).

12 For a guide, see J. M. Powell, Historical geography and environmental history: an Australian interface, *Journal of Historical Geography* **22** (1996) 253-73.

13 *Ibid.*, and Powell, Past imperfect, *passim*. One contextualization of the historiographical line is offered in J. M. Powell, *An Historical Geography of Modern Australia: The Restive Fringe* (Cambridge 1991).

14 O. H. K. Spate, *The Pacific Since Magellan* vol. 1, *The Spanish Lake* (Canberra 1979), vol. 2, *Monopolists and Freebooters* (Canberra 1983), vol. 3, *Paradise Found and Lost* (Canberra 1988). Professor Spate died in Canberra, in May 1999, shortly after this chapter had been written.

15 A. R. H. Baker, Rhetoric and reality in historical geography, *Journal of Historical Geography* **3** (1977) 301-5, and Reflections on the relations of historical geography and the *Annales* school of history', in Baker and Gregory, *op. cit.*, 1-27.

16 For the historiographical-biographical discussions I have in mind see the accompanying complete bibliography; on the cited intersections see, for example, A. R. H. Baker, On geographical literature as popular culture in rural France, c.1860-1900, *Geographical Journal* **156** (1990) 39-43.

17 A. R. H. Baker, Patterns of popular protest, *Journal of Historical Geography* **1** (1975) 383-87; Historical geography and environmental history, *Journal of Historical Geography* **20** (1994) 1-2; Baker and Biger, *op. cit.*

18 *Fraternity Among the French Peasantry* capped the best part of forty years research on rural France.

19 The point is touched upon in Powell, *Historical Geography of Modern Australia*; its application can be extended to many facets of Australian *mentalité* in the colonial and postcolonial eras.

20 Baker, *Fraternity Among the French Peasantry*, 320.

Appendix One

ALAN R. H. BAKER

Publications

On the Historical Geography of England

1962a   'Local history in early estate maps' *Amateur Historian* **5** 66-71

1962b   'Some early Kentish estate maps and a note on their portrayal of field boundaries' *Archaeologia Cantiana* **77** 177-184

1963a   'The field system of an East Kent parish (Deal)' *Archaeologia Cantiana* **78** 96-117

1963b   'Open fields in Derbyshire: some reservations about recent arguments' *Derbyshire Archaeological Journal* **83** 77-81

1964a   'Open fields and partible inheritance on a Kent manor' *Economic History Review* **17** 1-23

1965a   'Field patterns in seventeenth-century Kent' *Geography* **50** 18-30

1965b   'Howard Levi Gray and *English Field Systems*: an evaluation' *Agricultural History* **39** 86-91

1965c   'Some fields and farms in medieval Kent' *Archaeologia Cantiana* **80** 152-174. [Reprinted in 1968 in *Beitrage zur Genese der Siedlungs – und Agrarlandschaft in Europa, Erdkundliches Wissen* **18** 1-11. Reprinted in 1973 in M. Roake and J. Whyman (Eds) *Essays in Kentish History* (London) 11-35]

1966a   'The Kentish *iugum*: its relationship to soils at Gillingham' *English Historical Review* **81** 74-79

1966b   'Field systems in the Vale of Holmesdale' *Agricultural History Review* **14** 1-24

1966c   (with D. Roden) 'The field systems of the Chiltern Hills and of parts of Kent from the thirteenth to the seventeenth century' *Transactions of the Institute of British Geographers* **38** 73-88

1966d   'Some evidence of a reduction in the acreage of cultivated lands in Sussex during the early fourteenth century' *Sussex Archaeological Collections* **104** 1-5

1966e   'Evidence in the *Nonarum Inquisitiones* of contracting arable lands in England during the early fourteenth century' *Economic History Review* **19** 518-532

1969a   'Some terminological problems in studies of British field systems' *Agricultural History Review* **17** 136-140

1970a   'Cooperative farming in medieval England. Keys to the agricultural past' *Geographical Magazine* **42** 496-505

1970b   'Contracting arable lands in 1341' *Publications of the Bedfordshire Historical Record Society* **49** 7-18

1973a   (with R. A. Butlin, Eds), *Studies of Field Systems in the British Isles* (Cambridge)

1973b   (with R. A. Butlin) 'Introduction: materials and methods', in A. R. H. Baker and R. A. Butlin (Eds), *Studies of Field Systems in the British Isles* (Cambridge) 1-40

1973c   'Field systems of south-east England', in A. R. H. Baker and R. A. Butlin (Eds), *Studies of Field Systems in the British Isles* (Cambridge) 377-429

1973d   (with R. A. Butlin) 'Conclusion: problems and perspectives', in A. R. H. Baker and R. A. Butlin (Eds), *Studies of Field Systems in the British Isles* (Cambridge) 619-656

1973e   (with J. B. Harley) (Eds), *Man Made the Land. Essays in English Historical Geography* (Newton Abbot)

1973f   'Field systems in medieval England', in A. R. H. Baker and J. B. Harley (Eds), *Man Made the Land. Essays in English Historical Geography* (Newton Abbot) 59-68

1973g   'Changes in the later middle ages', in H. C. Darby (Ed.), *A New Historical Geography of England* (Cambridge) 186-247. [Reprinted in 1976 in H. C. Darby (Ed.), *A New Historical Geography of England before 1600* (Paperback edn, Cambridge) 186-247]

1979a   'Observations on the open fields: the present position of studies in British field systems' *Journal of Historical Geography* **5** 315-323

1980a   'Laxton: preservation for people' *The Geographical Magazine* **52** 321 and 324

1983a   'Discourses on British field systems' *Agricultural History Review* **31** 149-155

On the Historical Geography of France

1961a   'Le remembrement rural en France' *Geography* **46** 60-62

1968a   'A modern French revolution. Farm consolidation policy in France' *Geographical Magazine* **40** 833-841

1968b   'Agricultural policy in the European Economic Community during 1967' *Geography* **53** 310-311

1968c   'Établissements ruraux sur la marge Sud-Ouest du Bassin Parisien dans les premières années du XIXe siècle: description analytique des types' *Norois* **60** 481-492

1969b   'Keeping the past in the present. The preservation of French townscapes' *Town and Country Planning* **37** (7) 308-311

1969c   'Reversal of the rank-size rule: some nineteenth century rural settlement sizes in France' *Professional Geographer* **21** (6) 386-92

1971a   'Some shape and contact characteristics of French rural communes', in F. Dussart (Ed.), *L'Habitat et les Paysages Ruraux d'Europe: Les Congrès et Colloques de l'Université de Liège* **58** 13-32

1971b   'Distance between farmstead and field in some nineteenth century French communes' *Geography* **56** 293-298

1973h   'A relatively neglected field form: the headland ridge' *Agricultural History Review* **21** 47-50

1973i   'Adjustments to distance between farmstead and field: some findings from the southernwestern Paris Basin in the early nineteenth century' *Canadian Geographer* **17** 259-275. [Reprinted in 1975 in R. L. Singh and K. N. Sing (Eds), *Readings in Rural Settlement Geography. National Geographical Society of India Publication* **14** 340-352]

1975a   'Patterns of popular protest' *Journal of Historical Geography* **1** 383-387

1975b   'A nation of peasants' *Geographical Magazine* **48** 24-30

1976a   'The lessons are learnt and a nation emerges' *Geographical Magazine* **48** 409-414

1977a   'Rhetoric and reality in historical geography' *Journal of Historical Geography* **3** 301-305

1979b   'Rural settlements and early development of agricultural syndicalism: the case of Loir-et-Cher during the second half of the 19th Century', in P. Flatres (Ed.), *Paysages Ruraux Européens* (Rennes) 267-275

1980b   'On the historical geography of France' *Journal of Historical Geography* **6** 69-76

1980c   'Ideological change and settlement continuity in the French countryside: the development of agricultural syndicalism in Loir-et-Cher during the late-nineteenth century' *Journal of Historical Geography* **6** 163-177

1983b   ' Devastation of a landscape, doctrination of a society: the politics of the phylloxera crisis in Loir-et-Cher (France) 1866-1914' *Würzburger Geographische Arbeiten* **60** 205-217

1984a   'Fraternity in the forest: the creation, control and collapse of woodcutters' unions in Loir-et-Cher 1852-1914' *Journal of Historical Geography* **10** 157-173. [Reprinted in French in 1985 as 'Fraternité dans la forêt: la création, le pouvoir et l'échec des syndicats de bucherons en Loir-et-Cher (1852-1914) *Mémoires de la Société des Sciences et Lettres de Loir-et-Cher* **40** 95-116]

1986a   'The infancy of France's first agricultural syndicate: the Syndicat des Agriculteurs de Loir-et-Cher 1881-1914' *Agricultural History Review* **34** 45-59

1986b   'Les syndicats agricoles de la vallée de la Cisse (1883-1914)' *Vallée de la Cisse* **8** 59-71

1986c   'Sound and fury: the significance of musical societies in Loir-et-Cher during the nineteenth century' *Journal of Historical Geography* **12** 249-267. [Reprinted in French in 1996 as 'Le bruit et la fureur: l'importance des sociétés musicales en Loir-et-Cher au XIXe siècle' *Mémoires de la Société des Sciences et Lettres de Loir-et-Cher* **51** 191-216]

1990a   'Fire-fighting fraternities? The corps de sapeurs-pompiers in Loir-et-Cher during the nineteenth century' *Journal of Historical Geography* **16** 121-139

1990b   'On geographical literature as popular culture in rural France, c.1860-1900' *Geographical Journal* **156** 39-43

1992a   'Collective consciousness and the local landscape: national ideology and the commune council of Mesland (Loir-et-Cher) as landscape architect during the nineteenth century', in A. R. H. Baker and G. Biger (Eds), *Ideology and Landscape in Historical Perspective* (Cambridge) 255-288

1992b   'Les bibliothèques des gares en Loir-et-Cher avant 1914' *Mémoires de la Société des Sciences et Lettres de Loir-et-Cher* **47** 207-216

1994a   'Rural landscape as socio-cultural heritage: the late-nineteenth century *cité agricole* of Champigny-en-Beauce, Loir-et-Cher (France)', in J. Bethemont (Ed.), *L'Avenir des Paysages Ruraux Européens* (Lyon) 129-142

1995a   'Locality and nationality: geopieties in rural Loir-et-Cher (France) during the nineteenth century' in S. Courville and N. Séguin (Eds), *Espace et Culture* (Laval) 77-88

1996a   'Farm schools in nineteenth-century France and the case of La Charmoise 1847-1865' *Agricultural History Review* **44** 47-62

1998a   '"L'Union fait la force, aidons nous les uns les autres": towards an historical geography of fraternal associations in Loir-et-Cher (France) 1815-1914' *Cheminements Conférences: Centre Interuniversitaire d'Études Québécoises* 1-7

1998b   'Military service and migration in nineteenth-century France: some evidence from Loir-et-Cher' *Transactions of the Institute of British Geographers* **23** 193-206

1999a   *Fraternity Among the French Peasantry: Sociability and Voluntary Associations in the Loire Valley, 1815-1914* (Cambridge)

1999b   'Sociabilité et associations fraternelles dans le Loir-et-Cher, 1815-1914' *Annales de Géographie* **108** 300-304

1999c   'French remembrances of past periods, places and people' *Journal of Historical Geography* **25** 559-564

1999d   'Some English images of the French peasantry 1789-1915', in J-R. Pitte and A. L. Sanguin (Eds), *Géographie et Liberté: Mélanges en Hommage à Paul Claval* (Paris) 213-224

On the Theory and Practice of Historical Geography

1968d   'A note on the retrogressive and retrospective approaches in
         historical geography' *Erdkunde* **22** 243-244

1969d   'The geography of rural settlements', in R. U. Cooke and J. H.
         Johnson (Eds), *Trends in Geography: An Introductory Survey*
         (Oxford) 123-132. [Reprinted in German in 1983 'Die Geographie
         der Landlichen Siedlungen' in *Die Landliche Siedlung als
         Forschungsgegenstand der Geographie* (Darmstadt) 415-427]

1969e   (with R. A. Butlin, A. D. M. Phillips and H. C. Prince) 'The future
         of the past' *Area* **4** 46-51. [Reprinted in 1991 in D. Brooks Green
         (Ed.), *Historical Geography: A Methodological Portrayal* (Savage,
         Maryland) 126-131]

1970bc   (with J. D. Hamshere and J. Langton, Eds), *Geographical
         Interpretations of Historical Sources. Readings in Historical
         Geography* (Newton Abbot)

1970d   (with J. D. Hamshere and J. Langton) 'Introduction', in A. R. H.
         Baker, J. D. Hamshere and J. Langton (Eds), *Geographical
         Interpretations of Historical Sources. Readings in Historical
         Geography* (Newton Abbot) 13-24

1971c   'Today's studies of yesterday's geographies' *Geographical
         Magazine* **43** 452-453

1972a   (Ed.) *Progress in Historical Geography* (Newton Abbot). [Italian
         edition 1981 *Geografia Storica: Tendenze e Prospettive* (Milan)]

1972b   'Rethinking historical geography', in A. R. H. Baker (Ed.), *Progress
         in Historical Geography* (Newton Abbot) 11-28

1972c   'Historical geography in Britain', in A. R. H. Baker (Ed.), *Progress
         in Historical Geography* (Newton Abbot) 90-110

1973j   'Wheatley as symbol' *Area* **5** 101-104

1973k   'A cliometric note on the citation structure of historical geography'
         Professional Geographer **25** 347-349

1974a   'In pursuit of Wilbur Zelinsky and any other hysterical geographers'
         Historical Geography Newsletter **4** 17-19

1975c   *Historical Geography and Geographical Change* (London)

1976b   'The limits of inference in historical geography', in B. S. Osborne
         (Ed.), *The Settlement of Canada: Origins and Transfer. Proceedings
         of the 1975 British-Canadian Symposium on Historical Geography*
         (Kingston, Ontario) 169-182. [Reprinted in 1991 in D. Brooks Green

(Ed.), *Historical Geography: A Methodological Portrayal* (Savage, Maryland) 219-230]

1977b   'Historical Geography' *Progress in Human Geography* **1** 465-474. [Reprinted in 1991 in D. Brooks Green (Ed.), *Historical Geography: A Methodological Portrayal* (Savage, Maryland) 231-242]

1978a   'Historical geography: understanding and experiencing the past' *Progress in Human Geography* **2** 495-504. [Reprinted in 1991 in D. Brooks Green (Ed.), *Historical Geography: A Methodological Portrayal* (Savage, Maryland) 299-309]

1979c   'Settlement pattern evolution and catastrophe theory: a comment' *Transactions of the Institute of British Geographers* **4** 435-437

1979d   'Historical geography: a new beginning?' *Progress in Human Geography* **3** 560-570

1981a   'An historico-geographical perspective on time and space and on period and place' *Progress in Human Geography* **5** 439-443

1981b   'On the relations of historical geography and the *Annales* school of history', in T. Tanioka and T. Ukita (Eds), *Proceedings of Historical Geography – 24th International Geographical Congress, Section 9* (Tokyo) 318-322

1982a   'Period and place: reflections on historical geography and the Mediterranean world', in G. Ferro (Ed.), *Symposium on Historical Changes in Spatial Organization and its Experience in the Mediterranean World* (Genoa) 27-40

1982b   (with M. Billinge, Eds) *Period and Place: Research Methods in Historical Geography* (Cambridge)

1982c   'On ideology and historical geography', in A. R. H. Baker and M. Billinge (Eds), *Period and Place: Research Methods in Historical Geography* (Cambridge) 233-243

1983c   'Some facts about British historical geography' *Erdkunde* **37** 159-160

1984b   (with D. Gregory, Eds) *Explorations in Historical Geography: Interpretative Essays* (Cambridge)

1984c   'Reflections on the relations of historical geography and the *Annales* school of history', in A. R. H. Baker and D. Gregory (Eds), *Explorations in Historical Geography: Interpretative Essays* (Cambridge) 1-27. [Reprinted in 1989 in Hungarian as 'A torteneti geografia es az Annales torteneti iskola kozotti kapcsolatra

vonatkozo megjegyzesk' *Vilagtortenet* pp 6-28. Reprinted in 1999 in
S. Clark (Ed.) *The Annales School: Critical Assessments* Vol. II
(London) 96-129. Reprinted in Hungarian in 1999 as 'Megjegyzések
a történeti geográfia és az Annales történeti iskola közötti
kapcsolatokról' in L. Timár (Ed.) *A Brit Gazdaság és Társadalom a
XVIII-XIX Században* (Debrecen) 13-36]

1984d   (with D. Gregory) 'Some *terrae incognitae* in historical geography:
an exploratory discussion', in A. R. H. Baker and D. Gregory (Eds),
Explorations in Historical Geography: Interpretative Essays
(Cambridge) 180-194

1984e   'Individuals and groups: the problem of method in historical
geography, illustrated with particular reference to rural France during
the nineteenth century', in M. Rosciszewski (Ed.), *Transition from
Spontaneous to Regulated Spatial Organization* (Warsaw) 15-16

1985a   'Maps, models and marxism: methodological mutation in British
historical geography' *L'Espace Géographique* **4** 9-15

1986d   'Historical geography in Czechoslovakia' *Area* **18** 223-228

1987a   'Some clues to British historical geography 1966-1986' (in Czech,
with English summary) *Historicka Geografie* **26** 25-43

1987b   'The practice of historical geography' *Journal of Historical
Geography* **13** 1-2

1988a   'Twenty years of "Discussions" in Historical Geography' *Historical
Geography* **18** (2) 3-4

1988b   'Historical geography and the study of the European rural landscape'
Geografiska Annaler B **70** 5-16. [Reprinted in 1990 in U. Sporrong
(Ed.), *The Transformation of Rural Society, Economy and Landscape*
(Stockholm) 1-14]

1989a   'Cambridge Occasional Discussions in Historical Geography 1968-
1988' *Historical Geography* **19** (1) 7-12

1989b   'Editorial: "Legacie, or an enlargement of the discourse of historical
geography" [after Samuel Hartlib, 1651]' *Journal of Historical
Geography* **15** 1-3

1991a   'Historical geography in Canada' *Journal of Historical Geography*
17 92-94

1992c   (with G. Biger, Eds) *Ideology and Landscape in Historical
Perspective: Essays on the Meanings of Some Places in the Past*
(Cambridge)

1992d   'Introduction: on ideology and landscape', in A. R. H. Baker and
         G. Biger (Eds), *Ideology and Landscape in Historical Perspective*
         (Cambridge) 1-14

1993a   'Historical geography: an essay on its basic characteristics' *The
         Deccan Geographer* **30** (2) 13-21

1994b   'Historical geography and environmental history' *Journal of
         Historical Geography* **20** 1-2

1994c   'Environment, space and place: historical geography at the Annual
         Meeting of the Association of American Geographers, San
         Francisco, 29 March-2 April 1994' *Journal of Historical Geography*
         20 452-455

1994d   'Évolution de la géographie historique en Grande-Bretagne et en
         Amérique du Nord' *Hérodote* **74-75** 70-86

1995b   'The practice of historical geography', in J-R. Pitte (Ed.),
         *Géographie Historique et Culturelle de l'Europe: Hommage au
         Professeur Xavier de Planhol* (Paris) 31-49

1996b   'Historical geography', in A. Kuper and J. Kuper (Eds), *The Social
         Science Encyclopedia* (2nd edn, London) 364-365

1996c   'On the principles and practices of historical geography' *Annals of
         Geography: The Chiri Shiso* **37** (2) 33-50. [Reprinted in Chinese in
         the Chinese *Historical Geography* **14** 340-350]

1996d   'The identifying of spaces and places', in D. Vanneste (Ed.), *Space
         and Place: Mirrors of Social and Cultural Identities*, being *Acta
         Geographica Lovaniensia* **35** 1-2

1996e   'On the history and geography of historical geography' *Rekishi
         Chirigaku (Historical Geography)* **38** (3) 1-24

1996f   'Agendas for historical geography: reflections upon an International
         Conference of Historical Geography, Beijing, P. R. China, 16-20
         July 1996' *Journal of Historical Geography* **22** 479-483

1997a   '"The dead don't answer questionnaires": researching and writing
         historical geography' *Journal of Geography in Higher Education* **21**
         231-243

1997b   'Historical novels and historical geography' *Area* **29** 269-273

1999e   'Historical geographies of England and Wales, 1925-1995', in
         Y. Ben-Artzi, I. Bartal and E. Reiner (Eds), *Studies in Geography
         and History: Essays in Honour of Yehoshua Ben-Arieh* (Jerusalem)
         33-62

Miscellaneous

1970e 'First degree courses in geography at British universities', in
R. J. Chorley and P. Haggett (Eds), *Frontiers in Geographical Teaching* 2nd Edition (London) 334-343

1970f 'Some observations on geography in British universities 1968-70'
Area **2** 42-46

1971d 'Decision-making down on the farm' *Area* **3** 56-57

1975d 'Obituary: Professor Andrew Clark' *Geographical Magazine* **47** 714-715

1975e 'Francis John Monkhouse' *Emmanuel College Magazine* **57** 87-88

1977d 'Twenty years onward ... or revolution and reformation in geography' *The Times Educational Supplement*, 11 November, 33-34

1984f 'Clearing a path out of the jungle: why Emmanuel College opted out of the Cambridge entrance examination' *Times Higher Education Supplement* 13 April, 15

1986e 'Don's diary' *The Times Higher Education Supplement* January 3, 2

1986f 'Annales School'; 'enclosure'; 'inheritance systems', in
R. J. Johnston, D. Gregory and D. M. Smith (Eds), *The Dictionary of Human Geography (*2nd edn, Oxford) 14-15, 128 and 229-30

1992e 'Obituary: Professor Brian Harley' *The Daily Telegraph* 7 January 1992, 15

1992f 'Obituary: Professor Sir Clifford Darby' *The Independent* 28 April 1992, p.27. [Reprinted in 1992 in Japanese in *Rekishi-Chiri-Gaku* **61** 43-45]

1992g 'Obituary: Henry Clifford Darby 1909-1992' *Transactions of the Institute of British Geographers* **17** 495-501

1994e 'Normans', 'Bretons', 'French'. 'Burgundians'. 'Provençals', 'Corsicans', in F. Fernandez-Armesto (Ed.), *The Times Guide to the Peoples of Europe* (London) 50-53, 76-80, 94-101, 102-104, 170-174, 175-180

1994f 'Accountability – the Universities and the Government' *Emmanuel College Magazine* **76** 47-56

Edited Series: Studies in Historical Geography
Edited by A. R. H. Baker and J. B. Harley

Published by David & Charles, Newton Abbot
_____

1970   Baker, A. R. H., Hamshere, J. D., and Langton, J. (Eds)
        Geographical Interpretations of Historical Sources

1972   Russell, J. C. *Medieval Regions and their Cities*

1972   Baker, A. R. H. (Ed.) *Progress in Historical Geography*

1974   Perry, P. J. *British Farming in the Great Depression 1870-1914*

Published by Dawson, Folkestone and Archon, Connecticut
_____

1976   Christopher, A. J. *Southern Africa*

1977   Roberts, B. K. *Rural Settlement in Britain*

1977   Powell, J. M. *Mirrors of the New World: Images and Image Makers
        in the Settlement Process*

1977   Jones, M. *Finland: Daughter of the Sea*

1978   Parry, M. L. *Climatic Change, Agriculture and Settlement*

1978   Patten, J. *English Towns 1500-1700*

1979   Newcomb, R. M. *Planning the Past: Historical Landscape
        Resources and Recreation*

1980   Turner, M. *English Parliamentary Enclosure: Its Historical
        Geography and Economic History*

Published by Cambridge University Press, Cambridge
_____

(Cambridge Studies in Historical Geography)
Edited by A. R. H. Baker with J. B. Harley and David Ward (and then
with R. Dennis and D. Holdsworth)

1982   Baker, A. R. H. and Billinge, M. (Eds) *Period and Place: Research
        Methods in Historical Geography*

1982   Turnock, D. *The Historical Geography of Scotland since 1707*

1982   Guelke, L. *Historical Understanding in Geography: An Idealist
        Approach*

1984   Dennis, R. *English Industrial Cities of the Nineteenth Century*

1984   Baker, A. R. H. and Gregory, D. (Eds) *Explorations in Historical Geography: Interpretative Essays*

1985   Kain, R. J. P. and Prince, H. C. *The Tithe Surveys of England and Wales*

1986   Sack, R. *Human Territoriality: Its Theory and History*

1987   Watts, D. *The West Indies: Patterns of Development, Culture and Environmental Change since 1492*

1988   Powell, J. M. *An Historical Geography of Modern Australia: the Restive Fringe*

1988   Denecke, D. and Shaw, G. (Eds) *Urban Historical Geography: Recent Progress in Britain and Germany*

1988   Cosgrove, D. and Daniels, S. (Eds) *The Iconography of Landscape*

1989   Galloway, J. H. *The Sugar Cane Industry: an Historical Geography from its Origins to 1914*

1989   Ward, D. *Poverty, Ethnicity and the American City, 1840-1925*

1989   Cleary, M. C. *Peasants, Politicians and Producers. The Organisation of Agriculture in France since 1918*

1989   Phillips, A. D. M. *The Underdraining of Farmland in England during the Nineteenth Century*

1990   Robinson, D. J. (Ed.) *Migration in Colonial Spanish America*

1991   Kearns, G. and Withers, C. W. J. (Eds) *Urbanising Britain: Essays on Class and Community in the Nineteenth Century*

1992   Baker, A. R. H. and Biger, G. (Eds) *Ideology and Landscape in Historical Perspective: Essays on the Meanings of Some Places in the Past*

1992   Driver, F. *Power and Pauperism: the Workhouse System, 1834-1884*

1994   De Planhol, X. *An Historical Geography of France*

1994   Carter, F. W. *Trade and Development in Poland: an Economic Geography of Cracow, from its Origins to 1795*

1995   Hoppe, G. and Langton, J. *Peasantry to Capitalism: Western Östergötland in the Nineteenth Century*

1996   Overton, M. *Agricultural Revolution in England : The Transformation of the Agrarian Economy 1500-1850*

1996   Friedman, S. W. *Marc Bloch. Sociology and Geography: Encountering Changing Disciplines*

1997   Short, B. *Land and Society in Edwardian Britain*

1998	Cliff, A., Haggett. P., and M. Smallman-Raynor, *Deciphering Global Epidemics: Analytical Approaches to the Disease Records of World Cities, 1888-1912*
1998	Dodgshon, R. *Society in Space and Time: A Geographical Perspective on Change*
1999	Baker, A. R. H. *Fraternity Among the French Peasantry. Sociability and Voluntary Associations in the Loire Valley, 1815-1914*
1999	Bassin, M. *Imperial Visions: Nationalist Imagination and Geographical Expansion in the Russian Far East, 1840-1865*
2000	Meyer, D. R. *Hong Kong as a Global Metropolis*
2000	Campbell, B. M. S. *English Seigniorial Agriculture 1250-1450*
2000	Hannah, M. G. *Governmentality and the Mastery of Territory in Nineteenth-Century America*

Cambridge Topics in Geography: Second Series
Published by Cambridge University Press, Cambridge

Edited by A. R. H. Baker and Colin Evans

1982	Small, R. J. and Clark, M. J. *Slopes and Weathering*
1982	Daniels, P. *Service Industries: Growth and Location*
1982	Bromley, R. D. F. and Bromley, R. *South American Development: A Geographical Introduction*
1982	Bayliss-Smith, T. P. *The Ecology of Agricultural Systems*
1983	Hoare, A. G. *The Location of Industry in Britain*
1984	Ogden, P. *Migration and Geographical Change*
1986	Clout, H. *Regional Variations in the European Community*
1987	Smith, D. M. *Geography, Inequality and Society*
1988	Musk, L. F. *Weather Systems*
1989	Hansom, J. D. *Coasts*
1989	Herington, J. *Planning Processes: An Introduction for Geographers*
1989	Smith, G. E. *Planned Development in the Socialist World*
1991	Owens, S. and Owens, P. L. *Environment, Resources and Conservation*
1993	Townsend, A. *Uneven Regional Change in Britain.*

Appendix Two

ALAN R. H. BAKER

Research Students

Bruce M.S. Campbell (Ph.D. 1975): *Field systems in eastern Norfolk during the Middle Ages*

Peter Balmer (Ph.D. 1979): *Aspects of migration in some Surrey villages, 1841-1871*

Mark Overton (Ph.D. 1981): *Agricultural change in Norfolk and Suffolk, 1580-1640*

Mark D. Billinge (Ph.D. 1982): *Late Georgian and early Victorian Manchester: a cultural geography*

John G. Kinsbury (M.Litt. 1982): *Landed interests and the land question in Essex in the nineteenth and early-twentieth centuries*

Mark C. Cleary (Ph.D. 1983): *Agricultural syndicates in Aveyron (S.W. France) 1880-1960*

Michael J. Heffernan (Ph.D. 1986): *The politics of literacy: cultural change and political responses in nineteenth-century provincial France*

Christopher R. Husbands (Ph.D. 1986: co-supervisor Dr R. Schofield): *The hearth tax and the structure of the English economy*

Kevin Stannard (Ph.D. 1987): *Education and urban society: working-class schooling in nineteenth-century Deptford and Greenwich*

Jeremy Boardman (M. Litt. 1989): *A geography of agricultural cooperation in the Gers, southwest France, c. 1955-1986*

Angela Fahy (Ph.D. 1989): *The commercial organisation and social structure of Nantes, 1770-1830*

Sarah Bendall (Ph.D. 1989): *The mapping of estates: a case study of Cambridgeshire c.1600-1836*

Iain S. Black (Ph.D. 1991: co-supervisor Dr D. J. Gregory): *Information circulation and the transfer of money capital in England and Wales between 1780 and 1840: an historical geography of banking in the Industrial Revolution*

Michael M. Barkham (Ph.D. 1991): *Shipowning, shipbuilding and trans-Atlantic fishing in Spanish Basque ports, 1560-1630: a case study of Motrico and Zumaya*

Susan Jones (Ph.D. 1992): *Public hygiene and hygienists in Rouen (France) 1880-1930*

Caroline Windrum (Ph.D. 1994): *The decline of the landed estate in County Tyrone, c.1860-1915*

Matthew J. Sleeman (Ph.D. 1996): *The geography of citizenship strategies in a rural South Australian aboriginal comunity since 1990*

Richard H. Turner (Ph.D. 1998): *An historical geography of the rural tramways of Loir-et-Cher (France) from c.1880 to 1934*

Laura Cameron (Ph.D. 2001)*: Relating place and memory in the Cambridgeshire Fens, 1923-1940*

Current doctoral research student:
Simon J. Cross: *Geographies of Owenite socialism in Britain, 1829-1848*